American State Archives

ЛЛЛЛЛ

AMERICAN

STATE

ARCHIVES

BY ERNST POSNER

THE UNIVERSITY OF CHICAGO PRESS

Chicago and London

Published under the sponsorship of the Society of American Archivists and with
the support of the Council on Library Resources, Inc.

Library of Congress Catalog Card Number: 64-23425

THE UNIVERSITY OF CHICAGO PRESS, CHICAGO & LONDON
The University of Toronto Press, Toronto 5, Canada

To

MARGARET CROSS NORTON

Archivist of Illinois, 1922–1957

and to the memory of

MARY GIVENS BRYAN

Archivist of Georgia, 1950–1964

To provide for the safe and perfect keeping of the Public Archives is so obviously one of the first and most imperative duties of a legislature, that no argument could make it plainer to a reflecting mind. They are treasures of so sacred a character, that the public enemy who wantonly devotes them to the flames is, by all civilized people, branded as a barbarian; and of so priceless a value, that no money could purchase them of the poorest state in the Union, or replace them when once destroyed.

Richard Bartlett, *Remarks and Documents Relating to the Preservation and Keeping of the Public Archives* (Concord, 1837), p. 3

PREFACE

ЛЛЛЛЛ

This report presents the results of a study of state archival agencies and their programs that began on February 1, 1962, and was completed on November 30, 1963. Most of the facts and figures supplied refer to conditions that prevailed on June 30, 1963.

A study of this kind has long been desired by those concerned about the preservation of America's archival heritage. State archivists, the entire archival profession of the United States, and students of American history must acknowledge with deep gratitude the generosity and the farsightedness of the Council on Library Resources, Inc., in supporting the work of the survey, formally called the Study of State Archival Programs. Not only did the Council make the initial grant and extend it for an additional period of three months when such extension became necessary, but also the Council's President, Verner W. Clapp, took a very personal interest in the project. He read and commented on the manuscript, and his advice was invaluable at every stage of the work.

Four presidents of the Society of American Archivists, which received the grant, had an important share in the project: Philip M. Hamer submitted the successful application for the grant; Robert H. Bahmer and Leon deValinger, Jr., gave generously of their time while the survey was in progress; and Everett O. Alldredge helped to see it through to completion.

The author of the report is particularly indebted to his Advisory Committee. First composed of Morris L. Radoff, chairman, Christopher Crittenden, and David C. Duniway, it was soon joined by Olney W. Hill and Oliver W. Holmes. These men, distinguished members of the profession, attended the meetings of the committee in Washington, D.C., and read and commented on the manuscript of the report as it was being prepared. Their counsel, their recommendations, and their criticisms were both helpful and constructive.

As will be explained more fully in the introduction to the report, the heads of archival and records management agencies throughout the country supplied much information both written and oral, answered requests for additional data, and read and brought up to date the essays on their respective state agencies. Their unfailing courtesy and assistance are gratefully acknowledged. The author thanks particularly his many friends and former students among them, who made his visits to state archival agencies a memorable and enjoyable experience.

In accordance with the terms of the grant, the chapter entitled "Standards for State Archival Agencies" that concludes the report was approved by the Committee on Professional Standards of the Society of American Archivists. This committee, composed of the society's former presidents, examined the statement in an all-day session and improved it in many ways.

Administrative supervision over the project was vested in the Council of the society. It was a privilege to report to the Council at regular intervals and to receive its encouragement. H. G. Jones, treasurer of the society, skillfully administered the funds of the project. His promptness in handling the financial details and his sound judgment on other matters related to the project were most gratifying.

The editor of the society, Ken Munden, gave much valuable advice in regard to the formulation of the report; explored prospects for its publication; made available the expert help of his associate editor, Elizabeth Hawthorn Buck, for editorial revision of the manuscript; and himself scrutinized the completed copy. Both editors also read the proofs of the printed report and incidentally corrected errors and inconsistencies; Mary Jane Dowd, also an associate editor of the society, assisted most willingly in the final proofing; and Mrs. Buck unselfishly agreed to prepare the index. Mrs. Buck, Miss Dowd, and Mr. Munden have earned the gratitude of the author and the readers of this document.

The project staff enjoyed the use of a well-equipped office in the National Archives and free access to its library, where most of the needed literature was readily accessible. By authorizing such use the Archivist of the United States, Wayne C. Grover, greatly facilitated the progress of the survey.

From February 1, 1962, to November 30, 1963, Mayfield Bray participated in the project as research assistant, office manager, typist, and indispensable aide. She deserves a great share of whatever merit this report may have.

ERNST POSNER

Washington, D.C.
June 30, 1964

CONTENTS

ⅢⅢⅢ

INTRODUCTION

ЛЛЛЛЛ

Backgrounds, Objectives, and Methods of the Study of State Archival Programs

As the role of government in the life of the nation has increased, as its activities have expanded, and as the points of contact between the state and the citizen have multiplied, the importance of public records for both the government and the people has become increasingly clear. For the government official, records are a major source of "intelligence," enabling him to base his actions on precedent and to develop and maintain consistent policies; for the people, records constitute the basis of their rights and privileges. Indeed the modern state can carry out neither its day-to-day nor its long-range activities without making and having recourse to records, while its citizens must have access to them whenever their rights are jeopardized. In addition, records have become an important source to which the social scientist must turn in his attempt to diagnose and interpret the past for the benefit of the present and the future.

In the course of time, the growing bulk of records made it necessary to separate from those constantly in use for current business the records that, although less frequently consulted, needed and deserved to be kept permanently. Termed archives, these records were first set aside and administered as so-called agency archives by the agencies that had created them. Soon, however, it was found both expedient and economical to assemble the archives of national and provincial governments in "general" archival depositories and to entrust their custody and service to the professional care of the archivist. By the middle of the nineteenth century, most states of Europe had established systems of archival agencies co-ordinated with their governmental structures, and they had also liberalized access to archival holdings so that scholars and others legitimately interested might benefit from their use.

In the United States the need for archival institutions and service was not generally realized until the end of the nineteenth century, when

American scholars brought back from Europe an increasing awareness of the manifold uses of archival materials and of the necessity to care for them. At the turn of the century the American Historical Association through its Public Archives Commission undertook a survey of the archives of the states, and the Carnegie Institution of Washington initiated a similar survey of the archives of the federal government.

Although the National Archives of the United States was not established until 1934, over a third of the states took action to establish some kind of archival agency during the first two decades of the twentieth century. In doing so, most of them proceeded independently, rarely paying attention to any organizational arrangements that their neighbors had made for the preservation of their archives. In some states, the state libraries or state historical societies had already acquired historical source materials of various kinds, and this seemed to make them logical depositories for state archives. In other states, emphasis on the use of archives for historical research led to the establishment of departments of archives and history that were to administer archives as part of their historical endeavors.

Widely different programs for the administration of public records thus developed in the states, and existing differences were accentuated by the effectiveness or lack of effectiveness of these programs. They were further increased when, following the example of the federal government, certain states began to initiate programs for the management of current or semi-current records. As a result, in some states there are now combined archives and records management agencies with responsibilities comparable to those of the National Archives and Records Service; in others records management is not a function of the state archives but that of a general services or fiscal agency; and in still others records management programs have not been authorized or, if authorized, have not been activated.

More than ever before, our state archival programs now seem to differ in regard to their legal basis, their scope, and their effectiveness. Although there are several archival agencies with strong programs, their number is still relatively small. Neither their example nor that of the National Archives nor the normal activities of the Society of American Archivists will suffice to encourage more adequate care of archives throughout the nation and to contribute incidentally to the creation of an archival profession as well established as the library profession. If these goals are to be attained, all states must recognize their responsibility for the preservation of their documentary heritage and accept toward that end certain minimum standards to govern the status and functions of their archival agencies.

To develop such standards, based on an examination and evaluation of existing state archival legislation, organization, and practices, has long been the hope of American archivists. A plan for a state archives survey, suggested in 1930 by Solon J. Buck, was again presented by David C. Duniway to the Council of the Society of American Archivists in 1954. When that proposal was not accepted, Mr. Duniway suggested in 1958 a more limited survey of "the collections and the collecting and disposal policies of archives in state libraries." The Council referred this proposal to the State Records Committee, under the chairmanship of Robert M. Brown; and early in 1960 that committee prepared for submission to the Council on Library Resources, Inc., a more comprehensive plan for a "two-year study of the origin and operation of the archives of the fifty states." Implementation of this plan, however, had to wait until in September, 1961, Philip M. Hamer, then president of the Society of American Archivists, submitted to the Council on Library Resources, Inc., an application for a grant in support of a study of state archival programs. As authorized by the Council of the society at its meeting of April 10, 1961, Dr. Hamer recommended in his application that the present writer undertake the study.

In the words of the application for the grant, the aims of the project were to be:

1. to determine concretely the status of archival arrangements in every one of the fifty states of the Federal Union and its territories;
2. to measure their attainments against a set of realistic standards;
3. to embody the results in a document that will reveal the weaknessses of individual states as regards the care and preservation of archives and convince responsible government officials and others concerned of the necessity of taking appropriate action;
4. to contribute to the standardization of archival work and procedure throughout the Nation and to the maturation of the archival profession.

Acting favorably on the society's application, the Council on Library Resources, Inc., on December 8, 1961, made a grant of $42,000 to the Society of American Archivists for a study of state archival programs; [1] on December 28 the grant was announced simultaneously by the Council on Library Resources, Inc., and the president of the society; and on February 1, 1962, the office of the study was established in the National Archives, where the Archivist of the United States had made space and equipment available for the use of the Director of the Study and his assistant, Mayfield Bray.

At its meeting on December 28, 1961, the Council of the society authorized President Robert H. Bahmer to appoint an Advisory Committee of three to assist the Director of the Study. Dr. Bahmer thereupon named three distinguished state archivists, two of them past presidents of the society: Morris L. Radoff, Archivist and Records Administrator of the State of Maryland; Christopher Crittenden, Director of the North Carolina Department of Archives and History; and David C. Duniway, Archi-

---

[1] A supplementary grant of $3,897 was made on July 26, 1963, for the completion and checking of the manuscript of the study.

vist of the Archives Division of the Oregon State Library. In the expectation that Dr. Radoff would agree to serve as the committee's chairman, the Director of the Study, on February 1, 1962, discussed with him the general plan and procedures of the project. After these had been worked out during the month of February, they were discussed and approved at the first meeting of the Advisory Committee on March 2, 1962. Documents submitted to the committee at this time included: an over-all plan and time schedule for the project; a schedule of visits to state archival agencies; a scheme for organizing the research materials to be accumulated and the data to be obtained from them; and a statement concerning the nature and contents of the final report. Complying with the committee's request to enlarge its membership to five, the president of the society appointed Olney W. Hill, Director of Public Records of the State of Vermont, and Oliver W. Holmes, Executive Director of the National Historical Publications Commission (also a past president of the society), as additional members of the Advisory Committee.

Since archival agencies had already struggled with numerous questionnaires, it was decided to use a different technique; namely, to condense into state-by-state "digests" all information available on archival developments at the state level. Information was to be derived from the literature, from data obtained in 1961 by the society's State Records Committee in reply to a lengthy questionnaire, and from responses to the elaborate questionnaire of the Survey of Library Functions of the States, which its director, Philip Monypenny, had agreed to place at the Study Director's disposal.

During the month of February, "digests" for five of the archival agencies to be visited were compiled, and the Director of the Study, on March 12, 1962, was able to set out on his first survey trip. The dates of these trips and the states visited on each "circuit" were as follows:

March 12–April 3, 1962: North Carolina, South Carolina, Georgia, Florida, and Puerto Rico;

April 29–May 19, 1962: Michigan, Wisconsin, Illinois, Indiana, Ohio, and West Virginia;

June 22–July 18, 1962: New York, Vermont, Maine, Massachusetts, New Hampshire, Rhode Island, and Connecticut;

August 26–September 20, 1962: Minnesota, North Dakota, Montana, Utah, Idaho, Wyoming, South Dakota, and Iowa;

October 28–November 17, 1962: Missouri, Kansas, Nebraska, Colorado, Oklahoma, and Arkansas;

November 25–December 8, 1962: Tennessee, Alabama, Mississippi, and Kentucky;

January 12–February 25, 1963: Louisiana, Texas, New Mexico, Arizona, Hawaii, California, Nevada, Oregon, and Washington.

In April, 1963, state archival agencies of Pennsylvania, Delaware, Maryland, Virginia, and New Jersey were visited on short trips from headquarters in Washington, D.C.[2] Intervals between trips were used to draft semi-final essays on the states visited and to review "digests of information" for the states on the next circuit, digests that the Director's assistant had compiled during his absence.

Copies of the semi-final essays were sent to, and criticized by, the members of the project's Advisory Committee. Final drafts of these essays were mailed to heads of state archival agencies in June, 1963, with the request that they substitute or insert the latest data and that they object to any statements or evaluations made, if they wished to do so. The Director considered any such objections but felt free not to accept them when they were at variance with his own judgment. Much time was consumed in working the information from their replies into the state essays, for frequently it necessitated a partial rewriting of the essays. Upon completion of the state essays, the chapter on the history of the archives function (Chapter I) and the summary of findings (Chapter III) were drafted.

Problems encountered in surveying state archival operations and in drafting the report were discussed at meetings of the project's Advisory Committee. In addition to the organization meeting on March 2, 1962, the committee convened in Washington on July 30, 1962, on May 6, 1963, and on August 12, 1963. Part of the meeting on May 6, 1963, was concerned with plans for the publication of the study that were submitted by the editor of the Society of American Archivists; and most of the meeting on August 12, 1963, was devoted to a discussion of the statement of standards for state archival agencies.

A preliminary statement of standards had been reviewed by the Advisory Committee at its July, 1962, meeting. A first draft of the final statement was sent to committee members in June, 1963; it was revised and partially rewritten in July, 1963; and a new draft was reviewed and amended at the committee's meeting on August 12, 1963. Revised in accordance with the committee's suggestions, the statement was reviewed and approved by the Committee on Professional Standards of the Society of American Archivists on September 20, 1963, in accordance with the terms of the grant. In October and November, Chapters I and III of the report were completed, the appendixes (including a glossary of technical terms) were compiled, and the entire manuscript was editorially reviewed by Ken Munden and Elizabeth Hawthorn Buck, editor and associate editor, respectively, of the *American Archivist*.

While the study was in progress, the Council of the Society of American Archivists received four progress reports; and Robert H. Bahmer, its president in 1961–62, was present at the first three meetings of the Advisory

[2] In connection with one of his periodic visits to Alaska, Paul A. Kohl, Regional Director, National Archives and Records Service in Seattle, Washington, obtained for the Director information on archives and records management in that state. His help is gratefully acknowledged.

Committee. Unable to attend the committee's meeting on August 12, President deValinger sat with the Committee on Professional Standards on September 20, when the statement of standards for state archival agencies received the committee's final approval.

The Director of the Study was given an opportunity to acquaint the society's membership with the purpose and progress of the work through notices in the April and October, 1962, issues of the *American Archivist* and through a progress report in its July, 1963, issue. He also reported orally at the society's meetings in 1962 and 1963.

Throughout the preparation of the study, every effort was made to keep the Council on Library Resources, Inc., informed about the work completed. Copies of all parts of the study and of the progress reports were sent to the Council's President, Verner Clapp, who also honored most of the meetings of the Advisory Committee by his presence.

CHAPTER I

ЛЛЛЛЛ

The Genesis and Evolution of
American State Archives

To write a full history of the development of American state archives
would require many and detailed preliminary studies. The record-making
and record-keeping practices of colonial America should be investigated,
with particular attention to their relationship to the practices of the respective mother countries; so should the practices of the states during the
nineteenth and twentieth centuries. We also need histories of individual
archival agencies, their struggles, and their achievements. For the purposes
of the present volume, however, it is hoped that the following historical
sketch may serve to identify the main forces that have shaped the American state archives of today.

RECORD-KEEPING IN THE COLONIES

When the first colonists set foot on the North American continent, few
European countries had provided for the protection of their archives by
entrusting them to the custody and care of specialized agencies of the government. Records remained with the offices that had created them and
were thus exposed to the dangers of fire, theft, and neglect. Generally
speaking, the concept of the state archives as a necessary depository for
the preservation of records of lasting value developed in Europe during
and in the wake of the French Revolution, when a new order replaced the
institutions of the past, when for legal reasons records became the object
of official concern, and when romantic enthusiasm and emerging national-
ism began to regard them as monuments worthy of preservation. By and
large, archival administration in Europe was a child of the nineteenth
century, and it was not until after that century that it received recognition
in the United States.

Though it would be a rewarding task, no comprehensive study has been
made of record-making and record-keeping practices in the colonies along

[7]

the eastern seaboard. Information available in the journals and acts of legislative bodies reveals a picture of losses and of negligence. Not only was physical protection inadequate but, worse yet, colonial officials were amateurs and were little concerned about preserving, and having access to, records of past action. The frequent admonitions of legislators were bound to have little effect so long as officials kept their records in non-fireproof buildings and failed to turn them over to their successors when their terms of office expired. As Governor Arthur Dobbs of North Carolina complained in 1754, "whenever officers 'died, all papers die with them, for the Successors say they have got no papers, or, if any, those very insignificant, from their Predecessors.'"[1]

Responsibilities for the records of colonial governments were usually quite well established. As early as 1637, when Lord Baltimore organized the government of Maryland, John Lewger was appointed to "be our Secretary and Keeper of the Acts and proceedings of our Lieuten^t and Councell for the time being," and it was he who was to receive "all the several votes and suffrages upon record, and the record thereof" of the first general assembly summoned to meet in St. Mary's City in January, 1638. From then on the secretary remained "the principal record-making and record-keeping official in Maryland, and he retained this function throughout the colonial period,"[2] though in the course of time other offices of record made and kept their own records. In other colonies, too, the provincial secretary had, and continued to have, the role of the guardian of the basic records of provincial government.

Legislatures and officials were not unaware of the necessity of providing proper housing for their records, but in those provinces in which there was no stable seat of government their fate was bound to be precarious. Thus in North Carolina there was not "one Publick Office, nor one place to keep any record or Publick Papers, they all lye around disperst in private Houses," so that often it was necessary to send "a hundred miles for a Paper that is wanted."[3] In Maryland, on the other hand, a building to house the records and the secretary's office was provided as early as 1666, though it did not protect the papers from "damage upon the least Wet or Rain," and when the capital was moved to the new State House in Annapolis care was taken to ship the records "without any damage, loss, or prejudice." In the State House rooms were assigned for the records of the

[1] J. G. de Roulhac Hamilton, "Three Centuries of Southern Records, 1607–1907," *Journal of Southern History*, X (Feb., 1944), 9.

[2] Edna E. Jensen, "The Record Making Practices of Colonial Maryland" (typescript of an American University term paper, 1950), pp. 4 ff., citing William H. Browne (ed.), *Archives of Maryland*, I (Baltimore, 1883), 1, and III (Baltimore, 1885), 53 ff.

[3] Quoted in the draft of Christopher Crittenden's "General Introduction to the Series of the Colonial Records of North Carolina" (typescript, 1962), p. 5, which the Director of this Study was privileged to see.

various offices, and they were equipped for the purpose.[4] Similarly, the fourth State House in Virginia was to have a special room for the secretary and "for ye placing" of his records; and, after the Capitol in Williamsburg had been burned in 1747, a bill to erect a special building for the "Preservation of the Public Records and Papers of this Colony" was considered by a committee of the House of Burgesses.[5]

In Maryland, at least, the secretary's records were considered "public records," that is, records accessible to the public as the term was understood at that time. An act of the assembly of 1650 instructed him "to search or pmitt the Records to bee searched by any Inhabitant of this Province, Gratis, The party desiring such search being not impertinently troublesome." [6] This, however, may not have been the rule in other colonies.

From the first days of settlement, preservation of records pertaining to aspects of their everyday living was of course a matter of real interest to the colonists as landowners, taxpayers, and litigants. As early as 1639 the General Court of the Massachusetts Bay Colony

ordered and declared, that henceforward, every judgment, with all the evidence, be recorded in a book, to be kept to posterity. Item, that there be records kept of all wills, administrations and inventories; as also of the days of every marriage, birth, and death of every person within the jurisdiction. Item, to record all men's houses and lands, being certified under the hands of the men of every town, deputed for the ordering of their affairs.[7]

But even where records were made and kept, negligence and frequent fires were bound to frustrate the good intentions of the lawmakers. For North Carolina, Christopher Crittenden estimates that "to the present date more than one-third of the State's 100 counties (many of them formed later than the colonial period) have suffered by fire losses of their records, in whole or in part"; [8] and, in regard to the keeping of vital statistics in the same province, Governor Tryon stated quite categorically in 1767: "There is no regular register of births, burials, or marriages in any county in the province, although prescribed. . . ." [9]

As time went on, some colonial legislatures began to display increasing

[4] Jensen, loc. cit., pp. 14 and 22 ff.

[5] Oliver W. Holmes, " 'Public Records' — Who Knows What They Are?" American Archivist, XXIII (Jan., 1960), 19, n. 38, quoting from a term paper by Edna Jensen on "The Record Making Practices of Colonial Virginia."

[6] Jensen, "Record Making Practices of Colonial Maryland," p. 10. In England, the Acts of Parliament were easily accessible, while the journals were considered private and secret. R. B. Wernham, "The Public Records in the Sixteenth and Seventeenth Centuries," English Historical Scholarship (London and New York, 1956), p. 12.

[7] As quoted by Henry E. Woods, "The Massachusetts Laws and Commission on Public Records," in J. Cuvelier and L. Stainier (eds.), Congrès de Bruxelles 1910: Actes (Brussels, 1912), p. 101. See also G. Philip Bauer, "Public Archives in the United States," in William B. Hesseltine and Donald R. McNeil (eds.), In Support of Clio: Essays in Memory of Herbert A. Kellar (Madison, 1958), p. 50.

[8] Crittenden, op. cit., p. 6.

[9] Hamilton, loc. cit., p. 8.

zeal in safeguarding records and in recovering those not in their proper legal custody. In February, 1719/20, the legislature of South Carolina passed an "Act for Preventing the embezzellment of the Public Records of this Settlement and for obtaining the Same out of the Hands of such persons as now have the custody thereof," and in 1736 a committee was appointed to consider "the State of the Public Records of the Province . . . and of a proper means to preserve the Records in a better manner than has been heretofore usually done." [10] In the same vein and with good results, the Connecticut General Assembly in 1770 appointed two agents to assemble "all public and other papers relating to the affairs of this colony which properly belong to the colony, in whose custody soever the same may be found, except those in the hands of his honor, the present governor," and one year later the governor himself was requested "To collect all the public letters and papers which may hereafter in any way affect the interests of this colony." [11]

EMPHASIS ON "MULTIPLICATION OF COPIES"

During the seventeenth and eighteenth centuries the importance of preserving records was by no means disregarded, but good intentions rarely had the desired effects, records remained unattended once they had lost their importance for the business of the day, and no efforts were made to concentrate them in responsible custody. This situation did not change after independence had been gained, though European precedent might have showed the advantages of such responsible custody. In the 1790's the archives of France's *ancien régime* were gathered together in the Archives Nationales in Paris, and in the following decades many other countries of Europe organized complete systems of state archival repositories. Jefferson, Franklin, and other leading Americans might have been aware of this development. As a matter of fact — and archivists will say unfortunately — European precedent worked in quite a different direction. Large-scale printing of records had started after the Reformation, when both Protestants and Catholics tried to prove the righteousness of their respective causes by publishing what they considered pertinent documents. The trend continued during the seventeenth and eighteenth centuries, as evidenced by the great series of the *Acta sanctorum*, Muratori's *Scriptores*, and other vast collections, no longer brought together for polemical purposes but assembled in the spirit of that meticulous scholarship that Mabillon's *De re diplomatica* had expounded. It was in this vein that in England Thomas Rymer (1641–1713), after 1692 historiographer royal, undertook

---

[10] *Ibid.*, p. 10
[11] As quoted by George S. Godard, "Lessons from Connecticut," *Annual Report of the American Historical Association for the Year 1922*, I (Washington, 1926), 140–41. In 1795 the papers thus collected were presented to the Massachusetts Historical Society, and in 1921 they were returned to Connecticut with much pomp and ceremony.

the collection and publication of the famous *Foedera*, the first fifteen volumes of which were brought out during his lifetime.

Rymer's work was widely acclaimed. In the American colonies, it caught the attention of Ebenezer Hazard,[12] who in 1774 announced the publication of a collection of "American State Papers." Encouraged by the Continental Congress and promised a subsidy of $1,100, which he never received, Hazard assembled a vast body of documentation that he published ultimately in the two volumes of his *Historical Collections* in 1792 and 1794. As "surveyor of the post" in the eastern part of the United States, he had succeeded in obtaining copies of state documents, and copies of records in federal offices were furnished him at public expense.

Hazard's pioneer effort set the stage for the vast movement [13] to publish records that got under way during the first decades of the nineteenth century. It was carried forward by a wave of patriotic enthusiasm and by an apparently widespread interest on the part of the educated public that had its parallels in Europe. The publications of the British Record Commission of 1800 and its successor commissions, which entailed a fantastic waste of public money, Stein's plan for the edition of the *Monumenta Germaniae*, and the appearance of Pertz's famous first volume in 1826 are indeed comparable to the American publications of federal records that started with the *Journal of the Constitutional Convention* in 1818 and were all overshadowed by Peter Force's nine volumes of *American Archives*, apparently as profitable to him as the publications of the British Record Commissions had been to their respective compilers.

"The state governments responded much more slowly to the current enthusiasm." [14] Their collecting and publishing activities were necessarily handicapped by the fact that their own records were incomplete and hence could not furnish all the documents that were needed to tell the story, while the full records could be assembled only by tapping the archival depositories of England. As early as 1824 Joseph V. Bevan was appointed "to collate, arrange and publish all papers relating to the original settlement or political history of Georgia," and when those of the state proved incomplete the legislature approved his request to transcribe the pertinent

---

[12] David B. Van Tassel, *Recording America's Past* (Chicago, 1960), p. 32, n. 2. Referring to the untapped sources of Revolutionary history, Jared Sparks told the Phi Beta Kappa Society in Cambridge, Massachusetts, in the middle 1830's: "No Rymers have yet appeared among us who were willing to spend a life in gathering up and embodying these memorials." Justin Winsor (ed.), *Narrative and Critical History of America*, VIII (Boston and New York, 1889), 417.

[13] According to Michael Kraus, *The Writing of American History* (Norman, Okla., 1953), p. 97, it "had its distant origins in the work of Hazard."

[14] Lyman H. Butterfield, "Archival and Editorial Enterprise in 1850 and 1950: Some Comparisons and Contrasts," *Proceedings of the American Philosophical Society*, LXXXXVIII (June 15, 1954), 160. The author is much indebted to this study. See also George H. Callcott, "Antiquarianism and Documents in the Age of Literary History," *American Archivist*, XXI (Jan., 1958), 17–29.

documents in England.[15] In New York, Governor DeWitt Clinton proposed to the legislature in 1826 that copies of documents pertaining to the history of the state be obtained from British archival depositories. The project received legislative approval in 1839, and led to the appointment, in 1841, of J. Romeyn Broadhead, former attaché at The Hague, to do the work. It resulted in comprehensive copying of documents in Britain, France, and Holland and netted the state eighty volumes of transcripts,[16] which were turned over to the New York State Library. Broadhead returned to New York to receive a hero's welcome at the celebration of the New-York Historical Society's fortieth anniversary in 1844.[17]

Impressed by Broadhead's success, other states took steps to mine the British depositories, and there began "the unending pilgrimage of American scholars to British museums, libraries, and universities,"[18] the phenomenon disparagingly called "a national obsession — documania."[19] Such harsh judgment is hardly warranted, given the status of historical studies in the United States and the lack of experience in a systematic approach to the use of foreign archives such as even Europe did not develop until the Secret Archives of the Vatican were made accessible for research in 1881. The necessity of diligently searching foreign archives became as obvious to European scholars as it was to American legislators and historians, and over the years collaborators of the *Monumenta Germaniae* spent as much money, effort, and time on obtaining transcripts of medieval charters from widely dispersed monasterial archives and other depositories as did the agents of American states who worked in England, France, the Netherlands, and Spain. In one respect, however, there was a marked difference in attitudes toward the original documents. While the great editorial enterprises of England, Germany, and France were moving forward, state archival repositories were being established all over Europe. In fact, in England the publications in "record type" of the Public Record Commissions (1800–1836), which were meant to be faithful reproductions of the original documents and were "carried out to the pecuniary advantage of the officials, though at an unreasonable cost to the Nation,"[20] led to a parliamentary inquiry and subsequently to the establishment of the Public Record Office. In the United States, however, no thought was given to establishing archival depositories. To the American mind "multiplication of copies" must have seemed much more important than the preservation of the originals. It had been stressed by Thomas Jefferson in his famous

[15] Van Tassel, *op. cit.*, pp. 105 ff.
[16] Roscoe R. Hill, *American Missions in European Archives* (Mexico, D.F., 1951), pp. 18 ff.
[17] Butterfield, *loc. cit.*, p. 162.
[18] Van Tassel, *op. cit.*, p. 107.
[19] *Ibid.*, p. 103.
[20] Hubert Hall, *British Archives and the Sources for the History of the World War* (London and New Haven, 1925), p. 214.

letter to Ebenezer Hazard as the more significant service to the nation and more valuable than preserving the originals "by vaults and locks." Jefferson expressed the same insouciance with respect to his own papers when he asked Hazard on November 13, 1791, to return to him only those documents of his that Hazard did not intend to print.[21] That American officials cared little about their records, Alexis de Tocqueville also discovered. He was able to obtain them for the asking, and this fact led him to the conclusion that a hundred years later it would be more difficult to write the history of the United States than that of medieval France.[22] It seems, too, that American legislators presupposed the same indifference on the part of European officials, for the New York legislature, in 1839, expected that the agent to be sent over would procure "if possible, the originals, and if not, copies" of documents relating to the history of the state.[23] Pennsylvania furnished the most striking example of disrespect for original records, when these were used as printer's copy for the publication of *Pennsylvania Archives*, many of them never to be returned to official custody.[24]

EMERGING CONCERN

To Jared Sparks belongs the honor of having been the first to explore systematically the archives of the states, for he thought that the materials for the history of the American Revolution were "still in the archives of the states, and in the hands of individuals." [25] On his great tour, which in 1826 took him from New Hampshire to Georgia, he discovered in state after state that few records had survived and that those that had were neglected because of "ignorance and apathy on the part of the responsible officials." [26] Disappointed, he joined the many others who turned to foreign archives as the more important depositories of useful information. Sparks, too, found government officials quite willing to let him have original records in exchange for transcripts he made for them.[27]

[21] Fred Shelley, "Ebenezer Hazard: America's First Historical Editor," *William and Mary Quarterly*, 3d ser., XII (1955), 65.

[22] *Democracy in America*, I (New York, 1945), 69.

[23] The writer is obliged to Don Anthony, Chief of the Manuscripts and History Section of the New York State Library, for making this information available. According to *American Archivist*, XIX (Jan., 1956), 92, the Massachusetts legislature in 1845 sent its agent to France for the purpose of "copying and *gathering* early colonial records" (italics supplied).

[24] This information was received from Frank B. Evans, former State Archivist of Pennsylvania.

[25] Kraus, *op. cit.*, p. 109.

[26] Butterfield, "Draper's Predecessors and Contemporaries," in Donald R. McNeil (ed.), *The American Collector* (Madison, Wis., 1955), p. 7. On the desirability of having the entire Sparks journals published, see Butterfield, "Archival and Editorial Enterprise," *loc. cit.*, p. 160, n. 8.

[27] H. G. Jones, State Archivist of North Carolina, kindly referred the writer to an entry in the diary of Sparks made while he was in Raleigh, North Carolina, in 1826: "By the politeness of Mr. Secretary Hill I have been permitted to take (that is, make) copies of several letters, which have been deposited in the files, and the originals he has given to

It would be wrong to assume, however, that there were no efforts at all to provide for the safekeeping of state archives. To cite but a few of them, the General Assembly of North Carolina in 1817 authorized "a Fire Proof House for the Preservation of the Public Records belonging to this State," [28] into which the Secretary of State and his records were moved; in New York the Secretary of State transferred some records to the State Library in 1847; [29] in Massachusetts archives vaults were built into the State House in the late 1820's; [30] and in South Carolina the work of arranging and indexing the colonial and Revolutionary records was begun in 1850.[31] In New Hampshire the Governor was authorized in 1836 to recover alienated records and to have the records of the state arranged and bound. This action might have been provoked by the example of Massachusetts and by the advice of Richard Bartlett, who first tried to arouse the conscience of American legislators, hitherto negligent in discharging what to him seemed one of their important responsibilities.

Richard Bartlett (1792–1837) was a founding member of the New Hampshire Historical Society, and — as Deputy Secretary of State, Clerk of the State Senate, and from 1825 to 1829 Secretary of State of New Hampshire — he was familiar with the state's historical records and their value. Toward the end of his life he began his inquiry into the preservation of the archives of the states and the federal government, using questionnaires to find out what records had been destroyed by fire and how the statutes were being preserved. His findings, submitted in a paper read before the New Hampshire Historical Society on December 21, 1836, and subsequently printed in the society's *Collections* [32] as "Remarks and Documents Relating to the Preservation and Keeping of the Public Archives," told a sad story of loss and neglect.[33] He accused American legislators of shirking their sacred duty to provide for the safekeeping of the public records, yet they were men "who would not sleep till their own title-deeds were on record and their buildings insured against fire." [34] Besides criticizing conditions of record storage, Bartlett made some positive recommendations as to how records should be kept. He was impressed by what was being accomplished in Massachusetts, where the Reverend Joseph B. Felt had started on his misguided task of classifying and binding the archives of the Secretary of the Commonwealth.

---

me." Quoted in John H. Moore, "Jared Sparks in North Carolina," *North Carolina Historical Review*, XL (July, 1963), 292.

[28] Crittenden, *op. cit.*, p. 7.

[29] See p. 194.

[30] See p. 143.

[31] Bauer, "Public Archives in the United States," *loc. cit.*, p. 55.

[32] Also printed as a separate in Concord, 1837.

[33] Richard G. Wood, "Richard Bartlett, Minor Archival Prophet," *American Archivist*, XVII (Jan., 1954), 13–18.

[34] Bartlett, *Remarks and Documents*, p. 3.

It was not until the end of the century that the idea of concentrating state archives in officially recognized repositories was conceived and began to be executed. Independently, however, a movement aimed principally at the protection of local records started in some of the New England states with the approach of the centenaries of the Declaration of Independence and the adoption of the Constitution. In Connecticut, towns were asked in 1876 to prepare sketches of their history, and ten years later the Secretary of State and the State Librarian were charged with making an exhaustive survey of the records of the courts and of "any territorial organizations now or formerly existing" in the state.[35] As a further step, a Commission on Public Records was appointed in 1899 "to inquire and report to the next general assembly the condition of the public records of the State, including the court, county, town, society, and parish records, and recommend to the General Assembly of 1901 the best methods of preserving the same from loss or injury." To exercise control over the keeping of local records, a temporary examiner was appointed in 1903, and in 1911 the permanent office of Examiner of Public Records, to be appointed by the State Librarian, was created and was filled by Colonel Lucius C. Barbour. He was to see to it that the laws relating to the keeping, care, and custody of public records were respected and to prescribe the materials to be used in record making.

In Massachusetts, where the General Court had voiced its concern for local records as early as 1639 and where nineteenth-century acts had at various times urged care in making and keeping them, Carroll Davidson Wright, pursuant to an act of 1884, submitted five years later a report "upon the condition of all public records of the parishes, towns, and counties" of the Commonwealth. The report led to the creation of the office of the Commissioner of Public Records, ably filled by Robert Thaxter Swan (1889–1907) and Henry E. Woods (1907–19). An act of 1897 defined public records and established the responsibility of local custodians in providing fireproof housing, in the repair and binding of neglected records, and in the use of standard ink and paper. It also prohibited any destruction of records without the approval of the Commissioner of Public Records.[36]

In New York the appointment of a State Historian in 1895 led to the establishment of a Division of Public Records, headed by the Supervisor of Public Records, whose duty it was to keep an eye on the preser-

[35] Report of the Secretary of State and State Librarian to the General Assembly on Ancient Court Records (Hartford, 1889), p. 3.

[36] Henry E. Woods, "The Massachusetts Laws and Commission of Public Records," loc. cit., pp. 101–11. Shortly before Woods's death, the office of Commissioner of Public Records was abolished and its powers and duties were transferred to the office of the Secretary of the Commonwealth, who was to appoint a "Supervisor of Public Records."

vation of local records. Later, a law of 1913 specified the requirements to be met by the local custodians.

ARCHIVES AND THE SCIENTIFIC SCHOOL OF HISTORY

Systematic care of the archives of the United States and especially of the archives of the states has its taproot in the development of scholarly concern for the availability of original source materials, a cause of supreme interest to the school of scientific historians that emerged in the last decades of the nineteenth century. As pointed out before, the many American agents who were sent to Europe to obtain copies of records, and historians like Sparks and Bancroft who went on their own behalf did not urge the establishment of professionally administered archival depositories such as existed in Europe, though they had enjoyed and praised their services. In the 1870's, however, federal administrators began to realize that non-current records should be concentrated in *ad hoc* institutions and recommended the establishment for that purpose of a "Hall of Records"; and, about the same time, a historical profession began to develop in the United States. Historical writing had previously been mostly the business of the amateur and antiquarian, but a change took place when the "scientific school" of historical writing began to rise in the United States, bringing back from Germany and other European countries the tenets of the scholarly approach. Earlier Americans — such as Joseph G. Cogswell, George Ticknor, and Edward Everett — had failed to do this although they had studied in Germany and although Ranke's famous *History of the Romance and Germanic Peoples*, based on the critical use of archival sources, had already appeared. After the Franco-Prussian War of 1870–71, German universities became the mecca of American and European historical students; for they were convinced of the superiority of the German educational system, which seemed so clearly demonstrated by the outcome of the war. Among the Americans there were Andrew D. White, first president of Cornell University, and Daniel C. Gilman, first president of the Johns Hopkins University, and there were John W. Burgess, Henry Adams, and Herbert Baxter Adams. The impact these men had on graduate work and particularly on historical studies in the United States was far-reaching. They acquired, and brought back with them, an appreciation of the liberal curriculum of German universities in general and — equally important — an admiration of Ranke's seminar method, designed to introduce the student to the use and critical evaluation of original sources. Momentous also was the German seminar's emphasis on institutional history, a study for which the use of archival source material was obviously of prime importance. In the 1870's, too, contacts between German universities and archival institutions became much closer than they had been in the past. Trained historians began to be appointed to archival positions, particularly after Heinrich von Sybel had become Director of the Prussian State Archives in 1875; and, vice versa, such experienced archivists as Max Lehmann and Friedrich Meinecke were appointed to chairs of history in the universities. An identity of purpose united archivists and history professors.

Nobody was more thoroughly sure of the superiority of the German historical method than was Herbert Baxter Adams, who studied in Germany from 1874 to 1876. He had received his instruction from professors like Droysen, Erdmannsdörffer, and Treitschke, who had produced or were working on great historical works for which they had consulted the resources of the Prussian Privy State Archives. What he had observed and learned in Berlin and as a Ph.D. candidate at the University of Heidelberg Adams put to use when in 1876 he became a teaching fellow at the newly established Johns Hopkins University and there organized the first full-fledged historical seminar in the United States.

In the Hopkins seminar, Adams stressed the study of the history of institutions, so much so that he preferred to remain "Professor of Institutional History" rather than to be known as professor of American history when offered the latter title.[37] Obviously, institutional history could not be written without the records of the institutions involved; later on, Woodrow Wilson, student at Johns Hopkins from 1883 to 1885, complained, "These professors wanted to set everybody under their authority to working on what they called 'institutional history,' to digging, that is, into the dusty records of old settlements and colonial history."[38]

With their experience in seminar work and the use of archival material, the scientific historians "passed on to their disciples a respect for arduous industry in uncovering manuscript sources."[39] It was necessary, however, for the new generation of historians to organize itself before, from academic interest in "uncovering manuscript sources," it could and would speak up in favor of their preservation and accessibility for research purposes. Also, a leader was needed to serve incessantly and doggedly as spokesman of those concerned about the care of American official and non-official records. Such a spokesman the new historians were fortunate to find in Professor J. Franklin Jameson, then managing editor of the *American Historical Review* and one of the great historical statesmen of the Western world.

[37] H. Hale Bellot, *American History and American Historians* (Norman, Okla., 1952), pp. 18 ff.

[38] W. Stull Holt (ed.), *Historical Scholarship in the United States, 1876–1901: As Revealed in the Correspondence of Herbert B. Adams* (Baltimore, 1938), p. 90, n. 1, quoting Ray Stannard Baker, *Woodrow Wilson: Life and Letters*, I (Garden City, N.Y., 1927), 174.

[39] Harvey Wish, *The American Historian* (New York, 1960), p. 132.

The American Historical Association was founded in 1884, and from
its early days it stressed the importance of original sources, on which the
new historians were to rely — not only those in foreign depositories, on
which for decades interest had focused, but also those in the United States.
An organization similar to the Royal Historical Manuscripts Commission
in England seemed a desideratum. By 1895 Jameson was ready with a
concrete plan for the first standing committee of the American Historical
Association, its Historical Manuscripts Commission, which was to prepare
or supervise "a calendar of original manuscripts and records of national
interest relating to the colonial and later history of the United States." [40]
The Commission, formally constituted on December 27, 1895, resolved at
its June 1, 1896, meeting "that the Commission's first volume should contain a bibliography, or list of printed guides to the contents of American
archives or similar repositories of manuscript historical material in the
United States and Canada," which would enable "the Commission, and
other students, to learn as early as possible what unprinted materials
are now accessible to investigators." [41] The resulting "A List of Printed
Guides to and Descriptions of Archives and Other Repositories of Historical Manuscript," [42] compiled by Edmund C. Burnett, was a first
significant effort to establish control over archival as well as manuscript
material within the United States.

Rightly, however, it was felt that, once it became a matter of describing
the materials themselves, the task would call for the efforts of two distinct groups, one to deal with official sources and the other to discover
and describe private materials. At the 1899 meeting of the Association,
therefore, a Public Archives Commission was organized and "charged to
investigate and report, from the point of view of historical study, upon
the character, contents, and functions of our public repositories of manuscript records." [43] It was clear from the beginning that an enterprise so
vast could not be undertaken by the Commission of five members originally appointed; so the Commission was authorized to obtain the help
of adjunct members in the states and territories. These men, with the
additional help of associate members, were to do the actual work. Never
was so big an enterprise started and successfully carried forward with so

[40] *Annual Report of the American Historical Association for the Year 1895* (Washington, 1896), p. 10. (Hereafter in this chapter similar reports are cited as "AHA, *Annual
Report*," with the year for the report italicized and the place and date of publication
omitted.)

[41] AHA, *Annual Report, 1896*, I, 470.

[42] *Ibid.*, pp. 481–512.

[43] AHA, *Annual Report, 1899*, I, 24 ff.

little money, for the Commission's total financial support consisted of $500 for postal expense.

Promptly in 1900 the Commission submitted its first report,[44] to which there were attached preliminary survey reports on Connecticut, Indiana, Iowa, Massachusetts, Michigan, Nebraska, North Carolina, Pennsylvania, and Wisconsin and Osgood's comprehensive report of almost 200 pages on the archives of New York. The Commission found widely divergent conditions: some states had considerable accumulations of records, others very little; some took good care of them, others were guilty of total neglect. As the Commission had pointed out to its collaborators, the work was to consist of investigating the extent, condition, character, and availability of the numerous classes of public records in the states and important local communities and to do so in the hope that it would help arouse interest in the better care of archives. The Commission believed that at least at this point it would not be wise to propose for general application a "specific and detailed plan for public record keeping," for

So long as conditions present few points of similarity in any two States, it is hardly practicable to formulate a scheme which shall take account of any considerable number of them, while the proverbial reluctance of American commonwealths to profit by example makes it unsafe to assume that a scheme that has met approval in one State will, because of that fact, be favorably received in another.[45]

On the other hand, the Commission wanted to support actively any efforts aimed at improving existing conditions. Its work proceeded with great regularity and speed. By 1910 it had obtained forty-six survey reports for thirty-two states, two cities, and the Philippines, while those for fourteen states, eleven of them east of the Mississippi River, were still missing. These reports, though uneven in respect to workmanship and data furnished, constituted an incredible achievement. In addition, their preparation had elicited increasing interest in the states and had produced a great amount of pertinent legislation. Equally important, a great many states had made concrete provision for the administration of their archives.[46]

THE FORMATIVE PERIOD OF THE AMERICAN STATE ARCHIVES

The South preceded other regions of the country in taking constructive action. To facilitate the use of archival material by the American scholar

[44] AHA, *Annual Report, 1900*, II, 5–25.
[45] *Ibid.*, p. 24.
[46] According to the AHA, *Annual Report, 1909*, p. 340, departments of archives and history had been established in Alabama (1901), Mississippi (1902), and West Virginia (1905). Commissions, named Public Records or Historical Commissions, and archivists had been appointed in Pennsylvania (1903, advisory), Maryland (1904, discontinued 1906), Delaware (1905), North Carolina (1903), South Carolina (1905), Arkansas (1905,

through proper administrative arrangements based on sound legislation had been the basic intent of the Public Archives Commission, and this intent was first realized in Alabama. Interested in history from childhood though a lawyer by profession, Thomas McAdory Owen, Sr., had helped to organize the Southern Historical Society while in Washington, D.C. Resuming the practice of law in Alabama and serving as secretary of the ailing Alabama Historical Society, he prevailed upon the General Assembly to create the Alabama Historical Commission in 1898. As chairman of the Commission, he guided through the assembly legislation that established on February 27, 1901, the Department of Archives and History of the state, of which he became director, serving under a self-perpetuating board of trustees. The law gave the department a sweeping mandate which, in addition to the care and custody of official archives, included the collection of historical materials of all kinds, publication of official records and other historical sources, "diffusion of historical knowledge and encouragement of historical work and research." [47]

Assembling with remarkable success records not in current use and, as envisioned in the law, manuscripts, museum pieces, newspapers, and "relics and personal belongings of eminent Alabamians, as library desks or tables, chairs, knives, dirks, dueling pistols or other fire arms, stock, knee or shoe buckles, drinking cups, watches, chains, snuff boxes, and canes," Owen defended before the Public Archives Commission the concept of the state archival and historical agency as superior to any other administrative arrangement. He gave short shrift to the librarians. "How many librarians are fit to cope with musty archives?" he asked. "How many are equipped to edit your historical publications? How many are able to respond to calls for detailed historical or statistical information?" The state historical society could not accomplish the task either, for "no existing society, however useful its work and extensive its operations, undertakes or is in position to undertake the functions of archivist." Could an organization like the Public Records Commission of Massachusetts do the job? While "a useful and wise institution," Owen thought

---

1909), Illinois (1905, advisory), and Tennessee (1907, office of the archivist). The role of the state library as the state's archival agency had been established or confirmed in Pennsylvania (1903), Indiana (1905), Iowa (1906, 1907), Virginia (1905), Texas (1909), and Connecticut (1909). In Kansas (1905), Nebraska (1905), Wisconsin (1907), and Oklahoma (1908) the state historical society had become the depository for state archives, while in New York (1900, actually 1895), Maine (1907), and Arizona (1909) state historians had been appointed and instructed to collect, edit, and prepare archival material for publication rather than to have custody of the records themselves. Commissioners or supervisors of public — that is, local — records had been put in charge of records in Massachusetts, Connecticut, and Rhode Island. See also Waldo G. Leland, "The Work of the Public Archives Commission of the American Historical Association," in Cuvelier and Stainier, *op. cit.*, pp. 463–67.

[47] See pp. 38 ff. On Owen, see Peter A. Brannon, "The Alabama Department of Archives and History," *Alabama Historical Quarterly*, XXIV (Spring, 1962), 1–15.

it was "too limited in scope" and did "not undertake to view archives in any sense from the standpoint of the historical student," which, in accordance with the mandate given the Public Archives Commission, was to Owen the decisive point.[48]

In neighboring Mississippi, Franklin L. Riley, a former student of Herbert B. Adams, archives conscious and stimulated by Owen's success, urged the creation of a Department of Archives and History in his capacity of chairman of the newly established Historical Commission of the state, and he succeeded in having the legislature establish the Department of Archives and History by an act that used the Alabama act as a model. Dunbar Rowland, director of the department from 1902 to 1937, found it possible as early as 1914 to publish *An Official Guide to the Historical Materials in the Mississippi Department of Archives and History*,[49] the first state archival guide to be published in the United States.

The example of Alabama and Mississippi prompted other Southern states to organize historical commissions. That of Arkansas did not develop into a Department of Archives and History. In North Carolina the Historical Commission was renamed the Department of Archives and History in 1943, and in South Carolina a similar commission became the Archives Department in 1950. West Virginia provided a Department of Archives and History in 1905, Virginia established one as part of the State Library in 1904, and Tennessee appropriated funds for a department in 1907, though it did not formally create one. Georgia provided a Historical Commission and under it a Department of Archives and History in 1918. Delaware's Public Archives Commission was organized in 1903 in prompt response to public indignation that had been aroused by the investigations of the Public Archives Commission of the American Historical Association, then still in progress.

A different pattern of organization for archival service evolved in the Middle West, where state-supported historical societies had assumed many of the functions that in the South were handled by historical commissions and departments of archives and history. The first states to recognize the state historical society as a depository for non-current records were Kansas and Nebraska, where laws to that effect were enacted on March 4 and March 30, 1905, respectively. Further study is needed to identify the forces and individuals that backed these laws. Undoubtedly, the existence and functions of the Southern departments of archives and history were widely known, and characteristically the Nebraska act charged the State Historical Society broadly with serving as "the custodian of all public records, documents, relics, and other material which it may consider of historic value or interest and which are now or may hereafter

[48] Thomas McAdory Owen, "State Departments of Archives and History," AHA, *Annual Report, 1904*, pp. 237–57.
[49] See pp. 159 ff.

be" in any of the departments, institutions, county courthouses, city halls, or other public buildings.[50] Wisconsin and Minnesota, where the state historical societies, thanks to close working relationships with the universities, had become agencies of great scholarly and cultural rank, also provided for archival institutions. In respect to Wisconsin, one would like to find a connection between the society's becoming the archival depository of the state and the flowering of historical studies that followed Frederick Jackson Turner's return to Madison after he had been a fellow at Johns Hopkins, but no such connection seems to exist. In his "Report on the Public Archives of Wisconsin," however, Carl Russell Fish mentioned, as an alternative to creating a department of archives and history, the transfer of the "older records into the charge of the society, which has so amply shown its ability to care for them." [51] A law authorizing state officials to transfer to the State Historical Society records "five years after the current use of the same, or sooner in the discretion of the head of the department" (Wisconsin Laws, 1907, ch. 88) had little effect so long as the society lacked the space to house them.[52] In Minnesota, Herbert A. Kellar's "Preliminary Survey of the More Important Archives of the Territory and State of Minnesota" clearly showed the need for remedial measures.[53] An act to authorize the Minnesota Historical Society to act as custodian of the state and local archives was passed in 1919.

Many states followed the early example of Kansas, Nebraska, and Wisconsin and the later one of Minnesota. State historical societies were recognized as official repositories for state archival material in Oklahoma (1917), Utah (1917), New Mexico (1927), Ohio (1927), Colorado (1943), Nevada (1943), and Idaho (1947)[54] or were occasionally used as depositories without formal legal action, as happened in Kentucky, Maryland, Missouri, Montana, North Dakota, and South Dakota.

In the Middle West, Iowa and Illinois charted a course of their own. Thanks to the efforts of Charles Aldrich, working closely with Benjamin F. Shambaugh, a professor of history at the University of Iowa with a doctoral degree from the University of Pennsylvania, the state of Iowa created in 1906 the State Library and Historical Department and gave it "the custody of all original public documents, papers, letters, records, or other official manuscripts of the state executive and administrative departments" ten years after the date of current use of these documents.

[50] Herman V. Ames (comp.), "Résumé of the Archives Situations in the Several States in 1907," AHA, *Annual Report, 1907*, I, 175.

[51] AHA, *Annual Report, 1905*, I, 379.

[52] Theodore C. Blegen, *A Report on the Public Archives* (State Historical Society of Wisconsin, Bulletin of Information No. 94 [Madison, 1918]), pp. 89, 99 ff.

[53] AHA, *Annual Report, 1914*, I, 385–476.

[54] In Colorado, New Mexico, and Minnesota the historical societies lost the archives function to specialized agencies. In Oklahoma it went to the State Library. See below under the respective states.

Under the able administration of Cassius C. Stiles, the Department developed into one of the leading archival institutions of the country. Stiles's advice was sought by many states, and his *Public Archives: A Manual for Their Administration in Iowa* became the first American handbook in the field. In Illinois, George H. Harlow, Secretary of State of Illinois from 1873 to 1881, had organized a Division of Archives and Index in his office.[55] It later became nothing but an indexing department. Archival interest, however, received a major stimulus from the work of Clarence W. Alvord. Then an instructor at the University of Illinois, he had studied two years under Paul Schäffer-Boichhorst in Berlin. In 1905 he was sent by the Illinois Historical Society to Belleville, where he discovered the records of the French and Virginian periods of the Illinois region from 1720 to 1790.[56] Working with the State Historical Library, he prevailed on the legislature to appoint a commission to make plans for a new state education building. It was for this commission that Waldo Gifford Leland in 1913 prepared his report on the "Public Archives and Historical Interests of the State of Illinois." [57] The State Archives found a refuge in the new state building, not as the independent agency that Dr. Leland had suggested but as a department of the State Library under the Secretary of State, who serves as State Librarian.

While impressively prompt action thus was being taken in many states to cope with the problem of archival preservation, the Public Archives Commission continued to receive reports from the various states and to submit them to the American Historical Association for publication in the annual reports. By 1909 constructive steps had been taken in so many states, and so many persons had become actively engaged in archival work that the members of the Commission thought it appropriate and timely to organize as "an outgrowth of the informal conference of the public archives commission with its adjunct and associate members . . . a conference of archivists, open to the public." [58] It was at "this first formal gathering in America of archivists and of those deeply interested in American archives" that Dr. Leland read his paper on "American Archival Problems." [59] In it he developed the two types of problems he saw — those pertaining to the external regulation of the archives and those having to do with their internal economy. In a second and equally significant paper, "Some Fundamental Principles in Relation to Archives," read before the Fourth Conference of Archivists in 1912, Dr.

[55] *Blue Book of the State of Illinois, 1935–36* (n.p., n.d.), p. 692.
[56] Bellot, *op. cit.*, p. 24.
[57] See p. 98.
[58] "Tenth Annual Report of the Public Archives Commission," AHA, *Annual Report, 1909*, p. 330.
[59] *Ibid.*, pp. 342–48.

Leland further explored basic aspects of the nature of archives and their administration.[60]

The Public Archives Commission had been singularly successful in encouraging steps toward better care of archives in a good many states. The Conference of Archivists served the equally important purpose of uniting those engaged in archival work for the discussion of professional problems. Its work "marked the formal and conscious recognition of the administration of archives as a distinct profession similar to other custodial professions, but differing from them in demands and qualifications."[61] Because, during the years when the conferences were held, there was neither a national archival agency that could have served as a pacemaker nor a professional journal, the seminal effect of those gatherings was considerable.

THE NATIONAL ASSOCIATION OF STATE LIBRARIES

The Public Archives Commission and the later Conference of American Archivists had grown out of the American historian's awareness of the importance of archival material. At the time the first Conference of American Archivists was held, the National Association of State Libraries began to give attention to the field of archives. At its thirteenth annual meeting, on Mackinac Island, the association's secretary-treasurer, Asa C. Tilton of the Connecticut State Library, recommended "that the Association carefully consider the advisability of adding to its committees a Committee on public archives which shall collect material relating to archives and present the same to the Association in annual reports." [62] State libraries charged with the care of archives or to be charged with such care in the future, Tilton said, would benefit from knowing "what was being done in other states and countries." A motion to establish a Public Archives Committee of the association was carried, and in 1911 the committee, then consisting of A. C. Tilton as chairman, J. L. Gillis of California, Gaillard Hunt of the Library of Congress, H. R. McIlwaine of Virginia, and T. L. Montgomery of Pennsylvania, submitted its first report. It was based on a circular containing questions about legal provision for the centralization of state and local archives, the existence of permanent or temporary commissions concerned with public records, administrative arrangements for a central repository and staff, and arrangement and description work in progress.[63]

From then on, the annual reports of the committee furnished a nation-wide running account of new legislation and activities in the archives

[60] AHA, *Annual Report, 1912*, pp. 264–68.
[61] Waldo G. Leland, "The First Conference of Archivists, December, 1909: The Beginnings of a Profession," *American Archivist*, XIII (Apr., 1950), 115.
[62] National Association of State Libraries, *Proceedings and Addresses* (n.p., 1910), pp. 9 ff.
[63] *Ibid.* (1911), pp. 24–36.

field and an additional means of exchanging information among those working in it. Beginning in 1919, however, the committee suffered an almost complete eclipse although papers on aspects of archives work continued to be read before the meetings of the association. At the 1922 meeting, for instance, John M. Hitt of the Washington State Library, discussing archives in his state, acquainted his listeners with a patented process "of filming official papers, in consecutive order, showing clearly the serial numbers and also the pages of books on a single film." [64]

Perhaps the most important and influential paper to come out of these meetings was the one that Margaret C. Norton, Archivist of Illinois, read at the 1930 meeting in Los Angeles: "The Archives Department as an Administrative Unit in Government." [65] This struck a new and significant note. Although giving due credit to the work of the Public Archives Commission, Miss Norton felt that the emphasis it had given to the historian's stake in archival preservation was one-sided and that the time had come to stress "proper care of archives as an administrative problem of state government instead of as a mere adjunct to the historical library field." Such mistaken emphasis, she pointed out, did not do justice to the primarily administrative need for the existence of an archival agency, and indeed made financial support for such an agency more difficult to obtain. Criticizing again "the fallacy of treating archives merely as historical records," Miss Norton set forth her ideas of the "Scope and Functions of a State Archives Department" [66] at a joint session of the National Association of State Libraries with the A.L.A. Committee on Archives and Libraries in 1937. The latter committee, an outgrowth and adjunct of the A.L.A. Committee on Public Documents, held regular sessions on aspects of archival administration from 1937 to 1941. Both of Miss Norton's papers had an incisive effect on the thinking of American archivists.

THE HISTORICAL RECORDS SURVEY

In the meantime, the Public Archives Commission of the American Historical Association had continued its activities. [67] At the fourth Annual Conference of Archivists, held in Boston in 1912, Herman V. Ames, the Commission's chairman from 1903 to 1912, pointed with justifiable pride to its achievements, for two-thirds of the archives of the states had been surveyed and information concerning them had been presented in the Commission's annual reports. [68] With much of its original purpose accom-

[64] *Ibid.* (1922), p. 5.

[65] *Ibid.* (1930), pp. 44–48.

[66] *Ibid.* (Springfield, Ill., 1937), pp. 15–20, and American Library Association, *Public Documents with Archives and Libraries* (Chicago, 1937), pp. 262–75.

[67] For the following see Victor H. Paltsits, "An Historical Résumé of the Public Archives Commission from 1899 to 1921," AHA, *Annual Report, 1922*, I, 152–63.

[68] That much progress had been made in providing archival service in the states became apparent during World War I. In connection with and encouraged by the activities of the

plished, it seemed timely to Ames "that attention should be directed to the practical problems of archive administration." [69] From then on until the thirties the preparation of a manual on archives administration engaged much of the interest of the Commission and of the Conference of Archivists. A systematic proposal for "a manual of archival economy for the use of American Archivists," later reduced to "a primer," was submitted by Victor H. Paltsits, chairman of the Commission from 1913 to 1922; but, though some of the chapters he had planned were actually prepared, the work was never completed.

The Commission, suspended in 1919, was reactivated a year later "as a clearing house of information respecting archival matters," and the suggestion was made that "its reports should contain a summary of American legislation respecting archives, together with notes of important developments in this country and abroad." Thus the Commission continued its activities, organizing the annual conferences of American archivists and compiling annual surveys of archival legislation. The publication of surveys of state archives had stopped in 1917, before surveys for South Carolina, New Hampshire, Nevada, North Dakota, South Dakota, Utah, and Oklahoma had been published.[70] The Commission seemed to have lost its early vigor. In 1930, however, there emerged a plan for a survey of a new kind that might have breathed new life into the Commission. At that year's Conference of American Archivists Solon J. Buck pointed out that the survey reports were out of date and that the Joint Committee on Materials for Research of the American Council of Learned Societies and the Social Science Research Council had asked the Public Archives Commission for a new survey of state archives, to be published in one volume.[71]

. . . this survey should not attempt to present detailed inventories of the type included in the original reports, but should instead, for each state, summarize the important general and special legislation concerning the making, custody, and supervision of state and local archives; list the custodians and depositories of state archives with a general indication of the material in each and the situation with reference to condition, care and accessibility; list all reports, inventories, and catalogues, published or unpublished, of state and local

National Board of Historical Service many states recognized the importance of collecting and preserving the records of civil participation in the war. Arkansas, Iowa, Mississippi, and Nebraska relied on their archival agencies to do the job. In other states — Alabama, Connecticut, Michigan, North Carolina, and Wisconsin — ad hoc committees or commissions were affiliated with the state archival authorities and enjoyed their co-operation. Franklin F. Holbrook, "The Collection of State War Service Records," *American Historical Review*, XXV (Oct., 1919), 72 ff.

[69] AHA, *Annual Report, 1912*, p. 250.
[70] Report of the Public Archives Commission, AHA, *Annual Report, 1932*, p. 65.
[71] Buck was then superintendent of the Minnesota Historical Society and chairman of the Joint Committee on Materials for Research. A typed abstract of his remarks is in his file "U.S. State and Local Archives," now in the National Archives Library.

archives; and set forth the practice in the state with reference to the destruction of archival material considered not worthy of preservation.

As suggested by Buck, Lester J. Cappon and Margaret C. Norton offered to do pilot reports on their states, and Charles W. Ramsdell of the University of Texas, chairman of the Public Archives Commission, stated the case for a new survey before the Council of the American Historical Association. The proposal was rejected "on the ground that the project was too large, that it would be impossible to do the work adequately with any sum which the Association has or is likely to have at its disposal." Changing the signals rather abruptly, the American Historical Association instructed the Public Archives Commission, reconstituted under the chairmanship of A. R. Newsome, to compile "during the year 1932 a pamphlet on the preservation of county and other local records, with information as to good models of legislation on the subject, to be sent to the clerks of all such local subdivisions, to historical societies, and to historical commissions." [72] Reporting for the Commission on the completion of the pamphlet, *The Preservation of Local Archives: A Guide for Public Officials* (Washington, 1932), Newsome renewed the plea for the "new type of survey of State Archives" that would be "a brief description by States of the various State departments and agencies, the condition and location of the archives of each agency, the methods used to insure their preservation, the facilities for their use, and the laws which affect them." [73]

Newsome's 1934 report for the Public Archives Commission, in conjunction with a memorandum prepared by Francis S. Philbrick,[74] led, at the December 2, 1934, meeting of the Council of the Association, to the appointment of a special committee "charged with the duties of (1) considering the relationship of the A.H.A. to the whole problem of documentary publications and of national, state, local, and private archives, and of making specific recommendations to the council; (2) considering, formulating, and presenting plans for a nation-wide survey of archival material which might be made the basis for an appeal to the foundations." [75] The report, submitted on October 15, 1935, emphasized the important concern of the American Historical Association with the problem of public archives and historical manuscripts and proposed the

[72] AHA, *Annual Report, 1931*, I, 39; and Ramsdell to Buck, Nov. 29, 1931, *loc. cit.* Ramsdell did not think much of the project. "If I know county clerks and their like, they will promptly throw the pamphlet in the waste basket and resent the (to them) intrusive interference of a 'lot of impractical highbrows.' But that is the new program." It prompted Ramsdell to resign from the Commission.

[73] AHA, *Annual Report, 1932*, p. 66.

[74] Philbrick, Professor of Law at the University of Pennsylvania, was chairman of the Littleton-Griswold Committee of the American Historical Association and Secretary of the American Legal Society.

[75] AHA, *Annual Report, 1935*, I, 77.

creation of a standing committee on historical source materials charged with "the entire interest and effort of the Association in respect to State and local archives and historical manuscripts, exclusive of their publication," the committee to have subcommittees on public archives and on historical manuscripts. As for a nationwide survey of state and local archives, the Newsome-Philbrick committee did not wish to deal with it, because "approval by the Works Progress Administration at Washington of a nation-wide survey of State and local archives and historical manuscripts" was pending at that time.[76]

The idea of this survey began to take form in 1934, at a conference called by Robert C. Binkley of Western Reserve University as chairman of the Joint Committee on Materials for Research.[77] A number of state records surveys financed by funds of the Civil Works Authority and the Federal Emergency Relief Administration were already under way when Luther H. Evans submitted to Harry Hopkins a plan for a national survey of state and local archives. This resulted in the establishment, by Presidential Letter No. 1090 (November 15, 1935), of the Historical Records Survey of the Works Progress Administration. At an organization meeting on December 5, 1935, attended by A. R. Newsome, former Secretary of the North Carolina Historical Commission, Solon J. Buck and T. R. Schellenberg of the newly established National Archives, Robert C. Binkley, and Verne E. Chatelain of the National Park Service, it was suggested that the survey should start with "an inventory of county records or some other selected category of records found throughout the country."[78] With the careful planning, instructions, and supervision of Evans and Sargent B. Child, National Field Supervisor and Evans' chief assistant, an average of 3,000 clerical workers were employed from 1936 to 1939, when the Survey came to an end as a federal project and its work was continued as state projects. Of the many projects undertaken by the Survey, the survey of county archives was by all odds the most successful. Field work was completed in 90 per cent of the counties, and 628 volumes of county archival inventories were published by 1942.[79]

These production figures do not do justice, however, to the significance and after-effects of the Historical Records Survey. As a nationwide enterprise it succeeded in channeling manpower that otherwise would have

[76] "Report of the Special Committee to the Executive Council," Oct. 15, 1935, AHA, *Annual Report, 1935*, I, 175–80.

[77] The best evaluation of the work of the Historical Records Survey is found in David L. Smiley, "The W.P.A. Historical Records Survey," in Hesseltine and McNeil, *op. cit.*, pp. 3–28.

[78] *Ibid.*, p. 13.

[79] In addition there had been published 584 volumes of federal archives inventories, 28 volumes of state archives inventories, 180 volumes of municipal and town archives inventories, 107 guides to manuscript collections, 164 volumes of church archives inventories, and 49 volumes listing American imprints.

been idle into a national undertaking on a scale never before conceived. European countries facing the human problems of massive unemployment had not been able to develop plans of comparable magnitude. From the vantage point of archival administration, the importance of local records and the necessity of caring for them had been brought down to the grass roots, and many improvements had been made. State archival agencies had been provided with inventories of county records that to this day furnish the basis from which measures directed at their preservation must start. Yet perhaps one of the most significant results of the Historical Records Survey was the role it played as a training ground for future state archivists and state archives personnel. At the beginning, scholars long known for their interest and work with archives served as supervisors, among them Lester J. Cappon (Virginia), Christopher Crittenden (North Carolina), Curtis W. Garrison (Pennsylvania), Milo M. Quaife (Michigan), and William D. Overman (Ohio). As time went on, they were joined or replaced by men who were to play an important role in the history of state archival administration, such as John C. L. Andreassen (Louisiana), Morris L. Radoff (Maryland), Henry Eddy (Vermont), and Jesse E. Boell (Wisconsin). Until the Historical Records Survey went to work it was principally the New England states and New York that had developed practical solutions to the local records problem. The rich materials now accessible through the inventories of the Survey made it obvious that archivists in many states had been remiss in trying to provide for their care, even though the problem had been discussed at their conferences.[80]

A NATIONAL SOCIETY OF ARCHIVISTS

On November 1, 1935, Solon J. Buck, newly appointed Director of Publications of the National Archives, submitted to the first Archivist of the United States his correspondence relating to the proposed manual of archival economy and to the survey of state and local archives then being considered by the Public Archives Commission. In his memorandum he pointed out that "the difficulties that the Public Archives Commission had as a subsidiary of the American Historical Association, especially in attempting to promote these projects, are suggestive, I think, of the need for an independent organization of archivists."[81] An organizing committee appointed by A. R. Newsome at the 1935 meeting of the American Historical Association went to work on drafting a constitution

[80] Solon J. Buck, "Local Archives. Should They Be Centralized at the State Capitol? Advantages and Disadvantages of Such a Centralization," AHA, *Annual Report, 1913,* I, 268–71; Charles H. Rammelkamp, "Legislation for Archives," *ibid., 1914,* I, 361 ff.; and Theodore C. Pease, "The Problem of Archive Centralization with Reference to Local Conditions in a Middle Western State," *ibid., 1916,* I, 151–54.
[81] Buck's file, *loc. cit.*

for a society of archivists; and at a meeting held at Providence, Rhode Island, on December 29, 1936, the Society of American Archivists came into being.[82]

The work of the Historical Records Survey, the founding of the Society of American Archivists, and the establishment of the National Archives under R. D. W. Connor, former Secretary of the North Carolina Historical Commission, were bound to quicken the pace of archival development in the states. Maryland joined the states that had been leaders in the field when the Hall of Records was built in 1934–35 and the Hall of Records Commission was organized by an act of 1935. The Illinois State Archives, which under Margaret C. Norton had become an important center of archival work, moved into its new building in 1938, and its activities contributed significantly to a reorientation of archivists. For many years Miss Norton edited a section entitled "Illinois Archival Information" in *Illinois Libraries,* and most of the articles she wrote herself. Although some of them dealt with Illinois materials and topics, the majority touched on basic problems of state archivists and became a major source of information for them. Her articles continued to reflect the conviction that she had first stated before the National Association of State Libraries — that archival materials are primarily the government's legal and administrative documentation and only secondarily research material for the historian and that the philosophy and practices of state archival agencies must flow from this overriding consideration. Other leading state archivists[83] have elaborated this thought, which has become a generally accepted tenet of archivists in the United States. As the nature of archival material was assessed more realistically, state archivists and their staffs also began to understand more clearly the difference between archives and private papers on the one hand and between archives and library material on the other. Accordingly, where agencies were charged with responsibility for functions other than archives administration, a sharper separation of their various duties began to be made.

During the formative period of American state archives, different patterns of organization had been adopted. Some archives had developed as adjuncts to the office of the secretary of state, some as parts of the state library, and some within the state historical society; and still others had been established as independent commissions or as departments governed by such commissions. "A generation of uncorrelated, unsystem-

[82] Philip C. Brooks, "The First Decade of the Society of American Archivists," *American Archivist,* X (Apr., 1947), 115–28.

[83] Henry H. Eddy, "The Responsibility of the State Archivist to the Other Officers of His State Government," *American Archivist,* XI (Jan., 1948), 28–35; Christopher Crittenden, "The Archivist as a Public Servant," *ibid.,* XII (Jan., 1949), 3–8; and Dolores C. Renze, "The State Archivist — 3-D Public Servant," *ibid.,* XXIII (July, 1960), 271–75. See also Margaret C. Norton, "The Place of Archives in Government," *Illinois Libraries,* XXXIV (Apr., 1952), 153–60.

atic experimentation . . . [had] produced a wide diversity of legislation, administration, and achievement." [84] In his challenging presidential address to the 1938 meeting of the Society of American Archivists, Newsome reviewed the existing disparities and called on the society "to formulate the best existing archival legislation in the states and endeavor to mobilize all available support in obtaining uniform or similar laws in all of the states." [85] A Committee on Uniform State Legislation, authorized by the society's Council and chaired by Newsome, drafted a "Proposed Uniform State Public Records Act" for submission to the 1939 meeting of the society. It defined public records; dealt with their making, keeping, availability, recovery, care, and disposal; and stated the duties of the head of the state archival agency, who was to have general supervision over the "making, administration, and preservation" of records still in the agencies of origin.[86]

Subsequently, the Committee on Uniform State Legislation undertook the even more formidable task of drafting an act for the establishment of a state archival agency. Arguing that an archival-historical agency "is more practicable and suitable for the conditions that generally prevail in the states," it formulated "A Proposed Model Act to Create a State Department of Archives and History," which clearly took its guiding ideas from the laws enacted in some of the Southern states, although it spelled out the archival duties of the department with particular care.[87] It is obvious, however, that an act of this kind did not fit the situation in many states; therefore in 1946 the committee, more realistically renamed the Committee on Archival Legislation, presented a less ambitious "Model Bill for a State Archives Department." [88] According to this bill, the duties and objectives of such a department were limited to the assembling, administration, and publication of public archives, the improvement of standards for their creation and administration in the public agencies, and the stimulation of research in the field of state history.

The 1946 model bill was drafted at a time when the boundaries of the archivist's task were beginning to be redrawn. Impressed by the awesome fact that federal agencies were producing records on an unprecedented scale and of a kind that made selection of valuable records and their arrangement incredibly difficult, the National Archives had embarked on its program of records administration. This was aimed at convincing agency administrators of the need to institute sound programs of records management. The emergency and World War II periods — with the con-

[84] Albert R. Newsome, "Uniform State Archival Legislation," *American Archivist*, II (Jan., 1939), 1.
[85] *Ibid.*, p. 3.
[86] *Ibid.*, III (Apr., 1940), 107–15.
[87] *Ibid.*, VII (Apr., 1944), 130–33.
[88] *Ibid.*, X (Jan., 1947), 47–49.

comitant expansion of staffs, activities, and paper work—had already forced agencies to call in archivists who would assist them in organizing such a program.

In the case of the National Archives, the first step toward coping with the ever increasing quantities of records was the use of the disposal schedule to accelerate the elimination of repetitive series of records, a device that was authorized by the 1943 "Act to provide for the disposal of certain records of the United States Government" (57 Stat. 380). The act prompted many states to adopt the concept of the schedule and, in general, to enact effective disposal legislation.[89] Also, as the federal government began to establish records centers for storing and servicing records of limited retention value and as federal agencies began to appoint records officers to co-operate with National Archives liaison officers in setting up records administration programs, the usefulness of a records management program, including provision for a records center, began to be recognized in the states. Its acceptance was furthered by the report of the first Hoover Commission on Organization of the Executive Branch of the Government and by the establishment, in the General Services Administration, of the National Archives and Records Service, with the dual responsibility of serving as a staff agency in the field of records management and as a depository agency for the administration of federal records of enduring value.

RECENT PROBLEMS AND DEVELOPMENTS

Particularly in the states with well-established archival programs, the need for records management as a measure of economy and efficiency was readily seen. The question arose, however, whether records management responsibility should be vested in the archival agency or whether it would better be discharged by a department of finance, or, where such an agency existed, a department of administration. Finding a solution seemed to be particularly difficult in a state where archival holdings were administered by a historical society charged with many historical activities that had little relation to the management of current and semi-current public records. The problem, where it was attacked, was solved in different ways. Firmly established archival agencies, such as those of Delaware, Maryland, North Carolina, and Illinois, were able to take over the records management function in its entirety. In some states an administrative agency took it over. Still other states divided the complex of records management operations by combining the records center with the archival agency, as in California, Connecticut, and Oregon, and by giving the financial or general administrative agency responsibility for its other

[89] Christopher Crittenden and Nell Hines, "The Disposal of Useless State Archives," *American Archivist*, VII (July, 1944), 165–73.

components. Finally, in some states that had no archival service, records management helped to promote the cause of archives so that a combined records management and archival agency was created — as in Kentucky, New Hampshire, and New Mexico. Though records management proved its usefulness in some states, in others there was a dangerous trend to substitute for a records management program the wholesale use of microfilming — a costly and wasteful procedure.

A naturally related problem also presented itself: whether or not the archival agency (or, where provided, the records management agency) should concern itself with records management in the subdivisions of the state. With respect to local records, conditions were extremely diversified. Successful programs for the preservation of local records had been initiated in some of the New England states and in New York, and the Conference of American Archivists had tried to deal with the question of local records and had debated the *pros* and *cons* of their concentration in the state archival agency. The first problem was how to preserve local records of enduring value; a second and later one was how to provide records management assistance to local authorities.

In regard to the care of local archives, the states had pursued different policies. In Delaware and in North Carolina, concentration of local records in the state archival agency was adopted as the correct solution. Most states, however, considered it impossible to assemble local records at state archival headquarters. If such concentration was not feasible, what other solution was there to the problem of the local archives? State supervision, as practiced in New England and in New York, could be used to insure their proper protection and handling. Still another possibility, however, emerged as a result of the far-flung microfilming activities of the Genealogical Society of the Church of Jesus Christ of Latter-day Saints, hereafter referred to as the Utah Genealogical Society.[90] State archival agencies cooperating with the society's emissaries were able to receive prints of the films produced and thus to obtain security and reference copies of local records. A few states found it possible also to extend the operation to include records dated after 1850 — the society's cutoff date. Archival agencies in most states, however, were not able or did not try to obtain the necessary funds for large-scale microfilming of local records. In a state like New York, for instance, a project of this kind was considered far too expensive, and the problem, it was felt, could be solved only by encouraging the establishment of properly equipped and adequately housed county archival depositories.

Still another solution is now being tried in some states of the Middle West. The Wisconsin State Historical Society has established so-called

[90] Archibald F. Bennett, "The Record Copying Program of the Utah Genealogical Society," *American Archivist*, XVI (July, 1953), 227–32.

[33]

area research centers at several state colleges, Illinois is planning to have three regional centers at major educational institutions, and Ohio has begun to establish regional centers at a number of colleges and historical societies. Similar plans are under way in Michigan, Washington, and Kentucky. Where this device of the regional center is adopted, arrangement and description of holdings remain tasks of the archival agency, while the servicing is the job of the depository. Whether or not this innovation will prove satisfactory, it is too early to say.

In most cases, however, it was found that measures aimed at preserving local records could not be separated from assistance to local agencies in matters of records management. In many states archivists and their staffs were ready with advice and help if called upon by local officials. The principal aim had to be to aid local agencies in matters of records disposal. Where state laws brought local records within the scope of state archival responsibility, this aid could be in the form of retention and disposal schedules for records of local authorities. In an effort to solve the problem, North Carolina's Department of Archives and History developed, in cooperation with organizations of county and municipal officials, a county and a municipal records manual, listing the series of records on hand and suggesting (but not imposing) retention periods for records not to be preserved permanently. The North Carolina program developed in a logical sequence: the Public Records Act of 1935 gave the department authority in matters of public records disposal; an act of 1959 directed it to undertake a program of inventorying, scheduling, repairing, and microfilming county records of permanent value; and a 1961 law enjoined county commissioners and governing bodies of municipalities to establish and maintain records management programs in cooperation with the Department of Archives and History.

In the years since World War II, as the international situation seemed to grow more menacing and the danger of large-scale nuclear attack became a distinct possibility, the Federal Civil Defense Administration and its successor, the Office of Civil and Defense Mobilization, began to concern themselves with the protection of records essential to the continuity of state and local government. The former at first offered to match state funds for the microfilming of essential records; but, when it appeared that the proposals submitted differed widely in their concepts of essential records, the offer was withdrawn. Nevertheless, a draft manual [91] was prepared by Ken Munden with the co-operation of state archivists and of the Microfilming and the State Records committees of the Society of American Archivists. The manual defines the scope and nature of the

[91] Federal Civil Defense Administration, *Preservation of Records Essential to Continuity of State and Local Government* (May, 1958, proc.), 128 p. See also Ken Munden, "Records Essential to Continuity of State and Local Government," *American Archivist*, XXII (Jan., 1959), 25–37.

task, discusses preservation methods and mechanics of protection, and proposes standards for selecting records for preservation. In February, 1960, a "Preservation of Essential Records Act" was prepared in accordance with policy specifications provided by the Office of Civil and Defense Mobilization. The act was included as a supplement in *Suggested State Legislation, Program for 1960*, of the Committee of State Officials on Suggested State Legislation of the Council of State Governments as a model for pertinent state legislation and as a sequel to the Council's "Records Management Act." Such legislation was enacted in but a few states, however, and where it was enacted, funds were not necessarily provided for carrying it out. Yet in many states archivists co-operated with civil defense officials in putting into practice some of the several methods available for the protection of essential records. A few states rented space in commercially owned and operated security vaults. For certain agency records, on the other hand, the storage of security copies in field offices proved an acceptable and practical solution.

THE STATE RECORDS COMMITTEE OF THE SOCIETY OF
AMERICAN ARCHIVISTS

The society's role in promoting the cause of archives in the United States, in furnishing a forum for the discussion of common problems, and, through advice and the exchange of information, in assisting archivists to start and develop their programs, is a matter of record.[92] Aside from the annual meetings of the society and publication of its periodical, the *American Archivist*, the work of its State Records Committee has been of particular value and benefit to state archivists and to the advancement of state archival work.

Strangely enough, no "area committee" to concern itself with state archival problems and activities was appointed until 1950. The State Archives Committee then formed has been remarkably active and productive since its inception. Under the chairmanship of David C. Duniway, it was instructed "to gather administrative data for a manual and study other problems in the field." [93] In 1952 it compiled surveys of archival salaries, microfilm activities, and legal developments. In 1953 it held a breakfast meeting of state archivists, and in 1954 it prepared, for publication in the *American Archivist*, a "Directory of State and Territorial Archival Agencies," [94] which superseded the first directory, compiled by Lester J. Cappon,[95] and an earlier mimeographed one compiled in 1951.

[92] Dolores C. Renze, "A Brief History of the Society of American Archivists," Society of American Archivists, *Society Directory* (1963, proc.), pp. i–iii.

[93] Minutes of the Council of the Society of American Archivists, Oct. 10, 1950, *American Archivist*, XIV (Jan., 1951), 61.

[94] *Ibid.*, XVII (July, 1954), 209–19.

[95] *Ibid*, X (July, 1947), 269–77.

[35]

To reflect the expanding concern and broadened interest of the state archivist, the committee was renamed Committee on State Records in 1953 and State and Local Records Committee in 1962.

The committee's chairman from 1954 to 1957, Mary Givens Bryan, in 1955 and 1956 compiled a *Comparative Study of State and U. S. Territorial Laws Governing Archives* (proc., unpaged).[96] In addition to furnishing data on legal developments, this study brought up to date the information included in the directory referred to above. The committee prepared and published similar studies in 1957, 1959, and 1961, called, respectively, State Records Committee Reports, Directory of State Archival Agencies, and Guide to State and Provincial Archival Agencies.[97] While assiduously assembling and keeping up to date information not available previously, the committee also was instrumental in having the society establish its Committee on Federal-State Relations.[98] This committee held its first meeting on December 28, 1958, in Washington, and it distributed its "Report on Federal-State Relations in the Archival and Records Management Fields" on October 6, 1959.[99]

The State Records Committee also organized at the annual meetings of the society conferences and workshops of state archivists and others interested that gave special attention to state archival problems. Generally speaking, the activities of the committee resulted in an extraordinary strengthening of bonds between state archivists, in stimulating discussions of common problems, and in facilitating the initiation of neophytes into the field of state archival administration. Its work emphasized the importance of the preservation and sound administration of state archives throughout the nation. Its ultimate objective was to raise state archival administration throughout the country to a high level of excellence.

[96] Highlights of this study are found in her "Recent State Archival Legislation," *American Archivist*, XIX (Jan., 1956), 63–67.

[97] In 1956 the committee also reproduced reports on records disposal policies, microphotography, and salaries. Also, in 1961, 1962, and 1963 it issued a Directory of State and Provincial Archivists and Records Administrators, the first compiled by H. G. Jones and the later two by William T. Alderson.

[98] *American Archivist*, XXII (Apr., 1959), 253.

[99] *Ibid.*, XXIII (Jan., 1960), 100 ff.

CHAPTER II

.ⅎⅎⅎⅎⅎ.

Archival Agencies of the States and Puerto Rico:
Status, Functions, and Program

This chapter, the heart of the report and by far its longest part, is designed to deal concretely with archival conditions in the fifty states and in the Commonwealth of Puerto Rico. So that the reader may compare the programs of the different states and may find, within each state essay, the information in which he is interested, the content of the essays has been organized, insofar as possible, according to a standard pattern. Because of the great diversity in the history, status, and functions of our state archival agencies, however, it has not been possible to follow this standard pattern in all cases.

In dealing with independent archival agencies, each essay normally consists of the following parts: a "preamble" that, in a sentence or two, characterizes the archival organization in the state; a section entitled "Backgrounds," which traces the history of the archival agency to June 30, 1963, with emphasis on the development of the legislation that governs its activities; a second section devoted to organization, personnel, buildings, and any non-archival activities of the agency; a third section in which the agency's archival program is discussed; and a fourth section dealing with records management and records disposition. The essay concludes with comments that offer specific suggestions in regard to aspects of the archival agency's legal basis, organization, and program that, in the opinion of the Study Director, might be strengthened.

If the archival agency is a constituent part of a parent agency — a department of archives and history, a state historical society, or a state library — the essay normally includes a section on the parent agency. This, however, does not attempt to give a well-rounded picture of such an agency's activities; its purpose is rather to show the organizational framework within which the archival agency must operate.

Essays on states that have no legally constituted archival agencies or that have "underdeveloped" archival programs deviate somewhat from the standard pattern.

ALABAMA

Alabama was the first state in the federal union to establish a Department of Archives and History that, in addition to its other duties, was to serve as the official custodian of the state's archives.

BACKGROUNDS

Alabama archives that date from the time of the establishment of Mississippi Territory in 1798 to the creation of Alabama Territory in 1817 are in the Mississippi Archives. Until 1846, when the state capital was permanently seated at Montgomery, the capital of the territory and state was moved four times, with no substantial loss to the archives. During this period and subsequently until the creation of the Department of Archives and History, the Secretary of State was the only official who held records not originating in his office. In 1820 he was made custodian of the legislative records, and by 1900 he had in his custody the extant records of defunct state agencies and of the Governor. When, in 1849, a fire destroyed the Capitol and the holdings of the State Library located on the third floor, some old records evidently kept in the library were destroyed. Those of the departments, however, were saved and kept on "suitable shelves" in the new Capitol, which was finished in 1851.[1]

Thomas McAdory Owen, who in 1898 became the chief founder and the secretary of the Alabama Historical Society, convinced the legislature of the need for a commission to examine into the extent, condition, and location of the public records. The Alabama History Commission, appointed by the president of the historical society and chaired by Owen, investigated the records of the state and its subdivisions; those of educational, religious, and other institutions; and private personal collections. In 1900 the commission turned in a massive and comprehensive report, popularly known as the "blue book," in which it pointed out that records were poorly cared for in inadequate space and were badly in need of centralized attention. The commission recommended the establishment of a State Department of Archives and History; Owen drafted the necessary legislation and urged all "Friends of Historical Work in Alabama" to support his efforts by writing to their senators and representatives.[2]

An act of February 27, 1901 (Laws, 1901, No. 476), established the

[1] For the history of the Alabama archives, see Thomas McAdory Owen (ed.), *Report of the Alabama History Commission to the Governor of Alabama: Publications of the Alabama Historical Society, Miscellaneous Collections*, I (Montgomery, Ala., 1901), 87 ff.; and by the same author, "Alabama Archives," *Annual Report of the American Historical Association for the Year 1904* (Washington, 1905), pp. 487–553.

[2] Peter A. Brannon, "The Alabama Department of Archives and History," *Alabama Historical Quarterly*, XXIV (Spring, 1962), 1–15.

Alabama Department of Archives and History as part of the executive branch of the state government and made it responsible for

. . . the care and custody of official archives, the collection of material bearing upon the history of the state and the territory included therein from the earliest times, the completion and publication of the state's official records and other historical materials, the diffusion of knowledge in reference to the history and resources of the state, the encouragement of historical work and research. . . .

Under the act of 1901, the department is the official repository for all public records of the state and its subdivisions, and copies of records in its custody have the legal force of originals when certified by the Director. It publishes every four years the *Official and Statistical Register* of the state.

In 1907 the department was moved to a new annex in the State Capitol and was directed by the legislature to set up a legislative reference service and a library extension program. An act of 1915 required all public officers to correctly make and accurately keep all records, books, files, etc., that would provide information regarding the functions of the office; specified that books, documents, and files should be of uniform size and style and that materials used in records creation throughout the state offices should be of permanent quality; declared it the duty of all state, county, and municipal officers to turn over non-current records to the department; required officers to turn records over to their successors; and set penalties for violations. The year 1940 saw the completion of the World War Memorial Building, which the department now occupies as sole tenant. A 1945 act (General Acts, 1945, No. 293) provides for records disposal and replevin and for records management services to agencies. In 1955 the legislature authorized the establishment in the department of a central microfilm unit, permitted local units to do their own microfilming, created a State Records Commission and a County Records Commission, and provided retention and disposal procedures (Act No. 565).

THE DEPARTMENT OF ARCHIVES AND HISTORY

The Alabama State Department of Archives and History is governed by a self-perpetuating board of trustees, one from each congressional district, the members of which, with the approval of the State Senate, are appointed for staggered terms of six years. The Governor is a member *ex officio*. The business of the department is conducted by a Director, who is elected by the board for a six-year term and acts as its secretary. In addition to its archival duties, the department operates a museum, a library, and a publication program including a *Civil War Centennial Bulletin* and the *Alabama Historical Quarterly*, which is edited by the Director. It also does the historical spadework for the Conservation Department, which administers the historical sites of the state.

[39]

The budget of the department [3] ($95,000 for 1962–63) is prepared by the Director, who discusses it with the Budget Officer of the Governor. As part of the executive budget, it comes up for hearings before the Joint Committee of the legislature; here the Director has an opportunity to defend it. He also appears at subsequent hearings of the respective committees of the Senate and House.

The personnel of the department is under the state merit system. The present Director, who succeeded Mrs. Marie Bankhead Owen in 1955, has been with the department since 1911. His salary of $7,500 is not commensurate with salaries of comparable posts in other departments. The department's professional staff consists of an archivist in charge of civil archives, $4,560–$5,760; an archivist in charge of civil archives, specializing in newspapers and legislative records, $4,560–$5,760; an archivist in charge of military records, $4,560–$5,760; the librarian, $5,040–$6,300; a clerk typist I (Civil Archives Division), $2,500–$3,360; and a clerk typist II (Military Archives Division), $3,000–$3,912. For manual work the department has to rely on the use of trusties from the state prison; this is not conducive to good housekeeping in the archival areas.

The World War Memorial Building, built as a joint federal-state project, with the federal government furnishing 55 per cent of the total cost of $650,000, is the home of the department. The building was completed in 1940, stacks were installed in 1948 at an additional cost of $71,000, and air-conditioning and humidity control were provided in 1962 at a cost of $92,000. Executive offices, library, and memorial lobbies are on the first floor. The Military Archives Division and the Manuscripts Division occupy half of the second floor; the rest of that floor and all of the third floor are given over to the museum. There are 192,490 cubic feet of available archival storage space, 192,000 cubic feet of which are used.

THE ARCHIVES PROGRAM

The Department of Archives and History holds the non-current official records of the territory and state from 1818 to recent date. These include records of the executive offices, departments, commissions, bureaus, and boards; the judicial department; the legislature; constitutional conventions; state institutions; special commissions; and counties and municipalities. The agency also has some federal records, including those of the Land Office from 1807. Archival materials are housed in two large basement rooms and on the first, second, and tenth stack levels, while the other stack levels are used by the library. In addition, the entire basement space under the terrace of the building and a hallway adjacent to the archives

[3] The department does not pay for heat, light, and other maintenance expenses, nor does it provide janitorial and guide services for the building.

office have been filled with records that include State Auditor's vouchers from about 1819, State Treasurer's canceled warrants from at least 1819, Department of Finance requisitions and purchase orders, and other records that have been brought in with no attention to their retention value and that are not under schedule control. Here also are records of the State Board of Pardons and Parole, which, because they are very active, should not be in the department. Most of this material is stored in file cabinets or transfer cases. Furthermore, when the building was air-conditioned, considerable space under the ceiling of the basement had to be hastily abandoned, with the result that records are piled up in the aisles, where they impede traffic. To restore a minimum of order will not be a simple task, for quite obviously the basement has been filled without any real plan.

Control over the basement holdings is by means of accession inventories that were started in 1953. There is a card index for records on the tenth stack level and brief typed calendars for the records of every Governor during the Reconstruction period. The two staff members who work on the civil records keep busy answering requests for information, helping searchers, and trying to restore order "under the Terrace." They have no time for arrangement and description. Also the Civil Archives Division is burdened with taking over and distributing more than 250 copies of the state's slip laws.

The military records, beginning with the militia records of 1819, are well kept in a large room in the main building and are separately administered; those preceding World War II have been carded. Another room in the main building is used for the considerable collections of private and church papers, controlled by a card catalog. Whenever possible, collections are maintained in their original order.

The department answers yearly about 3,700 letters involving the consultation of records and sends out about the same number of form letters transmitting pamphlets, copies of legislative acts, etc. Some 3,000 telephone inquiries are handled and about 900 photographic copies of records are made each year. Nearly 5,000 persons a year consult 84,000 records and 85,000 reels of microfilm in the department's research rooms.

Act No. 565 of 1955 authorized the photographing or microfilming of public records, gave certified reproductions the legal force of the originals, established in the department a central microfilm unit, and authorized the purchase or lease of equipment for the program. No central unit has been set up, however; only antiquated microfilm and photostat equipment is available; and microfilming is used solely for internal purposes. There is no program for microfilming the newspaper holdings, estimated at 38,000 volumes and occupying an enormous amount of space. Even current newspapers are bound, at a cost of about $10.00 a volume.

Act No. 565 of 1955 created the State Records Commission. This consists of the Director of the Department of Archives and History (chairman), the Examiner of Public Accounts, the Attorney General, the Secretary of State, the Commissioner of Revenue, and a member each from the University of Alabama and the Alabama Polytechnic Institute named by the heads of the respective history departments. The act also created a County Records Commission consisting of the Director of the Department of Archives and History (chairman), the Examiner of Public Accounts, the Attorney General, one member each from the university and the Polytechnic Institute, two probate judges, two county tax assessors, one register in equity, and one circuit court clerk. The commissions are empowered to authorize the destruction of public records after microfilming, to make records surveys, and to issue regulations regarding retention and disposal periods. The commissions neither meet nor function, for in practice the department's Director, the Attorney General, and the Examiner of Public Accounts act as an executive committee and arrive at their decisions by correspondence.

Although the law furnishes the basis for developing retention and disposal schedules, no such regulations have been issued.

COMMENTS

1. Alabama needs a records management program including provision for retention and disposal scheduling.

2. There is urgent need for appraising and scheduling the vast quantities of records now cluttering up the basement of the World War Memorial Building.

3. Space freed in the basement should be equipped with shelving for the storage of archival material.

ALASKA

No standard archival program has yet been developed in Alaska, and as a result the sources of its history are dispersed. A records management program begun in 1957 has become largely inoperative.

BACKGROUNDS

In the Carter Act the Congress of the United States, on June 6, 1900, created a fund for the establishment of the Alaska Historical Library and Museum (henceforth called the library) and charged it with collecting "copies of all laws relating to the district, and all papers and periodicals published within the district, and such other material of historical interest as the Governor may consider valuable and appropriate for such collection." Pursuant to this act the library accessioned certain bodies of official territorial records, some archives of the Russian regime, and some private papers. Another accumulation of records developed when, on March 3, 1925, Congress abolished the office of Surveyor General, who had been *ex officio* Secretary of the Territory, and the Secretary of the Territory was formally appointed. Among his duties was that of preserving and recording "all the laws and proceedings of the legislative assembly, and all the acts and proceedings of the Governor in the Executive Department" (1455-48-USC). At the date of Alaska's statehood, the Secretary had in his vaults copies of all session laws from 1913, one Governor's report each for 1885 and 1918, and a complete set of such reports from 1923 to 1958.

Since 1953 the National Archives and Records Service has helped to preserve Alaska's archives by transferring a considerable volume of records to the Federal Records Center in Seattle, Washington; by servicing and partially describing them; and by encouraging the establishment, in Alaska's Department of Finance, of a records management program (Session Laws, 1957, ch. 147), which unfortunately began to wither away after the territory became a state.

Chapter 16, Session Laws of 1955, created a Department of Library Service, now the Alaska State Library. It has no archival responsibilities.

THE HISTORICAL LIBRARY AND MUSEUM

Originally seated in Sitka, the library was removed to Juneau when Juneau became the capital. Until 1922 it was considered a federal institution, but after the Attorney General of the United States had ruled, on September 30, that the library was a territorial institution, the territorial legislature by an act approved May 3, 1923 (Sess. Laws, 1923, ch. 87), created the Territorial Historical Library and Museum Commission [4] and the office of Librarian and Curator of the Territory of Alaska and provided funds for acquiring a building on Third and Seward Streets to house the library. From there it moved in 1931 to its present location on the second floor of the new Federal and Territorial Building, now the State Capitol.

In fiscal 1963 the library had a budget of $30,509, of which $29,909 was actually spent, and a staff of three: a Curator Librarian ($10,000), an Assistant Curator ($7,000), and a Historical Librarian ($7,800). Of the quarters the library occupies, 3,015 square feet are equipped with steel shelving for books and newspapers. The library has one microfilm machine for microfilming Alaska newspapers, which are subsequently destroyed. It has no repair or rehabilitation equipment.

[4] The commission was to "be constituted of the Governor of Alaska, the Secretary of the Territory, the Commissioner of Education, the Treasurer of the Territory, the Attorney General and one member of the Board of Managers of the Alaska Historical Association." Incorporated in 1920 and reorganized in 1925, it has been defunct since the early thirties.

Manuscript holdings include Alaska customs records, 1867–1914; "American Occupation, 1867" (reports and letters of the Collector of Customs at Sitka, 1867–69); "Consent Government at Sitka, Alaska, 1867" (charter, ordinances, tax and license records, and proceedings of the city council, 1899–1900); and private papers, 1821–1940. The library receives two copies of each document issued by any office of the state government or by the legislature, one of them to be forwarded to the Library of Congress. It maintains a collection of agency issuances and regulations.

Approximately 500 persons a year do research in the library.

THE FEDERAL RECORDS CENTER IN SEATTLE

After the National Archives and Records Service had, in 1953, established liaison with both territorial executive agencies and with federal agencies in Alaska, several record series were transferred or scheduled for periodic transfer to the Federal Records Center in Seattle. They include the Alaska Road Commission records; some of the Alaska Railroad records; records of the Bureau of Indian Affairs, including as well those of the Alaska Native Service; the complete records of the Territorial Governors, except for the records of about the last five territorial years, retained in the interest of orderly transition to statehood;[5] and the Sir Henry S. Wellcome Papers, 1856–1936, received from the Wellcome Trust and relating chiefly to the Metlakahtla Indians and to Father Duncan, lay missionary for the Anglican Church Missionary Society.[6]

Files of Alaska field offices of the Department of the Interior other than those referred to above are in part in the National Archives and in part in the Interior Department's Washington and Alaska offices.

RECORDS MANAGEMENT AND RECORDS DISPOSITION

Encouraged by the National Archives and Records Service, a territorial records management program was initiated in 1957 in the Department of Finance. By chapter 64, Session Laws of 1959, it was transferred to the Division of Budget and Management, Department of Administration.

The original program of 1957 provided that records officers of territorial agencies should supervise their respective agency programs and maintain liaison with two staff members of the Department of Finance. Two small records centers for semi-current records were set up, one in the basement of the Alaska Office Building, with negligible holdings, and one in the basement of the Juneau Memorial Library, accommodating approximately 500 cubic feet of records on wooden shelving. No service other than stor-

[5] Described in the processed *Preliminary Inventory and List of Records of the Office of the Governor of Alaska, 1884–1956* (Seattle, 1959), 34 p.

[6] Described in National Archives, *Preliminary Inventory* No. 150 (Washington, 1963, proc.), 13 p.

age is provided. Few records inventories have been taken, and only two control schedules have been developed.

Final authority over the disposal of state records is vested in the Commissioner of Administration. He has the power to receive archival records, but so far no attempt has been made to segregate them.

Inasmuch as the two staff members of the Department of Administration formerly employed in records management have been lost to the program, it has now all but vanished. Both the Commissioner of the Department of Administration and the Director of its Budget and Management Division appreciate the need for an active records management program; but, because of the shortage of funds, they see no possibility of revitalizing it in the near future.

COMMENTS

1. The records management program in the Department of Administration should be reactivated as soon as possible.

2. Chapter 147, Session Laws of 1957, should be amended to provide for a state archival establishment.

ARIZONA

The Arizona Department of Library and Archives discharges in a limited way the functions of a state archival agency. Since 1955 it has been administering a microfilm program of considerable proportions; this, however, is not related to, or controlled by, a program of records management.

BACKGROUNDS

Arizona became a territory on February 14, 1864, part of the area having been acquired from Mexico in 1848 and the rest in 1854. A Territorial Library, later named the State Law and Legislative Library, was created in 1864, and connected with it was a historical department. This was the forerunner of the Office of the State Historian, created in 1909. Both the State Library and the Office of the State Historian were housed in the State Capitol in Phoenix. The State Historian, appointed by the Governor for a period of four years, was to collect, preserve, and compile materials containing data for a new history of Arizona.[7] Archives, however, continued to be held in the departments of origin, and nothing was done toward their care and preservation beyond some casual collecting by the library and the State Historian until 1937. In that year the name of the

[7] See National Association of State Libraries, *Proceedings and Addresses*, Fourteenth Convention, Pasadena, Calif., May 22, 1911, p. 24; *ibid.*, Twentieth Convention, Louisville, Ky., June 22–26, 1917, p. 22; and *Proceedings and Papers, 1928–1929*, 32d Annual Convention, Washington, D.C., May 13–15, 1929, p. 14.

State Law and Legislative Library[8] was changed to the Department of Library and Archives (Arizona Session Laws, 1937, ch. 32). The law established the Division of Arizona History and Archives within the department and made it "the central depository of all official books, records, and documents not in current use of the various state officers and departments of the state, the counties and incorporated cities and towns, which shall constitute the state archives." No funds were made available to implement this law and no archivist was employed, but over the years considerable quantities of records were taken over. In 1955 an appropriation of $20,000 was made for microfilming and processing the backlog of archives, and in 1956 this was increased to $80,000. In 1961 an archivist was appointed.

To act on requests for the destruction of records, chapter 98, Session Laws of 1958, created the Board of History and Archives. It is composed of the Director of the Department of Library and Archives, the Attorney General, the State Post Auditor, and, whenever the records of a political subdivision are involved, the State Examiner.

The laws pertaining to the Department of Library and Archives have been codified as Arizona Revised Statutes, Annotated, 1956, Title 41, chapter 4, article 1, §41-701 to §41-727.

THE DEPARTMENT OF LIBRARY AND ARCHIVES

The Department of Library and Archives is governed by a Board of Curators consisting of three members appointed by the Governor for overlapping terms of six years. The Director of the department must be a person "technically trained in library work, or of not less than five years experience as chief administrator of a major library." He is named by the Board of Curators and confirmed by the Senate. The Director appoints all other personnel of the department.

The budget of the department is prepared by the Director after discussion with the division heads. Approved by the Auditor, it is submitted to the Governor for presentation to the legislature, which meets annually. The budget is presented in three parts, namely, library in general, including Arizona history; extension service; and archives and filming. A Division of Archives and History, as provided for in the 1937 law, does not exist. In fiscal 1963, $15,000 was made available for equipment and material used for archival and microfilming purposes. The 1963–64 budget provides $89,729 for the library, $50,000 for extension service, and $14,115 for microfilming.

Since Arizona does not have a merit or state personnel system governing recruitment, examination and certification of staff, position classification,

[8] In 1915 a Legislative Reference Bureau was established in the library. Its functions were transferred to the Legislative Council in 1953.

and the like, appointments in the department are made solely on the basis of an applicant's qualifications for a specific job to be filled. Also, there is no central system of wages and salary rates including in-grade increases. There is, however, provision for retirement benefits, with the state and the staff member contributing 3.5 per cent of the salary. The statutory salary of the Director ($7,200) has been raised to $8,400, together with other statutory salaries in the state. The newly appointed archivist receives $5,500.[9] Two clerks serving as microfilm operators earn $3,600 and $3,500, respectively.

Since 1939 the department has been housed in an annex to the Capitol built especially for that purpose. It badly needs additional facilities. There is no laminating and fumigating equipment.

The Library Division is composed of the following sections: Museum, Genealogy, Federal Documents, State Documents, Laws, Technical Processes, Arizona History, and General Reference. The Arizona History Section continues the functions of the former State Historian and administers materials that according to the law of 1937 should be in the custody of the Division of Arizona History and Archives, together with the state archives.

The Director of the department is a member of the Governor's Historical Advisory Committee, the State Landmarks Committee, and the Territorial Centennial Committee.

ARCHIVAL ACTIVITIES

The Department of Library and Archives has in its custody a considerable quantity of records, and it is engaged in extensive microfilming of state records. There is, however, no program designed to make it the depository of the state's permanent records and to equip it for discharging the normal functions of a state archival agency. To develop such a program should be the first and demanding duty of the department's archivist.

The archival holdings are kept on library stack equipment on the fourth floor of the library stacks, which provides 4,000 square feet of space. They include territorial records received from the Secretary of State, Governor's correspondence, legislative records, Supreme Court case files, and a considerable quantity of county records. About a third of the available space is taken up by warrants, all of which have been filmed and are kept solely for the expiration of the five-year retention period.

Until an archivist was appointed, the permanently valuable records were only partly arranged, and none of them had been listed or described in finding aids. The present incumbent is engaged in preparing inventories of the simplest kind. There is no guide to the holdings, and under

[9] The maximum salary for the position is $6,500.

[47]

the prevailing circumstances the records remain practically unused. No significant research seems possible at this time, and no count is kept of reference requests from agencies or individuals.

Much of the time of the archivist is devoted to the microfilm activities of the department. Arizona has gone in for large-scale microfilming with two rotary cameras, one planetary camera, and one reader-printer. The department microfilms current records for agencies without charge but demands that they obtain the necessary appropriations if quantities of back material are to be filmed. The entire filming operation is carried on without reference to a records management program and is therefore bound to be wasteful. A microfilm inventory of July 1, 1963, shows the following production totals:

	16 mm.	35 mm.	Total Reels
Security Copy Film [10]	2,504	37	2,541
Historical Collection [11]	43	576	619
State Records' Collection	6,866	402	7,268
	9,413	1,015	10,428

Of the microfilmed State Records' Collection, 2,796 reels are reproductions of records of the Auditor's Department. This collection is stored in modern cabinets in the archivist's office but is not adequately protected from fire hazards. A cardex file facilitates access to the collection.

The microfilm service provided is not a central microfilm service, for independent programs are under way in the Arizona Highway Department, the Employment Security Commission, and the Vital Statistics Bureau of the Department of Public Health.

DISPOSITION OF STATE AND LOCAL RECORDS

Under chapter 98, Session Laws of 1958, the destruction of official records, local as well as state, must be approved by the Board of History and Archives, composed of the Director of the Department of Library and Archives, the Attorney General, the State Post Auditor, and the State Examiner. The board had its first meeting on July 17, 1958, and frequent meetings, presided over by the Director of the department, were held until, on April 3, 1963, the board decided to have formal meetings only when "special" matters needed its attention. In the absence of such meetings, signatures on the disposition authorization form are obtained from the board members.

Forms to be used in the disposal process and "Rules for Disposition and Transfer of Public Records" have been approved by the board. There has also been some discussion of general problems pertaining to the state's records problems. For recurring records of the Highway Department and

[10] This is film produced for other state departments and transferred to their custody.
[11] Preponderantly Arizona newspapers.

the Unemployment Compensation Division of the Employment Security Commission, schedules have been approved.

1. Arizona needs a records management program, of which the present microfilm service should become a part.

2. If the Department of Library and Archives is to activate its archives program and if it is to assume records management responsibilities, it needs more space, funds, equipment, and personnel, including the services of an experienced archivist–records administrator.

3. Either the Division of Arizona History and Archives should be activated in accordance with §41-709 to §41-712 of the law, or a State Archives and Records Service under the Board of History and Archives, probably to be renamed the Public Records and Archives Board, should be established. In this case the Arizona History Section, including its non-archival holdings and activities, should remain in the library.

ARKANSAS

In addition to other functions assigned to it, the Arkansas History Commission serves as a depository for records of the state. The commission is not concerned with records management.

The Arkansas Historical Association was founded in 1903 at the University of Arkansas.[12] Because of its limited membership and income, the association found its field of operation so narrowly circumscribed that it appealed to the general assembly for help and obtained passage of a law of April 27, 1905, creating the Arkansas History Commission. This commission, composed of five members appointed by the president of the association, was to direct and surpervise the printing of the first volume of the association's publications, to ascertain the condition of all extant material on Arkansas history, and to report on the status of historical work in the state. The commission received an appropriation of $1,000 for publishing and $250 for expenses incurred by its members.

Finding the archives of the state in a deplorable condition, the History Commission in 1906 urged the state: (1) to establish, in the State House, a library, gallery, and museum for all books, papers, relics, and paintings pertaining to Arkansas; (2) to create a Department of History and Archives to classify, index, and care for the archives of the state; to collect

---

[12] The association became defunct before World War I. A second Arkansas Historical Association, founded in 1941, publishes the *Arkansas Historical Quarterly*. The editor and secretary-treasurer of the association is a member of the department of history of the University of Arkansas.

and arrange material in the library, museum, and art gallery; to locate and mark historical sites; to edit and publish a series of state papers; to serve as an information bureau; and to publish an official register of the state; (3) to give the Arkansas Historical Association a biennial appropriation for publications; and (4) to require counties to provide fireproof vaults for the protection of their records. An exhaustive inventory of the sources of Arkansas history was included in the report.[13]

In 1909 the commission's recommendations were partially carried out. Act 304 of that year made the commission a permanent agency of the state and charged it with the care and custody of the official archives, the collection of materials bearing on the history of the state, the editing of official records and other historical sources, and the encouragement of historical work and research in the state. Act 269 of 1917 added a legislative reference service to its duties, and Act 20 of 1955 gave the commission the authority to dispose of useless records in its custody. This act has been repealed and its provisions have been incorporated in Act 207 of 1963. The new law also directs officers of the state to notify the commission of their intention to destroy records and to give to it any that it considers to be of historical value.

It will be noted that in Arkansas the establishment of the History Commission did not lead to the creation of a Department of Archives and History, as had happened in Alabama and Mississippi and was later to happen in North Carolina and South Carolina.

THE HISTORY COMMISSION

Under Act 207 of 1963 the commission is composed of seven members, all appointed by the Governor for seven-year overlapping terms. Recent gubernatorial appointments seem to have been based on political considerations. Nevertheless, the presence on the commission of members with strong political connections is said to have added to its effectiveness in obtaining appropriations.

The commission, through its Executive Secretary, operates a museum, a portrait gallery, a reference library, and its holdings of archives and private papers. The 1917 act providing for a legislative reference service has been repealed.

The commission's budget has always been insufficient. Reviewed by the commission's budget committee, requests are submitted to the Governor to become part of the executive budget. Then, with the Governor's recommendations, the requests go to the Arkansas Legislative Council, where

[13] John Hugh Reynolds (ed.), *Report of the Arkansas Historical Commission*, I (Fayetteville, Ark., 1906), 309 p.; and John Hugh Reynolds, "Public Archives of Arkansas," *Annual Report of the American Historical Association for the Year 1906*, II (Washington, 1908), 23–51.

hearings are held. The council makes its recommendations to the general assembly, which meets in January of odd-numbered years and normally accepts the Governor's recommendations.

The staff of the commission consists of five persons including the full-time janitor. Present salaries are: Executive Secretary, $8,000; Research Assistant, $4,500; Librarian,[14] $3,300; secretary, $3,000; and janitor, $1,800. During the 1959–61 biennium four persons in succession were employed as secretary. The Executive Secretary is trying hard to have the pitiful salaries raised to an acceptable level. Staff members pay 4 per cent of their salaries into the state retirement system, with contributions matched by the state.

Since 1951 the History Commission has been housed in the west wing of the handsome Old State Capitol in Little Rock. In addition to office, reading room, and museum space, it now has a three-story archives annex, 30 × 40 feet, with temperature and humidity controls. Construction of the annex was begun in 1953 with an appropriation of $50,000. For its completion, an additional $25,000 was made available by Act 17 of the First Extraordinary Session of the General Assembly of 1961; this sum, however, did not suffice for buying and installing newspaper steel shelving and a booklift. For that purpose and for the acquisition of microfilm readers and film file cabinets $11,600 was appropriated for the 1963–65 biennium.

During the first fifty years of its existence, the collecting of private papers and research engaged most of the attention of the commission's secretaries. When the present Executive Secretary was appointed, he was instructed to improve the commission's public relations and to arouse interest in its objectives among the people of the state. To that end he has encouraged, and helped with, the establishment of local historical societies, of which there are now twenty-three. Some of the most successful have memberships of up to five hundred and publish their own quarterlies.[15] Since October, 1960, the Executive Secretary has also issued a monthly news sheet, *Arkansas History Commission News.*

At present the commission's museum, consolidated into one large room, is closed, because it has to be used for storing library material pending the completion of the annex. The portraits in the gallery of Arkansas have recently been cleaned and restored. If the museum and gallery functions are to be taken seriously, the commission should have the services of an experienced curator.

Much emphasis is given to a program of microfilming Arkansas newspapers, and members of the staff make field trips to borrow files or missing issues and to return them after they have been filmed.

[14] The Librarian also operates the microfilm camera.
[15] John L. Ferguson (comp.), *Directory of Arkansas Historical Societies, 1962* (Little Rock, July, 1962, proc.), 12 p.

The History Commission has a certain quantity of archival material, but it does not have an archival program. Nor is one likely to be initiated, for the Executive Secretary — the only professional staff member — is involved in too many other activities.

Present holdings consist of 1,020 volumes of non-current records of the territorial and state governments, 1823–1937, including Governor's letter books and other records of the Governor's office and militia and Confederate pension records. In addition, there are records of some counties and collections of private papers. Holdings were shelflisted by WPA workers, but the shelflist and part of the cards on which it was based were lost when the commission moved from the Capitol to its present quarters. As a result, any indication of what the commission now has would be nothing but a wild guess. Most Arkansas archival material is still with the agencies. The Secretary of State, for instance, has many corporation records and all the records of the Senate and House and keeps them under rather unsatisfactory conditions in the basement of the new State House.

Operating with one planetary camera, the commission emphasizes the microfilming of newspapers and early county records. Microfilming is also done in some of the major government departments, including those of the Secretary of State and the State Auditor. There is no co-ordination among these programs.

During the 1959–61 biennium 1,015 persons signed the commission's research register. They used chiefly the microfilm records of the U.S. Census, 1830–80; county tax rolls, 1821–69; and the military records of Arkansas for the Mexican, Civil, and Spanish-American wars.

RECORDS MANAGEMENT AND RECORDS DISPOSITION

As pointed out above, Act 20 of 1955 vests certain authority over disposal in the History Commission. In actual practice no disposal requests are received from the state agencies and the act is applied solely to the holdings of the commission, with the Executive Secretary deciding what is no longer needed. The following statement in his last budget request is likely to arouse some concern:

Microfilming is the only answer to the space, storage, and preservation problems of a modern archival agency. Without microfilm we would eventually require a complex of huge warehouses for storage of archival materials. Microfilming constitutes the very heart of History Commission operations.

There is no talk of a records management program for Arkansas.

COMMENTS

1. Arkansas needs a records management program and an archives program.

2. The Arkansas History Commission cannot undertake to initiate an archives program unless a professional archivist is added to its staff.

CALIFORNIA

In California, responsibilities for records management and archives administration are divided between the Department of General Services and the Secretary of State. The latter administers the archival program and operates records center facilities, while the former is in charge of the records management program.

BACKGROUNDS

The first act of the first session of the California state legislature in 1850 instructed the Secretary of State to receive all records, maps, and books of the previous administrations of California and to classify and keep them safely.[16] Three months later the legislature, by joint resolution, directed the Secretary of State to send "a suitable person" to Monterey to procure these archives. Their fate was unhappy because of the periodic removal of the state capital from one place to another, until it was finally located in Sacramento in 1854. The legislature of 1858 directed the Secretary of State to turn over the Spanish and Mexican archives to the U.S. Surveyor General for California for use in establishing land titles. When these records became the subject of controversy between the state and the Library of Congress, which wanted to have them removed to Washington, the state succeeded in having them retained by the U.S. Surveyor General for California. Most of them were destroyed in the 1906 San Francisco Fire,[17] and those that are left are now in the National Archives. Fortunately an act of 1866 had instructed the Secretary of State to arrange for copying and translating the Spanish-Mexican land-grant records and to furnish duplicate copies to the counties to which they applied; it also gave the copies and translations the legal force of the originals.

Legislation of 1889 (Statutes and Amendments to the Code, ch. 389) instructed the Secretary of State to have constructed in the Capitol a moisture-, fire-, and burglar-proof vault in which to preserve the archives of the state; created the office of Keeper of the Archives; and directed him to arrange and index the holdings. In 1915 Edwin L. Head, in charge of that office, reported to the Public Archives Commission of the American Historical Association that the Secretary of State had four rooms, two of

[16] For the following, see J. N. Bowman, "Preservation of the State Archives," *California Historical Society Quarterly*, XXVIII (June, 1949), 143–50; and W. N. Davis, Jr., "The California State Archives," *American Archivist*, XXII (Apr., 1959), 189–96.

[17] John Lombardi, "Lost Records of the Surveyor-General in California," *Pacific Historical Review*, VI (Dec., 1937), 361–71; and W. W. Robinson, "Land Grant Records That Survived a Great Fire," *Quarterly of the Historical Society of Southern California*, XXVI (Mar., 1944), 38–44.

them fireproof, in the Capitol basement.[18] To relieve overcrowding, another room was added in the same year.

During the 1920's the state agencies became so short of space that they began to turn to the Secretary of State for relief of their storage problems, and, as a result, record holdings in his custody spread into two floors of a state warehouse. To cope with this situation, the Secretary of State in 1939 obtained a revision of the 1889 act so that only records of historical value were to be received into his custody. For the storage of records of limited retention value, a facility of the records center type, also under the Secretary of State, was authorized in 1947. This is the present Central Record Depository.

Assembly and Senate interim committees and a joint legislative committee on governmental reorganization, created in 1949 and 1953, respectively, gave considerable attention to the archives and records management problems of the state. Influenced by the Task Force Report on Records Management of the first Hoover Commission, the committees recommended passing a records management act. It would have transferred the archives as well as the records center from the Secretary of State to a new Department of General Services and would have given it broad responsibility for the entire field of records management. A bill to establish such a department with staff responsibility for records management and with line authority over the records centers but not the archives, which would remain under the Secretary of State, was passed in the 1963 session of the legislature (A. B. No. 2006). Under the terms of the new act, however, the records centers are not to be transferred to the new department until January 1, 1967.

THE ARCHIVES AND CENTRAL RECORD DEPOSITORY

The Archives and Central Record Depository, henceforth called the depository, is under the Secretary of State. It is a double-headed operation, with the State Archivist in charge of the records center activities and serving as staff manager for the State Archives and with the Historian, State Archives,[19] in charge of the archives function. The two officers work together in an atmosphere of amicable symbiosis, both of them deriving their authority from the Secretary of State and reporting to him through the Assistant Secretary of State.

In addition to its regular session in odd-numbered years, the legislature has a budget session in even-numbered years. The depository budget is prepared by the State Archivist for submission to the Secretary of State. As part of his budget, it is transmitted to the Budget Division, Depart-

[18] "Report on the Archives of the State of California," *Annual Report of the American Historical Association for the Year 1915* (Washington, 1917), pp. 277–309.

[19] The Historian's position, held from 1945 to 1955 by J. N. Bowman on a contract basis, was made a permanent position in 1955.

ment of Finance, to be reviewed there and to become part of the Governor's budget. Both the State Archivist and the Historian attend the hearings before the Budget Division and the respective subcommittees of the finance committees of the two houses of the legislature.

The depository, with its Los Angeles annex, received an appropriation of $54,548 for 1961 and $55,831 for 1962. The budget for fiscal 1964 is $119,987; this sum includes provision for a San Francisco records center annex and other urgent needs of the agency that will be referred to below.

The staff attached to the depository and its Los Angeles records center annex numbers twelve:

Historian, State Archives	$8,604–	$10,440
State Archivist	6,120–	7,428
Assistant State Archivist	5,028–	6,120
Senior Clerk	4,788–	5,280
Intermediate Clerks (6)	4,140–	5,028
Laborers (2)	4,788–	5,280

In the early fifties, there was an approximately even balance between archives and records center activities and a corresponding distribution of personnel. Gradually, however, most of the manpower of the agency has been shifted to records center duties, so that now the Historian has the services of only one clerk and occasional typing help from the receptionist. A senior clerk on the payroll of the Secretary of State is in charge of the archives holdings in the basement of the Capitol.

The personnel of the depository is under the state merit system. Vacancies are advertised and examinations are held by the State Personnel Board; the agency then makes its selection from the top three on the eligible list. Privileges and benefits enjoyed are: one to three years' service, ten days' vacation; three to ten years', fifteen days; ten to fifteen years', seventeen days; fifteen to twenty-four years', nineteen days; over twenty-four years', twenty days; one day of sick leave per month, which can accumulate indefinitely; a state contribution of $5.00 per month to the health insurance plan selected by the employee. Within salary ranges, there is provision for four increases plus a higher bracket for meritorious service.

The depository shares with other agencies the former State Printing Plant, misleadingly called the Archives Building, which was renovated and partially equipped for use by the depository in 1956. Available storage space for about 90,000 cubic feet of center records and 18,000 cubic feet of archives is nearly exhausted. In addition, the archives rooms in the State Capitol basement are still in use.

The depository has no fumigating vault, nor has it been able so far to obtain appropriations for laminating equipment requested over a number of years. The 1963 legislature established a California Heritage Preservation Commission and named the Secretary of State its secretary. It is hoped that lamination work can be done by the commission under this act. One microfilm camera of the rotary type seems all that is needed, since there is a widespread network of independent agency microfilming operations. In the basement of the Archives Building, the Secretary of State has a photostat operation available to the depository as well as to other agencies.

THE STATE ARCHIVES

The State Archives holds primarily official state records. Exceptions are collections of court records of Sacramento, Humboldt, Nevada, and San Diego counties,[20] public school records at the district level, copies of Spanish-Mexican land-grant records, and papers of several California congressmen. The Archives has the letter books of many Governors and the papers of Governors Warren [21] and Knight. Archival material is arranged according to agency of origin.

In the available stack space the archival holdings are not clearly separated from center holdings. In storage these types of material are intermingled, and even archival records of the same agency may be scattered among various locations.

To all intents and purposes the State Archives is a one-man operation under the Historian. His workload, were he to do justice to it, would be utterly impossible. His "Evaluation of the Performance of the State Archives, 1962" frankly and realistically appraises the present situation:

H—functions of the Historian.
A—functions of the State Archivist.

1. Accessioning.
   Screening and appraisal of records. H. Ranges from satisfactory to below standard.
2. Preservation and repair.
   Housing for protection of records. A. Satisfactory.
   Repair. A. Nothing being done.
3. Classification, arrangement of material. H. Below standard to nothing being done.
4. Cataloging, inventories, guides. H. Nothing being done.
5. Reference.
   Enabling researchers to locate material. H, A. Below standard.
6. Research services for agencies, public. H, A. Satisfactory to below standard.

Much of the Historian's time has to be devoted to reviewing disposition schedules and identifying permanently valuable records. In these schedules he flags the items deemed of permanent value; frequently this process

[20] Inasmuch as the governing bodies of counties or cities may transfer to the Secretary of State items of historical interest (*Government Code*, sec. 12226), the Historian, State Archives, has been instructed to develop a program to implement this provision. Efforts so far have been directed at concentrating in the State Archives the records of California's pioneer courts at the county level.

[21] Restrictions on the use of these, some 600 cubic feet, terminated in 1963; hence the processing of the papers is a matter of considerable urgency.

is followed by further screening either on the premises or after the records flagged have been sent in.

With the exception of the records in the Capitol vault, for which indexes were prepared by WPA workers, the only finding aid available is the card catalog of "Selected Archival Material," for which brief entries are drafted by the Historian. It serves at the same time as an accession index and as a general finding medium. The Historian rightly calls it the "irreducible minimum of records control." Unless he receives additional help the present hopeless situation will not change.

Searchers calling at the depository sign a log, which, however, does not separate archival clients from those using records center holdings. A total of 312 archival reference letters were written in 1963; also, there were 286 visits to the research room, where 412 record items were produced; and photographic copies of 206 documents were furnished.

Since California has no position of State Historian, many requests that normally would go to such an official are referred to and handled by the Historian, State Archives, adding to his burden. He served as secretary for the Lincoln Sesquicentennial Commission and directed most of its year-long program. At present, he serves as chairman of the Committee on Historical Trends of the Department of Mental Hygiene and as Councilor, Pacific Coast Branch, American Society for Legal History.

THE RECORDS CENTERS

In addition to being in charge of general plant and personnel management, the State Archivist has charge of the records centers. During fiscal 1963 their total holdings amounted to 102,239 cubic feet. A Los Angeles records center annex, staffed with a senior and an intermediate clerk and now holding more than 10,000 cubic feet of records, has recently been expanded to a 16,500-cubic-foot capacity. Appropriation for a San Francisco center, with a similar staff, is included in the fiscal 1964 budget.

The Depository and the Organization and Cost Control Division of the Department of Finance have developed procedures and forms for the handling and servicing of records center holdings, and a manual containing these forms and appropriate instructions has been issued by the Secretary of State.[22] The extremely neat installation gives evidence of excellent housekeeping.

RECORDS MANAGEMENT AND RECORDS DISPOSITION

California's records management program was inspired by the efforts of J. N. Bowman during his years as Historian and was given further

[22] "Operating Instructions for Central Record Depository Facilities" (Jan., 1963, proc.), 30 p. First published as an appendix to "Management Survey" 1185.1 of the Management Research Section, Organization and Cost Control Division, Department of Finance (Dec., 1962, proc.).

impetus by the Task Force Report on Paperwork Management of the second Hoover Commission. Accordingly termed a paperwork management program, it was administered by the Department of Finance until 1963 legislation transferred it to the newly established Department of General Services.

The paperwork management program originated in 1960 when the Organization and Cost Control Division, Department of Finance, made a survey of existing record practices and recommended remedial action in a staff report entitled *A Program for Paperwork Management in California* (Survey 1098, Sacramento, Calif., April, 1961; 37 + 3 p.).The Governor transmitted the report to all state officers and department heads with the request that the recommendations included be implemented without delay. Instructions necessary to that effect were issued by the Director of Finance.

California's paperwork management program is administered by a unit of the Management Research Section of the Organization and Cost Control Division, Department of Finance. The unit is headed by a Senior Administrative Analyst ($10,440–$14,696) and staffed with two associate administrative analysts ($8,604–$10,440); two assistant administrative analysts ($7,080–$8,604); a delineator, in charge of drawing forms ($5,832–$7,080), who provides service for the entire department; and an administrative trainee ($5,280–$5,832). The unit handles paperwork management in a staff capacity, publishes the *State Administrative Manual*, has responsibility for the state forms program, and prepares management studies as requested.

Thus far the main achievements of the program have been the following: Agencies have designated record co-ordinators and have inventoried their records; an Interagency Paperwork Management Conference has been organized; and the Department of Finance has established controls for the purchase of file equipment, has issued a new paperwork management chapter [23] of the *State Administrative Manual* and assisted agencies in developing their records disposition programs, and has developed standardized personnel roster and position cards and a standardized personnel folder. The department has also provided records disposition training for agencies, including workshop sessions in San Diego, Los Angeles, San Francisco, and Sacramento; and has recommended that branch records centers in Los Angeles and San Francisco be established by the Secretary of State. According to a progress report to the Governor for the first six months of operations, July 1 through December 31, 1961, "45,000 cubic feet of records [were] destroyed and 20,000 cubic feet of records transferred from offices to low-cost storage." In the following year 109,500 cubic feet of

[23] "Paperwork Management 1600." It replaces the former records chapter of the *Manual*.

records were destroyed and 62,020 cubic feet of records were transferred to low-cost storage.

By the end of 1962, twenty-eight agencies of the government, about half of all agencies, had effective disposition programs, and all of the agencies were expected to have such programs by July 1, 1963. The department is now beginning to move into other areas of paperwork management, with preference given to forms and reports control. The department intends to reduce the records in offices by two-thirds.

Part of the act establishing the Department of General Services is a records management act based on the model act of the Council of State Governments. As part of the Management Research Section, the paperwork management staff will move to the new department. The present Central Record Depository and its branch offices will be transferred to the department after January 1, 1967.

Before an act of 1927 required Department of Finance approval for the destruction of records, agencies disposed of records as they saw fit according to their own needs. Some were destroying records before they could be audited, and the legislation was aimed merely at insuring that an audit had been made before destruction. Fortunately, the Department of Finance and the Secretary of State worked out in 1949 procedures to protect the state's historical interests. The agencies inventory their own records; appraise them for fiscal, legal, and administrative value to the agency; establish retention periods based on the appraisals; and develop retention and disposal schedules. The agencies then transmit the disposition schedules to the Archives for approval by the Historian, who enters "Hold for Archives" opposite the items the Archives wishes to screen and forwards the schedules to the Audit Division, Department of Finance, for a determination of the adequacy of the proposed retention periods for auditing purposes. The Audit Division returns the approved schedules to the agencies of origin with disposition instructions entered thereon.[24] The Archives and the Audits Division may act on all or part of the records listed, and their instructions for disposition are binding on the agency. Once approved, the record disposition schedules operate as a continuing authorization, and they remain so until modified or rescinded.

Under sections 2451, 26201, 26202, 26205, 26207, and 27205 of the Government Code, county records may be destroyed with the approval of the Board of Supervisors, and under section 34090 those of cities and local agencies with the approval of the city council and the city attorney. School districts must transmit lists of records they wish to destroy to the Historian, State Archives, who, within a sixty-day period, may select those he wishes transferred to the State Archives.

[24] The Attorney General is occasionally consulted for a legal opinion.

Article 12956 of the act creating the Department of General Services instructs the Director of the department to provide appropriate protection for "records designated by state agencies, with the concurrence of the director, as essential to the functioning of state government in the event of major disaster." Before the enactment of this law the Secretary of State, then responsible for the preservation of essential records, had rented space from Western States Atomic Vaults, Inc., a firm that had equipped a former railroad tunnel in the Santa Cruz Mountains as a security vault. A considerable number of agencies have taken advantage of this arrangement for storing 3,223 reels of microfilm of their essential records. The State Retirement System has a vault of its own. Other agencies are using their field installations for the safekeeping of security copies.

COMMENTS

While California has a strong and successful records management program, it lags behind many smaller states in providing for its archives. In regard to housing, personnel, and funds for operations, the present arrangements are entirely unworthy of the most populous state in the federal union.

COLORADO

Originally set up under the State Historical Society, the Division of State Archives and Public Records, the archival agency of the state of Colorado, is now a division in the executive department of the state.

BACKGROUNDS

In 1903 Frederic L. Paxson, professor of history at the University of Colorado, reported to the Public Archives Commission of the American Historical Association on the archives of the state.[25] Because Colorado did not have a law to provide for the safekeeping of its records, he found that those not needed for the dispatch of current business were sadly neglected. No action was taken except that the Secretary of State was instructed to keep all acts, resolutions, and journals of the legislature and to preserve all bonds, books, records, maps, registers, and papers of public character (Comp. Laws of Colorado, 1921). This act, however, was not construed as an assignment of statewide archival authority to him, and most records were still kept in the agencies of origin. After the sub-basement of the Capitol in Denver had been cleaned out in 1911, records

[25] *Annual Report of the American Historical Association for the Year 1903,* I (Washington, 1904), 415–37.

were stored there in open cupboards exposed to fire and theft, those of defunct agencies were inaccessible, and the archives as a whole were in chaotic condition.

In 1881 the legislature had passed an act (Laws, 1881, p. 31) to encourage the establishment of a state historical and natural history society and had appropriated $500 to assist it in starting a collection, ownership of its properties to be vested in the state. The State Historical and Natural History Society has had financial support from the state, except for the years 1885 and 1893, when the legislature failed to make appropriations to it. Yet, because of the society's Class B organizational position in the government, funds were not always available to meet appropriations. Made an educational institution of the state by an act of 1915, the society occupied in the winter of 1914–15 its new building, the State Museum, which had been erected at a total cost of $350,000.[26]

Though the depression of the 1930's seriously menaced the continued existence of the historical society, it proved a blessing in disguise for the cause of records in Colorado, as it did in other states; for the WPA Historical Records Survey, under the sponsorship of the Secretary of State, did the most complete job of surveying state, county, and municipal records ever done in the state. When the program was drawing toward its end, the State Historian and Curator of History of the society proposed to the board of directors in his monthly report of December 13, 1940:

I suggest for your consideration the advisability of having a law introduced in the coming legislature making this Society the Archives department of the State. State Archives work is becoming increasingly important, and many of the states have made special arrangements for the selection of State documents worthy of preservation, and for the care of the same. In such a law the Society might be declared one of the Executive Departments and thus be assured designation in the first-class, so far as appropriations are concerned.[27]

As a result of the work of a committee appointed to consider steps toward continuing the Historical Records Survey program, the board of directors of the society drafted legislation that was passed in 1943 as Senate Bill No. 50 (Session Laws, 1943, ch. 151).[28] Under this act the historical society was made responsible for the preservation, destruction, or microfilming of all public records of the state and its counties, municipalities, districts, or other legal subdivisions. Section I of the act carried the following provision: "For the purpose of determining the order of

[26] In 1927 the State Historical and Natural History Society was rechartered as the State Historical Society. Le Roy R. Hafen, "History of the State Historical Society of Colorado," *Colorado Magazine*, XXX (July, 1953), 161–85; XXX (Oct., 1953), 283–310; and XXXI (Jan., 1954), 37–68.

[27] *Ibid.*, XXXI (Jan., 1954), 51.

[28] This was a modified version of the "Proposed Uniform Public Records Act" recommended by the Society of American Archivists (see p. 31).

its appropriations, the State Historical Society of Colorado is hereby declared to be part of the Executive Department of State Government," and this provision removed the ever present threat that appropriations might not be paid even though made by the legislature. Although the legislation was permissive only, the society was able to accomplish a great deal with the help of increased appropriations.[29] For practical reasons, a Division of Archives was established, an archivist and a staff were appointed, and a microfilm program was initiated in 1944. Unfortunately, the archivist was almost immediately granted leave of absence to direct a major research project, and such archival work as was being done was left to his assistants.[30]

To provide proper storage for the state archives, the legislature in 1945 authorized construction of a storage vault in the sub-basement of the museum, equipped with air-conditioning, humidity control, a fumigation chamber, and cleaning facilities. By 1948 shelving had been installed, many valuable records of various state departments had been brought in, and a limited checklist of territorial and state printed reports had been prepared.

The public records act of 1951 (H.B. No. 98) officially established the Division of State Archives under the historical society; defined public records; gave the disposal authority to the Attorney General, the State Archivist, and the head of the department whose records were concerned; provided that records with legal, administrative, or historical value be transferred to the Archives and that lists of them be kept in the office of origin and in the Archivist's office; provided further that records of defunct agencies be destroyed or transferred to the Archives — the determination to be made by the Attorney General and the Archivist; required that the legal custodian preserve, repair, and renovate records and that materials used in records creation be of durable quality; permitted custodians to have records microfilmed according to standards set by the National Bureau of Standards and gave to such microfilm the legal force of the originals; conferred upon the Archivist the right of reasonable access to non-confidential records; gave the Attorney General the right of replevin; and provided that when a dispute arose concerning the value of state records, the Governor should be the final arbitrational authority. In 1955 the name of the Division of State Archives was changed to Division of State Archives and Public Records.

In 1959 (Colorado Statutes Rev., 1953: 131-3-1–131-3-10, as amended 1959) the Division of State Archives and Public Records was separated from the State Historical Society and set up as an agency in the executive department.

[29] $37,000 for 1943–45 biennium, an increase of $16,000.
[30] Hafen, *loc. cit.*, XXXI (Jan., 1954), 57.

THE DIVISION OF STATE ARCHIVES AND PUBLIC RECORDS

This division operates the State Archives, the State Records Center, and the State Microfilm Unit. Reporting to the State Archivist and Records Administrator, an Assistant Archivist is in charge of field work and permanent archival holdings, while another Assistant Archivist administers the records center and the microfilm unit.

The division's budget for fiscal 1963–64 is $105,847 ($88,738 for 1962–63), with an additional $70,250 in the microfilm revolving fund, making a total for the year of $176,097. There is no budgetary division between the archival and records management functions, although operations are programed with expenditures as follows:

Administrative $25,183
Archival Management 39,224
Records Management 32,740
Technical Services Related to Public Records.................... 8,700

Having obtained the budget requests of units heads, the State Archivist submits the division's budget to the Budget Office and consults with its analysts. As part of the Governor's executive department budget, the budget goes to the Joint Committee on Budget of the legislature, where the State Archivist defends it, customarily accompanied by members of the advisory committee [31] and occasionally by the assistant archivists. The State Archivist has not had any budget request substantially cut by the joint committee. Cuts on the floor of the House, generally minor, are usually restored by the Senate.

Since July 1, 1959, all employees of the division have been under the state civil service system. The State Archivist is appointed by the Governor after an open competitive examination consisting of three parts — a written presentation, an oral examination by experts, and the verification of professional status, education, and experience — each part having equal weight. Staff members are appointed by the State Archivist from civil service eligibility lists, with the approval of the Governor. Examinations for all professional personnel are similar to that for State Archivist, and positions must be filled from the top names on the respective lists. Employees may retire at half of the maximum five-year average salary with thirty-five years of service at any age, with twenty or more years of service at age sixty, and with thirty or more years of service at age fifty-five. There is no compulsory retirement age. Other personnel benefits available are optional group insurance, fifteen days of annual leave, and fifteen days of sick leave per year.

The division has eighteen employees, six of whom are professional. Salaries are as follows:

[31] See p. 66.

State Archivist .... $8,724–$11,136
Assistant Archivists (2) 6,840– 9,160
Archives Assistants (2) 5,100– 6,842
Archives Aides (2) 3,996– 5,355
Microfilm Operators (4 permanent, 3 as needed).............. 3,288– 4,410
Senior Photographer 5,364– 7,182
Stenographers, Clerks 3,804– 5,103

Within the grades there are increases through seven steps. Longevity increases are given after five years at the top step.

On August 26, 1963, the division moved from quarters in the State Services Building into its own building at 1530 Sherman Street, Denver. This is in effect two structures: a historic three-story mansion, the only one standing in the Capitol Building Complex; and a modern three-story fireproof and air-conditioned annex across the rear of the property. This will give the division much-needed additional space for its archival holdings, as all available space in the two-story vault in the sub-basement of the State Museum has been practically exhausted. The records center has remained in the State Services Building.

In co-operation with the department of history of the University of Denver and its Graduate School of Librarianship, the division offers a graduate course applicable to the M.A. or Ph.D. degree, with internships for students specializing in history, library work, or public administration. An annual archives institute, also offered in co-operation with the university, was initiated in 1962. The State Archivist is the director of the institute, and the State Archivist of Delaware serves as co-director. A small but comprehensive technical library in the fields of records management and archival administration has been assembled.

As for its status and achievements, the division derives much strength from the interest and support of the Public Records Advisory Committee. Appointed under authority of Colorado Statutes Revised, chapter 131-3-2 (4), the committee is composed of the State Archivist (chairman), the Attorney General, the Secretary of State, the State Auditor, the State Controller, and a representative of the State Historical Society. The committee has about two meetings a month, reviewing disposal requests and advising the Archivist in matters of importance to the program in general.[32]

Unfortunately the activities of the division, which are bound to be of interest to other archival institutions of the country, are too little known, since they formerly received inadequate attention in the annual reports of the State Historical Society and since "after secession" shortage of funds has not permitted their publication. A full report is said to be forthcoming in the near future.

[32] The Director of this Study was privileged to attend a meeting of the committee.

Holdings consist of 25,000,000 documents dated from 1840 to 1956, largely non-current public records of the territory, state, counties, municipalities, and other subdivisions of the state. There are also papers of former public officials who have deposited them in the State Archives because they were intermingled with public records. With the exception of four Governors whose papers are in the State Historical Society, papers of all the Governors from 1864 to 1960 are in the State Archives, as are the records of other constitutional officers. Even the Supreme Court and district and county courts have transferred non-current records to the State Archives. Since the separation of the State Archives from the State Historical Society, the state agencies have seemed quite willing to place public records in the Archives.

The archives vault in the museum sub-basement, built at a cost of $65,000 in 1946–47, has a gross content of 32,000 cubic feet, walls thirteen inches thick of brick lined with structural tile, seven-inch reinforced concrete floors, rolling steel fire doors on each level, fire signals and extinguishers, a 180-cubic-foot fumigating vault, and temperature and humidity controls. At present 6,700 cubic feet of space is available for archives storage in this vault, all of which is used, and there is an overflow into the records center, one-third of its space being occupied by archives. There are also two archives vaults [33] in the basement of the State Services Building, one housing the master negatives of archival holdings and the other used for county and municipal archival material. Pending the acquisition of laminating equipment, there are no preservation facilities beyond those for cleaning and first aid to documents.

Records are arranged by agency of origin. Effective in 1962 a "record group identification system" has been established, which uses a simple alphabetical-numerical system for identifying state (A-1 to A-133), county (C-1 to C-63), and municipal (M-1 to M-240) provenances and which is applied to all records from creation to retirement. A booklet explaining the system has been made available to agencies. Also a considerable number of inventories and collateral studies have been prepared, partly by archivists and partly by archival interns.

In fiscal 1963, 6,340 archival reference services were rendered (2,350 over the telephone, 2,672 by letter, and 1,312 to visitors). Records are used by legislators, lawyers, newspapermen, graduate students, scholars, writers, political parties, legislative committees, and individuals con-

[33] Under the new space allocation there will be three, since the large vault now housing two large planetary cameras will be vacated and will be converted by double-decking to archival use. The microfilm and photographic holdings will be transferred to a specially constructed area in the new headquarters building.

[65]

sulting birth and death statistics. Two-thirds of all reference services are for state agencies.

RECORDS MANAGEMENT AND RECORDS DISPOSITION

The authority of the division in the area of records management is broad, inasmuch as the State Archivist is empowered to "formulate and put into effect, to the extent authorized by law, within the division and otherwise, such program or programs as he deems advisable or necessary for public records conservation by the State of Colorado or political subdivisions thereof" (Colorado Statutes Rev. 131-3-3). Appointed by their agencies, records liaison officers [34] are to co-operate with the State Archivist "and to provide such other assistance and data as will enable the division properly to carry out its activities and effectuate the purposes of this article." So far the State Archivist and the staff have considered it their primary duty to establish close working relationships with the records liaison officers and have conducted workshops for state agencies on records management problems. Rules and regulations for scheduled disposition of public records have been promulgated, and a guide for the appraisal of agency records has been prepared and is in use. Similar advice and assistance are offered to local units as requested and to the extent that requests can be accommodated.

Comprehensive general and departmental schedules are prepared with the assistance of agency personnel, reviewed by the Public Records Advisory Committee, and finally approved by the State Archivist, the Attorney General, and the agency head. Only records of a regular, recurrent, and routine nature are scheduled on a continuing basis, and all schedules are subject to annual review. Inasmuch as the public records act applies to all public records of the state, records of the political subdivisions of the state are subject to the same disposal procedure; that is, records liaison officers prepare inventories and schedules under the direction of the State Archivist and the staff, and these are reviewed by the Public Records Advisory Committee. Disposal authority is vested in the State Archivist and the Attorney General. Every one of the 63 counties has a records program for one or more units of its government. At the discretion of the State Archivist, local records of limited historical value may be deposited in the State Archives or placed in an appropriate depository, e.g., the State Historical Society, various university libraries, public libraries, or the State Library.

Records deemed to have limited retention value but no longer needed for agency operations are placed in the records center, which has been

---

[34] The Study Director was given an opportunity to meet many of these liaison officers at an "open house" offered by the division, and he found their intense interest in the division's program very impressive.

in operation since 1957. Located since 1960 in the sub-basement of the State Services Building, it has a capacity of 14,000 cubic feet, all of which is used. In fiscal 1963 the center disposed of 2,942 cubic feet of records, received 4,010 cubic feet, added 500 cubic feet of archival material to the 5,000 cubic feet of such material already in the center, and rendered 9,729 reference services. A detailed system of reporting, on "Records Center Flow Sheets," is in force.

Colorado expects to participate in the essential records preservation program, and legislation to that effect was to be enacted by the 1963 legislature. The State Archivist has initiated microfilming of vital records in many departments, with security copies deposited elsewhere.

THE MICROFILM PROGRAM

Colorado has a central microfilm unit administered by an Assistant State Archivist under the State Archivist. In 1959 a revolving fund for the purchase of microfilm stock, photographic supplies, and related expenses was set up (H.B. No. 524). In 1962–63 this fund was $40,634. Employing six regular operators and collators, the division owns five rotary (16-mm.) cameras and two planetary cameras. An additional camera is rented as needed. The division does its own developing and bills the agencies at cost plus 2 per cent under the revolving fund act.

In fiscal 1963 the microfilm unit completed 687 reels of 16-mm. negative film, 513 reels of 35-mm. film negatives, and 620 reels of 35-mm. positive microfilm — a total of 1,820 reels. Besides microfilming, the unit does Thermofax, Xerox, Multigraph, and offset plate work from microfilm. A senior photographer, who is also the audio-visual archivist assistant, does original photographic work and is on call by state agencies for the recording of special events and the making of portraits.

Microfilm service is offered to local units on a limited basis; that is, only selected archival materials are microfilmed by the central microfilm unit. Other local projects are done on contract or in the office needing the work, in which case the State Archivist checks quality and assists with the training of personnel and in most instances accepts the security copy of the film for deposit and custody.

COMMENTS

1. Although in August, 1963, new headquarters and some space for archival purposes were provided for the Division of State Archives and Public Records, the effectiveness of its services suffers from the existing dispersal of its storage facilities.

2. To take care of a large volume of records in need of repair, the division needs a lamination and rehabilitation laboratory.

[67]

3. The activities and holdings of the division should be made better known through publication of annual reports and finding aids.

CONNECTICUT

The State Librarian of Connecticut is the legal custodian of the state's archives, he is a member and the secretary of the State Records Management Committee, he administers the State Records Center, and the Examiner of Public Records in charge of the local records program reports to him. This makes for a very desirable concentration of responsibility in the hands of a professional official of the state.

BACKGROUNDS

By constitutional provision, the Secretary of State has the care and custody of public records, especially the acts, resolves, and orders of the general assembly. After the first State Librarian had been appointed in 1854, the Secretary began to use the State Library at Hartford for the safekeeping of such records in his possession as he did not see fit to keep in his own office.[35] The library's role as an official depository of public records was confirmed by an act of 1909 (General Statutes, Rev. 1958, Title 11, secs. 1-6), according to which "any official of the state or of any county or town, or any other official, may turn over to the state librarian, with his consent, for permanent preservation in the state library, any official books, records, documents, original papers or files not in current use in his office."

This action had been preceded in 1886 by an investigation, conducted by the Secretary of State and the State Librarian, of the existence and condition of old court and colonial or state records. The report of the two officials [36] led to the creation, in 1889, of a Commission on Public Records, which concerned itself with the problem of town, probate district, and church records predating the year 1800. The commission recommended that the records of the jurisdictions visited be listed and indexed, that they be stored in fireproof vaults or safes, that those deteriorating be repaired, that a uniform system of record-keeping be installed in the probate court districts, and that their older records be sent to the State Library.[37]

A Temporary Examiner of Public Records appointed by the Governor in 1901 was to put the public records of the state in the condition prescribed by law. After he had visited towns and probate districts of the

[35] See the list of holdings of the State Library in "Report on the Public Archives of Connecticut," *Annual Report of the American Historical Association for the Year 1900*, II (Washington, 1901), 27–31.

[36] *Report to the General Assembly on Ancient Court Records* (Hartford, 1889), 38 p.

[37] *Report*, 1900, Public Document No. 41 (New Haven, 1900), 15 p.

state, he made his recommendations. They resulted in the passage in 1903 (ch. 165) of legislation designed to protect existing records and to insure the permanence of records to be created in the future. In 1911 the permanent position of Examiner of Public Records was created, and subsequent legislation, providing incisive penalties, increased this officer's authority.

In 1955 the general assembly charged a State Records Management Committee — consisting of the Commissioner of Finance and Control, the State Librarian, and the Attorney General — with certain records management responsibilities and with approving disposal and retention of records. Subsequently a records center for the storage of records of temporary value was created as a division of the State Library.

Senate Bill No. 1108, referred to the Judiciary Committee of the 1961 general assembly, would have established in the State Library a Division of Records Administration under a State Records Administrator to be appointed by the State Librarian with the approval of the State Library Committee. The division, composed of a State Records Section, a Local Records Section, a Records Preservation Section, and the Examiner of Public Records, would have been in charge of a complete records management program for all governmental agencies and offices of the state and its subdivisions, except with respect to judicial records, and also would have directed a program for the preservation of records essential to the operation of government in times of disaster. The bill died in committee. A similar bill introduced in the 1963 session of the assembly suffered the same fate.

THE STATE LIBRARY

The State Library is governed by the State Library Committee, which consists of the Governor and four members appointed biennially by the general assembly. This committee appoints the State Librarian. Under the State Librarian the Archives Section, the Office of the Examiner of Public Records, and the State Records Center are charged with archival and records management responsibilities.

The 1964 budget provides for archives and records management approximately $32,000, which sum includes the salaries of the Archivist ($6,700–$8,700), the Examiner of Public Records ($6,700–$8,700), and four persons in the records center. The Archivist, who must have an M.A. degree in history or an M.S. degree in library science, reports to the library's Chief of Public Services. Most of the library's personnel is under the state civil service. Salary increases are given on a merit basis.

The State Library and Supreme Court Building, in which the library has been housed since 1910, is one of the finest examples of modified Renaissance library architecture. Its storage facilities for archives consist of twenty vaults of various sizes. These afford good protection, but the

[69]

resulting dispersal of records is not very convenient from the standpoint of service. The library has acquired contiguous property on which a new wing will be constructed that will add much-needed space for general library as well as archival purposes, including adequate vaults.

The library's holdings consist of several million papers dating from 1631 to the present and include records of the general assembly through 1820 and records of offices of the colony and state. There are also considerable quantities of probate records, other court records, town records, and church records. Probate and town records have been accessioned under the authority of section 11-5 of the General Statutes, Rev., 1958, which permits any town clerk and any judge of a probate district to deliver to the State Librarian with his consent "any volume of land or probate records in his official custody, the age or condition of which renders its continued use by the public inadvisable," and to receive, in lieu of the original, certified photostat copies bound "to match the current volumes of land or probate records." The State Library also holds the Barbour index to Connecticut vital records to 1850 and the World Wars I and II records pertaining to Connecticut residents, for which a special section of the library is reserved.

In Connecticut the archives function of the State Library has been largely absorbed into the general operations of the library. Obviously the intention has been to treat archival material insofar as possible like other holdings of the library, to use the library's general catalog for controlling and making it accessible, and to enable the general reference staff to service it. Certain classes of material such as the probate and church records are handled by the library's Section of History and Genealogy. There is no archives division responsible for the processing, controlling, and servicing of *all* the archival holdings as in other state libraries charged with the state archives function. The policy of integrating archival material with the general collections of the library is illustrated by the way in which accessions are processed. A distinction is made between bound and unbound material. While the Archivist receives all records accessioned, bound material is sent to the Cataloging Section, and its classification conforms to the classification of the general library. If the material is and remains unbound, the Archivist processes, classifies, and catalogs it. The same distinction between bound and unbound material prevails in the filing of the catalog cards. Those pertaining to bound volumes are filed in the library's general catalog. A separate catalog holds the cards for unbound material, which physically is kept in file cases on the mezzanine floor above the general reading room and in an adjacent vault.

The library's most important group of records, the so-called Connecticut Archives, to 1820, has been accessioned and organized in two series. The first series, including documents up to the year 1790, was selected from the files of the general assembly about 1845 and was rearranged in accordance with a subject pattern providing such headings as Agriculture, Indians, Finance and Currency, Schools and Colleges, and so on. A second series was transferred from the office of the Secretary of State, when the library occupied its new buildings, and was "methodized" in the same fashion. Quite obviously, these records were classified as were the Massachusetts archives in the late 1830's and early 1840's. In the case of the Connecticut archives, the damage done has been remedied to a considerable extent by the compilation of complete and careful indexes prepared under the guidance of George S. Godard.[38]

The library has published a number of volumes of *Connecticut State Records*. Its *Bulletin* contains such items as lists and descriptions of records deposited in the library and in other jurisdictions, instructions for the care of archives in the library, and the history, progress, and work of the Emery Record Preserving Company. Under the heading of *Miscellaneous Publications*, selected laws of Connecticut relating to retention and reproduction of public records have been compiled and published.

Inasmuch as archival holdings are serviced by the library's general reading room staff, no separate statistics indicating their use are available. Inquiries answered by mail and telephone amount to several hundred a year. The library maintains in its Memorial Hall a permanent display; it includes the original charter of Connecticut and the engrossed copy of the state constitution of 1818. The library also prepared an exhibit for the "Freedom Train," which illustrated the colonists' desire for freedom from 1631 to the Revolution.

The State Library has its own bindery. For the restoration of records in need of repair, the Emery silk method[39] has been, and is being, used with considerable skill. The library also does its own photostating and microfilming, using two photostat machines, a Diebold rotary camera, a microfilm enlarger, and other pieces of equipment.

STATE RECORDS MANAGEMENT AND RECORDS DISPOSITION

Before the enactment of No. 339 of the Acts of 1955 (Gen. Stats., Title 4, sec. 34), heads of state agencies, with the permission of the Attorney General, the Comptroller, and the Treasurer, were permitted to destroy any records more than six years old. The new act created a State Records Management Committee consisting of the Commissioner of Finance and Control as chairman, the Attorney General, and the State Librarian, who

[38] The State Library's methods of filing and indexing records were described by Effie M. Prickett in her "Instructions for Care of Archives in the Connecticut State Library," *Bulletin*, No. 8 (Hartford, 1920), 14 + 2 p.

[39] Allen P. Hoard, "History, Progress and Work of the Emery Record Preserving Company, Taunton, Massachusetts, in Connection with the Public Records of Our Land," Connecticut State Library, *Bulletin*, No. 12 (Hartford, 1926), 11 p.

serves as secretary and because of his length of service [40] helps to provide consistency in the committee's decisions. The committee, "responsible for carrying out a records management program for the books, records, papers and documents of all state agencies within the executive department," may require the agencies to inventory their records and to submit for the committee's approval retention schedules based on the need for retaining them in agency space or "in a suitable records center." Requests for the disposal of records of no administrative, fiscal, legal, and historical value must be approved by the committee. Items that, in the opinion of the committee, have historical value to the state "may be transferred to the state library." At the second meeting of the committee, the then Commissioner of Finance put the State Librarian in charge of a records center to be established. One person in the Budget Division of the Department of Finance and Control works on retention and disposal schedules.

THE STATE RECORDS CENTER

The State Records Center, which is a part of the State Library, is located in Rocky Hill, Connecticut, within easy driving distance from Hartford. Its staff consists of a Manager, a Material Storage Manager I, a clerk II, and a store keeper I, the last paid from funds of the three state departments that require most service. The center has been in operation since 1958, when the "root cellar" of the Veterans Home and Hospital was made available to it, with a storage capacity of 9,120 cubic feet. To this a new wing, constructed at a cost of $50,000, has added another 11,600 cubic feet, giving the center a total capacity of 20,720 cubic feet. The shelving arrangement was planned to conform to the existing building, and calls for storing boxes two deep with the wide side toward the aisle. The center, while by no means fireproof, has a fire-detection system, which helped to prevent great losses when a fire started near the heating plant in the old building.

The performance of the center becomes apparent from the following statistics:

SUMMARY FIGURES SHOWING THE GROWTH OF THE RECORDS CENTER
FROM FISCAL YEAR 1958–59 THROUGH
FISCAL YEAR 1961–62

Year	Material (cubic feet)		Number of References	Inventory at Close of Year	Agencies Serviced
	Received	Discharged			
1958–59	7,152	1,231	6,747	8,255	19
1959–60	1,436	959.5	7,014	8,731.5	23
1960–61	5,965	1,451	11,704	13,245.5	31
1961–62	5,371.5	3,477.5	12,015	15,215.5	34

[40] This seems to be a happy tradition in Connecticut. Charles J. Hoadly served as State Librarian from 1855 to 1900, George S. Godard from 1900 to 1936, and James Brewster from 1936 to 1956.

With two minor exceptions, all the material in the center is under schedule control. Some of the retention periods set seem to be on the conservative side — fifty years for hospital records, seventy years for state prison records, for example — and in all likelihood the center will be completely filled by the end of 1965. The situation would seem to call for careful scrutiny of the center's reference service statistics with a view to reviewing and changing retention periods. Procedures for the transfer to, and servicing by, the center are simple and effective. In developing them, those of the Dupont Company center have been followed to a large extent.

Though the center staff is not engaged in records management other than the administration of the holdings, the Manager and the Material Storage Manager are called upon to help agencies with inventorying records and preparing retention schedules.

THE LOCAL RECORDS PROGRAM

Connecticut's local records program is administered by the Examiner of Public Records, who is appointed by and reports to the State Librarian and has his office in the State Library. With its sixty-year history, the program enjoys a national reputation. Continued in the distinguished tradition of Harold S. Burt and his predecessors, it is aimed at the protection and preservation of local records. It enters the field of local records management only to the extent that the Examiner furnishes to state and local officials lists of approved standard papers, standard inks, typewriter ribbons, and loose-leaf binders and decides on requests for the destruction of local records, after such requests have been approved by the chief executive of the local unit.

According to the law (Gen. Stats., Rev., 1958, Title 11-8), the Examiner "shall cause such action to be taken by the persons having the care and custody of public records as may be necessary to put such records in the custody and condition required by law and to secure their safety and preservation"; that is, he is responsible for the well-being of public records of all political units including the courts. In actual practice, the Examiner does not concern himself with the records of state departments and agencies or with those of the courts, though he may survey the vaults of courts upon request of the Chief Justice of the Supreme Court.

A travel allowance in the budget of the library enables the Examiner to visit local offices in a systematic fashion, spending if possible three days of the week on the road and using a state car for the purpose. In the opinion of the present incumbent of the office, the small and medium-size towns have made satisfactory provision for the safekeeping of their records; and, where arrangements are deficient, they can be remedied with reasonable ease. In the large places, however, the sheer bulk of the records poses a problem.

[73]

Considerable quantities of probate and church records have been accessioned by the State Librarian, who has the legal authority to receive them. They are part of the Section of History and Genealogy.

Until 1940, when it was discontinued for reasons of economy, the Examiner's *Biennial Report* was an excellent source of information on the Connecticut local program. Now the Examiner makes his annual reports to the State Librarian for incorporation in the latter's report to the Governor. A digest of this report is printed in the "Digest of Administrative Reports to the Governor," and it deals in two or three sentences with the Examiner's activities.

As in other states, the Utah Genealogical Society did a great deal of microfilming in Connecticut. It reproduced the land and probate records to 1850 and the library's collection of church records, and it gave positive sets to the library. Additional microfilming for security purposes is being done by many towns.

Excellent though it is, the local records program could be improved by providing records management assistance to local units. Senate Bill 1108 of the 1961 January session would have provided such service.

COMMENTS

1. The State Library is badly in need of increased facilities for the storage and handling of the state's permanently valuable records.

2. It is the policy of the State Library to incorporate the archival process in the general operations of the library. This, it seems, will have to be abandoned when major accessions of recent state records can be received. It will then be advisable to place all archival activities, including custody, processing, and servicing of all records, under a Division of State Archives that will be a self-contained unit of the library.

3. The local records program, which is now essentially conservative in nature, should be modernized to provide records management assistance to local units.

DELAWARE

Owing its genesis to the alarming findings of the Public Archives Commission of the American Historical Association, the Public Archives Commission of the State of Delaware has, over a period of sixty years, developed an increasingly active program of archives administration and records management. In addition, it has served successfully in many fields of historical endeavor, including the establishment of a museum and the preservation of historic buildings and sites.

BACKGROUNDS

In 1906 Professor Edgar Dawson reported to the Public Archives Commission of the American Historical Association that the records pertaining to the early history of Delaware were located in Sweden, Holland, New York, Pennsylvania, and Maryland; for the colonies making up the present area of Delaware had been under those successive jurisdictions from 1634 until, in 1776, the three lower counties of Pennsylvania seceded and formed the state.[41] The records still preserved in Delaware in 1906 were few, owing to carelessness, to vandalism, and to the dishonesty of students and antiquarians. Before 1873 those archives that had been accumulated were deposited in the loft of the State House at Dover (along with a collection of branding and cropping irons), only to be seriously vandalized during a remodeling in 1873–75. When they were moved to the basement in 1875, the janitor is alleged to have used them to start fires. Professor Dawson stated, "There is probably no State in the Union where one would find less material for writing its history than in Delaware, and there is certainly no one of the original thirteen in which so few records have been made and where so little care has been taken of those that have been made."[42] He also reported that the records in the three counties were much more complete than were the state records, although county clerks had inherited confusion and disorder and crowded, unsatisfactory conditions under which they did their best.

Aroused by Dawson's investigations then still in progress and by clamoring of patriotic societies, the legislature created the Division of Public Records (Laws, 1904–5, ch. 77), consisting of six members appointed by the Governor for terms of two years — later extended to four years — from the memberships of patriotic and historical societies in the state. The division was made custodian of all records predating 1800 and was instructed to classify, catalog, and preserve them, to make them available for reference, to make and enforce rules regarding them, and to report biennially to the Governor. The first appropriation of $500 to the division was made in 1906–7, and this was increased to $1,000 in 1908–9. Chapter 82 of 1911 changed the name of the Division to Public Archives Commission, extended the years of records to be entrusted to its custody to 1850, and authorized it to publish such of these records as it deemed proper and necessary.

The first archivist was employed in 1913. The Hall of Records was established and located in the fireproof basement of the library wing of the State House, also in 1913, and $1,000 was appropriated for the purchase and installation of steel shelving, cabinets, etc. (ch. 10). The same legislature changed the makeup of the commission to two from each of the three counties. Over the years, the powers of the commission were progressively increased. In 1917 it was given authority to remove all records prior to

[41] "Public Archives of Delaware," *Annual Report of the American Historical Association for the Year 1906*, II (Washington, 1908), 129–48.
[42] *Ibid.*, p. 129.

1850 [43] that were not in current use from state, county, and municipal offices and to classify, catalog, and publish them. Chapter 92 of 1937 provided that no records could be destroyed or sold without the written consent of the commission and gave the commission custody of the records of defunct agencies. Chapter 95 of 1939 provided that the membership of the commission should be one man and one woman from each of the counties and that no more than three might be from the same political party. In 1939 also the commission was housed in the new Hall of Records and given the authority to make photographic duplications of the records in its custody. Chapter 74 of 1943 authorized the disposal, with the approval of the State Archivist, of certain records after duplication, and gave these duplicates the legal status of the originals. Also in 1943 the commission was authorized to set standards for paper and ink and to furnish a list of approved products for use in records creation. The State Museum Division of the Public Archives Commission was established in 1949, and the museum was set up in the historic Old Presbyterian Church (built in 1790). The State Library was abolished in 1957, and its holdings of historical interest were transferred to the State Archives.

A 1959 amendment to the Delaware Code, Title 29 (ch. 33, 1960 Cumulative Pocket), required the commission to care for all non-current public records of historical value other than deed record books, instead of only records 75 years or older, to transfer semi-current records to records centers, and to operate a centralized microfilming program; and it provided a penalty for public officials refusing to relinquish public records.

THE PUBLIC ARCHIVES COMMISSION

The Public Archives Commission is charged with the administration of the state archives, a records management program including a records center in each of the three counties of the state, a central microfilm program, the State Museum Division including an increasing number of historic buildings and sites, a reference library, and a publication program.[44] Responsibility for all aspects of the commission's work is vested in the State Archivist, who is also Director of the State Museum. The manifold historical activities are designed to strengthen and to supplement the archives operation, which remains central to the commission's mandate.

From a budget of $6,000 in 1931, $16,865 in 1947, and $65,350 in 1959, the commission has progressed to a budget of $160,925.95 in fiscal 1963. This is broken down as follows: Archives, including records management and publications, $99,664.64; [45] State Museum, $27,487.84; John Dickinson Mansion, $19,473.45; and Fort Christina Monument, $14,300. The

[43] In 1933 the law was changed to read "all records 75 years old or more."
[44] A handsome illustrated folder (n.p., n.d.), 12 p., describes the holdings of the Hall of Records and the historical activities of the Public Archives Commission.
[45] This item includes the purchase price of the old Sussex County Court House.

commission received $151,090 for 1963–64, the difference being accounted for by several special items in the 1962–63 budget that are not included in that for 1963–64.

The State Archivist's budget requests are prepared for, and approved by, the Public Archives Commission; and the president of the commission and the State Archivist present them at hearings before the State Budget Commission. If they wish they may also appear before the Joint Legislative Finance Committee.

The staff of the commission is not under a state merit or civil service system. The State Archivist is appointed annually at the meetings of the commission, and he, in turn, appoints the staff members, who serve during good behavior. Under a policy adopted by the commission, salaries of the staff are not revealed. Salary increases are awarded by the commission, and there are other benefits in the form of a non-contributory pension system and participation in old age and survivors insurance.

The State Archivist, as over-all director, is in charge of a staff of twenty-five: in the Archives, the Assistant State Archivist, a junior archivist for administration, a junior archivist for research, a public records examiner, a secretary, a library assistant, a document restorer, a chief photographer, an assistant photographer, six junior photographers, and a clerk; in the State Museum, a Curator, a Historic Sites Supervisor, a secretary, a receptionist, an exhibit preparer, and a maintenance technician; and in the John Dickinson Mansion, a Building Supervisor, a receptionist, and a watchman. Though the State Archivist wishes to maintain a measure of flexibility in assigning duties to his staff, they perform for the most part the tasks specified in their respective job descriptions.

Since 1939 the Public Archives Commission has been housed in the Hall of Records, which was built with $160,000 appropriated by the legislature and a like amount of federal funds and which houses also the Corporation Department and the Franchise Tax Department. The commission's quarters contain two large air-conditioned and fireproof vaults and a basement vault, a well-equipped research room with a catalog room connected, offices and workrooms for the staff, an exhibition lobby, and basement space for photographic and repair operations. Equipment includes a Barrow laminator, three flatbed and five rotary cameras, a reader-printer, and nine readers. The commission desperately needs more storage space for its holdings. It had expected to take over the quarters now used by the Corporation and Franchise Departments after they moved into the old Board of Health quarters, but these departments are still in the Hall of Records. Because of the shortage of storage space, some archival materials are held in the commission's records centers.

The series of publications of the commission was started in 1911. It includes such substantial works as the *Calendar of Kent County, Delaware,*

Probate Records, compiled by Leon deValinger, Jr. (Dover, Del., 1944); three volumes of the *Calendar of Ridgely Family Letters*, edited and compiled by Leon deValinger, Jr., and Virginia E. Shaw (Dover, Del., 1948, 1951, and 1961); two volumes dealing with *Delaware's Role in World War II, 1940–1946*, by William H. Conner and Leon deValinger, Jr. (1955); and *Historic Houses and Buildings of Delaware*, by Harold D. Eberlein and Cortlandt D. V. Hubbard (Dover, Del., 1962).

Dedicated to the idea that the protection of the state's archives and the preservation of its historic buildings, historic sites, and artifacts constitute essentially one task the two phases of which lend strength to each other, the Public Archives Commission administers, as a separate division under the State Archivist as the Director, the Delaware State Museum, which was formally opened in 1950. It is now housed in the Old Presbyterian Church built in 1790 and the adjacent chapel built in 1880. For heavy exhibits, a third building, the original office of the Dover Gas Light Company, was opened as part of the 50th Anniversary Program of the Public Archives Commission. Displays and display techniques compare favorably with those of older and more affluent institutions. Among the historic sites and houses restored and administered by the commission, the John Dickinson Mansion and the Fort Christina Monument are particularly noteworthy. Restorations are carried out by commission personnel at minimum cost.

In addition to serving as Director of the State Museum and contributing significantly to the commission's publication program, the State Archivist is involved in a host of historical activities. He is a member of the Board of Directors of the Historical Society of Delaware. He is also secretary of the State Portrait Commission, the Lewes Memorial Commission, the Civil War Centennial Commission, the Delaware Society for the Preservation of Antiquities, and the Council of Presidents and Executives, which is the Governor's cabinet. Finally, he operates the historical markers program in the state and, in co-operation with the Chief Engineer of the Highway Department, supervises the care of the Mason-Dixon boundary markers. In 1962 and 1963 he was co-director of the Institute of Archival Administration offered by the University of Denver and the Colorado State Archives.

All agencies, departments, boards, and commissions of the state, counties, and municipalities are required by law to deposit with the Public Archives Commission two copies of the best edition of each publication issued by them.

THE ARCHIVES PROGRAM

As archival depository for the state, county, and municipal governments the Public Archives Commission holds 15,285 cubic feet of records, 11,005 reels of microfilm, 23,767 photographic negatives and positives, 1,569 sound recordings, and some motion pictures. These records date from 1674 to 1962.

Holdings include archival material of the colonial period, records of the executive department from 1776, legislative records, probate records and other early court and county records, genealogical records (church records and tombstone inscriptions), the very rich John Dickinson collection, and other private papers. For storage purposes four-drawer file cabinets and archives boxes are used. Microfilm holdings and sound recordings are kept in the mezzanine vault. All three vaults are crowded, and, even with a shoehorn, no new accessions of any size could be inserted. What small items are accessioned — mostly private papers — are listed in the commission's processed *Accessions List*, the latest issue of which is volume 12, number 4 (July, 1963).

Holdings are organized in record groups named after the agencies of origin and controlled by checklists. Indexes are available for wills and records of births and marriages, and information obtained from other sources has been incorporated in these indexes. There is a checklist of state and county records, a location guide, and detailed checklists for individual record groups. A summary checklist of Delaware microfilms and additional detailed checklists of microfilms of individual agencies have also been prepared. In fiscal 1963 archival reference services numbered 1,110, almost half rendered to visitors in the archives reference room and the rest to inquirers by letter.

Preservation and rehabilitation work is done through a deacidification and lamination program. In fiscal 1963 about 8,200 items were repaired and restored.

With the American Library Association, the Public Archives Commission is co-sponsoring a project to develop improved fiberboard for archival containers. The project, begun in 1961 and financed by a grant from the Council on Library Resources, Inc., is administered by the Library Technology Project of the association; and the research is being done by the Institute of Paper Chemistry of Appleton, Wisconsin. The ultimate aim of the project is to produce containers with reduced acidity and increased fire resistance, insect repellency, and mildew resistance.[46]

RECORDS MANAGEMENT AND RECORDS DISPOSITION

The beginnings of the records management program may be said to go back to a 1935 law that required custodians of public records to use paper and ink of standard quality. This led to the establishment by the commission of a paper- and ink-testing laboratory in 1944, and since then it has published annual lists of papers and inks approved for records cre-

[46] Library Technology Project, *Third Annual Report for the Period Ending June 30, 1962*, p. 19, 20.

ation, from which public officials must choose their materials. The disposal legislation of 1943 referred to above laid the foundation for a records management program formally authorized by a 1959 amendment to Title 29, chapter 33.

In discharging this function the commission, upon request, has assisted departments in solving their filing and other records problems by setting up, for instance, a central files system for the State Highway Department and others. Particularly noteworthy are the arrangements for the storage of semi-current records. A records center has been provided in each of the state's three counties. The Kent County Records Center near Dover, a building taken over from the State Highway Department, is completely filled with state and Kent County records, including some permanent records of the Adjutant General. The Sussex County Records Center near Lewes has, in a well-ventilated underground installation taken over from the Army, two rooms, to which a third one is likely to be added in the near future. The finest center is that of New Castle County, located in a World War II Command Post of Old Fort Dupont, now the Governor Bacon Health Center, which is protected by concrete slabs and thirty-six feet of earth and is temperature-controlled by means of a heat pump. The three centers are equipped with steel shelving from the defunct State Library.

No staff is stationed at these records centers. If records are requested, a member of the Dover staff meets with agency personnel on the premises or takes the records requested to the proper city, county, or state office — an arrangement which, given the short distances, seems to work well. Accessions in fiscal 1963 amounted to 1,076 cubic feet, practically all placed in the records centers; and 948.5 cubic feet were destroyed. In the same year 305 reference services were rendered to forty-two departments and agencies.

Microfilming is handled as an integral part of records management, over which the State Archivist asserts and exercises full authority, and it serves the purposes of creating reference and security copies and of reducing bulk. It is usually done at the Hall of Records, but if necessary, personnel and cameras are sent to the counties or municipalities.

The Utah Genealogical Society in the late 1940's microfilmed county records, 1680–1850, and the state microfilmed those for the period following in order to provide security copies.

In 1963 about 1,500 reels of microfilm were produced, making possible the disposal of 1,050 cubic feet of records. Prominent among these were individual income tax returns and dissolved corporation records of the Secretary of State. Treasurer's invoices, payrolls, canceled checks, income tax returns, motor vehicle licenses, and vital statistics are filmed as they accumulate. Films are stored in the Hall of Records and, upon a moment's notice, can be evacuated to one of the underground installations. Since the commission is nearly up to date on security copying, the intent of the essential records preservation program seems practically fulfilled.

Authority to dispose of useless records rests with the State Archivist; he considers it an essential attribute of a responsible archivist not to leave basic decisions to others. Where he sees fit, however, he confers with the Attorney General or, in the case of fiscal records, with the Budget Bureau. The device of the disposal schedule has not been adopted, for the State Archivist does not consider it desirable in a state like Delaware that does not have records officers in the various agencies.

COMMENTS

The otherwise fine program of the State of Delaware suffers from an acute shortage of storage space. To remedy this regrettable situation, the Public Archives Commission should be enabled to take over those parts of the Hall of Records building now occupied by other state agencies.

FLORIDA

Although legal custody of non-current records has been vested in the State Library, renamed the State Library and Historical Archives in 1963, that agency has not been in a position to develop an active archival program.

BACKGROUNDS

The movement in the Southern states for the preservation of state records that started in South Carolina and even more significantly in Alabama and that influenced developments in other states of the South has bypassed the state of Florida. The reasons for this are many. First of all, the state was stripped of practically all records of the Spanish and British regimes, and consequently its historians had to rely on the documentary resources of institutions outside their own state. Also, historical interest was slow in developing; not until 1856 was the Historical Society of Florida organized in St. Augustine. It lapsed during the Civil War; and, though an attempt was made to reorganize it in 1879, it was not revived until 1902.[47] More recently the influx of residents from other parts of the United States has tended to retard popular support of an archival program for the state. Efforts on the part of the Historical Society of Florida and the Southern Historical Society to arouse such support have not yet changed the picture.

A state archives might have originated in the Office of the Secretary of State, for an act of 1845 made it his duty "to cause all books and maps belonging to the state to be collected together."[48] In fact, legislative, cor-

[47] Watt Marchman, "The Florida Historical Society, 1856–1861, 1879, 1902–1940," *Florida Historical Quarterly*, XIX (July, 1940), 4–15.
[48] "Florida's State Library," *ibid.*, II (Apr., 1909), 44.

poration, and election records are in the custody of this official. Actually, however, the archives function was assigned to the State Library Board created by an act of 1925 and composed of three members who serve for overlapping terms of four years. The board's secretary acts as State Librarian.

Shortly after the board had been established, there must have been a plan to charge it with archival duties; for the board's *Report*, 1927–29, mentions as one of its aims that of preserving "the great mass of valuable material (books, maps, manuscripts, etc.) now in the custody of the Secretary of State." Possibly with this in mind, the General Appropriations Act of 1941 (Laws of Florida, 1941, General Laws, vol. I, ch. 20980) gave the State Library Board $5,500 "For Historical Program." Subsequently, an act of 1943 (General Laws, vol. I, ch. 21730) authorized the Library Board to negotiate for and receive official records from state departments and agencies, empowered public officials to turn over to the State Librarian all records not needed for the transaction of business, and required the State Librarian to give receipts for such records and to serve as their legal custodian. A further law of 1957 (General Laws, vol. I, pt. 1, ch. 57-66) was designed to prevent arbitrary destruction of public records. Under this law a "public records screening board consisting of the secretary of state, the attorney general and the state auditor is to pass on applications" for permission to destroy any public records with or without photographing prior to their destruction. Where permission is granted, the State Librarian is to be informed of such action and may then request for delivery into the Library's custody "any public records the destruction of which has been approved."

To resolve the problems of ever increasing quantities of records, the model records management act recommended by the Committee of State Officials on Suggested State Legislation of the Council of State Governments was introduced in the Judiciary Committee D as House Bill 1020 in 1961. Reported out unfavorably, it was later recommitted to the committee, then withdrawn and referred to the Committee on Government Organization, State, where it died. The fate of the bill may not be regretted, because a records management program without the existence and participation of an active archival agency would have been undesirable.

The legislature has now enacted chapter 63-39 of the Laws of 1963, establishing the "state library and historical archives" to be administered by the Florida Library and Historical Commission, its members to be appointed by the Governor in consultation with the Florida Library Association, the Florida Historical Society, and related organizations. The commission is to assume "leadership in" the collection, recording, and dissemination of information about the Florida history, "giving" parity to the historical and the library functions in its own endeavors and co-operating "with other agencies, groups, and individuals." This poorly conceived act does not take advantage of modern archives and records management laws enacted in other states. However, it might lead to a concentration of Florida's archives in the present State Library in Tallahassee and to an active archives program — provided, of course, that the necessary funds are made available. Members of the history departments of the University of Florida and of the Florida State University have stated that records of permanent value continue to perish while in the hands of the creating agencies and that historical research, including the writing of M.A. and Ph.D. theses, is severely handicapped because materials for research have not been concentrated in archival custody where they could be used. History and political science faculties may be willing to support more effective legislation. As one historian put it: "Since we have nowhere to go but up, there is much room for hope."

THE STATE LIBRARY

Neither the act of 1943 nor that of 1957 has benefited the State Library, nor has the library itself taken effective steps to contribute toward their implementation. This explains why an archives department does not exist as an identifiable unit of the State Library. Archival holdings share the quarters of the library in the basement of the Supreme Court Building; there is no separate budget for the archives; and, though one of the library's staff members has been trained in archival work, her main duties are in the library field. In fact, the archival holdings of the State Library are small (260 linear feet) and do not require a great deal of service. In addition to a group of private papers, they consist of executive papers, about 1876–1910, tax rolls, and records of the State Board of Health. Obviously, a policy of acquiring permanently valuable records does not exist, nor has it ever existed; and therefore most of the important documentation of the state's government is not in the custody of the State Library. Admittedly, no acquisition policy can be pursued so long as the State Library lacks personnel, space, and the will to exercise its prerogatives. Also, the Public Records Screening Board does not seem to prevent the arbitrary destruction of state records. Agencies seem to prefer to obtain authorization for the destruction of records by special bills rather than through the machinery of the board.

LOCAL ARCHIVES PROGRAM

On the local level, the Board of County Commissioners of any county was authorized by an act of 1953 (ch. 28306) to create a historical commission. Under this act, the clerk of the circuit court is "to file and record without charge historical data and material," and the county commissioners are "to provide a suitable place as a repository for such data and

[83]

material." Few historical commissions, however, have been organized as a result of this act.[49]

COMMENTS

Florida should enact a modern archives and records management law and provide the funds to administer it effectively. Chapter 63-39 as enacted in 1963 is no substitute for such a law.

GEORGIA

Handicapped by its totally inadequate premises, the Department of Archives and History has not yet developed a fully adequate archival program. It will be able to do so once it occupies the new archives building now being constructed in Atlanta.

BACKGROUNDS

In Georgia concern for the archives of the state emerged early in the nineteenth century. In 1824 Joseph Vallence Bevan was appointed "to search the archives of the State with a view to unfold its history." [50] Interest in the early colonial records manifested itself again when an act of 1837 made funds available for the copying of such records in London. Because the copies thus acquired were lost in a fire while on loan to a professor at Emory College, the Office of Compiler of Records was established in 1902 to assemble for publication the colonial, revolutionary, and Confederate records of Georgia. In 1918 this office ceased to exist with the passage of a law (Laws, 1918, p. 137) creating the Georgia Historical Commission and under it a Department of Archives and History (henceforth called the department), headed by the State Historian and Director. The commission was abolished by the Reorganization Act of 1931 (Laws, 1931, p. 38), and the department was placed under the Secretary of State. In 1951, however, the Historical Commission was re-created by an act of February 21 (Laws, 1951, p. 789), as a separate agency under the Secretary of State. A law of 1957 (Laws, 1957, p. 496) eliminated the designation of State Historian from the Director's title. At the same time the requirement of annual reports of the department was removed from the law.

THE DEPARTMENT OF ARCHIVES AND HISTORY

The Secretary of State participates actively in the department's administration and has furthered its interests in many ways. His role is reflected

[49] According to information received from the P. K. Yonge Library of Florida History in Gainsville, historical commissions have been organized in Alachua, Hillsborough, and Polk counties — in Gainesville, Tampa, and Benton, respectively.

[50] Mary Givens Bryan, "Recent Archival Developments in Georgia," *American Archivist*, XVI (Jan., 1953), 56.

in the integration of the department with his own office in matters of budget. The 1963–64 budget of the Secretary of State provides a lump sum of $1,063,100 for the department, the Microfilm Division of the Secretary of State, and the State Museum of Science and Industry. Since this amount includes $815,000 for "lease rental payments to the State Office Building Authority for the [new] State Archives Building in the amount of $815,000," [51] the sum of $248,000 is left for the operation of the three programs. In the absence of a detailed budget, a breakdown specifying the respective appropriations does not exist. An auditor's report for 1962 [52] shows that the total expenses of $950,613.69 for the operations of the Department of Archives and History included $2,570.77 for travel; $102,520.32 for personal services; $7,516.05 for supplies and materials; $3,097.72 for printing and publications; and $4,969.59 for repairs. Expenses for the Microfilm Division and for the State Museum were $61,577.23 and $25,681.42, respectively. As a matter of actual practice, the office of the Secretary of State, except for salaries, uses the appropriation for the three institutions as one fund and draws upon it as need arises.

The office of the Secretary of State, with all of its departments and divisions, is under the merit system, but not all the personnel of the department are covered by it. However, all enjoy the fringe benefits provided under the state merit system: fifteen days of annual and fifteen days of sick leave a year, hospitalization with the state sharing in the premium cost, and participation in a comprehensive retirement plan that includes social security benefits and membership in the state employees retirement system and is based on a salary deduction of 6.5 per cent, matched by an equal amount paid by the state. Salaries are low compared to those of major state archival agencies. The Director receives a salary of $9,600; the County Archivist, $6,000; the Assistant Archivist, $6,000; another Assistant Archivist, $6,000. Salary increases are given, without reference to any system, when additional funds become available.

The operation is already of such size that organization into several offices has become necessary. They are: the Laminating Division, the Microfilm Division (not to be confused with the Microfilm Division of the Secretary of State), the County Archivist's Office and Processing Department, the Surveyor General Department, and the Official Register Office. Two archivists and research assistants are in charge of processing records. The Assistant Archivist assists and substitutes for the Director when the latter is absent. A librarian and research assistant is in charge

[51] General Appropriations Act. No. 167 (House Bill No. 48), sec. 39C.
[52] Department of Audits, *Report of Examination, Secretary of State, Year Ended June 30, 1962* (proc.), 24 p. Total expenses also included $815,551.02 for "Rents — State Office Building Authority."

of the research room, which, considering the number of visitors — more than seventy on a given day during the summer — is much too small and not adequately staffed.

The so-called Rhodes Memorial Building, a twenty-room mansion inspired by a medieval castle on the Rhine, which is occupied by the department, is inadequate in every respect. Now, however, funds for a fourteen-story archives building with approximately 90,000 square feet of storage space have been made available, and the plans developed for it seem very satisfactory. Once completed, the building — to cost $5,759,000 not including equipment — will be a fine example of modern archival architecture and will attract the attention of experts in this country as well as abroad. Ground for the building was broken in May, 1962.

Even in its old building the department has an abundance of technical equipment. This includes: ten Recordak microfilm readers, one Remington Rand reader for checking film, a flatbed camera, a 3-M microfilm printer, a Presto heat film splicer, a Polymicro developer unit, a Photostat Corporation Itek 18.24 Reader-Printer, RF Model #1176, and a Xerox 914 copier, rented for $95.00 a month. The Laminating Division, staffed with a Head Clerk, an assistant head clerk, a Head Laminating Technician, and a laminating technician, has laminated an average of 100,000 pages of book records and loose documents a year. Much of the microfilming and laminating is done in connection with the county records program.[53]

Present holdings of the department consist of archives transferred from state agencies, counties, and other officials in accordance with chapter 40-8, section 40-805 of the law establishing the department.

As there is no guide or over-all finding aid to the holdings of the department, it is not easy to describe them in general terms. Among the most important bodies of records are the following: transcripts from the British Public Record Office; papers of the Governors; journals of the constitutional conventions; legislative journals; and judicial records. Of special note are the records of the Office of the Surveyor General, which office was consolidated with that of the Secretary of State by acts of 1861 and 1866. The records, including grant and survey books and a precious collection of original district and county maps, are administered by a staff member with the title of Deputy Surveyor General, who appears in the Auditor's Report for 1960–61 under the title of Head Clerk, Assistant Researcher. She certifies facts from the records that are in the department, using forms presigned by the Secretary of State in his capacity of Surveyor General. This body of records is well under control. Eighty thousand files of the State Division of Confederate Pensions and Records, abolished January 1, 1961, that were previously arranged by date, are being rearranged by county and thereunder by year, in order to provide

[53] See below.

easy access to them. More complicated is the task of bringing under control a vast series of state records including papers of the Governors, the Executive Department, the Military Department, and various other provenances that were "methodized" by previous archivists and arranged by names, subjects, or county. So far records of the Surveyor General have been removed from the series and combined with the other records of his department.

Reference service in the department is extremely active. The overwhelming part of it goes to genealogists, who receive every courtesy and who, as members of patriotic societies, support the department and its work in many ways. In fact, the success of the department in obtaining funds for the new building stems largely from the grass-roots enthusiasm of patriotic societies and local attorneys, who receive unstinted service at the department. The number of visitors is extremely large, and frequently the microfilm readers on hand are not enough to accommodate them. Visits amounted to 4,770 in fiscal 1956–57 and jumped to 7,586 in 1962–63.

The department's successful county records microfilming program has added immensely to its popularity as well as to its holdings. The program in the 159 counties uses the services of employees of the Utah Genealogical Society, who do the actual microfilming under the able guidance of the department's County Archivist. The department checks the films and obtains a positive or a second negative. In the process, loose papers are frequently obtained for transfer to the department, and volumes in need of repair are laminated. While operating in a county, the County Archivist invites churches and other organizations to give their records, the so-called special collections, to the department. As of June 30, 1963, there were in the Microfilm Section 10,563 rolls of film, two-thirds of which stem from the activities of the Utah Genealogical Society.

There is every evidence of the excellent press and other public relations of the department. Speeches of the Director before groups and on television, an exhibit in the lobby, and courtesies extended to visitors and searchers have contributed to make the department known. Its popularity is based on archival service, not on historical activities, for the Georgia Historical Commission, also in the office of the Secretary of State, has been assigned the task of promoting and publicizing the historical resources of the state, including the maintenance of historic shrines and museums, a total of fifteen, and the putting up of historical markers. In line with its concentration on the archives function, the department has published little. For use in connection with research, genealogical and other, a number of processed circulars have been prepared, as for instance a helpful thirteen-page document entitled "Genealogical and Historical Research in Georgia." As one of its duties, the department publishes for the Secretary of State *Georgia's Official Register*. The 1959–60 edition is a volume of 1,091 pages; and its compilation, under the supervision of the Director, required the services of two of the department's employees.

RECORDS MANAGEMENT AND RECORDS DISPOSITION

Although the Governor's Commission on Economy and Reorganization submitted, in 1959, an excellent staff study on records management,[54] no such program now exists, nor is one likely to develop until the department can enter the picture, which in turn depends on its moving into the new archives building. There is, however, a State Records Center close to the Capitol area, housed in the same building with the Microfilm Division of the Secretary of State. With a staff of seven and some part-time help, this division produces microfilm copies of current records. No personnel are specifically assigned to the center, and its expenses come out of the budget of the Microfilm Division, though they do not appear in the Auditor's Report. Most of the records stored are those of the Secretary of State. In addition, the department has had to place some bulky accessions in the center. Neither the Archivist nor the head of the Microfilm Division can encourage government agencies to transfer records so long as only a small area has been equipped with shelving and so long as there are no personnel specifically assigned to servicing the records. At present the center is a storage facility without supporting funds and staff. A large number of the records in the building are under the jurisdiction of the department.

An act approved March 6, 1960 (General Acts and Resolutions, No. 596), regulates the procedure for the destruction of obsolete state records by repealing all acts that have authorized destruction of records of individual state agencies and making destruction subject to the approval of the Secretary of State and the Director of the department. The law seems to work satisfactorily. Records retention and disposal schedules have not been developed, nor can there be an active program to solicit accessions while the department is in its present quarters.

COMMENTS

1. The task of accessioning and bringing under control the considerable volume of records to be expected after the move into the new building will call for a sizable expansion of the department's staff.

2. Georgia needs a records management act or, even better, a modern archives and records management act and funds for administering a records management program.

[54] Appendix A to the commission's processed report (Aug 13, 1959), 24 p.

[88]

3. The present records center should be fully equipped and staffed for the housing and servicing of records to be kept for limited periods of time.

HAWAII

Ironically, the Territory of Hawaii, now the youngest state in the federal union, preceded most of the states in caring for its archives and all of them in providing a fireproof building for the records' protection. Its archival program may be said to have developed slowly but consistently over a period of sixty years.

BACKGROUNDS

The first action to preserve the archives of Hawaii was taken by the Privy Council of the Kingdom in 1847, when, at the suggestion of Robert Crichton Wyllie, Minister of Foreign Affairs, it requested all the Hawaiian chiefs to collect their papers and send them to the Council for examination.[55] In January, 1903, five years after the United States had annexed Hawaii, Worthington C. Ford, Chief of the Manuscripts Division of the Library of Congress, visited the islands, and while there he apparently gave the impression that the Library of Congress wanted to take over the archives of Hawaii. Under the pressure of public opinion, aroused by what was considered a threat to these archives, the territorial legislature appropriated $36,000 in 1903 for an archives building, and, on its completion in 1906, it became the first building in the present United States specifically constructed as an archives. The 1905 archives act established a three-member Board of Commissioners of Public Archives with the Secretary of the Territory acting as chairman and executive officer of the Archives and the two other members being appointed for indefinite terms by the Governor with the approval of the territorial Senate. The board was instructed to collect all public records, historical documents, and other valuable papers relating to Hawaii; to arrange,

[55] For the following, see Jason Horn, "The Archives of Hawaii," *American Archivist*, XVI (Apr., 1953), 105–14; and Elizabeth H. Wray, "The Archives of the State of Hawaii," *ibid.*, XXIII (July, 1960), 277–84. According to Horn, *op. cit.*, pp. 106 ff., the Chief of the Bureau of Rolls and Library of the Department of State was sent to Hawaii to examine the archives and to transfer them to Washington. Advised that the land records were indispensable to the conduct of business on the islands, the department agreed to leaving the archives in Honolulu if the territorial government provided a fireproof building in which to house them. The Reverend Chester R. Young, author of an M.A. thesis on "The Origin and Development of the Public Archives of Hawaii: A Study in Administrative History," University of Hawaii, 1964, has kindly informed the Director of this study that the story as told by Horn and by others before him is nothing but a myth, for neither the files of the Department of State nor those of the Library of Congress reveal any intention on the part of these agencies to acquire the Hawaii archives. It seems that Ford was erroneously considered an official of the Department of State and that whatever remarks he may have made in Hawaii were mistakenly interpreted as a design to deprive the islands of their archives.

classify, file, and preserve them; to furnish information regarding this material; and to make the archives available to the public. A regular appropriation provided for a librarian of the Archives and a staff. A 1915 act made the Archives the depository for all territorial government publications.

By 1928 the building was full and records were being stored in the basement of the Iolani Palace. In 1930 the vault of the Archives Building was enlarged, a basement was built under it, and a new research room and a filing room for bound volumes of newspapers were added.

In 1921 the Historical Commission of the Territory of Hawaii was created by the legislature to collect materials pertaining to Hawaii's role in the First World War and to publish a revised history of the territory. This commission was instructed to deposit its materials in the Archives on completion of its work, which is still in progress. A War Records Depository Committee was created in 1943, and its collections were to be turned over to the University of Hawaii, probably because by then the Archives was again filled to capacity, with records stacked in bundles on the floor of the vault, in the mezzanine, and on the basement stairway. The present Archives Building was constructed in 1953.

The government of Hawaii is highly centralized, for it embraces such typical county functions as health, education, libraries, welfare, sanitation, land conveyances, and taxation; and consequently its archives are very inclusive. Also, the number of departments had multiplied to 103 by the time of Hawaii's admission to statehood in 1959. The constitution and the Reorganization Act of 1959 cut the number of departments to twenty, in addition to the Governor's and the Lieutenant Governor's offices, and put the Archives under the jurisdiction of the Department of Accounting and General Services "to manage the preservation and disposal of all records of the state."

THE ARCHIVES DIVISION

The Archives Division is part of the Department of Accounting and General Services, which is headed by the State Comptroller. It is divided into a Records Service Branch directly under the State Archivist and a Records Management Branch administered by the Assistant State Archivist, who is also responsible for the division's microfilm program. The division also operates a library, which is the depository for state government publications, collects newspapers, and provides guide service for the Iolani Palace and the Royal Mausoleum.

The division's budget is broken down by program, and in fiscal 1964 it received $73,009 for records service and $41,986 for records management. General administrative expenses and all of the State Archivist's salary are included in the records service program. Budgets are approved annually, there being a regular and a budget session of the legislature. The State Archivist, together with the fiscal officer of the department, presents the budget request to the Comptroller. It goes to the budget examiner in the Department of Budget and Review, where short hearings are held; and, modified by that department's recommendations, it becomes part of the Governor's budget request. Hearings are held by the House Finance Committee and the Senate Ways and Means Committee, and in the past the State Archivist has testified before these committees. Legislative review is thorough and frequently calls for a reworking of the budget.

Hawaii has a merit system under which employees are well protected, even when their positions are abolished. The Department of Personnel Services administers a classification system that covers state and county jobs and provides thirty-one salary ranges and, within ranges, six ingrade steps and three longevity increases. Employees are granted twenty-one days of annual and twenty-one days of sick leave and may participate in the Hawaii Employees' Health Fund, to which the state contributes $3.00 per month for a single individual and $10.00 for a family. The retirement system, which also includes federal social security benefits and to which state and employee contribute equal amounts, provides after thirty years of service a pension amounting to half the salary of an employee.

Positions are filled by examination, and the agency must select one of the top five on the list of eligibles, provided that there is such a list. A three-year residence requirement applies unless qualified persons cannot be obtained locally.

The Archives Division has a staff of twenty, five of whom are professional, with the following salaries:

Archivist	$8,256–$10,536
Assistant Archivist	6,468– 8,256
Hawaiian Translator	6,156– 7,860
Librarian I	5,076– 6,468
Librarian Aid	4,392– 5,592

There are three archives clerks ($4,392–$5,592) and one clerk II and one clerk I in the Records Service Branch. Under the "Supervising Duplicating Machine Operator (Microfilm)" [56] ($4,608–$5,868), five persons serve in the microfilm program; and the Records Service Branch has a stenographer, a bookmender, and two guides.

The division occupies a new building, completed in 1953 at a cost of $265,000. The basement (48 × 72 feet) is used as a storage area. The first floor (63 × 111 feet) contains the offices and reading room; and the second floor, the only air-conditioned area, consists of the 75 × 123-foot ar-

[56] The Department of Personnel Services insists on classifying microfilm operators as duplicating machine operators.

chives vault. Until a records center becomes available, the basement must be used for storing records of limited retention value. It also houses records hastily evacuated from the old archives building but not yet evaluated and duplicate copies of government publications. There is a fumigating vault on the first floor. There are, however, no laminating facilities, so that repair work must be done under contract by commercial firms.

The Archives Division enjoys close working relationships with the Legislative Reference Bureau, with the University of Hawaii, and especially with the latter's history department. Also, the State Archivist serves as secretary of the Hawaiian Historical Society and as a member of the Historical Markers Advisory Committee. The Archivist helped in the compilation by the Hawaiiana Section, Hawaii Library Association, of *Official Publications of the Territory of Hawaii, 1900–1959,* published by the Archives Division in 1962. Together with the university, the Library of Hawaii, and the three outer islands libraries on Hawaii, Kauai, and Maui, the Archives Division is a depository for all official publications of the state. It also issues the slip laws and certified copies of laws.

THE RECORDS SERVICE BRANCH

The Records Service Branch, directly under the State Archivist, is in charge of the archival holdings of the division. These comprise over 4,400 cubic feet of non-current official records of the kingdom, the provisional government, the republic, the territory, and the state from 1790 to 1962. Included in the figure are 150 cubic feet of private papers. Most records are kept in legal-size file cabinets, all with individual locks. In addition, there is open shelving for bound records and newspapers. The storage capacity of the archives vault could be doubled by putting in a mezzanine floor for which, in planning the building, provision was made.

Except for the land records still in the Department of Land and Resources — and this is the only major gap in the holdings — most of the permanently valuable records of the state are in the custody of the Archives Division. Legislative records, for instance, go back to 1840, and it has become a tradition for the Governors to transfer their records to the Archives upon the expiration of their terms of office. As the records management program of the division develops, more and more accessions will reach it through schedule and not as a result of sudden agency transfers. No accession book or register is kept in addition to correspondence with the individual agencies.

The finding aids developed are specified in the typed Departmental Manual. They include an elaborate, though not entirely complete, subject and name index to the Foreign Office and executive records, the Privy Council minutes, and certain other bodies of material; and name indexes to the naturalization and immigration records. Records of most agencies, boards, and commissions are listed with inclusive dates and brief explanatory remarks. For those of the Governors (1900–1960) a complete break-down of the filing pattern is given. It should not be too time-consuming to prepare a short guide to the holdings of the division. Unfortunately, the Archivist has no professional staff qualified for arrangement and description work, and this is perhaps the greatest shortcoming in an otherwise satisfactory setup.

Reference service statistics are well kept. In fiscal 1962–63 there were 2,798 visits from 570 government officials and 2,228 private persons, 920 telephone inquiries, and 124 inquiries by mail. Items used amounted to 2,033 documents, 3,124 newspapers, and 5,478 pieces of other types of material, including books. Sources most frequently used were legislative records, passenger lists, naturalization records, and a name index of births, deaths, and marriages reported in the newspapers. To facilitate the use of documents in Hawaiian, a translation program has been and is in progress.

No decision has been made about the preservation of local records except for certain tax records and Circuit Court case files that represent state functions and therefore are state records transferred to the Archives. A system of repositories on the main islands seems to be the most likely solution of the local archives problem.

RECORDS MANAGEMENT AND RECORDS DISPOSITION

A limited program of records management was initiated by the Archives Division in 1958 with the assistance of a staff member of the San Francisco Federal Records Center. Under the Reorganization Act, the Comptroller is authorized "to manage the preservation and disposal of all records of the State." Records officers have been appointed in all departments, and the process of inventorying and scheduling their records is under way. A great number of inventories have been prepared, and schedules for six departments with considerable accumulations of records have been completed and approved, in addition to a general schedule for fiscal and administrative forms. A general schedule for records common to all departments has been completed and distributed to the departments. Inventorying is done by the departments with help from the Assistant State Archivist.

For the time being, part of the Archives' basement is used as a records center, and 1,650 cubic feet of records have been moved in. In 1962 the sum of $8,000 was appropriated for planning a records center, and the final project is to be presented to the legislature in 1964.

Though some assistance is given to the departments, the Archives Division is not equipped to administer a broad records management program including controlled creation of records. Such a program is being considered by the Department of Budget and Finance in connection with its review of operations and methods of the departments.

Lists of records essential to the continuity of government have been

[93]

prepared by the Archives Division and presented to the departments. Nothing has been done, however, since a bill drafted by the civil defense authorities was introduced during both the 1962 and 1963 sessions of the legislature but failed to pass.

The 1959 Reorganization Act has given the final authority over records disposition to the Comptroller (Rev. Laws, 1955, as amended, 1959, secs. 7-5–7-10). Agency heads request the approval of disposal lists or schedules, the State Archivist reviews the requests, and the Comptroller then approves them. While the State Archivist consults informally with the Attorney General, both the Attorney General and the Legislative Auditor might well share the responsibility for records disposal.

The Assistant State Archivist in charge of records management also supervises the Ceneral Microfilm Unit for state agencies that was started in 1959. Work is done by two operators who use two rotary cameras and one planetary camera and are assisted by four preparation clerks. During the 1963 fiscal year, 628 reels of 16-mm. film were produced in duplicate, one copy going to the appropriate department and one being retained by the Archives. Microfilming is being used primarily for permanently valuable records that create space problems in the department. Records filmed include court records, National Guard records, and basic personnel records.

COMMENTS

1. The State Archivist needs additional professional help to pursue an active program of records arrangement and description.

2. The records center, now in the planning stage, should be constructed as soon as possible.

3. A records management program to assist agencies in matters of records creation and maintenance should be provided. If the Archives Division is to administer such a program, it needs additional trained personnel.

IDAHO

The Idaho State Historical Society at Boise is the legal depository for the state's archives. Archival funds have never been appropriated, however, and because of an acute shortage of storage space and personnel the society is not now in a position to do justice to its mission.

BACKGROUNDS

The Historical Society of Idaho Pioneers, organized in 1881 and originally restricting its membership to persons who had settled in Idaho before 1864, became an agency of the state in 1907 (Acts, p. 265), under the name of the Idaho State Historical Society. Chapter 161 of the 1947 acts assigned it "state archival authority," empowered all public officers to deliver to the society records and documents "not in current use," and authorized the society's Board of Trustees to require the deposit, by all public officials, of "official books, records, documents, or original papers not in current use, which are of definite historical importance, in the Idaho State Historical Society for preservation." The relatively strong act was drafted by a scholar not on the staff of the State Historical Society.

THE STATE HISTORICAL SOCIETY

The Idaho State Historical Society is governed by a board of three trustees appointed by the Governor. The board appoints the Director, who, in turn, appoints all other personnel. There is no civil service system for the State Historical Society staff, and it was not until 1956 that the Governor removed their positions from the political appointment category. This measure has ushered in a period of progress and modernization.[57] There being no law on the subject, a new administration could appoint a new board that, in turn, could dismiss the present staff and replace it with political appointees. Because of its now widely recognized services, however, the society's personnel seems reasonably well protected, except from some political upheaval.

The society has a staff of ten persons; but only one, the Historian and Archivist ($8,500), gives part of his time to work with the archives, reporting to the society's Director ($10,800). Since February, 1963, the Historian and Archivist has been assisted by a second person with good training in history and some experience in archival work. Staff members participate in the social security system, and a state retirement system was adopted in 1963 to become effective in 1965. The state pays for the staff members' Blue Cross hospitalization insurance and for their life insurance in the amount of the annual salary. Annual and sick leave arrangements are the same as for other state personnel.

The society operates on an appropriation of $153,500 for the biennium beginning July 1, 1963, and ending June 30, 1965. This represents a considerable increase over earlier appropriations of $56,695 for 1957–59, $96,425 for 1959–61, and $126,525 for 1961–63. Income from memberships and other sources is not worked into the budget, although it is audited by the State Auditor; it is always modest.

The budget, broken down into salaries, capital expenses, travel, and current expenditures, is prepared by the Director, approved by the Board of Trustees, and examined by a prelegislative budget committee of the outgoing legislature. Adding his own to the committee's recommendations, the Governor submits the "budget book" to the joint Senate-House Fi-

[57] H. J. Swinney, "The 26th Biennial Report of the Idaho Historical Society, 1957–58," *Idaho Yesterdays*, II (Winter, 1958–59), 11–15, 24–32; and Director, Idaho Historical Society, *Twenty-seventh Biennial Report* (Boise, 1960), 19 p.

nance and Appropriations Committee of the incoming legislature. It is customary for the Director to defend his budget request at the various hearings. In 1963 the joint committee cut the society's budget from $175,000 recommended by the Governor to $153,500, and this amount was appropriated by the legislature.

The society comprises a Museum; the State Archives; the Division of Manuscripts, which with its more than ninety collections is separate from the Archives; the Division of Newspapers; and Historical and Genealogical Libraries. Originally housed in the State Capitol, the society received an appropriation for a new building in 1939. This $100,000 building, a two-story reinforced concrete structure 176 by 56 feet, was started in 1942; but because of wartime restrictions it was not completed until 1950. By far the better part of the practically fireproof building serves the society's museum function. The lower level of one end is used by the State Library. A new building for the society is included in the state permanent building fund appropriation for 1963–65. Architectural plans for the building had not been made by July 1, 1963, nor was financing entirely available.

A microfilm program was started by the society with the publication on 16-mm. microfilm of a 30,000-entry index of territorial newspapers. Microfilming is done with a flatbed camera. There are four microfilm readers, three of which are in the Genealogical Library.

The society publishes a quarterly entitled *Idaho Yesterdays*, a monthly newsletter, and a biennial report, now of high quality.

THE STATE ARCHIVES

The State Archives has no separate appropriation, nor could one be provided in the budget; obviously, the State Historian and Archivist has non-archival functions. The Archives has 1,400 cubic feet of available storage space, partly in the library stacks adjacent to the offices and partly in a first-floor vault. Most of this space is now taken up. The space situation, fast becoming desperate, makes it impossible to accession systematically the permanently valuable records of the state. Construction of a new building should somewhat alleviate the demand for archival space.

In spite of existing limitations, the following important bodies of records have been brought in: nearly all existing territorial records, except the original territorial legislative journals and sessions laws still in the office of the Secretary of State; all the correspondence of the Governor's office to 1950; records of the State Treasurer and State Auditor for approximately the same period; and papers relating to some Carey Act irrigation projects. There are also the non-current records of the society, small groups of records from several other state offices, records of Alturas County, and some material from other counties and from mining districts.[58]

[58] For a listing of the early record holdings of the state see Thomas M. Marshall, "Re-

The process of bringing this material under control has started. A first list of "Idaho State Archives" was published in the *Twenty-fourth Biennial Report of the Idaho State Historical Department [sic], 1953–1954*.[59] It is now being superseded by an over-all arrangement that will provide a system of record groups for territorial and state records, county records, city and village records, and mining district records. Once the State Archives has facilities to accept regular accessions, these can be fitted in easily. Inventorying will have to be done in the future, but catalog cards for archival *fonds* have been prepared for the National Union Catalog of Manuscript Collections.

Inasmuch as the service on archives is not clearly separated from that on other record material of the society, figures regarding the use of archival material are not available.

RECORDS MANAGEMENT AND DISPOSITION

Chapter 127, Acts of 1941 (Code 67-2026–67-2031), empowers the State Board of Examiners — consisting of the Governor, the Secretary of State, and the Attorney General, with the State Auditor serving as secretary — to determine what state records are of current official value, what records are of official value but are used infrequently, what records have historical but not official value, and what records have neither official nor historical value. The last are to be destroyed five years after the time of their original filing. Records infrequently used may be removed by the board to "any suitable place of storage," while records of historical value will be transferred to the State Historical Society. The Board of Examiners exercises its functions without the State Historical Society's entering into the process; nevertheless, little of value seems to be destroyed.

An act of 1957 (Code 9-331–9-334) authorizes the duplication of county records not less then ten years old by microfilm, photographic, and similar processes in accordance with standards not below those approved by the National Bureau of Standards and permits the subsequent destruction of the originals by order of the competent district or probate court. Sixty days prior to such destruction, however, the Idaho State Historical Society is to be given written notice.

Idaho has no records management program. Recommendations for such a program were made by an official of the National Archives and Records Service in 1958. The political climate changed with the 1958 elections, however, and at present there is little or no prospect of getting a program set up. The Director of the society has hopes that "Eventually . . . a coordinated program of records management should be developed within the state, which will in its turn lead to an archival program on an ade-

port on the Public Archives of Idaho," *Annual Report of the American Historical Association for the Year 1917* (Washington, 1920), pp. 137–72.

[59] It is found on pp. 31–35 of the *Report.*

quate scale." In the meantime he warns against "indiscriminate filming of all kinds of records." [60]

COMMENTS

1. Idaho Code 67-4106 should be amended to provide for the appointment of the society's trustees for overlapping terms so as to eliminate the present danger of a complete renewal of the board at the pleasure of a new administration.

2. Though a good start has been made, the Historical Society needs additional space and personnel to carry out its mandate as the State Archives of Idaho.

3. Plans for the installation of a records management program including provision for a records center should be resumed.

4. It would be desirable for the State Board of Examiners to consult the society when questions of records destruction come before it.

ILLINOIS

The archives and records management program of the state of Illinois is known as one of the outstanding programs in the United States. It is under the jurisdiction of the Archives–Records Management Division of the Secretary of State's office at Springfield.

BACKGROUNDS

Based on provisions in the Illinois constitutions of 1818, 1848, and 1870, a Division of Archives and Index was established as early as 1873 in the office of the Secretary of State, the legal custodian of the state's records. The division soon concerned itself exclusively with the current records of the office and did not develop along archival lines. In 1912 Waldo Gifford Leland prepared his epochal "Report on the Public Archives and Historical Interests of the State of Illinois, with Especial Reference to the Proposed Education Building." [61] Here, for the first time in the United States, were outlined clearly the functions, needs, and most desirable status of a state archival agency. Leland's recommendation to create a Department of Archives under a board of seven trustees that was to have the counsel of an advisory commission on public archives was, however, not accepted. An act of the legislature of 1921 established the Archives Division in the State Library and did not change the division's close affiliation with the Secretary of State, inasmuch as he was, and still is, the State Librarian.

Although under this act the division was responsible solely for records of the Secretary of State, an act of 1925 broadened its responsibilities by providing that any agency of the state might turn over to the Archives

---

[60] *Twenty-seventh Biennial Report*, p. 13.

[61] Printed on pp. 11–53 of the *Report of the State Education Building Commission to the Forty-eighth General Assembly* (1913).

[98]

Division records of permanent value. A later act, of 1939, authorized ac-ceptance by the Archives Division of county, city, town, or village records.

The creation, in 1943, of a State Records Commission to concern itself with the disposal of useless records was a first step toward dealing with this important aspect of archival administration. After acting at first in an advisory capacity only, the commission in 1951 received exclusive juris-diction over the destruction of state records. A records management and paperwork survey conducted by the National Records Management Coun-cil set the stage for the State Records Act of 1957, which strengthened, redefined, and refined existing legislation. The act also designated the Secretary of State and State Librarian as State Archivist and Records Administrator.

To help administer the act, a records management unit was created in 1957 and was raised to division status in 1958. A recent reorganization (1962) has combined the Records Management and Archives Divisions of the State Library into the Archives–Records Management Division of the office of the Secretary of State. As for the records of local units, matters relating to their destruction and preservation have been regulated by the Local Records Act, approved August 16, 1961.

House Bill 1382, adding sections 13a and 15b to the State Records Act and approved on August 8, 1961, charged the Secretary of State and State Archivist with establishing a system for the preservation of records essen-tial for the continuity and re-establishment of state government in times of disaster. A statewide inventory of such records is now being taken.

THE ARCHIVES–RECORDS MANAGEMENT DIVISION

Responsible to the Secretary of State — who is State Librarian, State Archivist, State Records Administrator, and Local Records Advisor — the "Chief Clerk and Assistant State Archivist" supervises four sections of the division, which are in charge, respectively, of state archives, records man-agement, local archives, and management analysis. According to the most recent organization chart, the Assistant State Librarian no longer consti-tutes an intermediate authority between the Assistant State Archivist and the Secretary of State, though he still exercises general supervision over the archives–records management program and retains his role as a budget supervisor.[62] There is no reference to the State Library in the State Rec-ords Act of 1957.

In the current fiscal biennium, the division's budget cannot be separated from that of the State Library. The following are clearly expenses of the archives–records management function: $141,200 for the archives, $65,500 for records management including the records center, and $32,579 for the

[62] An organization chart in *Illinois Libraries*, XLI (Apr., 1959), 240, still placed the "Library Supervisor" between the Secretary of State and the then existing separate Archives and Records Management Divisions.

state microfilm program, plus a special appropriation of $30,000 for the local archives program (which in the future will be incorporated in the general budget). The state is adopting a system of functional budgeting, and this will make it possible to identify precisely the cost of the archives–records management operation.

Except for an Archival Assistant III and the administrative secretary, none of the members of the staff is under civil service, nor do they have letters of appointment that afford them a minimum of job security. Salaries of the professional personnel are as follows:

Assistant State Archivist	$7,980–$10,440
Archival Assistant V and Methods and Procedures Advisor (MPA) III	6,780– 8,760
Archival Assistant IV and MPA II	5,940– 7,800
Archival Assistant III	5,760– 7,080
Archival Assistant II and MPA I	4,920– 6,480
Archival Assistant I	4,140– 5,640

A system of five steps provides for increases on a merit basis.

Applicants for professional positions must meet requirements of education and experience determined by the State Department of Personnel and do not need political sponsorship for appointment.

The entire Archives–Records Management Division, with the exception of the records center and its staff, is housed in the State Archives Building,[63] the third building in the United States planned and constructed (1936–38) for the sole purpose of storing and servicing archival material and provided with modern fire-prevention and fire-fighting equipment and with ducts for the future installation of air-conditioning. It has a fumigating vault, photographic and restoration laboratories, workrooms, and office space. During the past twenty years, much office space has had to be turned over to other agencies. It is hoped that before long the last of these tenants — the Bureau of Vital Statistics — can be moved out. In the building but not controlled by the division are the so-called departmental vaults. They are at the disposal of departments that wish to store records of long-term value, the legal custody of which they want to retain. The building has a capacity of 140,000 cubic feet of records, 80,000 feet of which are now stored. Most of the archival stack space is equipped with legal- and correspondence-size file cabinets, consisting of six drawers each that necessitate the use of stepladders by those examining papers in the upper drawers. Since most of this equipment is legal size and most of the records are letter size, a good deal of storage space is lost. Departmental vaults and the special vaults for particularly valuable records use book-stack construction adapted to the needs of records storage.

The restoration and repair unit, administratively under the Records

[63] Margaret C. Norton, "The Illinois State Archives Building," *American Archivist*, I (Apr., 1938), 78–90.

Management Section as is the central microfilm unit, is staffed with an Archival Assistant II and equipped with a Barrow laminator. During the 1960–62 biennium it deacidified 38,353 and laminated 39,739 documents. Production continues on approximately the same level.

The archives program of Illinois owes some of its characteristics and much of its national and international reputation to the leadership of Margaret C. Norton, who developed it to a high level of perfection.

Limited entirely to the preservation of the official records of the state and thus relieved of all non-archival functions, the Illinois Archives has assembled practically all the permanently valuable records of the state.[64] Prominent among them are those of the Secretary of State and the various divisions of his office, the General Assembly, the Governor and the so-called code departments, the State Treasurer, and the Auditor of Public Accounts, whose records include the important land records. There are also county land records, most of them collected by the Illinois State Historical Society before the creation of the Archives Division, and security microfilm copies of important county records that have been deposited with the Archives.

Accession records consist of letters of transmittal from the agencies transferring records, receipts, and the accession documents proper, which are kept in loose-leaf binders. Such documents from now on will be bound. Accessions have been numbered consecutively from the time the Archives Division was activated.

For control and description a variety of media are used. Of basic importance is Miss Norton's "Legal and Administrative History of Illinois State Agencies" (typed). Holdings are described in "shelflist inventories" that enumerate the components of the various groups (series) and indicate their location. In addition, an elaborate card catalog "intended to be a guide to the subject and classification approaches to the series" with "a large number of secondary cards and cross references" [65] has long been in progress. New entries for the catalog are mostly based on the letters of transmittal referred to above. Preparation of cards, including subject cards, function-subject cards, analytics, and cross-references, consumes most of the time of an experienced cataloger and cannot keep pace with the influx of accessions. It is suggested that the technique now being used is too elaborate, that it follows library cataloging procedure too closely,

[64] See Theodore J. Cassady, "Records Holdings of Illinois State Archives," *Illinois Libraries*, XL (Apr., 1958), 295–303.

[65] Emma M. Scheffler, "The Card Catalog: A Useful Tool for State Archives," *Illinois Libraries*, XLI (Apr., 1959), 288–98. See also Illinois State Library, *Catalog Rules: Series for Archives Material* (Springfield, 1938), 51 p., proc., and its Revision No. 1 (Springfield, 1939), proc.

and that the size of the cards prohibits adequate description of the series cataloged. Because the card catalog is not up to date and the shelflist inventories give a description by location, indexes based on series entries as well as subjects are now being prepared. The entire system of control and description of records, as it now stands, might well be reappraised.

Name indexes to the 1850 federal census and to Civil War records are being compiled.

In regard to reference services rendered, the following figures are given for the last biennial period (Oct. 1, 1960–Sept. 30, 1962):

Secretary of State	11,882	
Other state agencies	1,995	
		13,877
Departmental vault entries		4,992
General public		
In person	5,857	
By mail	6,569	12,426
		31,295

In the past, biennial reports of the State Archives were included in those of the State Library, which in turn were part of the reports of the Secretary of State.[66]

A museum room in the State Archives Building displays material of historic interest to its many visitors.

STATE RECORDS MANAGEMENT AND RECORDS DISPOSITION

The former Records Management Division has been broken up into the Records Management and Management Analysis sections of the present Archives–Records Management Division of the office of the Secretary of State.

The Records Management Section, headed by a Methods and Procedures Advisor II, gives advice and assistance to agencies in the identification, inventorying, storage, microfilming, and legal disposition of records. Operating only on request, it is chiefly concerned with helping agencies to revise their retention and disposal schedules, many of which seem to have become obsolete, and to bring under schedule control the agencies whose records have not been scheduled. Agency heads are required by the State Records Act to maintain an active and continuing program for the economical and efficient management of their records and to submit to the State Records Commission lists and schedules of records no longer needed in the transaction of current business and not having sufficient value to merit further preservation. The agencies may use the records center for the storage and servicing of records.

[66] "The Biennial Report of Illinois State Archives and Records Management, October 1, 1958–September 30, 1960" was published in the January, 1961, issue of *Illinois Libraries* and also as a reprint.

Only records covered by disposal schedules may be transferred to the records center, which is conveniently located on two floors of the former power plant close to the State Capitol. Records are stored 14 boxes high on steel shelving. During the 1960–62 biennium the center received 17,309 cubic feet of records, removed and destroyed 18,094 cubic feet, and rendered an average of 4,187 reference services per month. The storage space — 29,000 cubic feet — is almost completely filled. It could be expanded if the License Plate Division, now occupying part of the first floor, were moved to some other location. There is great need for a records center in Chicago for state agencies in Cook County, but no suitable accommodations have yet been found for it.

The central microfilm unit works for agencies without charge, provided that they prepare their records for microfilming. It uses three flatbed and three rotary cameras and a reader-printer. Processing is done commercially. During the 1960–62 biennium, 1,799,969 frames were exposed.

The present Management Analysis Section was formerly part of the Records Management Division. Now directly under the Assistant State Archivist, it is staffed with three Methods and Procedures Advisors graded III, II, and I. In actual practice the systems arm of the Secretary of State, it works in the fields of systems analysis, space utilization in state-owned buildings that by statute is assigned to the Secretary of State, and forms control. The section is also writing a manual on operations for the office of the Secretary of State.

As the Archives–Records Management Division is now organized, its records management activities do not seem to live up to the intent of the State Records Act. With responsibility divided between the Records Management Section, which emphasizes the scheduling of records, and the Management Analysis Section, which limits its services to the office of the Secretary of State, little seems to be done "for the economical and efficient management of records of state agencies by analyzing, developing, promoting, coordinating, and promulgating standards, procedures, and techniques designed to improve the management of records," which, according to section 13 of the act, is one of the duties of the Secretary of State. With its present staff, the Archives–Records Management Division is not equipped to shoulder this responsibility; therefore a statewide system of "integrated paperwork controls" has not been established.[67]

The disposal of state records is governed by the State Records Act of 1957. It vests disposal authority in the State Records Commission, consisting of the Secretary of State as chairman, the State Treasurer, the Director of Finance, the Attorney General, and the Auditor of Public Accounts, or their authorized representatives. The State Historian serves

[67] Illinois, Secretary of State, *Illinois Moves Forward: A Summary Report of Installation of Integrated Paperwork Controls of Illinois* (1957), which is the report of the National Records Management Council's project staff headed by Thornton W. Mitchell.

as secretary of the commission, and the Assistant State Archivist has been designated by the Secretary of State to act as its chairman. In accordance with section 17 of the act, the commission has issued *Regulations* (second revision July 12, 1961, 26 p.) concerning procedures for compiling and submitting disposal lists and schedules and standards for microfilm reproduction of records to be destroyed.[68] Archival interests are well protected by section 19 of the act, which specifies that lists and schedules must first be referred to the Archivist (in practice the Assistant State Archivist), who "shall ascertain whether the records proposed for disposal have value to other agencies of the state or whether such records have research or historical value" that qualifies them for permanent preservation in the State Archives.

During the last biennium reported on (Oct. 1, 1960–Sept. 30, 1962) the State Records Commission, in fifteen meetings held, considered 134 applications covering 945 series of records. Of these, 30 series (214 cubic feet) were authorized for destruction on the basis of disposal lists, while 890 series (*ca.* 9,000 cubic feet) were approved for destruction in accordance with retention and disposal schedules. Over 400 cubic feet of nine series were to be destroyed in accordance with retention schedules after microfilming.

LOCAL RECORDS MANAGEMENT AND RECORDS DISPOSITION

The Local Records Act, approved August 18, 1961, expands the state's program of efficient and economical records management to "any court, and all parts, boards, departments, bureaus and commissions of any county, municipal corporation or political subdivision of the state." Under the act the Archivist — that is, the Secretary of State — serves as "local records advisor" and may appoint the assistants needed to carry out the intent of the law.

The act is to be administered by two Local Records Commissions, an "upstate" commission for Cook County — this is a separate local records commission provided by section 6 of the act for "those agencies comprising counties of 3,000,000 or more inhabitants or located in or coterminous with any such county or a majority of whose inhabitants reside in any such county" (not yet activated) — and one for "downstate," already appointed "by the Governor, the State Archivist, and the State Historian." It consists of a chairman of a county board; a mayor or president of a city, village, or incorporated town; a county auditor; and a state's attorney. The head of the Local Archives Section of the Archives–Records Management Division serves as the commission's secretary.

The Local Records Commission has prepared a set of *Regulations* (1962)

[68] Appendix A specifies minimum requirements for permanent record microcopying film based on the standards of the American Standards Association, Inc.

dealing with general rules, definitions, records disposal applications, destruction of records, and standards for microfilming. Its *Suggested Guide* (April, 1962) gives practical advice to local officials on how to fill out the "Inventory Work Sheet" as a basis for disposal applications, control cards, and finding aids. The commission is to pass on all applications for authority to dispose of local records — lists as well as schedules — and has started doing so.

Local records of permanent value may be deposited in the State Archives or in a regional depository. Southern Illinois University has informally agreed to serve as a depository for thirty-three of the southern counties of Illinois. Two more depositories — one at the University of Illinois, the other at Western Illinois University — are planned. There are advantages in restricting the number of regional depositories instead of operating with a considerable network of co-operating institutions, as is the case in Wisconsin and in Ohio.

COMMENTS

1. The records description techniques and procedures of the State Archives may well be in need of reappraisal.

2. Inasmuch as the Archives–Records Management Division is under an elected official, much can be said for placing the staff under the state's civil service system.

3. Records management responsibilities are divided between the Records Management and the Management Analysis sections of the division. It might be questioned whether in its present form the program carries out the intent of the State Records Act of 1957.

INDIANA

In Indiana the Archives Division is part of the State Library in Indianapolis.

BACKGROUNDS

Through much of Indiana's history the State Library had been taking over records,[69] until in 1903 the Board of Education, designated for library purposes as the State Library Board, established in the State Library a Department of Indiana Archives. It received legal recognition as the Department of Indiana History and Archives through an act of 1913 (ch. 116). The department was to assume the custody and care of official records, collect material bearing on the history of the state, and contribute to historical research and to making the history of Indiana better known. State,

[69] The following résumé is based on Christopher B. Coleman, "Indiana Archives," *American Archivist*, I (Oct., 1938), 201–14; the same author's "Some Problems of State Archival Administration," *ibid.*, IV (July, 1941), 149–58; and Margaret Pierson, "Indiana's State Archives," *Library Occurrent*, XVI (June, 1950), 313–16.

county, and other officials were authorized to transfer to the State Library for preservation by the department books, records, and newspapers not in current use. A 1925 act (ch. 58), which established the Library and Historical Board of five members appointed by the Governor — four of them on recommendation of professional and educational bodies — did not affect the activities of the department. Under the inspired guidance of Esther U. McNitt, its holdings grew so large that it had to be divided into the Archives Division and the Indiana Division, in charge, respectively, of official records and private papers.[70]

After the State Library had moved into its new building in 1933, the authority of the State Library as the archival agency of the state was firmly established by chapter 219 of the acts of 1935. This act created a State Commission on Public Records, composed of the Governor, the Secretary of State, the State Examiner of the State Board of Accounts, the Director of the State Library (who also serves as the commission's secretary), and the Director of the Historical Bureau (charged with publishing material on Indiana history). Besides giving the commission power to decide on the disposition of public records, the act made the State Library the repository for all records that, because of their official or historical value, were deemed worthy of preservation. A later act, of 1939 (ch. 91), created in each county a commission on public records and gave it authority to destroy records of the county and its subdivisions lacking official or historical value. Public records having such values were, on order of the appropriate commission, to be "removed" to the State Library. By an act of 1955 (ch. 319) amending that of 1939, the membership of the county records commissions was increased from four to six members.

THE ARCHIVES DIVISION

The Archives Division operates as a distinct unit of the State Library, though its budget is part of the library budget. In fiscal 1962 the division received $32,000 for its archival activity, $5,000 for "records management,"[71] $10,000 for its microfilm program, and $5,000 for its newspaper program. The Indiana Division is not included in these figures. Regarding preparation of the budget, the State Archivist submits all recommendations to the Director of the State Library, as do other division heads, and the Director presents them first to the Library and Historical Board to obtain its support and subsequently to the Budget Director of the state and the Budget Committee, composed of four members of the general assembly.

The Archives Division has its separate staff, consisting of the following

[70] "The Legacy of Esther U. McNitt," *American Archivist*, VI (Jan., 1943), 67–68, reprinted from *Library Occurrent* (Sept., 1942).

[71] By this is meant the servicing of records of limited retention value in the Archives Division's basement and warehouse space.

full-time employees: the State Archivist, two Assistant State Archivists, two clerk typists, a clerk, a photographic laboratory supervisor, a duplicating machine operator, an apprentice machine operator, and two student assistants. Salaries of the professional staff, though low, are above those in many other departments of the state. The State Archivist receives $6,900–$8,640; the Senior Assistant, $5,280–$6,600; and the Junior Assistant, $4,320–$5,520. Increases within a minimum-maximum range are granted each year, as funds permit. An act of 1907 (ch. 98) provides penalties for soliciting or receiving political contributions or for paying assessment to any person, organization, or political party. The act of 1925, referred to above, imposes these prohibitions on all personnel appointed by the Library and Historical Board. Professional employees are certified under the 1941 Library Certification Act, while the clerical staff is under the 1941 State Personnel (civil service) Act. The rules governing the two groups are, however, identical. The State Archivist, besides having a good knowledge of history and government and several years of practical experience, must be a library school graduate. The position is classified as Librarian IV, that of Assistant Archivist as Librarian II. The custodial staff is subject to political appointment and is not a part of the archives or library staff.

In addition to two stack levels (4,800 square feet) and the archives vault (925 square feet), the basement in the Library Building (6,700 square feet) and additional space in a warehouse (10,000 square feet) are used for storing records in transfer boxes and miscellaneous types of equipment.[72] As soon as the change can be effected, records will be transferred to boxes and put on shelves. The stack space occupied by the division in the Library Building meets requirements of safety. It is crowded, however, and the basement area should be equipped with shelving and be better ventilated if it is to be used as regular archives space.

The Archives Division has had considerable success in acquiring the major portion of the state's permanently valuable records, including the enrolled acts and related papers formerly in the custody of the Secretary of State (Acts, 1957, ch. 5). Records of the general assembly (original bills and registers of bills) are transferred from the Legislative Bureau to the State Library and placed in the Archives (Acts, 1945, ch. 88). Holdings also include the official correspondence of the Governors and of heads of executive offices, records of military service, land records,[73] and many valuable documents of other types. The division has successfully built up its holdings, now estimated at 15,000 bound volumes and 3,000 file drawers and storage boxes of records, which cover the period from 1790 to 1959. Con-

[72] Newspaper holdings require 6,000 square feet in the stacks and 1,100 square feet in the basement.

[73] Formerly deposited with the Auditor, these have been transferred except for records pertaining to land the state still owns.

siderable quantities of these records, such as World Wars I and II bonus records and state inheritance tax records, are quite active and should be held and serviced in a regular records center instead of being a burden on the Archives Division. In fact, such semi-active records with limited retention value are being transferred from the basement of the library to a records center; the space thus vacated will give the Archives Division an opportunity for the physical rearrangement and better organization of its holdings. Also, scheduling for all the state's records is in progress in order to make the Archives Division the repository of permanently valuable records only.

Arrangement of records follows accepted archival practice. Record groups have been brought into a system by assigning them numbers, and regular inventories are being prepared. Detailed shelf-lists are available for records of the Governor, Auditor, and Attorney General. A dictionary-type catalog, once attempted, has been abandoned, as has been calendaring except for the Governor's and Adjutant General's Civil War records.

In fiscal 1963 the Archives Division rendered service to 1,800 personal visitors using records or microfilms, prepared 1,100 letters in response to requests for information, and answered 1,700 telephone calls. It also issued 2,500 certified statements and furnished 1,200 photocopies to users outside the State Library.

The Archives Division administers a photographic laboratory set up by an act of 1949 (ch. 172) and equipped with one planetary and two rotary microfilm cameras, a microfilm enlarger, and transfer process equipment. In the last fiscal year, the laboratory produced 900,000 film images and 1,200 paper prints. About 90 per cent of the records microfilmed are records that can be destroyed. An act of 1947 (ch. 195) gives full legal recognition to microfilm copies.

The division's activities are solely in the fields of archives administration and records management, except that it houses and cares for the Indiana newspapers. Collection, processing, and servicing of private papers are handled by the library's Indiana (local history) Division, and the publication of historical materials is the duty of the Indiana Historical Bureau, "a separate but co-ordinate agency with the State Library under the same board and housed in the same building."[74]

RECORDS MANAGEMENT AND RECORDS DISPOSITION

Most recently the role of the Commission on Public Records has been affected by the creation of a State Department of Administration (Acts, 1961, ch. 269), which is responsible for records management in the state. Its General Services Division, in addition to other duties, is to conduct

[74] From the State Library's *Organization Chart*. On the genesis and early history of the Historical Bureau, see Indiana Historical Bureau, *Annual Report, 1944–1945*, submitted by Howard H. Peckham (Indianapolis, 1945), 24 p.

the statewide records management program and operate the state records center, establish a central microfilm service, assist agencies in forms control, and provide "other central office services to bring about efficiency and economy in state operations." [75]

The act of 1961, which was unexpectedly passed by the legislature, is based on a bill drafted at the behest of the Governor-elect by the University of Indiana — a bill that paid no attention to the respective roles of the Commission on Public Records and the Archives Division of the State Library. The fact that a manual of the new Department entitled *Functions and Organization* makes no reference to the authority of the commission in records disposal has prompted the Director of the State Library to obtain an opinion from the Attorney General with regard to the respective powers and duties of the commission, the State Library, and the Department of Administration under the new act. The opinion,[76] ill phrased in various respects, rules that the Commission on Public Records continues in existence though its powers are "reduced to reviewing all public records to prevent the inadvertent destruction of documents of less official use or historical worth" and that similarly the duties of the State Library have been limited to:

a. The management of State Archives devoted to historical documents, and
b. The examination and classification of the documents and records of the various departments which are no longer of immediate use, for the inclusion in the historical files of the state.

The Attorney General finally opines that the provisions of earlier acts that do not conflict with the 1961 act "should be worked into a harmonious system of standards and procedures which give full force and effect to the intent of the General Assembly."

To achieve that end the Department of Administration and the Commission on Public Records have now met. Also, in a conference with the State Librarian, the State Archivist, and the Study Director, the Commissioner of Administration agreed to examine the Michigan state records management program and, as a first step, to establish an organized records center, which is badly needed. There appears to be no intention on his part to eliminate or reduce the role of the Commission on Public Records in the disposal process.

Disposal of useless records is governed by the act of 1935. According to this act, "public records having an official value but which are used infrequently . . . shall, on order of the commission [on public records], be removed to the state library and added to its archives," while "records having no apparent official value but having a historical value shall be

---

[75] From a processed document, entitled "Department of Administration, Functional Organization," April 1, 1962, issued by the department for internal use.
[76] *Official Opinion* No. 23, March 23, 1962.

transferred to and shall constitute a part of the collection of the state library." However, in actual practice all records transferred go to the Archives Division, as was the original intent of those who sponsored the legislation. All state offices and institutions have been directed to present to the Commission on Public Records inventory lists of records on file in their offices and storage areas, and disposal seems to proceed expeditiously. "Instructions to State Departments and Institutions" issued by the commission on March 15, 1960 (one page, processed), explain the procedure involved in obtaining authority to destroy or transfer records. While not voting, the Archivist attends and participates in the proceedings of the commission, gives advice that is sought and followed, and otherwise gives much time to disposal matters.

So far, the Archives Division has not been able to assume responsibility in the area of local records, though it has acted in an advisory capacity. The act of 1939, amended in 1955, provided for the disposition of local records without giving a voice to the State Commission on Public Records or the State Archivist. Disposal authority was vested in the county records commission, composed of the judge of the circuit court, the president of the board of county commissioners, the county auditor, the clerk of the circuit court, the county superintendent of schools, and the city controller of the county-seat city or the clerk treasurer of the county-seat city or town where there was no controller. Under the terms of this act it was only through co-operation with county officials that the State Archivist was informed of local records developments. An act of 1963 provides that before county records may be disposed of, the county historical society must be notified. If the society cannot care for the records, they may, on request, be transferred to the State Archives.

A considerable quantity of county records has been microfilmed by the Genealogy Division of the State Library.[77] Original county records are housed in the Archives Division.

COMMENTS

1. The role of the Commission on Public Records as the final authority over the disposal of state records must be safeguarded.

2. In connection with the records management program of the Department of Administration, establishment of a *bona fide* records center is of the essence. Pending action on the part of the department, the Archives Division is planning to move more records from the library basement to the Kentucky Avenue warehouse, to place a regular staff member and a part-time assistant there, and to operate it as a temporary records center.

3. Relieved of considerable quantities of semi-active records, the Ar-

[77] See Carolynn Wendel and Dorothy Riker, "County Records in the Genealogy Division of the Indiana State Library," *Indiana Magazine of History*, LIII (June, 1957), 181–96, and LIV (Mar., 1958), 56–65.

chives Division will be able to have more space and an opportunity to organize its holdings, provided that the library basement is properly equipped.

4. Indiana needs a new local records act that will provide both better control over the disposal of local records and assistance in the management of current records.

IOWA

Until 1938 in the vanguard of American states that had made efforts to care for their archives, Iowa has fallen back since then to a place of far less importance.

BACKGROUNDS

The archives of Iowa suffered badly from their many removals from city to city as the capital of the state was shifted, and from Capitol building to Capitol building within those cities. Requested by the general assembly in 1860 to examine into the safety of the records from fire, the Committee on Public Buildings reported that the records in the various offices were in great danger and recommended that they be housed in a fireproof building. In the same year $3,500 was appropriated for such a structure. It was built but subsequently destroyed by fire in 1884. Completion of the State Capitol in the same year, with vaults in the most important offices, provided insufficient storage space for the rapidly increasing records.[78]

Early in the twentieth century a vigorous movement for the preservation of the state's records was started jointly by Charles Aldrich, Curator of the Historical Department of the State Library, and Benjamin F. Shambaugh, professor at the State University and Curator of the State Historical Society in Iowa City. Their hope to see a "Hall of Archives" established did not materialize. Prompted by Aldrich's suggestions, however, the thirty-first general assembly of the state passed, in 1906, "An act providing for the care and permanent preservation of the public archives, and making an appropriation therefor." The law gave the State Library and History Department, at Des Moines, the custody of official records of the state's executive and administrative departments "ten years after the date of current use of such public documents," empowered the Executive Council to order the transfer of records before the expiration of the ten-year limit or to rule that they be retained in the offices beyond this period, and directed the council to furnish rooms and equipment for the archives in the Historical, Memorial, and Art Building then being erected. A law of 1924 (Code of Iowa, ch. 233, secs. 4512-4531) changed the name of the

[78] For the early history of the Iowa archives, see Benjamin F. Shambaugh, *A Report on the Public Archives* (Des Moines, 1907), pp. 24 ff.: Ora Williams, "The Iowa Historical Department," *Annals of Iowa*, 3d ser., XXIII (Apr., 1942), 267–86; and William J. Petersen, "Iowa — the Challenge of the Archives," *American Archivist*, XXVI (July, 1963), 327–31.

agency from State Library and History Department to Historical, Memorial, and Art Department of Iowa. The department was reorganized in 1939 and is now called the Iowa State Department of History and Archives (Acts, 1939, ch. 113).

THE DEPARTMENT OF HISTORY AND ARCHIVES

The department is governed by a Board of Trustees composed of the Governor, a judge of the Supreme Court, and the Superintendent of Public Instruction, which appoints the Curator for a six-year period. The following divisions are operated by the department: the State Historical Library, the Newspaper Division, the Census and Early Archives Records Division, the State Archives (actually a records center), the Manuscripts Division, the Museum, the Microfilm Division, and a Publications Division, which publishes the *Annals of Iowa*.[79]

Appropriations are made biennially, and the department had a budget of $100,000 for July 1, 1961, to June 30, 1962. Of this, $15,000 was used for archives and records management. The Curator of the department submits his budget to the Governor, Comptroller, and Fiscal Director of the state, and then defends it in hearings before the Governor and the Comptroller and subsequently before a joint House and Senate committee. The budget, which becomes part of the whole state budget, is of course subject to amendment by the general assembly.

The department has twenty employees, of whom six work in the records and archives field or are classified as archivists — two in the records center, two in the Census and Archives Division, and two (the superintendent and his assistant) in the Newspaper Division. Staff salaries vary from $3,060 to $4,140. The Curator's salary is $6,600. While the department is not under civil service, there is provision for merit increases in four to five basic steps; there are four longevity steps.

The Historical Building, in which the department operates and which it shares with the State Traveling Library, was built in 1906 — the already mentioned Historical, Memorial, and Art Building. Only a small part of the building has been available for archival purposes, and as a result holdings long ago overflowed into vaults, closets, sub-basements, and attics of the Capitol, and even into its so-called "east tunnel," where water seepage and dampness affected them. As early as 1913 an archives addition was planned and approved (Acts of 1913, ch. 14), but it was never built. Finally, in 1942, the Kasson Memorial Building, formerly St. Mark's Church, was leased for the storage of records, and in 1943 it was bought for $9,520. This building, built of brick but with wooden supports and wooden shelving, is misleadingly called the State Archives Building. Though it has been strengthened somewhat by additional supports, it is still a firetrap

[79] State of Iowa, Department of History and Archives, *Thirty-fifth Biennial Report*, July 1, 1958, to June 30, 1960 (Des Moines, 1960), 24 p.

and a constant danger to the records as well as to the persons working with them. The Curator has not failed to call this perilous situation to the attention of the general assembly.[80]

THE STATE ARCHIVES

Cassius C. Stiles was appointed Superintendent of Archives when the Public Archives Division of the State Library and History Department was established in 1907, and he retained the position until February, 1938. He organized the earlier records of the state by classifying them within departments, as set forth in his *Public Archives: A Manual for Their Administration in Iowa*.[81] In doing so, he followed suggestions offered by Benjamin F. Shambaugh in his noteworthy reports on the public archives of Iowa.[82]

The records of the Governor, Secretary of State, Auditor, and other officials are kept in steel containers on the third floor of the department's building, together with the census records and the archives of the Grand Army of the Republic. They are made accessible through an elaborate system of index, calendar, and record storage cards. Though Stiles's system of classifying records has been superseded by modern methods of arrangement and description, undoubtedly in its time it was a great achievement and the envy of other states.

All available space in the Census and Archives Division is used, and some permanently valuable records have to be kept in the records center. Some additional storage space will be gained as a result of the intensive program for microfilming newspapers that now occupy considerable shelf space in the basement. Two planetary cameras are used for that purpose.

There are no facilities for the rehabilitation of records. Occasionally volumes of census records have been rebound.

During the 1960–62 biennium the division "handled more than 1,000 personal requests, plus 541 telephone calls and thousands of letters." [83] Search of the census records is subject to a fee of twenty-five cents, which is considered too low by the Curator.

RECORDS MANAGEMENT AND RECORDS DISPOSITION

Iowa has no records management program for either state or local records. It does have a records center in the so-called State Archives Building and, connected with it, an extensive microfilm program which uses one planetary and two rotary cameras. All the holdings of the records center,

[80] *Ibid.*, pp. 8 ff.; and *Thirty-sixth Biennial Report,* July 1, 1960–June 30, 1962 (Des Moines, 1962), p. 27.
[81] Reprinted from the *Annals of Iowa,* 1928. 181 p.
[82] The *Report* referred to above; and *A Second Report on the Public Archives* (Des Moines, 1907), 8 p. There is appended to the latter a *Guide to the Administrative Departments, Offices, Boards, Commissions and Public Institutions of Iowa* (355 p.), an extremely useful tool compiled by John C. Parish at Shambaugh's request.
[83] *Thirty-sixth Biennial Report,* p. 26.

except the records considered to be routine, are being microfilmed, and the films produced are stored in cabinets in the same building. This practice, as pointed out above, is far from safe. Furthermore, in such a wholesale operation, records of fairly limited retention value are likely to be included. Transfers to the center, requested by the departments concerned on transfer forms that describe the material in question as "deemed legally or permanently preservable," must be approved by the Curator of the Department of History and Archives.

Neither the records center nor the microfilm operation can be considered sound, for professional archival judgment does not enter into the determination of the retention value of the records involved, nor has the department been able to hire personnel trained in the essentials of modern records management.

In accordance with the Code of Iowa, 1962, section 303.10, department heads are directed to transfer non-current records to the Curator of the Department of History and Archives. First, however, a list of them must be submitted to the Curator, and he may recommend to the Board of Trustees the destruction of any records listed that have no legal, administrative, or historical value. In actual practice, departments use either the transfer procedure mentioned above or the "disposal form" on which they request permission "for disposal of material having no administrative, legal or permanent value, without filing in the archives." Disposal requests are normally approved by the Curator without referring them to the Board of Trustees. In fact, the disposal form does not call for the trustees' signatures.

The device of the retention and disposal schedule has not been legalized in Iowa.

COMMENTS

Practically all the elements of a sound program in records management and archives administration are lacking in Iowa, and no remedial action seems to be in sight. An adequate plan would call for:

1. a records management program;
2. a fireproof records center;
3. an archives building; and
4. a trained records management and archives staff (such a staff, however, cannot be obtained unless the miserable pay scale of the department is radically improved).

At present Iowa is out of step with developments that even in less affluent states have served the cause of good management as well as scholarship.

KANSAS

The Kansas State Historical Society at Topeka has a well-developed archival program. It also assists state agencies with their records management problems, though it is not charged with that responsibility. In the words of Walter Muir Whitehill, the society "attends to its affairs in a workmanlike and realistic manner, with a delightful freedom from boastfulness or portentous solemnity." [84]

BACKGROUNDS

Setting a precedent for Oklahoma and Missouri, the Kansas Editors and Publishers Association in 1875 founded the Kansas State Historical Society for the purpose of collecting complete files of newspapers and such other historical records as it might secure. It obtained quarters in the State Auditor's office, where one bookshelf was set aside for its collections; and it received its first modest appropriations from the legislature in 1877 and 1879. Chapter 167, Laws of 1879, made the society a trustee for the state, and even more significantly chapter 358, Laws of 1905, authorized state, county, and other officials to turn over to the society non-current records not required by law to be kept in the agencies. This made the society the acknowledged depository for the state's permanently valuable records.[85]

Constantly expanding and housed first in one place and then another in the State Capitol, the society never had adequate space until in 1908 the legislature appropriated $700,000 for the construction of a Memorial Building to house the society and several patriotic organizations — an amazingly far-sighted action. Approximately two-thirds of this amount was reimbursement by the federal government to the state for equipping Kansas troops during the Civil War. Documents to prove the state's claim had been furnished by the society.

Though comfortably housed, the society remained understaffed and inadequately equipped; hence its archival activity consisted mainly of accepting archival material and placing it either on the few available shelves or on the floor. In 1931, however, two new clerks were provided to arrange and catalog archives and private papers, and during the depression WPA workers did much listing and describing of records and private papers. They also indexed the 1855 and 1860 censuses.

In 1939 chapter 307 authorized the destruction of certain bodies of records and empowered the society's Secretary to select any of these for permanent preservation. Under a 1945 law (ch. 306) requests for the disposal of records at least six years old were to be reviewed by a board composed of the Attorney General, the State Librarian, the Secretary of the Historical Society, and the head of the agency seeking disposal authorization. After

[84] Walter Muir Whitehill, *Independent Historical Societies: An Enquiry Into Their Research and Publication Functions and Their Financial Future* (Boston, 1962), p. 281.
[85] On the history of the society, see William E. Connelley and Mary Embree, *The Kansas State Historical Society and Department of Archives* (Topeka, 1928), 48 p.; and the society's annual reports.

they had been reviewed, these requests were submitted to the legislature, which would approve destruction and print in the statutes complete lists of the records thus approved. The present organization of the State Records Board and its powers are based on Senate Bill 375 of 1957 (ch. 75, art. 3502-3504, in the 1961 Supplement to the General Statutes of Kansas, 1949).

THE STATE HISTORICAL SOCIETY

The State Historical Society is governed by a board of ninety-nine directors elected by the membership. The board elects a President and first and second vice-presidents; it also elects, for two-year terms, the Secretary and the Treasurer. The President appoints a five-member executive committee for two-year terms. The Assistant Secretary of the society now serves as Treasurer. Most of the past secretaries who have directed the work of the society have served for many consecutive terms and thus have provided continuity in its policies and activities. Staff members are appointed by the Secretary of the society, but their number is controlled by the legislature through appropriations. For the operation of its Reference Library, Newspaper Section, Division of Archives and Manuscripts, Archaeology Section, Photoduplication Section, and historic sites, the society in fiscal 1962 had an appropriation of $298,000, of which $31,000 was allocated to the Division of Archives and Manuscripts. This sum provides primarily for salaries and certain specific archival supplies, such as manuscript boxes.

Since the legislature has a thirty-day budget session in even years in addition to its regular sessions in odd years, budgets are prepared and approved annually. The budget requests, based upon recommendations of the department heads, are presented to the State Budget Director in the Department of Administration, who makes his recommendations to the Governor and keeps the society informed. Both the Secretary and the Assistant Secretary of the society appear at the Governor's budget hearings, at which members of the Ways and Means Committees of the two houses may also be present. They appear again to defend their budget before the Ways and Means Committee of the Senate, which introduces the society's appropriations bill. The bill is usually then passed by the legislature with little or no change. In addition to appropriations, the society has private income from bequests and membership fees (annual membership, $5.00; life membership, $50.00). It also has a "general fees fund" derived from the sale of microfilms, photographs, publications, and other materials, which is budgeted with appropriated funds for the regular operations of the society.

There are forty-five staff members of the society, four of whom, trained in history, work in the Division of Archives and Manuscripts. Salaries for fiscal 1964 are:

Executive Secretary	$10,920
Assistant Secretary	9,456
State Archivist	8,568
Assistant Archivist	6,060
Manuscript Cataloger	6,684
Assistant Manuscript Cataloger	4,515
Archives and Manuscript Clerk	3,888

The personnel of the society is "classified exempt"; that is, it is under the state civil service only in regard to the establishment of salaries. Within salary ranges there are eight in-grade steps. Longevity increases are granted after five, ten, twenty, and thirty years of service, each increase the equivalent of one step in the range. While selection of personnel is governed by job descriptions, the Executive Secretary enjoys complete freedom in matters of appointment. A pension system to which the state contributes 5.35 per cent and the employee 4 per cent of the salary of the position has been in effect since January 1, 1962. Retirement is mandatory at age seventy.

The State Historical Society occupies nearly all of the Memorial Building, which was remodeled in 1959–60 and is in excellent condition. Offices and the Newspaper Section are on the first floor, with the newspaper stacks extending into the basement, where there are also a sorting center and extensive storage space; the library uses the second and part of the third floors; and the main museum is on the fourth floor. Four stack areas and two vaults are available to the Division of Archives and Manuscripts.

In addition to the main museum, the society operates several others at historic sites in the state, a program for historic sites and markers (in cooperation with the Highway Commission), an archeology program, and a publication program. Recent publications include: *Kansas, a Pictorial History* and *Kansas in Maps* (both in 1961) and *Kansas in Newspapers* and *Why the West Was Wild* (both in 1963). The older biennial *Kansas Historical Collections* (17 vols., 1875–1928) has been replaced by the *Kansas Historical Quarterly* (1931 to date), the spring issue of which carries the society's annual report. The bimonthly four-page newsletter, the *Mirror*, paid for from private funds, is sent to members only.

The society enjoys close relationships with educational institutions of the state, for the State Archivist and the Archaeologist teach part-time at Washburn University, while the Assistant Secretary is in charge of an extension course at the University of Kansas.

THE STATE ARCHIVES

Both the archives and private papers are administered by the Division of Archives and Manuscripts, though in location and in servicing they are separated. Archives are kept in a four-story stack area in the central part of the building while private papers are stored in two two-story

[117]

vaults. Of the total storage space of 8,700 cubic feet, 5,700 are in use. Holdings consist of non-current official records of the Governors, 1854–1955; [86] the Board of Agriculture, 1862–1962; the Attorney General, 1882–1905 and 1927–58; the Adjutant General, 1861–1903 and 1932–45; and other state officers and agencies. The Manuscript Section has the private papers of many men who served as federal and state officials, including those of Governor Landon, and papers of Kansans in other walks of life. As a matter of convenience, state census records are kept and serviced by the Newspaper Section, which also co-operates in the society's continuous newspaper microfilm project. On the other hand, the Division of Archives and Manuscripts administers 41,000 photographic items, 5,700 maps, and 2,300 reels of microfilm, primarily material filmed for security reasons. All microfilm is centralized in a second-floor reading room adjacent to the library, where reading machines are available to researchers.

Accessions, reaching the society through the disposal process to be discussed later, through agency initiative, or, in the case of private papers, through gift, are entered in an accession journal. They are not numbered. In the arrangement of records and papers the basic principles of archival administration are observed. Control of archival holdings is by means of a simple shelf-list on cards, arranged by agencies. Records are kept in Hollinger boxes provided with labels identifying the contents in considerable detail. Control of private papers is by means of a card catalog with author and subject entries.

Research room facilities are adequate. Each year some 350 searchers consult 5,570 record items and 60 microfilm items, and approximately 300 letters are written in answer to inquiries involving consultation of the records by staff members. Certified copies of census and state employment records are furnished for a fee of $1.00.

Although there are no modern facilities for the rehabilitation of records, a flatbed microfilm camera and other photographic equipment of the Photoduplication Section are available for the needs of the Division of Archives and Manuscripts.

RECORDS MANAGEMENT AND RECORDS DISPOSITION

Kansas does not have a records management program, though the State Historical Society on request helps agencies with their records problems.[87] A 1957 law (ch. 459) authorized a records center under the supervision of the society, and in 1959 the center was "transferred" to the Department of Administration. No money was ever appropriated for the actual establishment of a center, however, for in the opinion of those responsible in gov-

[86] Records for two gubernatorial terms are missing.

[87] For the following, see Robert W. Richmond, "Kansas — the Administration of the Public Records," *American Archivist*, XXVI (July, 1963), 333–37.

ernment agencies and in the society, the space problem has been solved by disposal scheduling.[88] The law, however, is still on the books.

Under the disposal act of 1957, referred to above, control over the disposal of state records is vested in the State Records Board. It is composed of the Attorney General (chairman), the State Librarian, the State Auditor, the Secretary of the Historical Society, or their designated representatives, and the State Archivist (secretary), plus a representative of the agency requesting disposal action. The State Archivist assists agencies in preparing disposal schedules. It is he who calls the meetings of the board. The board has the power to order destruction, reproduction, or temporary or permanent retention of records; to approve schedules for the orderly retirement of records; and to adopt regulations to accomplish the purpose of the act. No forms are used in the process. The minutes of the board meetings are prepared by the State Archivist and filed with the Revisor of Statutes.[89] After a thirty-day waiting period records may be destroyed. Since 1957 the State Records Board has acted on requests from forty-six agencies. Of these, twenty-eight have been granted continuous authority on a scheduled basis.

As for local records, county commissioners have the authority to dispose of records more than twenty years old (1961 Supplement to the General Statutes of Kansas, 1949, ch. 19, art. 254), after the State Historical Society has exercised its right of review and has taken what it considers permanently valuable. Other local records are accessioned by the society if offered. Of the 105 counties in the state, the larger ones have microfilm programs, and a good many of them — an estimated 80 per cent — have storage facilities for records not in current use. According to society officials, most counties keep their essential records well, and a statewide county microfilm program is not contemplated at this time.

Kansas has legislation pertaining to the continuity of government in an emergency (1961 Supplement to the General Statutes of Kansas, 1949, ch. 48, articles 12–15). It has not been implemented, however, nor has an essential records preservation law been enacted.

COMMENTS

1. Kansas operates without a records center and without a records management act. Constant attention should be paid to the need for establishing the former and for enacting a records management bill.

2. Kansas authorities should anticipate the possible need of a county microfilm program.

[88] Some agencies, such as those in charge of social welfare and highways, use rented space for storing semi-current records. Others have adequate storage space.

[89] This requirement has taken the place of approval of records disposal by the legislature, which had to be obtained under the law of 1945.

KENTUCKY

In recent years Kentucky has joined the ranks of those states that have made arrangements for effective administration of their records. In the absence of the requisite storage facilities, however, the program is still limited to the area of records management.

BACKGROUNDS

As in many other states, in Kentucky the Secretary of State long served as custodian of his own records, executive papers, and legislative records, while other records remained with the agencies of origin. Severe losses were suffered when the Capitol burned in 1813 and 1824; when fires occurred in the offices of the Governor, the Secretary of State, and the Clerk of the Court of Appeals in 1865; and when, during the Goebel affair in 1900, troops quartered in the Capitol used public records as mattresses and pipe lighters.

In 1910 Professor Irene T. Myers reported to the Public Archives Commission of the American Historical Association [90] that most state records had been moved from the basement of the old Capitol into the new Capitol Building in Frankfort, where, on the whole, they were accessible. She pointed out, however, that in spite of vastly improved conditions records were still in jeopardy because officials had neither the time nor the inclination to arrange and care for the records of their predecessors.

A 1926 executive order of the Governor transferred the Governors' papers (1792–1915) from the Secretary of State to the Kentucky Historical Society. In 1936 the Historical Society became a division of a newly established Department of Library and Archives headed by Emma Guy Cromwell, and when the department was abolished in 1954, the society retained its archival holdings until a new agency could be established. Important fiscal, administrative, and legal records were salvaged during the 1930's by Thomas D. Clark, head of the history department of the University of Kentucky, and James W. Martin, director of the university's Bureau of Business Research. Informed that trucks were to take these records to Louisville, Kentucky, where they were to be destroyed, they obtained authorization from the Governor to transfer them to the University of Kentucky.

As a first step toward coping with the state's records problem, chapter 205, Acts of 1950, established a Records Control Board composed of the Commissioner of Finance, the Attorney General, the Auditor of Public Accounts, the Clerk of the Court of Appeals, and the Secretary-Treasurer of the Kentucky Historical Society. The board was instructed to issue regu-

[90] This and the preceding paragraph are based on Professor Myers' "Report on the Archives of the State of Kentucky," *Annual Report of the American Historical Association for the Year 1910* (Washington, 1912), pp. 331–64.

lations concerning the disposal of records and to authorize the destruction of the records of any agency of the state; and agencies were empowered, in the absence of legal prohibitions, to destroy records after a finding by the principal officer that they were useless. A central microfilm program, started at the same time, was abandoned in 1952, when it was discovered that microfilming was too expensive as a primary records control device.

It was at the urging of Dr. Clark, who had aroused the interest of the Governor and the Lieutenant Governor, that the Legislative Research Commission prepared a substantial report on *Records Management and State Archives.*[91] The report recommended enactment of legislation providing for replevin of records; establishment of a records and archives program under the Department of Finance; creation of an advisory commission to formulate policy; statutory provision for an archivist and records manager; establishment of a central records repository; appointment of records officers by the agencies; establishment of schedules for the controlled flow and deposit or disposal of state records; creation of a central microfilm unit; protection of confidential state records; transfer of the central documents depository to the jurisdiction of the archivist; placing the control of creation, flow, and disposal of state records in the hands of an archivist and records manager and making mandatory the compliance of state agencies with the program; and giving the records manager authority to review requests for the purchase of file cabinets and other records equipment and orders for printed forms.

This very effective report led to the passage of the Kentucky State Archives and Records Act of 1958 (Kentucky Revised Statutes, 1959, 171.410–710), which created the State Archives and Records Commission and, as its operating arm, the State Archives and Records Service. The Reorganization Act of 1962 (S. B. No. 153) assigned "the functions of the state relating to archives and records" to the Commissioner of Finance, and consequently the State Archives and Records Service became "an administrative unit" in his department.[92]

THE STATE ARCHIVES AND RECORDS SERVICE

Under the Reorganization Act of 1962, the duties of the State Archives and Records Commission have been confined to advising the Department of Finance "on matters relating to archives and records" and to determining "whether a particular record or group of records should be destroyed." The commission is now composed of the Commissioner of Finance as chairman, the Attorney General, the Auditor of Public Accounts, the chairman of the Legislative Research Commission, and the Chief Justice

[91] This is Research Publication No. 50 of the commission (Frankfort, Dec., 1957), 55 p.
[92] Charles F. Hinds, "Kentucky — the Archives and Records Service," *American Archivist*, XXVI (July, 1963), 339–43.

of the Court of Appeals. In addition, the Kentucky Historical Society, the Kentucky Library Association, the University of Kentucky, and the five state colleges (as a class) have one representative each on the commission.[93] The fact that the Director of the State Archives and Records Service is neither a member nor the secretary of the commission can only be explained as a strange oversight in legislative drafting.

The Director, an appointee of the Commissioner of Finance and now designated as Executive Officer I though permitted to use his legal title in parentheses, plans to organize the service as follows. There will be two sections in charge of, respectively, the records management and the archives functions. An Assistant State Records Administrator will have the services of a System and Procedures Officer, a Scheduling Officer, a Local Records Officer, and a Records Center Supervisor. The Assistant State Archivist's staff is to consist of a Senior Archivist, a Search Archivist, an Archives Librarian, and a Superintendent of Microfilming and Manuscript Repair. The following positions have been authorized:

Executive Officer I (Director)	$7,716–$10,344
Systems and Procedures Officer	5,760– 7,716
Scheduling Officer..	4,980– 6,672
Search Archivist	4,512– 6,048
Stenographer-Clerk	3,696– 4,980

Within salary ranges, there is provision for five merit increases. Longevity increases are also granted.

Members of the staff enjoy state retirement and social security benefits and, except for the Director, are protected by the state's merit system. Prospective appointees, who must have passed appropriate tests, are interviewed by the Director and approved by the Executive Assistant of the Commissioner of Finance; thereupon appointment forms are sent to, and executed by, the Department of Personnel.

In fiscal 1961–62 the State Archives and Records Service had an appropriation of $27,168. This was increased to $41,810 for 1962–63 and will reach $43,515 for 1963–64. Only $6,360 for 1962–63 and $6,672 for 1963–64 are earmarked for the archives function, though part of the Director's salary would also have to be charged to it.

The Director discusses his budget with the Executive Assistant of the Commissioner of Finance, and there his influence tends to end. In recent years no budget hearings have been held by legislative appropriations committees, for it has become customary for the Governor's budget recommendations to be approved by the legislature.

[93] Dr. Clark represents the University of Kentucky and Dr. Jacqueline Bull, Head, Special Collections Division, University of Kentucky Library, represents the Kentucky Library Association. Both of them have worked incessantly for a solution of the state's records problems that will do justice to scholarly and administrative needs.

Plans for a State Archives and Records Center building especially designed for that purpose are being considered by the Commissioner of Finance and the Governor.

THE ARCHIVES SITUATION

The State Archives and Records Service does not at present hold any records. Until it can obtain the necessary facilities the Kentucky Historical Society, the University of Kentucky, and the agencies of origin will continue to serve as temporary depositories.

The Kentucky Historical Society has in its custody some of the basic documents of the state. These include the first two state constitutions; enrolled bills, 1792–1920 (405 volumes); papers of Governors, 1792–1923 (1,180 docket files and 204 executive journals); records of the Confederate Pension Department; tax lists, 1781–1871; and a small collection of personal papers. Holdings at the University of Kentucky (11,000 cubic feet) consist of administrative, fiscal, and judicial records, among them papers of the Bank of Kentucky, 1806–40; assessment records of Kentucky counties, 1910–36; records of the State Court of Appeals, 1865–1931; circuit court records of Pike County, 1860–67; and Kentucky District Superior Court records, 1783–86.

Accessioning, arrangement, description, and servicing of archives will have to wait until archival holdings have been concentrated in the future Records Center–Archives Building. Given the role that the department of history of the University of Kentucky and the university library have played in getting the state's records and archives program started, a continuing close relationship between them and the Archives and Records Service can be anticipated, and from this relationship graduate research and local and regional historical studies will undoubtedly benefit.

Western Kentucky State College, the University of Kentucky, and the University of Louisville are serving as holding areas for local records that have been filmed. Microfilm copies will be used for purposes of reference service.

Once provided with the necessary facilities, the Archives and Records Service will be in a position to accept, in accordance with Revised Statutes of Kentucky, 171.620, private papers of Governors and former state officials, "other papers relating to and contemporary with any governor or former governor of Kentucky," and other appropriate materials, such as motion picture films, still pictures, sound recordings, maps, and private papers. In addition, the service is to collect "all reports and publications,[94] except the Kentucky Revised Statutes editions, issued by any department,

[94] The University of Kentucky Library acts as the central distributing agency for these publications.

[123]

board, commission, officer or other agency of the commonwealth for general distribution . . ."

RECORDS MANAGEMENT AND RECORDS DISPOSITION

According to Kentucky Revised Statutes, 171.470, as amended by the Reorganization Act of 1962, the Department of Finance

is authorized to make continuing surveys of government records and records management and disposal practices and to obtain reports thereon from state and local agencies; to promote . . . improved records management practices and control in such agencies, including the central storage or disposition of records not needed by such agencies for their current use. . . .

The State Archives and Records Service as the official agent of the Commissioner of Finance is now engaged primarily in making inventories and schedules and giving advice and assistance in the area of records creation. Plans call for an expansion of the program to include filing systems, the management of forms, reports, directives, correspondence and mail, office equipment, data processing, and microfilming.

Disposal authority is still vested in the State Archives and Records Commission. Its *Rules and Regulations* [95] govern the inventorying, scheduling, and disposal of public records. A survey of state records with the intent to bring all agency holdings under schedule control was completed by August, 1963. It is estimated that there are 145,652 cubic feet of records in the seventy-five departments, agencies, commissions, and boards of the state government and that 36,413 cubic feet of these can be destroyed. Of the approximately 30,000 cubic feet of records being created each year 7,500 will be disposed of under the present plans.

Local records are also subject to Kentucky's program of records management and disposal. When requested to do so, the Director of the State Archives and Records Service provides assistance to counties and municipalities in matters of records management, pending the appointment of a local records officer. So far records of the circuit court in Warren County have been inventoried and appraised to serve as a basis for a permissive schedule, which would have to be agreed upon with the Organization of County Officials.

A program for the preservation of essential records is still in the discussion stage. Vital statistics records to 1865, in some instances to 1959, and county clerks' records have been, or are being, microfilmed by the Utah Genealogical Society. Positive copies are given to the University of Kentucky and to the county where records have been microfilmed.

In the future, central microfilm service to state agencies and local units

[95] They are attached to a document (available in the records of the commission) prepared by Charles F. Hinds, "Records Management in Kentucky" (Frankfort, Jan. 1, 1961), unpaginated, which is a progress report of the commission to the Governor, the Honorable Bert Combs.

will be provided under the State Archives and Records Act, but provisions of this act do not necessarily preclude microfilming in other state agencies where justified.

COMMENTS

Kentucky's primary need is for a facility that will serve as a combined records center and archival depository. Once such a facility has become available, the state's archives — now held by the University of Kentucky, the Historical Society, and departments and agencies of the state — should be assembled there.

LOUISIANA

The Secretary of State, in presenting in May, 1956, the second report of the *Louisiana Archives Survey*, pointed out that Louisiana "has sound general archives and records laws on the statute books, but it needs a professional group of employees to implement the law." Yet Louisiana still lacks the personnel and the facilities to carry out fully the intent of the excellent Act No. 337 of 1956.[96]

BACKGROUNDS

Only fragmentary records of the French and Spanish regimes of Louisiana remain within the state, and state records suffered losses as a result of numerous moves of the state capital until 1879, when it was finally located in Baton Rouge. Still other losses occurred in 1862, when the Capitol, then used as lodging for Union troops, was destroyed by fire.

Act No. 273 of 1855 charged the Secretary of State with keeping a register of the acts and resolutions of the general assembly, which apparently were meant to remain in his custody after copies had been sent to the State Printer. Act No. 329 of the same year established "a public library of the State of Louisiana" and put the librarian in charge of "all books, statutes, manuscripts, plans, maps, papers, and documents of every description belonging to the state." The latter act was apparently not intended to make the library an archival depository, for William O. Scroggs reported to the Public Records Commission of the American Historical Association in 1912[97] that he found records stored in rooms in the basement and other parts of the Capitol, unsorted, unclassified, and inaccessible. There were a few fireproof vaults, where records were at least safe from fire. Many of the old Spanish archives were in the archives room of the New Orleans City Hall, on wooden shelves, dusty and moldy, and at the mercy of fire. Scroggs found some very important old records in

[96] Materials as well as information kindly made available by John C. L. Andreassen were of great help in preparing this section of the study.

[97] "The Archives of the State of Louisiana," *Annual Report of the American Historical Association for the Year 1912* (Washington, 1914), pp. 275–93.

local custody, the most notable of which were the parish records at the Natchitoches and Baton Rouge courthouses. Losses, he stated, were not all due to moves and fires, but frequently to the fact that officials, interested only in the records of their own incumbencies, stored records haphazardly and sometimes even threw away older ones to make room for the more recent.

According to the findings of Grace King,[98] the parishes had made no provision whatsoever for the preservation of their records, and courthouses had been burned so many times that few parishes had records older than fifty years — indeed, in one the records were no more than twenty years old, files having apparently been stolen bodily and the courthouse deliberately burned. Where parish records were in existence they were disordered and impossible to use.[99]

No effective remedial action was taken. Act No. 90 of 1900, creating the State Museum, authorized the Governor to lend to or deposit in the museum historical documents, relics, or works of art; and a 1912 act (No. 242) defined public records, stated the duties of persons in charge of them, and provided for their protection.

A few bodies of archival material found their way into the library of the Louisiana State University between 1922 and 1932.[100] Professor Edwin A. Davis of the history department of the university was so successful in his attempt to collect historical source material for the university that in 1936 the Department of Archives and Manuscripts was officially established as a division of the university libraries, and the legislature passed Act No. 258, which authorized the department to "perform certain services in the way of preserving state and parish records" and, to that end, to "receive and collect public records or documents bearing upon the history of the state." By 1938 the department held a large collection of private manuscript material and some fifteen million documents received from state and parish officials. The Department of Archives and Manuscripts, however, had neither funds nor the space that in the long run would have enabled it to serve as the state's archival agency. Most of the records transferred to the department were those rescued from the basement of the old State Capitol by Historical Records Survey workers; and, generally speaking, the inventories and other publications produced by the survey under John C. L. Andreassen, as State Supervisor of the survey

[98] "The Preservation of Louisiana History," *North Carolina Historical Review*, V (1928), 363–71.

[99] John C. L. Andreassen and Edwin A. Davis, *Louisiana Archives Survey*, Report No. 2, *Findings and Recommendations* (May, 1956), 20 p. The survey revealed that conditions may not be so bad as Miss King's findings indicated. Thirty parishes were found to have records dated as early as the years 1716 to 1811, but no indication of the quantity or continuity of these holdings is given.

[100] Edwin A. Davis, "Archival Development in the Lower Mississippi Valley," *American Archivist*, III (Jan., 1940), 39–46.

project in Louisiana and later as Regional Supervisor for the Southern states except North Carolina, laid the foundations for a future archives program in Louisiana.

Realizing that the permissive legislation of 1936 could not meet the need for such a program, Dr. Davis almost yearly tried to have sound archival legislation introduced. Thanks to the interest of Secretary of State Wade O. Martin, Act No. 381 of 1954 was passed and approved by the Governor on July 7, 1954. The act authorized the Secretary of State to make a survey of state, parish, municipal, colonial, territorial, and federal records in Louisiana in order to ascertain their condition, location, and availability and to report to the legislature with recommendations. The Secretary of State appointed Andreassen and Dr. Davis to make the survey, and in 1956 they made two reports to the legislature, the first containing a survey of the records and the second consisting of findings and recommendations. They recommended that a general archives and records management administration program be established under the Secretary of State with the guidance of an Archives and Records Commission consisting of three or more elected state officials, that an Archives and Records Service be established as its administrative agency, and that an Archives Division, a Records Administration Division, and a Historical Division be established in the service.

Accepting this report, the legislature in 1956 passed Act. No. 337 (cited as Rev. Stats. of 1950, Title 44, ch. 5, secs. 401–409), creating the Archives and Records Commission and defining its powers and duties, creating and establishing an Archives and Records Service and defining its objectives and responsibilities, authorizing the establishment of a State Archives and Records Center, and outlining the duties of the state and local officials with regard to the management of records and archives.

Unfortunately, appropriations to implement the act were vetoed by Governor Long in 1956, and for two years Andreassen, logical candidate for the position of Director of the Archives and Records Service, worked as Consultant in Records Management to the Secretary of State and other officials. On June 11, 1957, the Archives and Records Commission appointed him Archivist without compensation. An appropriation in the amount of $36,640 became available July 1, 1958.

Effective August 1, 1960, Andreassen was dismissed. According to a newspaper statement [101] his successor "has been in the oil lease business 12 years and is familiar with records. He was a parish leader for Gov. Davis in the gubernatorial campaign." The law (Rev. Stats. 1950, Title 44, ch. 5, 406) calls for the appointment of a "professionally qualified director." Letters protesting the dismissal of Andreassen and the appointment of his successor were sent by the president and the secretary of the

[101] Baton Rouge *State-Times*, July 27, 1960.

Society of American Archivists to the Governor of the state and to the members of the commission.

The commission is now composed of the Secretary of State, the Attorney General, and the State Comptroller. It has the power to establish procedures for submission of disposal lists and schedules, to authorize the disposal of public records, and to set standards for the photoreproduction of records. It appoints the Director and Associate Director. The former acts as secretary to the commission. The Director is to make continuing surveys of public records and records management and disposal practices and to promote the adoption of good records management techniques; to have custody of a state archives and records center building; to "prescribe" the policies and principles to be followed by state and local governmental agencies in the conduct of their records management programs; and to establish standards for the selective retention of records and assist in their application. He may also appoint advisory groups, inspect or survey public records, accept public records for deposit in the future state archives and records center, and effect the transfer to the commission of any records more than fifty years old, unless the head of the agency concerned certifies in writing that they must be retained by it "for the conduct of its regular current business."

Although Revised Statutes 1950, Title 44, chapter 5, section 406, creates "an archives and records service" as an executive arm of the commission, no such instrumentality exists.[102] The personnel working under the commission are as follows:

Director $9,600
Assistant Director [103] 9,600
Typist Clerks II (2) .... 2,760–$ 3,660
Records Preservation Technicians II (3) 3,300– 4,200
Records Preservation Technicians I (12) 2,760– 3,660

The technicians are used mainly in the microfilm operation. One of them is stationed in the New Orleans Branch of the commission. Because the present Director does not actively participate in the work of the commission, operations are headed by the Assistant Director.

With the exception of the Director and the Assistant Director, all employees are under the state's merit system. Benefits for full-time personnel are hospitalization and life insurance (with the state paying 50 per cent of the premium) and retirement, to which the state contributes 6 per cent and the employee 5 per cent of the gross salary. Employees in

[102] The letterhead of the commission lists the Director and Assistant Director but does not refer to them as the staff of the Archives and Records Service.
[103] Not an Associate Director as provided in the law.

the classified service receive eight hours a month of annual and eight of sick leave, increased after three years to ten hours. Within salary ranges there are five step increases, to which after two years at maximum pay a longevity increase is added.

In addition to its regular sessions the legislature has a budget session in odd-numbered years. Budgets prepared by the Assistant Director are reviewed in detail by the Secretary of State, approved by the commission upon his recommendation, and submitted through the Division of Administration to a joint legislative committee. The Secretary of State and the Assistant Director are required to appear before the committee, whose recommendations are normally not changed on the floor. For fiscal 1964 the commission received $45,920, plus $45,000 as an extra appropriation.

The commission is housed on the second floor of Peabody Hall, a building on the old campus of the Louisiana State University. The place is a firetrap; so the records kept or processed there are by no means safe.

The Director is an *ex officio* member of the Civil War Centennial Commission, the Cultural Resources Commission, and the Stonewall Jackson Memorial Fund. The State Archives and Records Commission's Senior Consultant edits *Louisiana History*.

THE STATE ARCHIVES

The official archival holdings of the state of Louisiana are dispersed. Lacking adequate facilities, the Archives and Records Commission has only about 120 cubic feet of archival material, including captured Louisiana state records returned by the National Archives, records of the Louisiana State Prison at Angola, 1862–1900, and colonial records of Avoyelles and St. Landry parishes. Those of Avoyelles have been very briefly described in the *Calendar of Louisiana Colonial Documents*, Volume I (1961), compiled by Winston De Ville. Understandably there are few reference service requests — only some 300 a year.

More voluminous are the archives held by the Department of Archives and Manuscripts of the Louisiana State University Library, which is housed in the fine new library building. In addition to 250 cubic feet of records of the Survey of Federal Archives and the Historical Records Survey projects in Louisiana, it has approximately a million state records from the most important agencies of the state, 1825–1933, and about 88,000 records from six parishes of the state. Holdings are listed in the first Louisiana Archives Survey on the basis of entries in the Historical Records Survey *Guide to Manuscript Collections in Louisiana: The Department of Archives, Louisiana State University*, Volume I (1940; 55 p., proc.). Most of the records are kept in the old library building; about 25 per cent of the parish records and the heavily used records of the Department of

Education are in the modern stacks of the library's Department of Archives and Manuscripts. Besides accession documents, more or less detailed inventories have been developed by the professionally trained and experienced staff of the department. A card index provides access to the case records of district, parish, and probate courts. Generally speaking, however, the department places emphasis on the processing of private papers.[104] Inasmuch as the permissive legislation under which the department may receive state records was not revoked by the act of 1956, it will presumably continue to hold those now in its custody.

Non-current records of the Office of the Adjutant General of Louisiana and other military records are in the Adjutant General's Military Archives at Jackson Barracks. Official records of the colonial and state periods, among them those of the Superior Council of Louisiana, 1717–69, are in the custody of the Louisiana State Museum; and the Louisiana Historical Association has records of the Confederate States of America and of the Confederate Army.

RECORDS MANAGEMENT AND RECORDS DISPOSITION

Although the act of 1956 envisages a strong and comprehensive records management program, little of it has been implemented, and the program is essentially a microfilm program for which the State Archives and Records Commission furnishes the manpower. The program, operating with a revolving fund of $3,000, has grown steadily since 1958, until now eight cameras and a Kalvar processor are in use and four "records preservation technicians" are employed, one of them in the New Orleans Branch located in the Old Civil Courts Building in that city. Records filmed at the behest of agencies include those of the major departments of the state, prominent among them the Comptroller's copies of parish assessment rolls. To date sixty-five guides to records microfilmed have been published; these can be considered useful inventories of the records themselves.

The program is by no means a centralized microfilm service. Not only the Highway Department but also small agencies buy equipment, which at times sits idle; and filming is not always done properly.

The disposal function is still undeveloped. Disposal requests are approved by the commission and the Senior Consultant, but few agencies apply for authority to destroy records and only one of them, the Forestry Commission, has had a disposal and retention schedule approved. Ten disposal actions were taken in fiscal 1963.

There is practically no records management service to local agencies. Some parishes have requested microfilming of records, and it is planned to provide service by lending cameras and training persons to operate them.

[104] V. L. Bedsole, "Collections in the Department of Archives and Manuscripts, Louisiana State University," *Louisiana History*, I (Fall, 1960), 328–34.

On January 28, 1963, the Archives and Records Commission received a grant of $32,560 from the Louisiana Civil Defense Agency for a "pilot project" of microfilming essential state records,[105] and as a result the microfilm program was expanded considerably for the remaining months of the fiscal year. It was to be staffed with one Clerk II, two Typists II, four Records Preservation Technicians II, and 21 Records Preservation Technicians I, and to be equipped with five planetary cameras, seven 16-mm. rotary cameras, and two Kalvar 35-mm. copiers. A detailed study of records to be filmed under this first phase of the civil defense microfilm project has been conducted. Engineering drawings of the State Highway Department and the New Orleans Port Commission will be placed in low-cost storage.

COMMENTS

1. Major parts of the program of records management and archival administration, as authorized in the act of 1956, still remain to be implemented.

2. The position of Director under the Archives and Records Commission calls for the services of a trained and experienced archivist who will give leadership to the program.

MAINE

On the archival map of the United States, the venerable state of Maine appears as a blank spot, for it has neither an archival nor a records management program. This is so because, according to one of the state's officials, "Maine is progressive but only if it does not cost money."

BACKGROUNDS

Concern about local records, which are older than those of the state (admitted to the union in 1820), made itself felt when an act of the legislature of 1821 required counties to provide "fireproof buildings of brick or stone . . . [for the housing of the records of] the offices of registers of deeds, and of probate and insolvency, and of the clerk of courts, with separate fireproof rooms and suitable alcoves, cases, or boxes for each office." [106] Much later, in 1897, the legislature passed a law stipulating that towns and cities of more than 1,300 inhabitants provide safes or vaults where the records were to be kept when not in actual use. Since non-compliance with the law called for a fine of ten dollars only, it remained practically inoperative.[107]

Chapter 88, Public Laws of 1907, established the position of State His-

---

[105] At the time of this writing an additional grant of $35,000 was expected for fiscal 1964.
[106] Allen Johnson, "Report on the Archives of the State of Maine," *Annual Report of the American Historical Association for the Year 1908*, I (Washington, 1909), p. 281.
[107] *Ibid.*, p. 304.

torian and instructed him to compile historical data and encourage the teaching of both state and local history in the public schools. The first historian, Henry S. Burrage, made two reports,[108] in the first of which he strongly urged the establishment of a state archives, describing in great detail the deplorable condition of those records of the state that had survived.

A bill to create at Augusta a Bureau of Maine Archives was sponsored by Jerome G. Plante of Old Orchard Beach, House minority leader, in 1959 and 1961. Both times it was reported out unanimously by the Committee on State Government, but the legislature postponed action indefinitely. The 1961 bill (Legislative Document No. 737, One-hundredth Legislature) would have established the Bureau of Maine Archives, charged with "the collection, preservation and administration of public archives; the editing and publication of such public archives; the improvement of standards for the making, care and administration of public archives in Maine; and the stimulation of research, study and activity in the field of archives." Though "under the supervision of the Secretary of State," the bureau would have been "under the control of a board of advisors consisting of five persons especially interested in the history of the state," which in addition to other duties specified was "to adopt policies designed to fulfill the duties and obtain the objectives of the bureau as established by law." The director, to be appointed by the Secretary of State, would have had "the qualification of special training or experience in archival or historical work." The bill provided an appropriation of $7,000 for fiscal 1961–62 and of $10,000 for fiscal 1962–63. The same legislation was again rejected in 1963.

A bill for the preservation of essential records against destruction in the event of disaster (Legislative Document No. 1376, One-hundredth Legislature) also failed of passage.

The sponsor of the abortive archives bills of 1959, 1961, and 1963 will continue his efforts, and the fact that Maine is now the only New England state that has no public records and archives law will certainly be of assistance to him. From past experience he may bear in mind, however, that the legislative climate of Maine is not favorable to enacting an archives bill pure and simple. The chances of enactment would apparently be much better for a combined records management and archives bill similar in scope, though not necessarily in specifics, to the New Hampshire law of 1961 (see below).

THE ARCHIVES SITUATION

The office of the Secretary of State is the official depository for all records of the Executive Council, a holdover from colonial times that

---

[108] *Report of the State Historian, 1907–1908* (Waterville, 1909), 21 p.; and *Report of the State Historian, 1909–10* (Augusta, 1910), 18 p.

supposedly serves as a check on the Governor; for legislative bills and resolves; for records of appointments and qualifications of members of boards and commissions; and for corporation records, election records, and other important series. Except for the bills and resolves (1820 to date) — which, being in a former elevator shaft, are difficult of access — records are reasonably well housed in various premises in the State Capitol, and the secretary to the Secretary of State is well informed about their whereabouts and contents.

The archives of the Secretary of State — for his records constitute an assemblage of permanently valuable records, non-current as well as current — did not develop into a general state archives of Maine. On the contrary, certain records of his office and of the Governor and Council were transferred to the State Library, established by an act of the legislature of 1861 (Public Laws, 1861, ch. 25, sec. 5). Included are the state constitution of 1819; some papers of Governors King and Kent; papers pertaining to the northeastern boundary, 1700–1842; election returns on the adoption of the constitution, 1819; and plans for the Maine State House. This material fills about half of one shelf.

The records of all other agencies of the Maine government are either inaccessible or kept under conditions that are haphazard and unsafe. Great losses have undoubtedly occurred, as borne out by the fact that evidence of the promulgation of certain constitutional amendments cannot now be discovered and that frequently reports of departments cannot be found. Upon expiration of their term of office the Governors have customarily taken all of their papers with them, a practice which is said to have caused embarrassment and difficulties. And, needless to say, both scholarly research in the history of the state and the work of the Office of Legislative Research are greatly handicapped.

Thanks to the interest of the Maine Historical Society, of Portland, local records have fared a little better. In its fairly adequate quarters at 485 Congress Street, the society administers a considerable quantity of town records and 199 microfilm reels of land and probate records. It also has positive copies of church records, proprietors' records, vital statistics, and family papers that were filmed by the Utah Genealogical Society, in some instances down to 1900 (38 reels). The Maine Historical Society also has the papers of the first Governor of Maine, Governor William King (24 boxes and 2 packages) — the only sizable body of Governor's papers in proper custody.[109]

RECORDS MANAGEMENT AND RECORDS DISPOSITION

Maine has no records management program except that Maine Revised Statutes, 1954, chapter 1, section 15, provides for the disposal of records.

[109] For detailed information, see Elizabeth Ring, *A Reference List of Manuscripts Relating to the History of Maine* (3 vols.; Orono, 1938).

Under this law, department heads may destroy records not in current use and having no legal or historical value, provided that the written approval of the Attorney General, the State Auditor, the Commissioner of Finance and Administration, and the State Historian has been given. The laws of Maine do not provide for the destruction of records on the local level but do require their preservation (Rev. Stats. 1944, ch. 79, secs. 16, 17).

A small amount of microfilming for other departments is done in the Bureau of Accounts and Control of the Department of Finance and Administration. The State Controller has expressed some interest in a records management program for state agencies.

COMMENTS

Inasmuch as efforts to create a Maine State Archives have failed three times, those interested in archives should support legislation establishing a combined records management and archives program, which may have a better chance of being passed.

MARYLAND

Operating under the Hall of Records Commission, the Maryland Hall of Records enjoys an enviable reputation as one of the leading state archival agencies.

BACKGROUNDS

Because of its concern about the records of the state, the general assembly ordered repeated examinations of the public records during the seventeenth and eighteenth centuries.[110] Their condition, however, remained precarious, and in 1834 the State Librarian was directed to survey and list the records in the state offices and to recommend steps conducive to their better preservation. Complying with these instructions, David Ridgely, State Librarian, made two reports;[111] in the second he said, "Already have documents, heretofore supposed to be lost forever to history, sufficient to form several volumes of the civil and documentary history of the province and the state, been brought to light"[112] from vaults, attics, and cellars, many of them from offices unrelated to the agency of origin or to the subject matter contained. He found some records in utter

[110] The early history of Maryland's archives and that of the formative years of the Hall of Records are well discussed in *First to Fourth Annual Reports of the Archivist of the Hall of Records* (1946), 52 p.

[111] *Report of D. Ridgely, Librarian, to the Executive of Maryland, in relation to the Collection of Documents, Papers, etc., etc., ordered to be deposited in the Council Chamber* (Annapolis, 1836), 13 p; and *Second Report of D. Ridgely, Librarian, of examination of Public Offices, for Records, Papers, etc., etc., made to the Executive of Maryland the 10th of October, 1835* (Annapolis, 1836), 8 p.

[112] *Second Report of D. Ridgely . . .* , p. 6.

decay and completely useless and many very valuable documents dumped under the stairway in the dome of the State Capitol.

Though at least some of Ridgely's recommendations were carried out and though in 1866 Colonel Brantz Mayer submitted other recommendations aimed at the protection of the state's records, nothing constructive was done until in 1878 Dr. Lewis H. Steiner, supported by the Maryland Historical Society, urged the general assembly to deposit the oldest records in the vaults of the society at Baltimore. Acting on his recommendation, the general assembly transferred the colonial and revolutionary records to the society, and, equally important, made an appropriation to the society for their care and publication. The society thus became the *de facto* archival agency of the state and received accessions as late as 1927, though for the most part records were retained by the agencies of origin. The Land Office also served as a quasi-archival depository for proprietary land records and the colonial probate court records, while county records continued to be neglected and exposed to destruction and loss.

"Stimulated by the investigations of the public archives commissions in other States," [113] the general assembly, in 1904, created a Public Records Commission and instructed it to examine into the condition and completeness of the public records and make a report with recommendations for their better custody, arrangement, and preservation. The detailed report of the commission was lost, but a condensed report by the chairman, Hester Dorsey Richardson, to the American Historical Association in 1905 found that the colonial records were fairly intact, that some post-revolutionary county records had perished in fires in county courthouses, and that on the whole the records had lacked proper care. The report recommended a central depository for old records and stated that a bill to establish such a depository had been drafted. No further appropriation for the work of the commission was made, however, and nothing was done about central housing for state records until the approach of Maryland's tercentenary celebration.

As a result of plans begun in 1928 to mark Maryland's three hundred years of history, St. John's College provided land on its campus in Annapolis, the Hall of Records was constructed, and the Hall of Records Commission was created (Acts, 1935, ch. 18). The commission was instructed to operate the Hall of Records, to appoint an Archivist and other employees, to provide space for the use of the Land Office, and to collect old court records, official documents, reports and other records, and old newspapers, church records, private papers, and other historical material pertaining to the history of the state from the earliest times. The legisla-

[113] Hester Dorsey Richardson, "Report of the Public Records Commission of Maryland," *Annual Report of the American Historical Association for the Year 1905*, I (Washington, 1906), 367

tion empowered state, county, city, town, and other officers to transfer to the commission records not needed in the current operation of their offices, gave the commission authority to copy records in its custody, and provided that the certified copies should have the legal force of the originals.

During the formative period of the commission, Carroll T. Bond, Chief Judge of the State Court of Appeals, rendered distinguished service as its chairman, as did James A. Robertson as the first Archivist of the Hall of Records (1935–39). In subsequent years the powers and responsibilities of the commission have been considerably increased. In addition to being made responsible for the destruction of useless records, subject to the final approval of the Board of Public Works [114] (Acts, 1941, ch. 825), it became a mandatory custodian of courthouse records antedating April 28, 1788 (Acts, 1945, ch. 248), certified photocopies of which it was to supply to the counties (Acts, 1945, ch. 896). It was also made custodian of all reports and publications of state agencies [115] (Acts, 1947, ch. 651), and the task of compiling and editing the biennial *Maryland Manual* was assigned to it by executive order.

When, in 1949, the general assembly authorized disposal of record material by schedule, once the schedule had been approved by the Board of Public Works (Acts, 1949, ch. 755), the Hall of Records Commission began to enter the area of records management. The Records Management Act of 1953 (Acts, 1953, ch. 436) explicitly charged the commission with developing and administering a records management program for state agencies and, upon request, with providing records management service to local units. To enable the commission to carry out one important phase of the new assignment, records centers at Annapolis and Baltimore were opened in 1958 and 1959.

THE HALL OF RECORDS

The Hall of Records, archival and records management agency of the state, is governed by the Hall of Records Commission, an aristocratic body composed of the Governor, the State Comptroller, the Chief Judge of the Court of Appeals, and the presidents of the Johns Hopkins University, St. John's College, the Maryland Historical Society, and the Peabody Institute. Given the nature of the group, it normally meets only once a year. It appoints the Archivist and Records Administrator responsible for the operation of the agency. Under the Archivist an Assistant Archivist is in charge of the archives program, including documentary repair and rehabilitation and the photographic laboratory. The Assistant

[114] A high-level group composed of the Governor, the Comptroller of the Treasury, and the Treasurer of the state.

[115] In accordance with chapter 96, Acts, 1960, all local codes, both county and municipal, must also be deposited with the Hall of Records Commission.

Records Administrator is responsible for the records management program, the records centers, and a microfilm unit. The three key officials, all of them respected members of the profession, have been in their posts for long periods of time — the Archivist since 1939 — and this tenure has contributed significantly to the continued and systematic growth of the Hall of Records activities.

Budget requests are developed by the Archivist in consultation with his two principal assistants. They are reviewed in hearings before the Department of Budget and Procurement and become part of the Governor's budget. Further hearings are held before the Senate Finance and House Ways and Means Committees. In recent years the committees have not cut the agency's budget requests, since it enjoys an outstanding reputation for honest budgeting. From a modest $28,432 in fiscal 1935, appropriations for the Hall of Records have increased to $144,412 in 1962. Approximately $180,000 will be available to it in fiscal 1964. The annual cost of watch and maintenance service, which the Hall of Records receives from the Superintendent of Public Buildings and Gounds, amounts to about $22,000.

The Hall of Records has twenty-two employees, ten of whom might be considered professional, namely, the Archivist, five persons in archives administration, and four in records management. The following salaries became effective on July 1, 1963:

Archivist and Records Administrator .... $10,160–$12,698
Assistant Archivist 8,560– 10,698
Assistant Records Administrator 8,560– 10,698
Public Records Examiners (2) 7,040– 8,802
Senior Archivist 6,286– 7,849
Junior Archivists (4) 5,040– 6,302
Manuscript Repair Technicians II (2) 4,040– 5,052

Photographer, clerk, and stenographer salaries range from $2,870 to $5,254. Six increases are provided within salary ranges, and after three years in the maximum brackets a longevity increase of 5 per cent of base pay is granted. Increases are automatic, not *de jure* but *de facto*. Though Hall of Records employees are not under the state's merit system, all its regulations except those having reference to appointment and severance apply to them. The qualifications for the position of Archivist have not been expressly stated. However, the Hall of Records Commission would certainly insist on his having the Ph.D. degree. For professional employees the B.A. or B.S. degree is a minimum requirement. Staff members participate in Blue Cross–Blue Shield health benefits and in the employees retirement system, to which both the state and the employees make contributions according to a sliding scale. Each employee is granted ten days of annual leave — increased to fifteen after four years of service and to twenty after twenty-five years of service — and thirty days of sick leave, which may accumulate up to a hundred days.

Located on the campus of St. John's College, the Hall of Records Commission is housed in a colonial-style but fireproof building eighty feet square, consisting of three floors and a basement with brick bearing-walls, steel girders, and reinforced concrete floors and roof slabs, erected at a total cost of $233,831.81. The air-conditioned stack area is isolated from the rest of the building by firedoors and brick walls and has six tiers with a total storage capacity of 29,280 cubic feet, of which 26,000 are in use. Appropriate areas have been provided for administration and staff offices, a research room, a catalog room, and rooms for the repair and preservation of documents and for photoreproduction. The vestibule serves as an exhibit room. There is a Barrow laminator, and there are facilities for flattening documents and for binding. In fiscal 1962, 25,238 pages were laminated and 76 record volumes were bound.

The Hall of Records has an outstanding publication program. Its *Annual Reports* are fine examples of informative reporting, strengthened by sound critical self-inspection. The agency has taken over from the Secretary of State the compilation, publication, and distribution of the biennial *Maryland Manual* [116] and has made it a good source of information on the legal and administrative history of the state government and the counties. Professional publications include: the *Calendars of Maryland State Papers* (7 vols., 1943–58); *Land Office and Prerogative Court Records of Colonial Maryland* (1946); *Buildings of the State of Maryland at Annapolis* (1954); and *The County Courthouses and Records of Maryland, Part One: The Courthouses* (1960). *Part Two: The Court Records*, containing a general description and history of basic records, is approaching publication. The Hall of Records is co-operating with the Littleton Griswold Committee of the American Historical Association in the publication of the Proceedings of the Court of Prince George's County, *Liber A*, 1696–99.

The Hall of Records makes a *viva voce* contribution to the cause of archives and their use by playing host to classes and institutes of The American University in archival administration and genealogical research and to such groups as the International Cooperative Workshop in Administrative Management. Fortified by an experience of well-nigh twenty-five years, the Archivist explains to these groups the operation of the Hall of Records and discusses basic aspects and techniques of state archival administration. As a quasi-historical agency for the state, the Hall of Records participates in planning for historical celebrations and the restoration of monuments and historic houses and, in general, supplies historical data when needed for the conduct of the state's business.

[116] The 1961–62 *Manual* is a volume of 732 pages. A 1963 supplement has 118 pages.

As mentioned before, the various departments and agencies of the state must deposit in the Hall of Records their printed reports and documents. Annual reports of agencies of which the Hall of Records did not have and could not obtain copies have been filmed. The Hall of Records is also the official repository for local codes, both county and municipal.

THE ARCHIVES PROGRAM

The Hall of Records holds 15,000 volumes, 8,000 reels of microfilm, and 3,000,000 pieces, 1635–1962, consisting of non-current official records and other papers relating chiefly to the history of Maryland. There are colonial records from 1635; records or photocopies of records of all counties, many from the colonial period; non-current executive, legislative, and judicial records of the state into the twentieth century; church records, 1664 to date (400 volumes); business records, 1752–1912 (300 volumes); family papers, 1641–1954 (12,000 pieces); [117] maps, 1606–1912 (200 pieces); and photographs (3,000 pieces). As a matter of practice, established in 1947, the Governor of the state has transferred his official records to the Hall of Records when his term of office expires.[118]

All courthouse records antedating April 28, 1788, have been concentrated in the Hall of Records. Land and basic probate records through 1850 were filmed by the Utah Genealogical Society, and copies were given to the Hall of Records. Its county land and probate record project, taking up where the Mormon project left off, is designed to microfilm all land records from 1850 to 1949. Filming is done in the counties under the supervision of employees of the Hall of Records or by Hall of Records staff members. To accelerate the project for insurance purposes, the Board of Public Works has furnished the Hall of Records funds for an additional photographer, film, and travel expenses. At the end of fiscal 1962, work remained to be done in seven counties and in Baltimore City. During that year there were produced for archival purposes and for the use of searchers 7,075 pages of photostats, 279 projection prints, and 101,725 microfilm images of county records and material in the Hall of Records.

In the organization of archival holdings, the principle of provenance has been followed. The *Catalogue of Archival Material, Hall of Records* (1942), compiled soon after the agency's establishment, is out of date as a general finding aid and will be replaced by a new guide.[119] Other finding

---

[117] Though under the act of 1935 the Hall of Records may receive non-public records and private papers and has in its custody a great deal of such material, it does not pursue an active policy of acquiring these. A collection of Methodist, Protestant Episcopal, and Quaker records, mostly on microfilm, is being assembled.

[118] Morris L. Radoff, "How To Transfer the Governor's Papers," *American Archivist*, XXIII (April, 1960), 185–89.

[119] It will not include courthouse records, which will be listed in the forthcoming second volume of *The County Courthouses and Records of Maryland*, referred to above.

aids consist of accession books in which accessions, now over 16,000, have been and are being entered, one accession to the page, beginning with No. 1 in 1935. These are supplemented by a card index, which is organized by agency provenance and indicates the numbers of all accessions received. Shelf-lists, primarily for staff use, are kept in the stack alcoves in which the records are stored. The material exposed to heavy use by genealogists — the probate records, testamentary proceedings, and other similar series — has been made accessible by means of indexes that expedite the handling of requests for personal data. Card as well as volume indexes of a general kind are listed and explained in a mimeographed bulletin that has been published repeatedly in increasingly useful form. *Index to Holdings 1963* is No. 12 in this series. Unique among finding aids recently prepared and published by American state archival agencies are the *Calendars of Maryland State Papers*,[120] that is, of the "Rainbow Series," a bound assemblage of papers of the colonial period named after the color of the bindings.

In fiscal 1962 the Hall of Records had 2,102 visitors, for whom 12,326 records were serviced; and, in reply to inquiries, it sent out 1,328 reference letters, about half of which were form letters. With a good deal of reluctance two such form letters have been adopted.

RECORDS MANAGEMENT AND RECORDS DISPOSITION

In 1952 the general assembly provided $48,000 for a survey of records and record-keeping practices of the state government, and Records Engineering, Inc., was employed to make the survey, with a special commission, of which the Archivist was chairman, appointed by the Governor to act as liaison. As a result of this study the Records Management Act was passed in 1953 instructing each state agency to develop a records management program and establish retention and disposal schedules. The Hall of Records Commission was given general supervisory control over the program, and a Records Management Division was established in the commission to take over this work. The division inspects record-keeping practices in all state agencies and advises them on records procedures, filing systems, record systems, record-keeping and duplicating equipment, and, on request, on design and control of forms. In order to insure the destruction of records scheduled for disposal, the re-use of equipment thus released, and the suitability of new equipment requested, the division reviews requests to the Department of Budget and Procurement for the purchase or rental of record equipment, services, and space for record storage. On request, advice to the Comptroller of the Treasury

---

[120] Morris L. Radoff's "A Guide to Practical Calendaring," *American Archivist*, XI (Apr., 1948), 123–40, and "A Practical Guide to Calendaring," *ibid.* (July, 1948), 203–22, are important by-products of this great calendaring venture.

is given on proposed expenditures by counties for record equipment, supplies, and services in the offices of registers of wills and clerks of court. The Records Management Division prepares inventories and schedules — and they are of high quality — providing detailed information concerning the content and use of the series described. Where applicable, schedules indicate what series are to be microfilmed and at what time this will be done, and, in the case of series of records eligible for retention in the Hall of Records, those parts of the series already in its custody are identified. During fiscal 1962 eighteen schedules controlling 126 series, sixteen of them revisions of State Roads Commission schedules, were prepared.

The Hall of Records offers advice and assistance through the Records Management Division to county officials on all phases of record-keeping and duplicating equipment, and from time to time on the use of space, air-conditioning, fire prevention, and vault construction. Participation by local agencies is voluntary, but increasingly the assistance of the Hall of Records is being sought in controlling record growth, providing adequate storage, and insuring disposal of useless records while assuring the preservation of those with permanent value. The records of the city of Rockville have been surveyed and scheduled and those of the city of Cumberland will be done next. In 1962 the application of schedules to the records of state, county, and municipal agencies released 9,479 cubic feet of storage space on agency premises.

There are two records centers, one at Baltimore and one at Annapolis, both ideally located in basement areas of the respective state office buildings and both having offices, research rooms, and stack areas with a combined storage capacity of 18,543 cubic feet, of which 12,745 cubic feet are used. All the holdings are scheduled. The centers are air-conditioned and have smoke-detector and fire-warning systems. In 1962 the two centers handled 109 requests for information and 2,092 requests for the loan of record units or films.

In order to provide the Commissioner of the Land Office with microcopies of currently recorded county land records, as required by chapter 504, Acts of 1949, a microfilm division was established in the Hall of Records in 1952 and was placed in the Records Management Division in 1953. Besides supervising the microfilming of all current county deeds, mortgages, and releases of mortgages, inspecting the film, delivering it to the Commissioner, and providing positive copies of deeds of certain counties to the Department of Assessments and Taxation for tax map purposes, the unit provides microfilm services to state agencies and advises and assists them in setting up their own programs. Three cameras are owned by the division and operated by two full-time operators. Commercial developing is used. Four hundred reels of 16-mm. and five reels of 35-mm. film are produced each year. In 1962 the unit exposed 1,391,611 images for state agencies.

Chapter 825, Acts of 1941, provides that, if the Hall of Records Commission declines to accept records offered for permanent preservation, they may be destroyed with the written consent of the Board of Public Works. Lists of records destroyed are to be filed with the Archivist, and no records less than five years old, permanent books of account, records of courts of record, or records required by law to be kept permanently may be destroyed. In 1949 the retention period was reduced to three years, scheduled disposal was authorized, and the destruction of non-record material by the custodian without the consent of either the Hall of Records or the Board of Public Works was provided for (Acts, 1949, ch. 755). The Attorney General had ruled consistently that microfilm copies of records required by law to be kept permanently might not be substituted for the originals and the originals destroyed. Chapter 82, Acts of 1956, removed this block to disposal by providing that certain records that were required to be maintained might be microfilmed and the originals might then be destroyed.

At the request of the Board of Public Works, attention is being given to the preservation of records essential to the continuity of government, and consequently the process of microfilming county records has been accelerated. Some agencies have deposited security copies of records in the Hall of Records, while the Department of Health is storing, in one of the state hospitals, copies of vital statistics, which are being filmed as they are received. In the future, the services of a commercial company providing suitable accommodations may be used for the storage of security copies of essential records.

COMMENTS

1. Co-operating with other agencies of the government, the Hall of Records should accelerate the program aimed at the identification and safeguarding of records essential to the continuity of government.

2. The Hall of Records has only a limited number of records of the general assembly, namely, the proceedings of the House and Senate and the recorded and engrossed laws. It might consider acquiring other legislative material, such as petitions to the general assembly and committee records, insofar as they exist and can be obtained.

MASSACHUSETTS

Although in size and importance the archival heritage of Massachusetts exceeds that of many other states of the Union, the state now ranks low in respect to arrangements for the care and preservation of its valuable records.

Chapter II, Section IV, Article II, of the Massachusetts constitution of 1780 made the Secretary of the Commonwealth, successor to the Provincial Secretary under the Royal Charter, the custodian of the commonwealth's records. Bound by the same article of the constitution to "attend the Governor and Council, the senate and house of representatives," the Secretary concentrated in his office the records of the General Court from the inception of the colony, and accordingly the legislature took considerable interest in their maintenance. In 1821 it required the Secretary to report on their condition, and in 1826 it appointed a committee to examine into the records in the Secretary's office. Its report and that of a later committee prompted the legislature to authorize "a fireproof edifice to be erected on the northern front of the State House . . . best calculated for the safe-keeping of the records and papers of the Commonwealth." This building, actually an extension of the State House at Boston, was constructed in 1831, at a cost of $6,919.33, and contained "four rooms for the safe-keeping of the records and papers . . . vaulted with brick. . . ."[121]

One of the first fireproof installations in the United States, the structure was removed when work was started on the north extension of the State House, and the holdings were shifted to far less adequate rooms in the main building. Before that happened, however, the early records, the so-called Massachusetts archives, had been rearranged (1836–45) by the Reverend Joseph B. Felt, forced into a system of his making, and bound in 328 folio volumes. Interest in the archives manifested itself again when an 1884 resolve, chapter 60, of the legislature empowered the Governor to appoint a commission of five persons including the Secretary of the Commonwealth to investigate the condition of the records in the Secretary's department. While accepting scholarly criticism of Felt's work, the commission found the records in as good a condition as could be expected, considering the facilities and help available to the Secretary.[122]

Except that the title of the head of the Archives was changed from Third Clerk in the Secretary's office to Chief of the Archives Division (Acts, 1897, ch. 351), the status of the Archives and the scope of its responsibility remained unchanged; that is, it served as the depository for the records of the Secretary's department, the council, and the legislature. In the late 1930's the Chief's position began to be filled with political appointees, unable to do justice to their duties. Now chapter 18, Acts of 1962, stipulates that the Chief of the Archives Division shall be "a qualified archivist and shall be known as the Archivist of the Commonwealth." Furthermore,

[121] John H. Edmonds, *The Massachusetts Archives* (Worcester, 1922), p. 18. This is a reprint from American Antiquarian Society, *Proceedings* (Apr., 1922).

[122] Commissioners Appointed under Resolve, ch. 60, 1884, *Report to the Legislature of Massachusetts, Jan., 1885* (Boston, 1885), 42 p.

chapter 427, Acts of 1962, establishing the Records Conservation Board, in addition to setting up procedures for the disposal of records, provides "for the transfer to the archives, in whole or in part, of public records no longer needed for current business." It thus potentially transforms the Archives Division of the Secretary of the Commonwealth into the state's general archives. The 1963 legislature created a special commission to study the records laws of the state (Resolves, 1963, ch. 60).

THE ARCHIVES DIVISION OF THE OFFICE OF THE SECRETARY
OF THE COMMONWEALTH

In 1961–62 the sum of $61,819 was appropriated for the division. Its budget is prepared by the Secretary of the Commonwealth in consultation with the Chief of the Archives Division; reviewed by the Bureau of the Budget, which is part of the Executive Office of Administration and Finance; and forwarded to the House, which sends it to the Committee on Ways and Means.

All positions on the Archives Division staff, except that of the Chief, are under the state's civil service system. Present salaries of the professional personnel are as follows: $6,331 for the Chief of the Archives Division and Archivist of the Commonwealth, $7,891 for the Curator of the Archives, and $5,369 for a principal archival assistant. A photoduplication clerk receives $6,825. At present there are eleven persons in the division, including clerks, clerk-typists, and photographers. A revision of the salary arrangement seems in order.

For many years the division occupied wholly unsuitable premises on the fourth floor and in the basement of the State House. In 1957 the legislature appropriated $1,005,000 for planning, constructing, and equipping a three-story depository for the Archives Division, its museum, and the State Library. The division uses one large area on the street level for the museum and the lower of the two underground vaults for storage purposes. The vault has a storage capacity of 41,500 cubic feet, of which 38,500 cubic feet are already in use. Records are still housed in one of the old offices on the fourth floor and in another storeroom. A room on the first floor near the museum serves inadequately as a combined research room and office for some of the staff. The vault is furnished with steel cabinets and steel drawers for folded documents, a wholly unnecessary expense. In fact, the entire installation disregards modern requirements for the housing of archives. Even if the Archives Division were to acquire the vault now used by the State Library, it would have to rely on the use of office space in the State House once it began to take over sizable accessions from state agencies.

The Archives Division is still essentially the depository for the records of the Secretary of the Commonwealth, the legislature, and the council.

The Treasury records, dating from 1657 and measuring at least seventy-five linear feet, which the division acquired recently, constitute the first large accession of departmental records outside the Archives' original field of competence. In the past, accessions amounted only to a trickle. This may change when the law establishing the Records Conservation Board has had its effects. Present practice is to keep two accession books, one for proclamations and one for other accessions. Accessions are not numbered.

There is no guide to the holdings of the Archives Division. For the "Massachusetts archives," a so-called "calendar" on cards, with cross-references, has been in progress over a long period of time. Only about one-fourth of the job has been done. An index to the "Court Records," 1692–1833, is being created.

Research room arrangements are inadequate, since users share a moderately large office with some of the division's personnel. About 3,000 reels of microfilm and 5,000 other items are used in the 2,700 visits to the research room each year. Some 1,500 reference letters are written annually, and no form letters are used.

Under the new law (Acts, 1962, ch. 18), the Archivist of the Commonwealth is instructed to prepare material for publication as directed by the Secretary of the Commonwealth. He is also to supervise the operation of the Archives Museum, opened on September 14, 1961, and this consumes much of his time, since the museum is a station on the "Freedom Trail" for Boston tourists. The Chief of the Archives Division believes that in a given year the museum will be visited by 8,000 persons in groups and 2,000 individuals. Because the bulky supporting columns obstruct the view, effective guarding of the museum is difficult.

Formerly the Emery silk method was used for restoring documents. At present, the division has neither staff nor up-to-date equipment for the purpose. On the other hand, it has good facilities for photographic reproduction: two photostat machines, a planetary and two flow cameras, a heat process Kalvar printer for producing positive film from negative film, and two reader-printers.

RECORDS MANAGEMENT AND RECORDS DISPOSITION

After chapter 104 of the Resolves of 1955 had authorized the Secretary of the Commonwealth to conduct a survey for the purpose of recommending a uniform records management program for the state and for counties, cities, towns, and districts in Massachusetts, a survey confined to state records was made by Leahy and Company. It had no immediate effects. In the latter part of 1957, the Commissioner of Administration directed his Management Improvement Section to undertake a records management study, and accordingly analysts from that office inventoried the records of many state agencies. Also, in 1958, a records center was established on the grounds of the Norfolk Correctional Institution. After two years the program began to slow down, for the personnel assigned to it was shifted to the fields of systems analysis, budget analysis, and other general management areas.

In the first two years of the program, 15,000 cubic feet of inactive records were accessioned by the center, a former dormitory. It is now filled to capacity, but only 10 per cent of the records are under schedule control. One person is stationed at the center to handle reference requests of agencies. In all probability, the building will have to be returned to the prison authorities within a year's time.

Chapter 757, Acts of 1962, established in the Executive Office of Administration and Finance, formerly the Commission on Administration and Finance, a Central Services Commission; this in due time may revitalize the records management program.

Under chapter 30, section 52, of the General Laws, Annotated, obsolete records could be destroyed with the approval of a board composed of the State Librarian or his delegate, an Assistant Attorney General designated by the Attorney General, the Supervisor of Public Records, and the Chairman of the Commission on Administration and Finance or his representative. This section has been replaced by section 2 of chapter 427, Acts of 1962. It creates the Records Conservation Board, consisting of the State Librarian, the Attorney General, the State Auditor, the Chief of the Archives Division, who is to be the board's secretary, and the Supervisor of Public Records, or persons designated by them.

Said board shall have power to require all departments of the Commonwealth to report to it what series of public records they hold, to set standards for the management and preservation of such records, and to establish standards for the destruction, in whole or in part, and transfer to the archives, in whole or in part, of public records no longer needed for current business. Nothing in this section shall affect judicial or legislative records, lessen the existing powers of the commission on administration and finance, or compel any department, division or commission to surrender public records it deems of current use.

As already provided in the old law, disposal of records is preceded by a brief description of them published at least thirty days earlier in a Boston daily; and, upon petition of twenty-five or more citizens, a public hearing must be held for all persons interested.

THE LOCAL RECORDS PROGRAM

As early as 1639 the General Court of Massachusetts Colony ruled that

. . . henceforward, every judgment, with all the evidence, be recorded in a book, to be kept to posterity. Item, that there be records kept of all wills, administration, and inventories; as also of the days of every marriage, birth, and death of every person within the jurisdiction. Item, to record all men's houses and lands, being certified under the hands of the men of every town, deputed for the ordering of their affairs.

At various times during the nineteenth century the legislature passed acts requiring fireproof protection for local records. A petition of prominent persons of the state, in 1884, obtained passage of a resolve calling upon Governor and council to appoint a person "who should report to the next legislature upon the condition of the public records of the parishes, towns, and counties of the commonwealth." [123] A further resolve of 1889 extended the appointment for three years, and in 1892 it was made permanent. The duties and authority of the Commissioner of Public Records and the responsibilities of the local custodians were defined by chapter 437 of the Acts of 1897 and more fully by chapter 485, Acts of 1913. Chapter 350, General Acts of 1919, Part III, section 24, abolished the position of Commissioner of Public Records and gave his duties to the Secretary of the Commonwealth, who was to appoint a Supervisor of Public Records. His duties are governed by chapter 66, General Laws of Massachusetts, Annotated.

Under the several capable commissioners the acts of 1897 and 1913 provided excellent care for the local records of the state. They required the use of ink and paper of specified quality in record-making, restoration of worn records, storage of records in fireproof facilities or safes, and formal surrender of records by the retiring officer to his successor. As a result, many new fireproof buildings were erected and old ones remodeled, fireproof safes were purchased, decaying records were repaired and rebound, and recording was done on durable paper with non-fading inks and ribbons, all of which served the purpose of "bringing the records into prominence, and making them of the importance with which they ought to be regarded." [124] Regulations were enforced through periodic inspection and through fines of from twenty to fifty dollars for violations and additional fines of twenty dollars per month of non-compliance.

Long the pride of Massachusetts and the envy of other states, the program lost much of its strength after its administration was turned over to the Supervisor of Public Records, an official in the office of the Secretary of the Commonwealth. The Supervisor no longer visits cities and towns at regular intervals to enforce regulations. His work consists mainly in approving proposals for the destruction of records and for the installation of vaults. Other duties imposed upon him [125] prevent the Supervisor from

[123] For the history of the local records program, see Robert T. Swan, "The Massachusetts Public Record Commission and Its Work," *Annual Report of the American Historical Association for the Year 1901*, I (Washington, 1902), 95–112; and Henry E. Woods, *The Massachusetts Laws and Commission of Public Records* (Boston, 1910).

[124] Woods, *op. cit.*

[125] Chapter 9, section 4, General Laws, Annotated, states that the "Supervisor, under the supervision of the secretary, shall perform the duties required of him, by law, and such other duties as the secretary determines."

administering the law vigorously and assisting towns and cities in solving their records management problems. A few towns have developed disposal schedules. Others have done some microfilming without reporting it to the Supervisor.

COMMENTS

1. If the Archives Division of the Secretary of the Commonwealth is to develop into a general state archives, it will need, in addition to its unsuitable new installation in the State House, expanded facilities, an increase of its staff, and an improved pay scale.

2. The local records program should be revitalized and possibly placed under the Archives of the Commonwealth to provide greater unity of action.

3. The state records management program should be fully reactivated. Also, it would be appropriate to transfer retention and disposal scheduling to the Archives Division, if it can obtain the necessary funds and staff.

4. A new records center must be provided.

MICHIGAN

Only in recent years has Michigan taken steps to provide for the effective management of its records and archives. The legislation adopted and the administrative arrangements made to implement it have been of considerable interest to other states of the Middle West and are likely to influence their future action.

BACKGROUNDS

No provision had been made for the preservation of Michigan's archives until in 1913 the legislature passed Act No. 271, creating the Michigan Historical Commission of six members appointed by the Governor. The law authorized the commission to collect historical material of all kinds and enjoined all public officials to assist it in acquiring non-current records not less than thirty years old that were of historical value. The staff of the commission, consisting of the Executive Secretary-Editor, a Museum Curator, an Archivist, assistant editors, and clerical help, was to operate in the State Library, which had already outgrown its quarters in Lansing. The commission's archival program lapsed during the depression and World War II, even though a 1943 amendment to the act of 1913 required agency heads to submit lists of non-current records not less than ten years old to the commission so that it might requisition those of historical value.

In 1951 a fire in the State Office Building and the water used to fight it destroyed or damaged many valuable records. Together with the recommendations of a National Records Management Council study — "Operation Red Tape," which had been authorized in 1949 — this disaster dramatically reversed the state's attitude toward the care of its records. The legislature passed a comprehensive state records act (Acts, 1952, No. 178), which gave broad authority to the Department of Administration to conduct a records management program but which continued the archival responsibility of the Historical Commission. The commission benefited directly from the records management program, however, because it received space for its holdings in the new records center built in 1954. More recently Act No. 68, Public Acts of 1959, gave the commission authority to take over county and local as well as state records.

Since the new constitution, which became effective January 1, 1964, limits to twenty the number of executive departments — excluding those of the Governor, the Lieutenant Governor, and institutions of higher learning — the Michigan Historical Commission will probably lose its independent status.

THE ARCHIVES PROGRAM

The Michigan State Archives Division is under the Historical Commission. The Chief, Division of Archives, reports to the Executive Secretary–Editor of the commission, as do the heads of its other divisions. The Executive Secretary prepares the commission's budget, based on the adjusted budget proposals of the divisions. Except for salaries ($40,728 in 1963–64), the expenses for the Archives Division cannot be separated from the total budget of the commission.

The Archives Division has a staff of three professional and two clerical workers. Professional salaries and civil service titles are as follows:

Chief (Archivist III A) .... $7,475–$9,563
Research Archivist (Archivist III A)[126]........................ 7,475– 9,563
Reference Archivist (Archives Executive II) 5,742– 7,224

Staff members are under the state civil service system and enjoy salary increases in five steps plus longevity pay after five years of service. Article XI, section 6, of the new constitution reduces the power of the Civil Service Commission in relation to the executive and the legislature.

The Archives Division is rapidly running out of space, and this shortage will soon be its greatest problem. It needs a new facility with a regular research room, temperature and humidity controls, and a fumigating vault. There is ample space to build an archives repository adjacent to the present records center.

The deficiency of space in the Archives may be slightly bettered by the provisions of Act No. 68, Public Acts of 1959. While stating the power of the Historical Commission "to collect from the public offices in the state, including state, county, city, village, and township offices, such records,

[126] At present the Research Archivist is in charge of historic sites and editorial work under the Executive Secretary of the commission.

files, documents books and papers as are not in current use, and are of value in the opinion of the commission," the act authorizes the commission to place such material in "a public institution having a fireproof building and suitable arrangements for carefully keeping" it. On the basis of this authorization, a system of depositories for local records is being developed, and the first regional depository agreement has been signed with Western Michigan University. A budget for a "Local Records Section" of the Archives Division was not adopted.

As of June 30, 1963, the Archives Division held 2,972 cubic feet of records. These consisted of the permanent records of all agencies of the state, four cities, four townships, and fifteen counties; some private papers; 3,797 reels of microfilm; and an excellent collection (55,141 items) of photographs, received from official as well as from private sources. A summary statement prepared at the end of the calendar year and entitled "Permanent Records of All Units of Michigan Government" lists the records of state agencies and local government units on hand, with an indication of the dates covered and the quantities received (typewritten report, June 30, 1963, 5 p.). An up-to-date conspectus of all holdings is thus readily available. Missing from them are the official records (1949–60) of Governor G. Mennen Williams, which, together with his private papers, he has given to the Michigan Historical Collections at Ann Arbor.[127] An Attorney General's opinion (No. 3590, Nov. 14, 1962) ruled that only the Department of Administration could initiate action to recover these records; that they would then be returned to the office of the Governor; and that the Historical Commission could then obtain them only by refusing to authorize a disposal request from that office.

Except for early Governors' records that were reorganized according to Cassius C. Stiles's Iowa subject classification,[128] records are left strictly in their original arrangement. Besides a control file consisting of cards for all state agencies, counties, cities, and townships that have released records to the archives, and a file of "records progress cards" that keeps track of records from the time of first contact with an agency through their accessioning, the Archives Division uses the inventorying procedure of the National Archives. Accessions, somewhat misleadingly called record groups, are described in inventories each of which consists of an administrative history, series-by-series descriptions, and sometimes a container list.[129] These accession inventories will be combined into complete agency

[127] Ruth B. Bordin, "Michigan — the G. Mennen Williams Papers," *American Archivist*, XXVI (July, 1963), 345–54. The article includes extracts from the opinion of Frank J. Kelley of November 14, 1962 (Opinion No. 3590), upholding the legality of the Governor's action.

[128] See Philip P. Mason, "Report on the Archives of the Historical Commission," *Michigan History*, XXXIX (June, 1955), 221–32.

[129] For example, *Finding Aids No. 3* and *No. 4* are for the Girls' Training School, Adrian, Michigan, 1880–1941, and the Michigan State Planning Commission, 1934–56.

inventories once retention and disposal schedules have become available. Some inventories have been made generally available through near-print publication.

The photograph collection has its own elaborate card catalog. Its contents are briefly described in *A Guide to Photographic Resources in the Michigan Historical Commission Archives* (Lansing, 1960; 8 p., proc.).

During the first six months of 1963 the Archives Division handled 408 letters and 77 telephone inquiries involving the use of archival materials, and 250 visitors consulted 1,019 record items.

The Archives Division has made its services known through a flyer entitled *Introducing the Michigan Historical Archives.* The division also installs exhibits, holds open house and all-day conferences about its activities, and assists in the distribution of the many publications of the Historical Commission, such as *Michigan History,* service-type bulletins, and booklets. The annual reports of the commission, published until 1961 in the December issue of *Michigan History,* do not separate the activities of the Archives Division from other functions of the commission.

RECORDS MANAGEMENT AND RECORDS DISPOSITION

In fiscal 1962–63 the sum of $66,027 was budgeted for the records center, which is in the Office Services Division of the Department of Administration.[130] The center is staffed with twelve persons, four of whom are professional — the Records Center Supervisor and the three administrative analysts. Present salaries range from $9,423 for the supervisor to $4,212 for a typist. The budget is a separate part of the budget of the Department of Administration, Office Services Division.

All staff members are under the state's civil service system,[131] have duties defined in job descriptions, and enjoy the same protection and benefits as those of the Archives Division.

The aims of the records management program are: (1) to develop procedures for, and give assistance to, agencies in the examination and appraisal of records systems; (2) to establish facilities and procedures for the systematic retention, reference, and disposal of records; and (3) to provide safeguards against the destruction or loss of records that have legal value or that have been deemed appropriate for preservation by the Historical Commission. In order to implement this program, the Department of Administration envisaged the following stages: (1) establishment of a state records center; (2) disposal of useless papers; (3) transfer of inactive and semi-active records by the agencies to the center; (4) processing of retention and disposal schedules; (5) prompt and efficient reference service to the agencies of the state government.

[130] The budget recommendation for fiscal 1964 calls for $68,900 for the records management program.
[131] State of Michigan, Civil Service Commission, *Rules* (1959), 61 p.

Under the program [132] agency records officers prepare inventories of the records in agency custody, draft retention and disposal schedules with the assistance of the records center staff, and, once these are approved, get the material ready for disposal or transfer to the center. Procedures are clearly outlined in the department's *Administrative Manual*, chapter 6, section 2, subjects 01-03, entitled, respectively, "State Records Center — General Information," "Establishing Retention Periods for State Records," and "Transfer of Records to the State Records Center."

In addition to offering storage facilities and reference service on records stored, the center staff has conducted surveys or studies in major departments, such as the Highway Department, the Department of Conservation, and the Department of Health. These surveys have been undertaken in order to establish retention and disposal schedules; to analyze filing systems; to recommend better methods in creating records systems; to institute better procedures in forms controls; and to promote more efficient methods in processing records.

The records center is a rectangle 100 by 215 feet with a smaller rectangle 40 by 138 feet attached, which houses the archives. There are 94,000 cubic feet of shelf space, of which 4,600 are assigned to the Historical Commission. Of the 89,400 left to the center, 80,100 are in use. It is the depository for all semi-active records, whether ultimately destined for destruction or for the Archives. It was constructed at a cost of about $300,000, including equipment; this sum was appropriated at the 1953 session of the legislature. The activity of the center is illustrated by the following figures:

Year	References	Material Received (cu. ft.)	Material Destroyed (cu. ft.)
1955–56	10,647	6,834	2,929
1956–57	14,480	11,881	7,409
1957–58	20,910	12,706	7,929
1958–59	25,618	10,736	6,487
1959–60	25,214	10,555	6,871
1960–61	25,950	13,383	8,631
1962–63	33,562	11,601	8,856

The center also serves as a central microfilming facility, although some departments whose work load justifies it are permitted to do their own microfilming. The program, started in 1956, microfilms records for the state agencies at cost. It has three microfilm cameras and three operators, produces approximately 1,500 reels of 16-mm. and 600 reels of 35-mm.

[132] Its evolution is well told by P. R. Peck, Deputy Controller, State Department of Administration, in a lecture given in the Michigan records management training program entitled "Organization of the State Record Program in Michigan" (May 20, 1958), 9 p., proc.

images each year, and does its own developing. For making photostat copies, the facilities of the University of Michigan are used.

Both the records center staff and the Archives Division are involved in the disposal of state records, which is governed by Act 178 of the Public Acts of 1952. The procedure followed involves the following steps: Agencies with the assistance of the records center staff prepare disposal schedules or, where appropriate, disposal lists in accordance with the *Administrative Manual*, chapter 6, section 2, subject 03. Retention periods on the schedules submitted are examined by the Auditor-General's Department, by the Attorney General's Department, and finally by the Historical Commission, which designates and takes possession of the records to be retained for historical purposes. On the basis of the recommendations of these three agencies, all retention schedules are finally approved or disapproved by the State Administrative Board, consisting of the eight elected officials of the state. This very elaborate procedure should provide all possible safeguards against wanton destruction of valuable records.

LOCAL PROGRAM

At present the Archives Division is principally concerned with the records management problems of local government. An earlier act (Public Acts, 1955, No. 59) required local units to present to the Historical Commission disposal schedules or lists of records deemed useless, whereupon the commission was to select those it considered of value. Actually the State Archivist travels about the state, examining records both current and non-current, and assists the local units in preparing lists and schedules. Retention and disposal schedules for counties, municipalities, and school districts are being developed on a statewide basis. The Archivist has also drafted a *Local Records Manual* (15 p. plus appendixes), which has been submitted to local officials for their comments.

In a memorandum dated May 10, 1962, the Archivist proposed establishing a local records program. The commission has adopted the idea of a decentralized program under which local records of value will be deposited "in an existing depository in a defined region." In a further memorandum dated May 28, 1962, the Archivist proposed establishing a local records section to assist local units in records retention and disposal. This would have required a special appropriation for fiscal 1964 of $28,586.80, which failed to pass.

COMMENTS

1. The internal operations of the Archives Division of the Michigan Historical Commission have much to recommend them. Control of holdings by means of finding aids is virtually complete.

2. The Archives Division lacks almost everything that a modern archi-

val agency should have: adequate storage and office space with humidity and temperature controls, a research room, a fumigating vault, and laminating equipment. To provide all these facilities a new archives building is needed. It might best be erected adjacent to the present records center.

MINNESOTA

Operating under the State Archives Commission, the State Archives and Records Service is charged with responsibility for records management as well as archival administration.

BACKGROUNDS

The Minnesota Historical Society was the first archival agency of the state. It received its charter from the first territorial legislature in 1849, was given a room in the Capitol in 1855, and in 1856 received its first annual appropriation. The first Capitol burned in 1881; state functions outgrew the second; and the Historical Society, along with other state agencies, moved into the third in 1905.

In 1914 Herbert A. Kellar reported to the Public Archives Commission of the American Historical Association that most of the state's records were still in existence but that they had suffered losses owing to the fire of 1881, to general carelessness, and to removal by some officials who had considered them as their personal property. Most of the extant records, he felt, were in danger from possible fire and water.[133]

One year earlier the legislature had appropriated $500,000 — and the society had contributed $75,000 for land and equipment — for a Historical Building in St. Paul that was to house the society, the State Library, and the Supreme Court. In 1915, when it appeared that the Supreme Court would remain in the Capitol, the appropriation act for the society, at the recommendation of Solon J. Buck, Superintendent of the society, was amended to include the words "care, preservation and protection of the State Archives." This made the society the potential custodian of state records. In 1919 it received formal authority to take over records, both state and local.[134]

Although the deposit of obsolete records with the Historical Society was not mandatory, many agencies took advantage of the opportunity to transfer considerable quantities of material to the society. Since the society, however, had no funds for screening, arranging, and describing the accessions, they were simply stored in whatever containers they arrived in. They were never intermingled with the society's collections of private papers.

[133] "A Preliminary Survey of the More Important Archives of the Territory and State of Minnesota," *Annual Report of the American Historical Association for the Year 1914*, I (Washington, 1916), 390.

[134] Robert M. Brown, "The Development of an Archival Program in Minnesota," *American Archivist*, XVI (Jan., 1953), 40.

Chapter 553, Laws of 1941, authorized the society to dispose of records more than six years old and having no legal, administrative, or historical value, and required it to pass on disposal requests of the agencies. The society, however, found it impossible to carry out its mandate, for it received no funds for the purpose.

House Resolution No. 9 of April 20, 1943, created the Interim Committee on State Administration and Employment, which made its report in 1944.[135] Finding the agencies burdened with 9,865 file drawers of records only occasionally used and with 6,592 file drawers of records never used, the committee concluded that the state needed a workable disposal law "and that the Historical Society, which is the final administrative authority of chapter 553, Laws of 1941 . . . is not equipped to carry out the provisions of the law," under which "no department can be forced to destroy useless records." The committee recommended the creation of an Archives Commission to "properly safeguard the preservation of essential records and supervise the destruction of useless records." The Archives Act (Laws, 1947, ch. 547) did create the Minnesota State Archives Commission as an independent agency and gave it custody of the state's archives, although physically they remained in the sub-basement, unfinished rooms, and stack areas of the society's building. Pressed with requests for the disposal of records, the commission could not give its attention to the archives, until in November, 1950, a professional archivist was employed to begin work on making them accessible.

Chapter 184 of the Laws of 1955 transferred responsibility for local records from the society to the State Archives Commission, and then the Historical Society had no further responsibility for public records except that archival holdings were still stored in its building. In 1960, however, larger quarters were obtained in the former Ford Motor Company assembly plant close to the Capitol and the Historical Building. There the archives could be moved and a records center could be opened. Finally, an act of 1961 (Minnesota Statutes 138.13–138.24) clarified the commission's authority with regard to local records and created the position of State Archivist and Records Administrator, and chapter 675 of 1963 directed him to conduct a records management program. Thus evolved the present archives and records management program of the state of Minnesota. With some minor exceptions, the powers of the State Archives Commission extend to all public records of the state.

THE STATE ARCHIVES COMMISSION

The State Archives Commission is composed of the Commissioner of Administration as chairman, the State Auditor, the Attorney General, the

[135] Dec., 1944, proc., 101 + 2 p. "One agency stated [to the committee] that they were keeping all their records for sentimental reasons."

Public Examiner, and the Director of the Minnesota Historical Society. The State Archives and Records Service [136] is under the jurisdiction of the commission and is headed by the State Archivist and Records Administrator. Working closely with the chairman, the Archivist prepares disposal requests and other pertinent matters for the commission's action and records the minutes of the commission's meetings.

The State Archives Commission had a budget of $129,154 for the 1963–65 biennium.

All the personnel of the State Archives and Records Service are classified under the Minnesota civil service system. They are the State Archivist and Records Administrator ($8,328–$10,128); the Assistant Archivist ($6,072–$7,392); an Archives Assistant, classified as Clerk III ($4,272–$5,196), who services the records center; a Documents Restorer ($5,196–$6,312); two clerks ($3,504–$4,272), and a Microfilm Supervisor ($4,620–$5,616), who is assisted by two clerks ($3,372–$4,104).

Both the State Archives and the records center are housed in the substantial Ford Motor Company building at 117 University Avenue in St. Paul, which had been adapted to office use before they moved in. Besides space on the first floor used for receiving and fumigating records, the State Archives has the second floor for office use, storage of records, and laminating and microfilming facilities. The archival storage area, not all of which is equipped with steel shelving, now has a capacity of 15,000 cubic feet. The records center, on the third floor, has a capacity of 18,000 cubic feet, 15,000 of which are in use.

THE ARCHIVES FUNCTION

The State Archives holds 15,000 cubic feet of official territorial and state records and of certain county and municipal records. There are the records of the decennial state censuses, 1865–1905, and those of the 1880 federal census. The 1850, 1860, and 1870 federal census records for Minnesota and the records of the U.S. census of Minnesota Territory, 1857, are on indefinite loan to the Minnesota Historical Society.

Accessions are numbered and entered in a book. There is no list of the holdings, most of which are unarranged. In fact, no arrangement work has been done since 1955, and a good deal of material has not been unpacked since it was taken over from the Historical Society. The explanation is that the only two professional staff members — the State Archivist and the Assistant Archivist — are so deeply involved in inventorying and scheduling the current records that there is nobody available to work on the archives. As a result the archival holdings are practically inaccessible for scholarly research, except for the official papers of the Governors before 1930, which are covered by an inventory.

[136] Robert M. Brown, "Minnesota — the State Archives and Records Service Reconsidered," *American Archivist*, XXVI (July, 1963), 355–60.

During the year ending June 30, 1963, some 1,500 letters or form letters were written in response to requests for information involving consultation of finding aids or records, 300 form letters were written in response to such requests but not involving consultation of finding aids or records, and there were about 400 visits to the search room involving consultation of 3,500 records including microfilm. A fee of $1.50 is charged for an original search of the census records and for a certification from them.

Although some local records have found their way into the State Archives, the local archives problem remains to be attacked. The State Archivist feels that ultimately half a dozen regional depositories might be established for their preservation and that the state should move into a local microfilming program.

RECORDS MANAGEMENT AND RECORDS DISPOSITION

A records management program is being initiated under chapter 675, Laws of 1963, which directs the Archives Commission to administer a program of paperwork management — from creation to disposition of public records. The commission now offers advice to state and local agencies on filing procedures, filing equipment, permanent ink and papers, and related matters. It is not advertising this service, however, because of the shortage of personnel, and it concentrates on the scheduling of records. The Budget Division of the Department of Administration consults the State Archivist whenever agencies request new filing equipment.

The records center is in full operation. Only semi-current records with fixed retention periods are eligible for storage. Inventories are prepared in the agencies, with practically all the work being done by the Archives staff; and retention and disposal schedules are approved by agency heads and the Archives Commission.

Records in the center are arranged for rapid reference and are available to agency personnel and, with the permission of the agency concerned, to searchers. From February, 1960, through August 24, 1962, reference service requests amounted to 14,000. Agencies may make requests for service by telephone, and hourly inter-office mail delivers the records that have been asked for. The records center staff checks on the frequency of use of the records stored there.

The State Archivist also offers advice to local government units concerning their records management problems and assists them in the preparation of inventories and schedules. No microfilming of local records has been done by the Utah Genealogical Society. Local units that wish to microfilm their records for security purposes may turn to the State Archivist for advice.

In Minnesota the preservation of records essential to the continuity of government has received considerable attention. After a study had revealed that only a small percentage of the records on hand was necessary for the continuity of government and the protection of its rights and those of the state's citizens, funds were requested for microfilming them in 1961. Although these funds were deleted from the budget proposal, two later emergency appropriations totaling $25,500 were granted, and the program is now under way with two operators and two cameras. Chapter 675, Laws of 1963, gave legal sanction to the program already begun and gave the Archives Commission supervisory authority over it. By August 15, 1962, certain series of the offices of the Governor, State Auditor, State Treasurer, and Attorney General and of the State Board of Investment had been filmed, and the master negatives had been placed in security storage at a state school and hospital. According to the State Archivist, the program has progressed more slowly than had been expected. Considerable delay is caused by the necessity of carrying records from the State Capitol to the State Archives, and this will be greater when records in other locations are to be filmed. Portable microfilm equipment is needed in order to film records *in situ*.

Minnesota Statutes 138.13–138.24 give the State Archives Commission final authority over destruction, photoreproduction, and storage of all public records of the state and its subdivisions, except those of the University of Minnesota, the Minnesota State Agriculture Society, the Minnesota Historical Society, the State Library, and the Supreme Court. The commission may hold hearings and subpoena witnesses and records. It has the power "to direct the destruction, the sale for salvage or disposition by gift or otherwise of public records . . . [and] may also cause any of such records to be reproduced by photographic or other means," and may direct the disposal of the originals.

Since its organization, the commission, by June 30, 1963, had acted on 1,097 disposal lists and schedules and thereby had cleared 251,652 cubic feet of records from state offices and storage rooms. As of the same date approximately 35,000 cubic feet of records, of a total of about 100,000 cubic feet in the Twin Cities, had been placed under schedule control.

Disposal requests and schedules are circulated among the members of the State Archives Commission for approval, and approval is confirmed at the commission's next meeting, at which time items of major importance are fully discussed and decided upon.[137]

COMMENTS

A potentially excellent program is severely handicapped by shortage of professional personnel, as a result of which work on the archival holdings

[137] The Director of this Study was privileged to attend, on August 29, 1962, a meeting of the State Archives Commission at which the disposition of certain files of the Rural Credit Office was discussed. Representatives of the office were present to explain the nature of the files and justify the disposal request they intended to make. The commission invited a disposal request, which was to include a list of the essential records to be retained.

has practically come to a standstill. The State Archives and Records Service needs at least two more professional staff members to organize, arrange, and inventory the state archives and to implement a local records program.

MISSISSIPPI

Profiting from the experience of the state of Alabama, Mississippi established its Department of Archives and History at Jackson in 1902. Conditions beyond the department's control have prevented it from effectively carrying out its archival mandate.

BACKGROUNDS

In 1897 Franklin L. Riley, who held a Ph.D. degree from the Johns Hopkins University, was appointed the first professor of history in the University of Mississippi. Through his efforts the defunct Mississippi Historical Society was resurrected, and two years later the society prevailed on the legislature to establish a Historical Commission similar to the one established in Alabama. As chairman of the commission, Riley in 1902 submitted a report urging the creation of a Department of Archives and History. A bill to that effect was enacted and was approved by the Governor on February 26, 1902.[138]

This act (Laws, 1902, ch. 52), which used the Alabama act as a model and which still governs the activities of the department, places it under a self-perpetuating Board of Trustees whose members, with the consent of the Senate, are elected for six-year terms. The board, said to be completely non-political, appoints the Director of the department for a six-year term. The objectives of the department are defined as follows:

. . . the care and custody of official archives, the collecting of materials bearing upon the history of the state and of the territory included therein, from the earliest times, the editing of official records and other historical materials, the diffusion of knowledge in reference to the history and resources of this state, the encouragement of historical work and research and the performance of such other acts and requirements as may be enjoined by law.

After the department had been moved into the New Capitol in 1903, Dunbar Rowland, its Director from March 15, 1902, to November 1, 1937, devoted his energies to assembling and arranging records and private papers. Ten years later he was able to publish *An Official Guide to the Historical Materials in the Mississippi Department of Archives and History*,[139]

[138] For the history of the department to 1948, see Wm. H. Weathersby, "The Preservation of Mississippi History," *North Carolina Historical Review*, V (Apr., 1928), 141–50; and William D. McCain, "History and Program of the Mississippi State Department of Archives and History," *American Archivist*, XIII (Jan., 1950), 27–34.

[139] This is published with the *Eleventh* and *Twelfth Annual Reports* of the Mississippi Department of Archives and History (Nashville, Tenn., 1914).

a remarkable achievement and probably the first such guide published in the United States. "After 1912 Rowland seemed to lose interest in acquiring State archives, private manuscripts, or printed materials, and in placing in order anything which drifted into the Department," [140] and engaged in a prolific program of publications. When Rowland's successor, William D. McCain, appraised the situation confronting the department, he was led to the following policy decisions:

1. Inasmuch as even in the War Memorial, to which the department was to move in 1941, no record accumulations of any size could be stored, only small and valuable groups of state records were to be accepted, "pending a solution of the space problem."

2. In the meantime, private manuscript holdings and the library were to be built up.

3. The museum of the department, on the first floor of the New Capitol, was to "remain in a dormant state" until the Old Capitol could be taken over for that purpose.

4. Money available for publication was to be used for buying equipment, books, and manuscripts, though the department began to reissue its *Biennial Report* and, within a year, to publish the *Journal of Mississippi History*.

Neither the legal basis on which the department operates nor its prerogatives have been changed significantly. Under chapter 161, Laws of 1938, it was made responsible for the protection of prehistoric and historic sites. In the field of records disposal, chapter 318, Laws of 1950, has given department heads the power to have records over six years old microfilmed by the State Board of Public Works and to destroy records after the Director of the Department of Archives and History has been given time to select for preservation any documents to be destroyed or to demand that additional reproductions be made for the department. A law of 1952 has empowered the State Board of Public Contracts to destroy records after six years *without* microfilming, provided that the Department of Archives and History gives its approval.

On the local level, county boards of supervisors were authorized by an act of 1950 (ch. 240) to microfilm and then destroy records six years old or over "except marriage licenses, registration books, and certain other books or records." [141]

THE DEPARTMENT OF ARCHIVES AND HISTORY

The department's governing body, the Board of Trustees, holds regular quarterly meetings and is said to give its full support to the Director of the agency. Under the Director, the department is organized into the follow-

[140] McCain, *loc. cit.*, p. 29.
[141] *Biennial Report, 1959–61*, p. 40.

ing divisions or units: Archives, Library, Historic Sites, Museum, Publications, and Photoduplication.

The biennial budget of the department is formulated by the Director and submitted to the Board of Trustees for approval. During the summer preceding the session of the legislature, the Director justifies the requests in hearings before the Commission on Budget and Accounting, which in turn makes its recommendations to the legislature. Normally the legislature appropriates what the commission recommends.

Biennial appropriations for the department, which in 1920–21 had amounted to $50,000, dropped to a low of $36,800 in 1930–31. They increased under Dr. McCain's directorship, and this upward trend has continued in recent years, as the following figures show:

	Biennial Appropriation
1950–51	$ 77,100
1956–57	87,820
1958–59	95,160
1960–61	249,095 [142]

The last and very much larger increase included the cost of installing the historical museum in the Old Capitol.

In the absence of a merit system, the department is free to hire staff members in accordance with existing job descriptions. Employees enjoy the benefits of the state's public employees' retirement system, old age and survivors insurance, and workmen's compensation. They are entitled to three weeks of annual leave.

For many years the salaries paid were pitiful. The department's Board of Trustees, referring to Dr. and Mrs. Rowland, complained to the Governor and legislature of the state: [143]

With all the Department's record of achievement the man and woman who made it were inadequately paid for their services. A living wage has never been granted. . . . They have trod the path of pain and struggle without a murmur.

Present salaries are:

Director of the Department	$9,000
Chief Curator of the Museum	8,000
Archivist	6,000
Research and Editorial Assistant	5,400
Librarian	3,720
Microfilmer	3,000
Microfilm Clerk [144]	2,700

[142] In addition to its regular appropriation for the last biennium, the department received $2,500 for the work of the Historical Commission, $20,000 for the Stonewall Jackson Memorial Fund, and $15,000 for the Civil War Memorial Fund.

[143] Mississippi Department of Archives and History, Board of Trustees, Statement and Recommendations (n.p., n.d.), p. 6. Rowland had received an average salary of $2,100 a year.

[144] The microfilm clerk gives some of his time to archival work

Of the fourteen professional and clerical employees of the department, ten have at least Bachelor's degrees. While salaries of the Director and the Curator are certainly not overly generous, there seems to be too large a gap between their pay and that of the professional staff members. Enthusiasm for the work of the department, however, and the fact that most of the employees are married women make it possible for the agency to retain competent personnel at lamentably low salaries.

Since 1941 the department has been housed in the War Memorial, which it shares with a number of veterans' organizations. The building, erected with $150,000 of state funds matched by a grant from the federal government, is badly in need of remodeling "so that Mississippi's archives may be protected from the hazards of fire, dampness, theft, insects and other threats of a poorly equipped archival establishment." [145] Offices and reading room are quite inadequate and stack and basement storage space are almost completely filled. Storage space could be increased if the department obtained funds to air-condition and equip the former Hall of Fame on the second floor, which became vacant when the department's museum was installed in the restored Old Capitol.

The department's Photoduplication Division has considerable equipment, including a photostat camera and two planetary and two 16-mm. rotary microfilm cameras, some of which it inherited in 1957–58 from the discontinued State Microfilm Department. The division films newspapers, which take up a great deal of storage space, census records, tax rolls, and Confederate military records. By the end of the 1959–61 biennium it had produced 3,250 reels of microfilm.

The State Historical Museum is an important and very popular division of the department. Housed in the splendidly restored Old Capitol and formally dedicated on June 3, 1961, it is under the care of a professional curator and archeologist. The sound policies that govern its administration and activities were formulated by the Director and adopted by the department's Board of Trustees in October, 1958.

In 1938 the Mississippi Historical Society was resuscitated through the efforts of the then Director. The present Director serves as secretary-treasurer of the society and editor-in-chief of its *Journal of Mississippi History*. The Director is also chairman of the State Historical Commission, established in 1948 and charged with marking historic sites and buildings, secretary-treasurer of the Stonewall Jackson Memorial Board, and a member of the Mississippi Commission on the War Between the States.

In addition to co-operating with the Mississippi Historical Society in publishing its *Journal*, the department has published folders such as *Re-*

[145] Mississippi Department of Archives and History, *Biennial Report, 1959–61*, p. 52. The basement walls must be waterproofed. Also, beneath the foundations, water is retained in the marl, which expands and contracts and causes the basement floor to buckle. Test pits in the basement show that the building is actually "floating" on water.

search in the Mississippi Department of Archives and History (11 p.,n.d.), and *Guide Lines for a Historical Society* (1962, proc.); and since March, 1959, it has issued the monthly *Mississippi History Newsletter* (1–2 p., proc.). The last two of these publications will aid the many local and specialized historical societies in the state. Also, *Mississippi in the Confederacy* (2 vols.; Baton Rouge: State University of Louisiana Press, 1961) has had the editorial care and supervision of the department's Director.

THE ARCHIVES FUNCTION

Because of the persistent shortage of stack space, complete concentration of the state's archives has not been possible. In fact, only a few major accessions have been brought in since 1912. Present holdings include: records of land titles and other records of the French, British, and Spanish administrations, 1699–1798 (102 volumes); records of Mississippi Territory, 1798–1817 (112 volumes); executive, legislative, and judicial records of the state, 1817–1940 (4,000 volumes and 2,500,000 pieces); and military records, especially of the Civil War period, including Confederate pension applications. In addition, there are considerable holdings of private papers. These are described, collection by collection, in loose-leaf binders; and in size and importance they exceed those of the Mississippi Collection of the University of Mississippi.

Regarding the arrangement of records, Dunbar Rowland in his *Guide* described his system as follows:[146]

The records of the state period are arranged in a series for each office of the state government. In all series there is a chronological arrangement of each document. In other words, the records of the departments and offices of the state government are arranged just as if they had been carefully and systematically arranged from the beginning.

Recent accessions of official and private documents have been processed in accordance with modern archival principles.

Because no sizable archival accessions have been absorbed since 1912, Rowland's *Guide* still serves as a reasonably adequate general finding aid, though it might well be brought up to date. It has been used to good advantage in the compilation of a *Guide to Civil War Source Material in the Department of Archives and History, State of Mississippi* (Jackson, 1962; 71 p.), which also covers other types of material in the custody of the department.

To the detriment of other activities, reference services absorb an unusually large amount of staff time.[147] Here are illustrative statistics:

[146] *Eleventh Annual Report*, 1911–12, p. 12.

[147] In October, 1948, Dr. McCain stated: "During the past 129 months we have written 33,118 letters and have had 35,959 registrations of researchers. There are times when we wonder if we have overemphasized this feature of the work, for it forces us to neglect our efforts to increase our collections and the efficiency of the Department."

[163]

	Written Requests	Searcher Registrations
1941–43	7,143	8,028
1949–51	7,966	7,555
1955–57	10,055	10,070
1959–61	12,510	10,092
1961–63	11,029	11,183

Copies of all reference letters and telephone replies (an average of five a day) are placed in a "subject file" set up in about 1938 to accommodate informational items of all kinds.

RECORDS MANAGEMENT AND RECORDS DISPOSITION

The department has recommended the adoption of a statewide records management program, rightly urging the development of retention and disposal schedules "before any more money is spent on a state-wide microfilm program." [148] As matters stand now, the department has neither authority nor staff to concern itself with records in government agencies. Considerable quantities of records are difficult of access, stored in the basement of the State Capitol. In addition, a former cafeteria building, now privately owned and rented at $1,100 a month, serves as a record dump with space assigned to agencies by the Building Commission.

Valueless records may be disposed of by agencies in accordance with the legislation mentioned above. To what extent this is done, however, is not known to the Department of Archives and History.

COMMENTS

1. Mississippi does not have a records management program, and as a result great quantities of records are not under schedule control.

2. Because of inadequate storage facilities the Department of Archives and History has not been able to absorb accessions of any size. Consequently, many of the permanently valuable records of the state are not in its custody.

MISSOURI

Archivally speaking, Missouri belongs to the "underdeveloped" states of the federal union.

BACKGROUNDS

In 1820 the Secretary of State was made custodian of the laws and resolutions of the general assembly, of the seal of the state, and of all public records, rolls, documents, etc. He was also instructed to keep a register of all commissions issued and of official acts of the government and to have all original rolls bound, properly labeled, and safely preserved in his of-

[148] *Biennial Report, 1959–61*, p. 54; and Charlotte Capers, "Records Management for Mississippi," *Journal of Mississippi History*, XXV (July, 1963), 202–7.

fice. These provisions were never interpreted strictly, and hence most records were kept by the agencies of origin.

The original Capitol of Missouri in Jefferson City was burned in 1837 and along with it the records in the office of the Secretary of State.[149] A new Capitol was built, and there Jonas Viles surveyed the records for the Public Archives Commission of the American Historical Association. He reported that they were piled up in the basement, dirty though dry and vermin-free, that many were stacked in front of the trash chute, and that only bad housekeeping had saved them from being thrown away. He recommended the creation of a central archival agency, but nothing had been done by 1911, when the Capitol burned again. This fire caused small but serious losses. Viles, a trustee and officer of the State Historical Society of Missouri, salvaged more than 100,000 pieces, many of them charred and "water soaked, frozen, and covered with dirt" [150] — and sent them to the society's headquarters in Columbia.

Except for these records and some small groups of papers later given to the State Historical Society, Missouri's records have remained with the agencies of the state government. In 1955 the record holdings of the various departments amounted to 250,000 cubic feet and occupied a total of 200,000 square feet of space — 35 per cent of all the space used by the state for all purposes.[151] The most important accumulation of records is that of the Secretary of State, kept in different vaults and rooms of the Capitol. It includes legislative records, with the House and Senate journals dating from 1819, extradition and appointment records, election returns, petitions, and corporation records. Because the Secretary of State is the official keeper of the land records, there are also original plats, field notes, and records pertaining to swamp lands, school lands, and land claims and grants. These records have been partly organized by a librarian from a Missouri college, and work on them is expected to continue.

In 1963 the House passed House Bill No. 496, to provide a records management program for the state, but it died in the Senate without coming to a vote.

THE STATE HISTORICAL SOCIETY OF MISSOURI

Although in 1917 the society was made a trustee of the records salvaged from the Capitol fire in 1911, and although some small bodies of records

[149] For the history of Missouri's archives, see Jonas Viles, "Report on the Archives of the State of Missouri," *Annual Report of the American Historical Association for the Year 1908*, I (Washington, 1909), 319–64.

[150] Jonas Viles, "Lessons To Be Drawn From the Fire in the State Capitol, Jefferson City," *Annual Report of the American Historical Association for the Year 1911*, I (Washington, 1913), 339; and Floyd C. Shoemaker, *The State Historical Society of Missouri: A Semi-centennial History* (Columbia, 1948), p. 51.

[151] Ben F. Cutcliffe, "Missouri — a Coordinated Records Program Needed," *American Archivist*, XXVI (July, 1963), 362.

have been given to it since by the Secretary of State, it is not, and is not likely to become, the archival agency of the state.[152]

As in Kansas and in Oklahoma, an association of the state's newspaper editors founded the State Historical Society. At a meeting of the Missouri Press Association at Eureka Springs, Arkansas, in May, 1898, the constitution and by-laws of a State Historical Society were approved. In the following year the society was made a trustee of the state, to "hold all its present and future collections and property for the state" (Laws, 1899, p. 222). Although, according to section 14903, Revised Statutes, 1939, ch. 114, the society is to

collect books, maps, and other papers and material for the study of history especially of this state and of the middle west; to acquire narratives and records of the pioneers, to procure documents, manuscripts and portraits, and to gather all information calculated to exhibit faithfully the antiquities and the past and present conditions, resources and progress of this state,

and although it is to receive "sixty bound copies of the several publications of the state and of its societies and institutions, except the reports of the supreme court and the courts of appeal" (sec. 14904), the Historical Society has never been designated as the archival depository for the records of the state.

Beautifully housed in the new east wing of the University of Missouri Library, while retaining space on the ground floor of its original building, the society's facilities include a research library, an art gallery, a large newspaper collection, and a manuscript collection consisting of 251,000 original manuscript pages, 1,645,598 manuscript pages on microfilm, 150,000 state archival items, and 71,000 letters.[153] Archival items, consisting primarily of the material salvaged in 1911, comprise records of the Governors, the Auditors, and the Adjutants General and election returns of the Secretary of State's office. In the 1930's they were indexed and placed in eighteen four-drawer filing cabinets. In addition, some territorial papers have been obtained from the Secretary of State in connection with a cleaning-up operation in his office, and other small accessions may be received in the future. The society is in no way prepared, however, to carry out the regular functions of a state archival agency. Its manuscript collections, well organized and well housed, are significantly supplemented by the university's Western Historical Manuscripts Collection, started in 1943 with grants from the Rockefeller Foundation and the University of Missouri. In his capacity of Associate University Librarian, the society's Secretary will have the administration of this collection.[154]

[152] Spanish Governors' letters and papers and the land records of two of the original districts of Missouri are in the privately supported Missouri Historical Society at St. Louis.
[153] David H. Spies, "The State Historical Society of Missouri Annual Meeting and Dedication of New Quarters," *Missouri Historical Review*, LVI (Jan., 1962), 126.
[154] See the *Guide to the Western Historical Manuscripts Collection*, 1952 and 1956

The 1953 legislature passed an act establishing a State Reorganization Commission to study the executive offices, departments, and agencies (Laws, 1953, p. 676). After the commission had identified records management as one of the major problems of the state government, Leahy and Company was employed in 1955 to make a limited records survey, and a few of its recommendations were adopted. A space survey made by Lawrence-Leiter and Company in 1960 led to the introduction in the legislature of House Bill No. 318. The bill would have established a board consisting of the State Comptroller and Budget Officer, the Secretary of State, the Secretary of the State Historical Society, the Attorney General, and the State Auditor, with authority over records disposal; and it would have authorized a records management program in the executive department under the Comptroller. It was defeated in the Senate, presumably because that body was not adequately briefed with regard to the bill's importance. There is some feeling that the Secretary of State, given his significant role as record keeper, looks with disfavor on a program to be administered by an appointed officer in the executive department. A State Reorganization Commission was established by the 1963 legislature; this commission has the power to examine into the records management situation in the state.

Before the introduction of the records management bill in 1963, some specific steps had been taken to improve records management in the state government. A records management clinic for key personnel [155] was held by the Regional Director of the National Archives and Records Service in Kansas City in December, 1961, and was addressed by the Governor. Agency records officers were then appointed, and two employees in the Comptroller's office worked intermittently on records management. Under the new bill a continuous operation would have been set up in the Comptroller's office. The Comptroller hopes to carry out some of the objectives of the bill, however, without specific legislation. The bill did not provide for a records center, nor did it create a regular state archives.

Although the new act would have given record disposal authority to a board consisting of the Comptroller, the Secretary of State, the Secretary of the State Historical Society, the Attorney General, and the Auditor or their representatives, it would not have repealed existing laws on the subject. Unaffected, then, would have been the power of certain agencies to dispose of specified bodies of records; the legislature's conferral of authority to destroy the records of the Secretary of State, the State Auditor, and the State Comptroller; and retention periods set up by law. Continuous

(University of Missouri Bulletins, "Library Series," Nos. 22 and 24; Western Historical Manuscripts Collection, Bulletins Nos. 6 and 7).

[155] It was preceded, in 1958, by a special clinic for personnel of the Division of Employment Security.

destruction of certain types of records has already been authorized after retention periods of three or five years or "a reasonable period" (Rev. Stats., 1949, Vol. I, secs. 28.100, 29.160, 33.150, 138.480, 142.330, 143.320, 287.650, 288.400, 301.360, and 301.530).

According to Revised Statutes of 1949, Volume I, sections 109.150, 111.630, and 113.380, county courts must approve the destruction of county records. There is no provision for disposal of municipal records.

COMMENTS

1. Missouri is an archival no man's land.

2. As a first step toward changing this unwholesome situation, a records management program should be enacted.

3. Inasmuch as the proposed records management act would not have provided for the establishment of a state archives, a bill to that effect should be introduced.

MONTANA

The state of Montana has no archival agency, though some archival material has drifted into the library of its Historical Society at Helena. A records management program was established in 1963 under the newly created Department of Administration. The Attorney General and the Director of the Historical Society are charged with authorizing the destruction of obsolete records.

BACKGROUNDS

By an act approved on February 2, 1865, the first territorial legislature created the Historical Society, and in 1873 an appropriation was given it for the purpose of acquiring manuscripts and books pertaining to the history of the territory. An act approved March 4, 1891, authorized the society to give title to its holdings to the state. The collections themselves, however, were to remain in the custody of the society, and in 1893 those of the Montana State Library were combined with them.

Before 1889 the territory's capital was frequently moved, and with each move records were destroyed by the departments without regard for anything but current needs. This attitude continued, and in some cases even records designated for preservation by law were destroyed. In 1912 Paul C. Phillips, reporting to the Public Archives Commission, thought it "beyond doubt that unless some plan for the preservation of Montana archives is acted upon, the State government will never have a history." [156] He urged the establishment of a department of archives in the Historical Society's library and the appointment of a trained archivist. For over fifty years his recommendation has remained without effect. "An Act to Perpetuate

[156] "The Archives of the State of Montana," *Annual Report of the American Historical Association for the Year 1912* (Washington, 1914), p. 300.

the Historical Society of the State of Montana as a Public Department of the State . . ." (Laws, 1949, ch. 134) charged the society with collecting, assembling, arranging, and preserving "books, pamphlets, maps, charts, manuscripts, journals, diaries, papers, paintings, engravings, photographs . . ." but did not make it the official archival depository of the state.

As a result of the work of Montana's Commission on Reorganization of State Government (Laws, 1951, ch. 185) and its budgeting and accounting task force, the legislature passed chapter 189, Laws of 1953, Montana's first records destruction act. It provided machinery for the disposal of valueless records and established a Microfilm Division of the Historical Society. In spite of budgetary limitations and lack of experience, both microfilming and records disposal made good progress during the first year of operations; a slowdown occurred during the second year; and reduced appropriations in 1955 led to a cessation of all microfilming by the division in May, 1956. The records destruction program also lost momentum, and no records management program developed,[157] until passage of Senate Bill No. 10 (Laws, 1963, ch. 271).

THE HISTORICAL SOCIETY

Under the act of 1949 the society is governed by a Board of Trustees of fifteen members, five appointed "from nominations by the Chancellor of the greater University of Montana," five appointed by the Governor, and five elected by votes of the two preceding groups. In 1963 the Governor was given sole appointive power over the board. The board appoints the Director of the society, who has authority "to hire and fire," though he clears appointments with the State Board of Examiners. Montana has no state merit system except in agencies expending federal funds.

The budget for 1963–65 provides the society with a yearly income of $200,500, of which $83,849 comes from state funds. The society depends to a very considerable extent on income from other sources, including the sale of its magazine *Montana*, of which no less than 60,000 copies are printed annually. The Director of the society receives a salary of $10,000.

What archival material there is in the society is administered by the library staff, consisting of a professional librarian ($7,000), a library assistant, a stenographer, a stack boy (not full-time), and a part-time assistant for the photographic files.

The archival holdings, of which there is no comprehensive description, include such miscellaneous groups as territorial licenses and tax receipts, 1865–89, county fund vouchers relating to payment for the killing of predatory animals, records of the Commission on Reorganization of State Government, post records of Fort Assiniboine, and materials of the WPA

[157] The preceding is based on an excellent analysis by John Hakola in *A Report Concerning State Microfilming in Montana* (Helena, Jan., 1957), 17 p.

Historical Records Survey. There are also collections of private papers, among them the vast collection of banking records of S. T. Hauser, exceeding in quantity the state records held by the society. Most of the state's records are still with the agencies of origin. The Secretary of State has all the legislative records, corporation records, election records, and other important series, stored in two vaults in the Capitol. He also has the constitution of 1889, which is badly in need of lamination.

In 1952 the Historical Society moved from inadequate quarters in the Capitol to its new Veterans Pioneer Memorial Building, erected at practically no cost to the state.[158] It houses the offices of the society and those of various veterans' organizations, the society's impressive "Formal Museum" with its dioramas depicting phases of Montana history, the "Informal Museum" on the ground floor, the society's art galleries, and the large display of works of Charles Marion Russell, Montana's "cowboy artist." [159] The library, in addition to a well-lighted reading room, has five floors of fireproof stacks. Manuscript material is kept in locked space on the fifth floor, and most of the archival material is stored in transfer boxes, tin containers, and file drawers on the first floor. Not all of the space is equipped with shelving. It is estimated that about 7,500 cubic feet of records could be accommodated if the society were to become the statutory repository for the state's archives.

The library has a planetary camera and two Copease machines but no other reproduction equipment.

Since the Library staff is much too small to do any arrangement and description of records, the archival holdings are virtually in dead storage. Furthermore, no accessions are received except photographs from the Fish and Game and the Highway Departments. All departments are required to give copies of all their reports, printed and non-printed, to the society.

RECORDS MANAGEMENT AND RECORDS DISPOSITION

Chapter 189, Laws of 1953, created a committee consisting of the Historical Society's librarian (actually the Director), the Attorney General, the Secretary of State, the State Bank Examiner, the State Comptroller, and the State Auditor "to determine what records shall be authorized to be destroyed," authorization to be unanimous, and directed all agencies of the executive branch to prepare lists of records that in the judgment of the respective executive officers were of no administrative or historical

[158] The ground, part of some tax-delinquent land near the Capitol, was bought by the Sons and Daughters of Montana Pioneers and the Montana Pioneers Society for about $150 and deeded to the state. Income that the veterans' organizations had received from prize fights and wrestling furnished the money for the building.

[159] Vivian A. Paladin, "Historical Society Reaches Maturity," *The People's Voice*, Aug. 5, 1960, p. 4.

value. The committee did not meet, and its members acted individually on the lists submitted on a one-page mimeographed form. Only a few lists were processed during the year.

The State Legislative Council published its *Executive Reorganization Report No. 7* in November, 1962. Beyond developing a long-range plan for reorganization of the state's 114 agencies, this document dealt specifically with finance and general administration. It included a bill creating a Department of Administration headed by the Comptroller and charging him with establishing a records management program. This bill (passed as ch. 271, Laws, 1963) abolished the State Records Committee and vested authority over records destruction in the Comptroller, the Attorney General, and the Director of the Historical Society, with the Comptroller's decision overriding the approval or disapproval of the two other members of the group. The law makes no provision for a records center, nor does it establish the Historical Society as the archival depository of the state.

COMMENTS

1. Although a records management program was approved by the 1963 legislature, provision has not been made for a records center.

2. Montana has no archival agency. Since the Historical Society is a "Public Department of the state" and has some storage space in its modern building, it might well be declared the official depository for the state's archives, and it could so serve if it should receive funds for the necessary equipment and for the hiring of trained personnel.

NEBRASKA

The Nebraska State Historical Society, the official archival agency for the state, has entrusted the archives function to its Division of Library and Archives.

BACKGROUNDS

When Nebraska became a state in 1867, the capital was moved from Omaha to Lincoln. Early in the twentieth century, A. E. Sheldon of the Nebraska State Historical Society [160] found territorial and early state records in great disorder, dusty, mildewed, and decaying, as a result of crowded conditions in the old State Capitol at Lincoln. Recent records were as a rule well cared for, but the non-current material was largely neglected. Those of the Secretary of State and of some few other offices were complete and well kept.

At the time of Sheldon's survey, the Nebraska State Historical Society had been made the official custodian of state and local records (Laws,

[160] "Report on the Archives of the State of Nebraska," *Annual Report of the American Historical Association for the Year 1910* (Washington, 1912), pp. 365–420.

1905, ch. 157). With newspaper editors and publishers displaying particular interest, the society had been organized in 1867 as the State Historical Society and Library Association. In 1878 it was reorganized as the Nebraska State Historical Society and was housed at the State University. It became a state institution and was given an appropriation in 1883. Declared the repository for non-current state and local records of historical value in 1905, it was authorized in 1909 to make and certify copies of the records in its custody, the copies to have the legal force of the originals. Since the 1905 legislation was permissive only, however, and applied solely to records of historical value more than twenty years old and liable to damage or destruction, its passage had no immediate substantial effects. The situation changed when the society, never before adequately housed, moved into its present building, which was financed by a special mill levy (1945) and was occupied in 1953.

As a step toward regularizing the destruction of public records, a 1947 opinion of the Attorney General stated that it was the intent of the legislation (Rev. Stats., 1943, chap. 84-713) that neither county and city officers nor state and institutional officers should destroy any records without first notifying the Historical Society. In 1961 there was passed a records management act (ch. 455), which is a combination of the Records Management and the Essential Records Preservation Acts of the Council of State Governments. It names the Secretary of State as Records Administrator for state records, establishes an essential records preservation program for the state and an assistance program to local units for establishing similar programs, and creates a State Records Board. Except where other units of government are specifically named, the act applies solely to the state's executive department.

THE STATE HISTORICAL SOCIETY

The Nebraska State Historical Society is governed by an Executive Board, which chooses a Director to conduct the business of the society. The society operates a museum and a historic site at Fort Robinson, an Education Division, and a Division of Library and Archives.

For the 1963–65 biennium the society has a total budget of $364,822. Since there is no breakdown, it can only be estimated that the Division of Library and Archives receives a fourth to a third of the total appropriation. Supplied with the requests of the divisional heads, the Director presents his budget proposal to the society's board, which concerns itself mostly with salaries, and then to the Governor, who holds his budget hearings and then submits his budget to the unicameral legislature. The legislature's budget committee holds its own hearings in March. The Director has insisted on having representatives of the board with him at the different hearings. He feels that in the matter of appropriations the society has fared as well as other agencies of the state. It received a spectacular increase for 1951–53, which made it possible to add an archivist to the society's staff. Since then, no sizable expansion of the staff has been authorized.

The staff of the society consists of twenty-seven employees, thirteen of them in the Division of Library and Archives. The Director of the society, who is on indefinite appointment, receives a salary of $10,200–$10,500; the Directory of Library and Archives, $9,400–$9,600; and the Archivist, $7,200–$7,500. In the absence of a firm salary pattern, the Executive Board of the society has approved a policy under which professional staff members receive increases of $300 per biennium. Staff members are under the social security system, may participate in Blue Cross insurance, and enjoy two weeks of annual leave, an additional week for keeping the building open on legal holidays, and a fourth week after ten years of service. There is no compulsory retirement age.

The society publishes the quarterly *Nebraska History*, a *Historical Newsletter*, and books, monographs, and pamphlets about the history of Nebraska and the prairie region. The Director of the society also writes a weekly column, "Out of Old Nebraska," which appears in the press of the state. The society's annual report is published in the December issue of *Nebraska History*.

Through its Education Division the society conducts an extensive program providing a television "Western Heritage Series," guided tours, puppet shows, and educational leaflets. It has two museums, one in its headquarters at Lincoln and another at Fort Robinson. In fiscal 1961 the main museum was visited by 83,018 persons. The museum also undertakes important archeological research projects under agreements with the National Park Service, with the State Game, Forestation and Parks Commission, and with the highway authorities in matters of the highway salvage program. The society has assisted in the restoration of the William Jennings Bryan House, in the establishment of local historical societies, in the work of the Civil War Centennial Commission, of which the Director is a member, and in the historical markers program under the Historical Land Marks Council.

THE DIVISION OF LIBRARY AND ARCHIVES

The society's book and newspaper collections and its archives and private papers are administered by the Director of Library and Archives. In regard to archival activities, the program is undernourished, if only for lack of personnel. Until recently the staff member holding the Archivist's position under the Director was in charge of the division's general reference service; he could spare a little time for the acquisition of private papers but none for the processing of archival holdings. Such processing and the handling of private papers was left to a records assistant and a student assistant under the supervision of the Director, who participated in the work as time permitted. The appointment in August, 1963, of a new Archivist, with none but archival duties, has presumably brought about an improvement in this situation. Another records assistant is in charge of the picture collection; and all accessions, including those of archival material, are recorded by a third records assistant, who, however, has other duties as well.

The Archives Section of the division might well be granted a greater measure of independence.[161] Archival material and private papers are intermingled in the stacks, archival accessions are handled through the division's "gift record," [162] and cards for them are entered in the general catalog. In addition, however, most archival bodies and collections of private papers are briefly described in a series of loose-leaf binders entitled "Manuscript Records." They give, mostly on one page each, a brief description of the material and its quantity, the date of receipt — accessions are not numbered but are identified by date — and a brief indication of its content. Some of the accessions are analyzed in greater detail.

Among the holdings — consisting of 5,600 volumes, 3,700 letter and manuscript boxes, 600 filing cases and cartons, 400 packages, and 1,800 small collections (one envelope each) — the major state agencies are well represented. There are, for example, 109 boxes and 58 letter books of executive papers, a quantity of legislative records, 5 file cases and 60 packages of corporation records, and records of the Bureau of Securities. There are also U.S. Land Office records, 1834–1933, some county records, the Kuska Collection of Burlington Railroad records, and great quantities of private papers.

Archival and manuscript holdings are stored on the second and third levels of the six-level modern stack, which is equipped with library shelving. Available space for archives and private papers amounts to 8,000 cubic feet plus an additional 4,000 being used for the temporary storage of newspapers. At present, 6,000 cubic feet of this space is in use. Control is by means of location symbols. As for arrangement, a "Manual of Library Procedures . . ." (1961, typed) prescribes that "Archives will be housed in their original cases where possible and the original working order and organization maintained." The same procedure is to apply to manuscript collections, "insofar as possible." Archival principles also govern the treatment of the very large picture collections, which are organized in

---

[161] The society's flyer *See the Nebraska State Historical Society Museum* (n.p., n.d.; 6 p.) says that the society "maintains an excellent reference library composed of books, manuscripts, archives, newspapers, genealogical materials, and photographs related to the history of Nebraska and the West." This statement seems to need revision.

[162] Gifts are listed in detail each month in the society's *Historical Newsletter*.

groups according to their origin and are made accessible by means of lists and a card index based on these lists.

The society has a binding and repair shop but no laminating equipment. A microfilm program is applied chiefly to the filming of newspapers. It is operated by three persons with one camera and has in the course of eleven years produced 7,847 reels of film.[163]

In fiscal 1963 the holdings of the division were used by 4,761 persons in the reading and newspaper rooms, and 957 mail inquiries and 2,050 oral inquiries were answered. No separate record of archival reference work is kept, but it is believed that most services involve the use of printed information.

RECORDS MANAGEMENT AND RECORDS DISPOSITION

Chapter 84–713 of the Revised Statutes of Nebraska, 1943, gave the Governor and the Attorney General final authority over the destruction of state records. This provision has been superseded by the Records Management Act of 1961.[164]

The new act, which applies only to the executive branch except where other agencies are specifically mentioned, calls for "a records management program which will apply efficient and economical methods to the creation, utilization, maintenance, retention, preservation, and disposal of State records," for a program to select and preserve essential state records, and for assistance in similar programs in local subdivisions of the state. The act furthermore names the Secretary of State as Records Administrator; gives him broad regulatory powers over all phases of record creation and record-keeping; makes him secretary to the State Records Boards, created for disposal purposes; and authorizes him to make and certify preservation duplicates of essential records in the executive department, to assign a place of storage for them, and to service them. The legislature and the Supreme Court may request and receive the same essential records preservation service. The act, furthermore, creates the State Records Board, consisting of the Governor (chairman), the State Records Administrator (secretary), the Attorney General, the Auditor of Public Accounts, and the Director of the Nebraska State Historical Society, or their representatives. The board is to review lists of records proposed for destruction, and it may designate certain classes of records to be authorized for destruction by the State Records Administrator without action of the whole board.

[163] From 1954 to 1962 the State Purchasing Agent offered a central microfilm service to state agencies. This has gone out of existence, but a few agencies have their own programs. Before they may destroy any records filmed, however, they must notify the Historical Society.

[164] An analysis of the act is in John B. White, "Nebraska — the Records Management Prospect," *American Archivist*, XXVI (July, 1963), 365–69.

Because the 1961 legislature passed the act without appropriating any money for its administration, it still awaits implementation. The Secretary of State is eager to assume his new responsibilities and for that purpose asked the 1963 legislature for an appropriation of $33,000 for the next biennium. This, however, was denied.

On the local level, the new law provides that the governing bodies of all local units shall administer programs of records management and essential records preservation. Records must be disposed of, however, only in accordance with Revised Statutes of Nebraska 1943, 1961 cumulative supplement, chapter 23-356, -357, which give disposal authority to the district judges.

COMMENTS

1. The Records Management Act of 1961 should be implemented as soon as possible.

2. In the processing and storing of materials by the Division of Library and Archives of the State Historical Society, a consistent distinction should be made among library material, archives, and private papers.

NEVADA

Under a 1943 law the Nevada State Historical Society at Reno serves as the archival agency of the state. Shortage of funds, space, and personnel has prevented it from discharging this function under any plan or system.

BACKGROUNDS

The Nevada Historical Society [165] was founded in 1904 under the auspices of the Social Science Section of the now defunct Nevada Academy of Sciences. [166] In 1907 it was recognized a quasi-state institution, with an appropriation of $2,000; and in 1915 it was given authority over the State Museum, previously under the Superintendent of Public Instruction. In 1927 the society's holdings were displayed in the Highway Exposition Building, which meant "the sacrifice of the valuable collections to commercial and political interests." [167] There followed a period of inactivity during which the materials remained unattended in the basement of this building, then occupied by the Washoe County Library. The society was reactivated in 1934; and, with the aid of Federal Emergency Relief Administration and Works Progress Administration helpers, its collections

[165] Apparently the terms Nevada State Historical Society and Nevada Historical Society are used interchangeably. The seal used on the 1960–62 *Biennial Report* reads Nevada State Historical Society, while throughout the report the designation Nevada Historical Society is used.

[166] The genesis of the society is told in detail in its *First Biennial Report*, 1907–8 (Carson City, 1909).

[167] *Twelfth, Thirteenth, and Fourteenth Reports*, 1935–40 (Carson City, 1942), p. 10.

were put in usable condition again. "Nobody can ever describe the filth and wreckage that was encountered." [168]

Chapter 67, Statutes of Nevada, 1943, named the Historical Society as the archival agency of the state, authorized its executive officers to make copies of records in its custody, and gave certified copies the legal force of the originals. Because of insufficient space and personnel, however, the provisions of this law remained largely inoperative. In fact, at one time Jeanne E. Wier, secretary and curator of the society, had to "utilize an apartment in her own home and also a garage to temporarily take care of large articles." [169]

A 1957 law (ch. 252) authorized destruction, after a period of six years, of obsolete notes taken by official reporters, ballots, county warrants, and such other papers and records of no further legal force or effect as the district courts might designate, with the proviso that the Nevada Historical Society should be notified and should have the privilege of selecting those worthy of retention.

Lacking funds and adequate quarters, the Historical Society has been unable to build up systematically its holdings of permanently valuable records of the state.

THE NEVADA STATE HISTORICAL SOCIETY

The society is governed by a Board of Trustees elected by the members at their annual meeting, and the daily business is conducted by the Director of the Executive Staff, who also serves as Executive Secretary of the society. The society has a considerable library, including a newspaper collection, a museum, and archival holdings that are not organized as a separate division.

Most of the society's funds stem from state appropriations.[170] They amounted to $29,738 in fiscal 1961 and $37,823 in fiscal 1962.[171] A goodly part of the money appropriated to operations goes into the publication of the *Nevada Historical Society Quarterly*, which must be printed in the State Printing Office. Budget requests, after approval by the Board of Trustees, are reviewed by the State Budget Director and become part of the Governor's budget. The society's Director may be asked to appear before a joint meeting of the Ways and Means Committees of the two houses of the legislature.

The staff of the society consists of three unclassified employees: the Director ($7,260), an Assistant to the Director ($5,280), and a half-time "Researcher" ($2,640). The secretary, an attendant, and a half-time attendant are in the classified service and are appointed after competi-

[168] *Ibid.*, p. 11.
[169] *Seventeenth Biennial Report*, 1944–46 (Reno, n.d.), p. 13.
[170] There are only about two hundred dues-paying members of the society.
[171] The 1962 appropriation included a considerable amount for equipment.

tive examinations. Employees participate in the state retirement system and are given fifteen days of annual leave and sick leave in the same amount.

The society is housed in the State Building (formerly the Highway Exposition and later the Washoe County Library Building), which it shares with the Washoe County Library, the Justice of the Peace Marriage Information Office, and various other offices. At first occupying unbelievably cramped quarters in the basement, in 1958 it received additional space, which somewhat relieved the pressure. Seven thousand dollars was appropriated at that time for renovating and equipping the society's quarters, but even so they are probably more crowded than those of any other state historical society.

The society collaborates closely with the University of Nevada, whose students consult its collections for work on Master's theses in Nevada history. About 500 researchers use the society's library each year, and 560 make inquiries by mail. The society did the historical research for the Pony Express and Virginia City centennials, and in 1961 it recognized the Territorial Centennial by devoting an issue of its quarterly to Territorial Governor James W. Nye and Secretary of State Orion Clemens. The Director also serves as adviser to the Centennial Markers Committee for the State Centennial.

ARCHIVAL ACTIVITIES OF THE SOCIETY

The archives do not constitute an identifiable department of the society. Some are intermingled with the library holdings, some are in the Rare Book Room, and some are kept in an adjacent room where they await processing. Archival holdings consist of a small quantity of state and county records and some valuable collections of private papers, including the papers of U. S. senators and representatives from Nevada. To these have been added the early school-land records and maps of the Bureau of Land Management (acquired in 1962), illustrative of the history of the office from the beginning to the 1920's, and early records of the Comptroller. The society, however, is in no way equipped to pursue a systematic program to concentrate and preserve the state's archives. There is no list of present holdings, nor are there any finding aids that would facilitate their use.

Starved since its inception, the society has no rehabilitation or photoreproduction facilities.

THE ARCHIVES OF THE SECRETARY OF STATE

The Secretary of State has a considerable accumulation of early records, including records of oaths and bonds, records of mining incorporations,

1863 to date, election returns, and records of the Carson County Court from 1855. Kept on the mezzanine floor in his main office, these valuable records are not adequately protected. Realizing the need for an effective archival establishment, the Secretary of State was instrumental in having placed before the legislature Senate Bill No. 166 (February 28, 1961). The bill, which was killed in the Finance Committee, would have provided for a division of archives within the office of the Secretary of State and would have authorized him to receive in the archives any material deemed by him to be of historical value and any other material "when so directed by the State Board of Examiners," composed of the Governor, the Attorney General, and the Secretary of State. The bill called for an appropriation of $20,000 to support the proposed division during the 1961–63 biennium.

The Secretary of State expects to have the bill reintroduced during the 1965 session of the legislature.

RECORDS DISPOSITION

Nevada has no records management program, nor is one contemplated at this time. Requests for disposal of state records must be approved by the State Board of Examiners. In 1944 Jeanne E. Wier reported that the

. . . present law concerning the *destruction* of obsolete archives is very defective. Useless records may be destroyed by the State Board of Control upon the request of any State board or officer. . . . The weakness is that no agency or person competent to pass upon the historical value of the records is included.[172]

In actual practice, the Historical Society is given an opportunity to scrutinize destruction requests.

COMMENTS

Nevada needs legislation under which effective records management and archival programs can be carried out.

NEW HAMPSHIRE

In 1961 New Hampshire joined the ranks of those states that have taken steps to provide for the management and preservation of their public records.

BACKGROUNDS

Under the state constitution, the Secretary of State became the custodian of the records of the legislature and the Governor and Council and of those of his own office. Although the constitution (pt. 2, art. 68) also said, "The records of the state shall be kept in the office of the secretary,"

[172] *Sixteenth Biennial Report*, 1942–44 (Carson City, 1944), p. 46.

this was never construed to cover departmental papers; hence these remained in the custody of the respective departments of origin. Concern about public records manifested itself first in regard to provincial records when an 1897 act provided that "the records of all the courts of the province of New Hampshire and all the records of deeds and all the probate records, and all the original papers of the province of New Hampshire prior to the . . . division . . . into counties . . . shall be kept by the Secretary of State in the vaults of the State Library or some other place provided by the Governor and Council."[173] Under this law the New Hampshire Historical Society holds an impressive assemblage of records, which includes executive and legislative records to 1840; a magnificent collection of provincial court records; deeds, wills, and inventories, originals as well as copies, in 100 volumes; and town records. A considerable quantity of executive, legislative, and judicial records is in the State Library at Concord. Both the State Library and the Historical Society, however, serve merely as depositories of the records in their custody.

In 1955 the legislature granted funds to the State Library to conduct a study of the records management and archives problems of the state, and accordingly the services of Leahy and Company were engaged for a survey of the records situation. The firm's 1956 report recommended "a Records and Paperwork Management Program," which would provide:

1. The preservation of historical records in a State Archives.
2. An orderly system of disposing of valueless records and for storing in a low-cost Records Center those papers not needed in offices.
3. A central records management service.
4. A central State Archives and Records Center.
5. That a single new law be enacted to amend or supersede the existing laws on disposition of records.[174]

In view of this report, the Governor in 1960 appointed a committee consisting of the chairman of the State Historical Commission, the State Comptroller, the State Business Manager, the Deputy Attorney General, and the State Librarian to study the proposed plan, to draft necessary legislation and assist in its passage, and to plan a building and program. The legislation was passed as chapter 266, Laws of 1961.[175]

THE DIVISION OF RECORDS MANAGEMENT AND ARCHIVES

The 1961 act establishes in the Department of Administration and Control a Division of Records Management and Archives, the Director of

[173] New Hampshire, Revised Statutes Annotated, 1955, Title 3, chapter 5:19.
[174] Quoted from a summary of the Leahy report, which is attached to the *Report of the Study Committee for Historical and Fiscal Records Management* (Nov. 21, 1960).
[175] This chapter amended the Revised Statutes Annotated by inserting the new chapter 8-B after chapter 8-A (supp.) as inserted by 1957, 284:1.

which is to be appointed by the Comptroller with the approval of the Governor and Council. In addition to a continuing appropriation of $16,000 for a records management study under the supervision of the Comptroller, the new division has a budget of $19,065 for fiscal 1963, the Director to receive a salary of $6,890–$7,930, a clerical worker $3,081–$3,575, and a warehouse man $3,311–$3,801. The sum of $143,352 was appropriated for building, equipping, and furnishing a records center, which was occupied in February, 1963.

The act assigns to the Director of the division the duty of establishing, for all agencies of the executive branch, standards, procedures, and techniques for effective records management, including the setting up of standards for the preparation of retention and disposal schedules and the formulating of procedures for the transfer of records with permanent or historical value. The Director is also to administer the records center and to promulgate rules and regulations governing its organization and services. Agency heads are directed to establish and maintain, under the supervision of the Director, active continuing programs for the economical and efficient management of records, for making and keeping definitive records that will protect the legal rights of the state and its citizens, for submitting retention and disposal schedules based on legal, fiscal, administrative, and historical considerations, and for complying with the rules and regulations of the Director.

A manual of rules and regulations necessary to carry out the intent of the act is to be submitted to a board composed of the chairman of the State Historical Commission, the State Librarian, and the Attorney General.[176] Once approved by the board, the manual must be submitted to the Governor and Council for their approval, and thereupon it will be binding upon all officers and employees of the state.

The New Hampshire records management program is now well under way. The Director, an able man of considerable managerial experience, has been appointed. Beginning in January, 1961, and working with a staff member of Leahy and Company, he had, by the end of June, 1962, almost completed the inventory and disposal schedules for state agencies. The schedules will be incorporated in the *Manual of Procedures: Records Management and Archives,* an addition to the *State Manual of Procedures,*[177] that is to receive the approval of Governor and Council. Leahy

[176] Inasmuch as the State Historical Commission is composed of political appointees, historical judgment is not necessarily represented on the board.

[177] Part C, Archives 2, defines archives as records of "permanent and historical value," but it continues, "This does not mean that all those records designated as permanent in the Records Disposition Schedules are archives. Most such designated records are listed as permanent, because no sound judgment can be made as to the date they will lose their administrative, fiscal or legal value." Such use of the term "permanent" seems misleading. Records of the kind referred to would be better characterized as "indefinite."

and Company prepared the draft of this *Manual* as well as that of an *Operations Manual* for the records center.

The records and archives center, located on the grounds of the New Hampshire State Hospital, was ready for occupancy in February, 1963, and by June nearly 3,000 cubic feet of inactive records and about 200 cubic feet of archival material had been accessioned. Approximately 65 by 100 feet in size, the building, of fire-retarding construction, provides a humidity-controlled archives vault for 800 cubic feet of records and a records storage area for 18,000 cubic feet. The latter is two stories high, and its second level extends over the archives vault. Neither a sprinkler system nor fire-detection devices are provided. In the storage area, records center–type boxes can be stored sixteen high. Heat is obtained from the central heating plant of the hospital.

The immediate purpose of the records center is to receive and service records of the executive branch that are to be disposed of in accordance with approved retention and disposal schedules. As to the records of the Secretary of State, the law (8-B:16) states:

Subject to the limitations of the constitution, the secretary of state may, to the extent he deems desirable, and consistently with the rules and regulations of the director, arrange for the transfer of any of his records to the records center.

This paragraph finds its justification in the fact that in New Hampshire the Secretary of State is elected by the legislature and therefore is not considered to be in the executive branch. It does not, of course, answer the question of whether and when the Secretary of State will transfer to the new division the archival materials already deposited with the State Library and the New Hampshire Historical Society. At this time, the division is not anxious to take them over. Also, it is to be hoped that its archives section will have on its staff at least one person trained in historical research as well as in archives administration before the division attempts to service a considerable quantity of records of great historical significance.

Under the act, the Division of Records Management and Archives may, upon request, render records management services to the judicial and legislative branches of the state government and to local government units. For the time being, however, the division does not plan to encourage such requests.

COMMENTS

If the archives function of the Division of Records Management and Archives is to be implemented, the division must have an appropriate increase of its professional staff.

[182]

NEW JERSEY

Scheduled to move into the new State Library Building in 1964, the Library's Bureau of Archives and History will soon be able to carry out more fully its functions as the state archival and records management agency.

BACKGROUNDS

The governing powers of the Proprietors of East and West Jersey, based on patents issued in 1664 to John Lord Berkeley and Sir George Carteret as joint proprietors, were not renewed after the end of the regime of Sir Edmund Andros as Governor of the Territory and Dominion of New England, into which the Jerseys had been incorporated in 1688. This, however, did not affect the property rights of the Proprietors, and accordingly records of land warrants and surveys are to this day kept in the respective Proprietors' offices, which are housed in stone buildings in Burlington and Perth Amboy.[178]

The public records of the state suffered from frequent moves of the seat of government, from the burning of nearly all courthouses during the Revolutionary War, and from the usual neglect of officials. After Trenton had been designated the state capital (1790), the legislature in 1795 provided for the erection of a "convenient house" for the Secretary of State and the Clerk of the Supreme Court and for the preservation of the public records. Further interest in the old records of the state manifested itself in 1872 in an appropriation of $3,000 for the purpose of obtaining copies of colonial documents from London and other places, and continued financial support made possible the publication by the New Jersey Historical Society of the impressive series of *New Jersey Archives*.

Concerned about the actual preservation of records, the legislature in 1897 authorized a survey of public records. This was conducted by a Public Record Commission chaired by William Nelson, corresponding secretary of the New Jersey Historical Society, second editor of the *New Jersey Archives*, and for thirty years editor of the society's *Proceedings*. Neither this survey nor the one made by Nelson for the Public Archives Commission [179] had any immediate results, and an act to establish a State Department of Public Records and Archives (Laws, 1913, ch. 180) was apparently never implemented. More effective was the 1916 report of a committee of citizens "on the Condition of Public Records of the State

[178] Board of Proprietors of the Eastern Division of New Jersey, *The General Board of Proprietors of the Eastern Division of New Jersey* (n.p., 1954), 8 p.
[179] Public Record Commission of New Jersey, *First Report* (Somerville, N. J., 1899), 116 p.; and William Nelson, "The Public Archives of New Jersey," *Annual Report of the American Historical Association for the Year 1903*, I (Washington, 1904), 479–541.

[183]

of New Jersey," which bitterly criticized the negligent treatment of the public records, state as well as local, the carelessness of officials, the alarming "abstraction" of public documents by private individuals, and the mutilation of many by autograph hunters.[180]

Most certainly influenced by this report, the legislature re-enacted with minor changes the act of 1913, establishing the Public Record Office (Laws, 1920, ch. 46). It was to be responsible for the records of defunct agencies, to establish rules and regulations with regard to the care of records, to accept records of state or local agencies no longer in current use, to acquire and preserve historical records, and to authorize the destruction of public records. Carlos E. Godfrey became the first Director of the office and served until he died in 1941. Upon his death the Public Record Office became a division of the State Library, which had been established in 1813 and which since 1902 had been operating under the Public Library Commission. The present Division of State Library, Archives and History was created in 1945 and was placed under the Department of Education.

After a survey of the state's record situation by William Benedon of the Lockheed Aircraft Corporation, chapter 410, Laws of 1953,[181] created the State Records Committee (i.e., the State Treasurer, the Attorney General, the State Auditor, the Director of the Division of Local Governments in the Department of the Treasury, and the head of the Bureau of Archives and History, or their designees); defined public records; and provided that no public records might be sold, destroyed, or otherwise disposed of without the consent of the Bureau of Archives and History, which must act in accordance with the rules and regulations of the State Records Committee. Under the same law, the bureau is instructed to make, in co-operation with the departments, studies of records and to prepare continuing disposal schedules for approval by the State Records Committee. With the approval of the State Records Committee the Bureau of Archives and History is to set standards for photographic reproduction.

THE DIVISION OF STATE LIBRARY, ARCHIVES AND HISTORY

The Division of State Library, Archives and History, under the Department of Education, is legally charged with maintaining a law library, providing a legislative reference and research facility, promoting library service throughout the state, maintaining New Jersey's basic historic docu-

[180] Nelson B. Gaskill et al., "Report on the Condition of the Public Records of the State of New Jersey," Annual Report of the American Historical Association for the Year 1916, I (Washington, 1919), 163–99. Included are revealing calendars of public papers in private possession and of those sold or offered for sale in auction houses after 1900.

[181] The act supersedes earlier legislation governing the destruction and reproduction of records, namely, chapter 135, Laws of 1924, and chapter 44, Laws of 1941. Chapter 205, Laws of 1928, gave replevin power to legal custodians of records, and chapter 21, Laws of 1936, extended it to the Public Record Office.

ments, and supervising the retention of public records of the state and its political subdivisions. In compliance with these charges, the division operates the Bureaus of General Reference, Law and Legislative Reference, Public and School Library Services, and Archives and History. The last bureau has custody of the state archives, develops retention and disposal schedules in co-operation with state and local agencies, administers the records centers for the storage of semi-current records, and operates a microfilm program.

In fiscal 1963 the division had a budget of $427,436, of which the Bureau of Archives and History received, for salaries only, $46,437. The budget is prepared for the Commissioner of Education by the Assistant Commissioner in charge of Business and Finance, with the help of the Director of the Division of State Library, Archives and History, who has discussed their needs with the heads of his bureaus. It conforms to guidelines drawn by the Director of the Division of Budget and Accounting in the Department of the Treasury, which is the agency to which the budget is submitted. The Director of the Division of State Library, Archives and History and his Administrative Assistant defend the budget in hearings held by the Division of Budget and Accounting. The Department of Civil Service also reviews the budget. Legislative review is by the Office of Legislative Budget and Finance.

The division has sixty employees, nine of them in the Bureau of Archives and History. All members of the staff are under the state civil service system and enjoy the following benefits: state retirement on a contributing basis, social security, group health insurance (including participation in a major medical expenses plan) and life insurance with all premiums paid by the state, twelve days of annual leave (increased to fifteen days after ten years of service, and to twenty days after twenty years of service), and fifteen days of sick leave, which may accumulate indefinitely.

At this writing the division occupies wholly inadequate quarters in the State House Annex, consisting of some office space, a fair-sized reading room, and the north and south stacks. The new State Library Building, part of a six-million-dollar cultural center, will be opened in 1964. The reinforced concrete building is being constructed by the Teachers' Pension and Annuity Fund for lease to the state, under authorization by the legislature of 1960. The gross area of the new building will be nearly 100,000 square feet, including two basement levels. It will be constructed on a modular system designed for flexibility of use. Rooms for non-storage functions, such as division administrative offices, archival exhibit space, and law and general reference reading rooms, will be located on the first floor; the second floor will house stacks for the division's book collection and an employees' lounge; the third will have offices for school and public library services and some stack areas for books. The entire upper basement will be used by the Bureau of Archives and History and its microfilm unit, and the lower basement will have shipping and receiving facilities, duplicating machines, and some unallocated stack space (5,000 square feet). The Bureau of Archives and History will have 700 square feet for administrative purposes, 3,000 for exhibits, 10,000 for archives stacks, 500 for vaults, 800 for archives preparation, 1,500 for a research room, 1,000 for photoduplication and restoration, and 1,250 for the microfilm unit.

The division no longer publishes its annual reports.

THE BUREAU OF ARCHIVES AND HISTORY

The Bureau of Archives and History has four employees, two of them professional, in its archives program; and five, one of them professional, in its records management program. Archival salaries are:

Bureau Head	$9,405–$12,225
Archival Examiner	6,684– 8,688
Supervisor, Microfilm Service	5,774– 7,508
Clerks and Microfilm Operators	3,042– 4,839

At present the bureau has at its disposal 306 square feet of office space and 500 square feet of stack space in the State House Annex, a 209-square-foot vault in the State House, 3,787 square feet for a records center and a microfilm unit in the Switlik Building, and a 3,569-square-foot records center at the School for the Deaf in West Trenton, making a total of 8,371 square feet, less than an eighth of which is used for archives.

Holdings consist of records from 1674 to 1956 and include colonial, state, and local material, chiefly pre-1860, engrossed acts, and other papers relating to the history of New Jersey. Although earlier records of the Governors are scattered, papers from 1878 are on hand. The bureau now has custody of more than 10,000 cubic feet of records including those at the records centers, and needless to say a vast increase is anticipated when the new building is ready for occupancy. In planning for the move, the bureau has accessioned large groups of records of permanent value now in the office of the Secretary of State, who is eager to have them removed from his vaults. The bureau plans to have a central core of permanent non-current records arranged and described before it moves.

Accession documents are kept in chronological order in a loose-leaf binder. A more formal accession book, with accession numbers assigned, is planned. All the present holdings are listed in short finding aids, assembled in a loose-leaf binder. Inventories of the official correspondence of Governor A. Harry Moore, 1932–35 and 1938–41, are ready for publication; and over 2,000 copies of *Genealogical Research: A Guide to Source*

Materials in the New Jersey State Library and Other State Agencies [182] have been distributed.

No exact figures are available for archival reference service by mail and on the premises. The number of users will increase sharply when, in the new building, the New Jersey History and Genealogy Collection, now in the General Reference Bureau of the Library, is transferred to the Bureau of History and Archives. At that time a staff member and a page will be added to the bureau staff.

The bureau has assisted in the preparation of the "Historymobile" now touring the state and in the work of the New Jersey Tercentenary Commission, with the Archival Examiner serving on its Historical Advisory Committee. Contacts with Rutgers University and other institutions of higher learning should be strengthened when the bureau has acquired greater quantities of research material.

RECORDS MANAGEMENT AND RECORDS DISPOSITION

In accordance with the 1953 act the bureau serves as the records management agency of the state. For the time being, its pertinent activities are limited to helping agencies inventory their records and to developing retention schedules. Though in the smaller agencies the bureau may do the inventorying, in the larger ones it is done by the departmental records officers with the bureau's assistance. To provide guidance a *Local Records Manual* (1962, 23 p., proc.) and a *State Records Manual* (1963, 18 p., proc.) have been issued.

For the storage of semi-current records, records centers have been established in the Switlik Building, a former parachute factory whose premises the bureau shares with the Public and Library School Services Bureau of the division, and in the basement of the Administration Building of the School for the Deaf, both of them two miles away from the State Capitol and jointly providing space for some 12,500 cubic feet of records. Inasmuch as the facility at the School for the Deaf is used for more or less inactive records, all of the records center staff is in the Switlik Building. In 1961–62 records of twenty-nine state agencies were deposited in the centers and 1,400 reference requests were processed. Policies with regard to accepting records for storage are firm. No records will be received in the centers unless they are in good order and have been scheduled, unless they must be kept for at least three years, and unless they do not demand more than eight reference services a week. It is estimated that annually about 1,200 cubic feet of records are received in the centers and that an equal quantity is disposed of.

Because the centers are too small and are otherwise inadequate, the

[182] Compiled by Rebecca Schlam and K. W. Richards (1957, proc.), 22 p.

bureau has prepared a plan (Nov., 1962) for a new records center for New Jersey, to be located in a place that the civil defense authorities do not consider a prime target area. The center would also have a security vault for the storage of copies of records essential to the continuity of government. For the time being, 7,000 reels of security microfilm have been deposited in the vaults of the Iron Mountain Atomic Storage Corporation. A "Preservation of Essential Public Records Law," fashioned after the Council of State Governments' model act, was introduced in the legislature on May 6, 1963 (S. B. No. 278), but was not acted upon.

The microfilm unit of the Bureau of Archives and History, operated with a revolving fund in the Switlik Building, is staffed with a supervisor and two operators. It is equipped with three planetary and three rotary cameras and produces about 1,000 reels of film a year. Agencies pay for material and labor, and some of them have continuing projects going on. No microfilming will be done for an agency unless its records have been scheduled. All state agency requests for microfilm equipment or microfilm service contracts are brought to the bureau's attention, and counties and municipalities have been asked to seek its advice in matters of microfilming.

As stated above, authority over the disposal of records is vested in the State Records Committee, composed of the State Auditor, the State Treasurer, the Attorney General, the Director of the Division of Local Governments, and the head of the Bureau of Archives and History, or their designees. The committee passes on the schedules prepared by, or with the assistance of, the Bureau of Archives and History. It meets at regular intervals and deals with county and municipal schedules as well as with state schedules.[183] In fiscal 1963 it received 328 requests for disposal of over 70,000 cubic feet of records and approved 17 new schedules.

COMMENTS

Although the bureau will have good accommodations, it will need a sizable expansion of its staff in order to assimilate the greatly increased number of accessions, to implement the records management program, and to carry out its responsibilities with regard to the records of the subdivisions of the state.

NEW MEXICO

New Mexico's program of records management and archives administration is one of the most recent in the United States. It reflects the increasing uniformity of professional thinking fostered by the activities

[183] The Director of this Study, who was privileged to attend the committee's meeting on April 30, 1963, was impressed by the interest of the committee members — all of them representatives of the designated state officials — and by the effective handling of the agenda prepared by the Archival Examiner.

of the Society of American Archivists and by the standards set by the National Archives and the more advanced state archival agencies.

When the territory of New Mexico was acquired by the United States in 1846, all existing records of the Spanish and Mexican periods were transferred to the custody of the United States.[184] Left with the territorial authorities, however, they lay neglected and scattered about the "Old Palace" in Santa Fe on open shelves and on floors. In 1854 the office of the Surveyor General was created, and the Spanish and Mexican land records were segregated and placed in the General Land Office. The rest of the records stayed with the territorial officials, and in 1870 the territorial Governor permitted them to be dumped in the Plaza and sold as wrapping paper. A good many of them were recovered, however, and others stayed in the offices. When the Territorial Capitol was completed in 1900, the remaining old records were moved into a vault in the office of the territorial Secretary, roughly arranged by date, tied in packages, and carefully stored. In 1903, when the Secretary needed the vault space and the Library of Congress wanted to obtain the archives, the U.S. Department of the Interior had them sent to the Library of Congress on the ground that they were the property of the federal government. They were returned to New Mexico in 1924.

John H. Vaughan reported to the American Historical Association in 1909 that the Secretary of the Territory was custodian of the executive records, records of the Office of Bonds, corporation records, Commissioner of Deeds and Board of Public Works records, original bills, laws, resolutions of the legislature, etc., and that other records were still in the offices of origin. He also reported that records were missing from almost all groups examined, that indeed in almost none were there records dated before 1850, and that in some cases there was evidence that no records had ever existed and in others that they had been stolen by curio seekers, scholars, and litigants in land cases. Although there was great confusion in the old records, those of recent date were well cared for and under adequate protection.

In the meantime the Historical Society, after its reorganization in 1882, had begun to collect records and other materials pertaining to the history of the state. For their storage, the society was given two rooms in the State Museum of New Mexico, and in 1927 public officials were authorized to turn over to the society non-current records not required by law to be kept in the agency of origin (N.M. Stats. Annot. 4-12-15). Some material

[184] Most of the following information is derived from John H. Vaughan, "A Preliminary Report on the Archives of New Mexico," *Annual Report of the American Historical Association for the Year 1909* (Washington, 1911), pp. 465–90.

was indeed placed in the custody of the society in accordance with this act. Most of it, however, remained unprocessed, and the bulk of the non-current records continued to occupy office space in the State Capitol.

As a first step toward coping with this unwholesome situation, chapter 185, Laws of 1947, provided for the microfilming and disposal of public records. Subsequently chapter 245, Laws of 1959,[185] created a State Commission of Public Records, composed of the Secretary of State, the Director of the Department of Finance and Administration, the State Law Librarian, the Director of the State Museum of New Mexico, the State Auditor, the Attorney General, and a professional historian of recognized stature. The commission was empowered to employ a State Records Administrator, who was to set up a records center and take custody of the public records transferred to him. Disposal authority was to rest with the commission, while the Attorney General was given the right of replevin.

THE STATE RECORDS CENTER AND ARCHIVES

Appointed by the State Commission of Public Records, the State Records Administrator operates both the records management and the archives program, though he has delegated responsibility for the latter to the Senior Archivist.

The 1959 records act contained an initial appropriation of $20,000 for equipment and $25,000 for each year of the biennium. For 1961 the budget was $45,000 and for 1962 $50,000. The budget for fiscal 1964 is $68,500.

Budget requests, after approval by the State Commission of Public Records, are reviewed by the Budget Division of the Department of Administration and Finance, before which the State Records Administrator is heard. He also meets with the Appropriations and Finance Subcommittee of the House and Senate before it makes its recommendations to the entire Appropriations and Finance Committee. The committee drafts House Bill No. 300, the appropriations bill.

The entire personnel of the State Records Center and Archives with the exception of the Administrator is under the state's merit system, administered by the State Personnel Board. The state provides a retirement program to which employee and state each contribute 5 per cent of the amount of the employee's salary; and a combined health, accident, and life insurance program with the premium based on the employee's salary. Fifteen days of annual and twelve days of sick leave are granted. Within salary ranges there are eight in-grade steps. Longevity increases of 3 per cent are earned after ten, thirteen, and sixteen years in the top bracket of the salary range.

In fiscal 1963, agency personnel consisted of:

[185] This is cited as the Public Records Act, New Mexico Statutes (Annot.), Vol. 10 (1959 Pocket Supplement, 71-6-1 through 71-6-19).

Records Administrator .... $10,800–$14,460
Administrative Assistant 5,280– 7,200
Typist II 2,880– 3,960
Senior Archivist 6,600– 9,000
Archivist 5,760– 7,920
Records Analysts (3).................................... 4,560– 6,300
Records Storage Man 3,600– 5,040
Records Storage Helper 2,400– 3,312

The State Records Center and Archives[186] is housed in a fire-resistant warehouse in Santa Fe, obtained by the state for that purpose. The records center and offices are at street level, and the Archives with its research room occupies the basement floor. Though modest, the accommodations may be considered satisfactory. Documents of special interest to visitors are on display in the main entrance hall and in an adjacent exhibit room.

The State Commission of Public Records publishes a processed *Annual Report* that in a few pages reviews the progress of the records management and the archives programs.

THE NEW MEXICO ARCHIVES

Under the State Records Administrator, the State Archives is administered by the Senior Archivist, who holds a Ph.D. degree in history and is fully conversant with the history of the Southwest. The incumbent served previously with the New Mexico State Historical Society.

Holdings (764 cubic feet) comprise the following: the old Spanish archives, 1620–1821, returned to the state by the Library of Congress and deposited with the Historical Society, consisting of correspondence, decrees, and many other types of records; Mexican archives, 1821–46, including Governors' letter books; territorial and state archives, consisting of records of the three branches of government; some county archives; and certain records of the city of Albuquerque. Until recently, when he released twenty cubic feet of territorial records, 1851–1912, the Secretary of State had transferred to the Archives only scattered materials. All archival material and collections of mixed private and public papers formerly in the Historical Society have been turned over to the Archives Division. The division solicits and accepts, with the approval of the chairman of the State Commission of Public Records, private papers as gifts or loans.

The archives vault is equipped partly with Vertifile equipment with doors and partly with center-type shelving. Within the compartments of the former, Spanish and Mexican documents are stored flat in boxes. Hereafter, Vertifile equipment without doors is to be installed. The use

[186] See the illustrated brochure *The New Mexico State Records Center and Archives* (n.d., n.p.), 8 p.

of standard archives boxes for modern records, however, might be more practical than an open-shelf system.

The Archives does not have a well-developed finding aid program. For the Spanish archives, there is the second volume of Ralph E. Twitchell, *The Spanish Archives of New Mexico* (Cedar Rapids, Iowa, 1913), prepared while the documents were still in the Library of Congress; for the Mexican archives, there is a partial card index. There are also a catalog of all collections, with some item-by-item entries, and a calendar for recent acquisitions. Otherwise, finding aids are practically non-existent. As a first step toward establishing over-all control of the holdings, the Senior Archivist plans to publish a guide of at least sixteen pages, and by means of yearly additions to keep it up to date.

The Archives Division has a well-equipped research room, named the Dorothy H. Woodward Research Room in honor of the late distinguished New Mexico historian. It is now supervised by the Senior Archivist, an unsatisfactory arrangement because the Archivist cannot leave the desk for any length of time. During fiscal 1963 the facilities of the division were used by 347 persons, 52 of whom required extensive service. In addition, 179 mail inquiries and 427 telephone inquiries concerning archival or historical documents were handled. Copies of archival material when requested are produced with a Verifax.

The Senior Archivist, who is an authority on New Mexico history, serves on the Research Committee of the Santa Fe Historical Foundation and teaches part time at St. Michael's College in Santa Fe. Holdings of the Archives Division are frequently used by students and faculty members of the University of New Mexico.

RECORDS MANAGEMENT AND RECORDS DISPOSITION

The records management program administered by the experienced State Records Administrator is well under way. Initially the emphasis has been on the preparation of inventories and disposal schedules, which are tied together in one document. Fourteen inventory-schedules have been completed and twenty are now being processed. These are prepared by the Records Analyst, working with departmental personnel including the respective records officers, are signed by the agency and division chiefs, and are sent to the Attorney General for his examination. They are then submitted to the State Commission of Public Records for final approval at one of its quarterly meetings. The State Records Administrator prepares the material for the meetings of the commission and attends them, while the Administrative Secretary serves as a recording secretary. Under the public records act, a unanimous vote of the commission is required for the destruction of records. Copies of the disposal schedules must be filed with the Supreme Court thirty days prior to destruction. The operation of the schedules approved is checked periodically.

Pending implementation of a full program, the State Records Administrator has prepared, and the commission has published, *A Guide to Records Disposition* (21 p., proc.) and *A Guide to Efficient Filing* (29 p., n.d).

Under the 1959 act, the State Records Administrator has been concerned solely with the management and preservation of state records. The Twenty-sixth Legislature, however, passed House Bill No. 40, which authorizes the Administrator to advise and assist the counties in the formulation of programs for the disposition of public records maintained in county offices. This program formally began on August 1, 1963, with an appropriation (sec. 3 of H.B. No. 40) of $8,500 for the first fiscal year of its operation.

The State Records Administrator operates the records center, which has a total storage capacity of 60,000 cubic feet. In fiscal 1963 the center received 2,969 cubic feet of records, disposed of 4,193 cubic feet, and handled 1,589 reference requests. At the end of that year, total center holdings amounted to 11,048 cubic feet. The center has a research room for the convenience of agency personnel, and with its own truck it can provide fifteen-minute delivery to nearby agencies that wish to borrow records.

An essential records preservation act was recently drafted but was not adopted because 1963 seemed to be "a bad money year." It may be introduced in the next legislature.

COMMENTS

1. The Senior Archivist, in consultation with experienced archival agencies of other states, should plan and implement a finding aid program for the archival holdings.

2. An increase in travel funds would enable the Senior Archivist to attend and profit from the meetings of the Society of American Archivists.

3. After completing the inventorying and scheduling of state records in agency custody, the State Records Administrator will be able to develop other phases of records management.

NEW YORK

New York State has no integrated program for the management and care of its records on both the state and local levels. At this writing, responsibility rests with three different units of the state's government.

BACKGROUNDS

The University of the State of New York and its governing body, the Board of Regents, created in 1784, absorbed the State Library in 1884.

When the legislature finally concerned itself with the preservation of the state's records, it directed the Secretary of State in December, 1847, to deliver to the Regents, for preservation in the State Library at Albany, "all such documents of historic value relative to and connected with the annals of the State" that were then kept in the Secretary's storeroom and were in his opinion "proper to be so transferred and delivered." Though at first the records thus delivered were administered by a worker in the Secretary's office, an act of 1881 authorized the trustees of the library "to appoint a suitable person to take charge of the records." This was the beginning of the Manuscripts and History Section of the State Library.

The library's role as depository of records of the state and particularly of those of the legislature was further emphasized by chapter 321 of the Laws of New York, 1859. It was jeopardized, however, by subsequent developments, for in 1895 the appointment of a State Historian responsible for collecting and publishing New York records pertaining to military and naval operations and to the state's external relations (Laws of 1895, ch. 393) threatened to impinge upon the State Library's archival responsibility. After the disastrous fire of March 29, 1911, which destroyed about two-thirds of the library's manuscript holdings, recommendations by the president of the university (i.e., the Commissioner of Education) led to the passage of chapter 380, Laws of 1911. It created in the Department of Education a Division of History and a Division of Public Records and gave to the department "control of all public records of extinct State agencies and of records transferred to the Department by municipalities." Subsequently chapter 424, Laws of 1913, gave the Division of Public Records broad powers to insure the protection and preservation of the public records of the state's political subdivisions and required all state and local officials to dispose of public records only with the consent of the Commissioner of Education.[187]

In 1915 the Board of Regents by administrative action combined the Division of Public Records and the Division of History into the Division of Archives and History and assigned to it the administration of the law of 1913. At the same time, Arnold J. F. van Laer, Archivist in the State Library, was moved, "title and all, upstairs to occupy quarters with the State Historian, an entirely practical but utterly confusing combination under which for over thirty years the Archivist of the State of New York has had no official connection with the New York State Archives housed in the Manuscripts Section of the State Library." [188]

[187] The preceding two paragraphs are based on Edward F. Rowse, "The Archives of New York," *American Archivist*, IV (Oct., 1941), 267–74; and New York, Temporary State Commission on Coordination of State Activities, *Interim Report, March 6, 1947* (Albany, 1947), pp. 17–20.

[188] Henry Howard Eddy, *The Proposed New York Records Office*, reprinted from *New York History*, July, 1946.

For the disposal of local records the act of 1913 served its purpose. A 1945 opinion of the Attorney General, however, questioned the power of the Commissioner of Education to authorize the destruction of records and cast doubts on the legality of the disposal program. The uncertainty thus created was one of the problems that engaged the attention of the Temporary Commission on Coordination of State Activities, created by chapter 1002 of the Laws of 1946. Its first *Interim Report* dealt with the Division of Archives and History and the management of state and local records. Referring to the chaotic conditions under which many public records were kept, it recommended that a central records repository be provided for state records of enduring value and for "non-current or inactive records," that a Division of Records Administration in the Executive Department be charged "with responsibility for the preservation of State records of enduring value and the prompt and systematic disposal of useless records," and that this division also have "the duty of giving advice and assistance to local officials with regard to the preservation of local records" and "power to authorize the disposal of useless local records." [189] On the other hand, an advisory committee, appointed by the Commissioner of Education in December, 1946, and composed of Margaret C. Norton, Luther H. Evans, and Solon J. Buck, recommended combining the archives function, state records management, and local records management in a single State Records Office, to be established in the Department of Education and to have status equal to that of the State Library.[190]

Neither report had any direct effect. Independently, chapter 223, Laws of 1950, established a state records management program under the Division of the Budget. In 1960 this program was transferred to the jurisdiction of the Office of General Services. The local records program, however, is still under the Division of Archives and History of the Education Department, while the Manuscripts and History Section of the State Library retains, but adds little to, its archival holdings.

THE STATE ARCHIVES FUNCTION

Historically the State Library, under the Commissioner of Education, has been the depository for non-current valuable state records and has exercised this function through its Manuscripts and History Section.

As an integral part of the State Library, the Manuscripts and History Section has no separate budget except for the purchase of manuscripts, maps, books, and related materials. The head of the section makes his budget request to the State Librarian. Applicants for positions on the staff must qualify under the minimum requirements of the Department of

[189] New York, Temporary State Commission, *op. cit.*, p. 15.
[190] Advisory Committee on New York State's Records System, *Report* (Albany, 1947, proc.), 15 p.

Civil Service and must pass competitive examinations to receive appoint-ment. To be admitted to the examination for section head — designated as Associate Librarian (Manuscripts and History) — a candidate must have, or must be eligible for, a state public librarian's professional certificate, a Master's degree in library science, and a Ph.D. degree or teaching or li-brary experience. Applicants for the position of Assistant Librarian (Man-uscripts and History) are tested in principles and techniques of manuscript work, library materials and their selection, and principles and practices of library science and administration. Patronage and political pressure are absent. All staff members have degrees in library science and, effective Au-gust 1, 1963, they receive the following salaries: Associate Librarian, Manu-scripts and History, $9,480–$12,147; Senior Librarian, Manuscripts and History, $7,350–$9,513; and four Assistant Librarians, Manuscripts and History, $5,910–$7,723. In-grade salary increases are granted on a merit basis, and longevity payments are accorded after ten and fifteen years of service.

The extensive holdings of the Manuscripts and History Section occupy 40,000 cubic feet of space. In addition to the rich manuscript collections, maps and atlases, historical prints and photographs, and sheet music, they include records of the Dutch and English colonial periods; land papers, 1692–1803; and many other important series. The original laws are kept in a maximum-security vault. The bulk of the archival material is stored in the stacks, wherever space has been found for it. On some of the stack levels accessions have been piled up — still in the containers in which they happened to arrive.

Only 80 per cent of the accumulations are controlled by a card catalog with author, title, and subject entries. These entries are based on inven-tories prepared in 1951 as an outgrowth of WPA activities, some of them covering whole groups, some of them classes or series. The card catalog serves as a general finding aid, while the inventories are consulted for more detailed information. Another set of inventories was developed for the New York State Inventory Project initiated by the Bureau of the Budget in 1955; this covers records series of twenty-five or more linear inches. These inventories, while not referred to in the card catalog entries, are readily available to staff and patrons.

Reference service consumes much of the staff's time. Each year about 5,800 letters are written in response to requests for archival information including that from genealogical and census records; approximately 4,100 persons visit the research room; and an average of 1,700 telephone in-quiries are answered.

For photoreproduction, the section uses the photocopying unit admin-istered by the State Librarian's administrative assistant. The unit has a Xerox machine and two flatbed microfilm cameras, and a Xerox horizontal camera is available to it. A rotary camera is rented when needed. Fumigating and laminating equipment has not been provided. Documents in need of repair are sent to a commercial firm for laminating.

Engrossed acts and "bill jackets" are still being accessioned. Otherwise the Manuscripts and History Section is unable to carry out its mandate to "acquire, maintain and preserve for research, reference and cultural purposes a comprehensive and integrated collection of New York State Archives. . . ." [191] In fact, the more recent accessions are kept under indefensible storage conditions; and some of them, such as the vast file concerning civilian activities during World War II, should have been thoroughly screened before acceptance.

It is difficult to see how the State Library could be enabled to reassume its archival function. Storage space is the crucial problem. It could be solved only if the museum were moved out of the Education Building and the space it occupies (about 2,000,000 cubic feet) were turned over to the library. Furthermore, the Manuscripts and History Section's present staff could not be expected to implement a modern archives program; it is hardly adequate to administer the present extensive holdings.

THE STATE RECORDS MANAGEMENT PROGRAM

Under the act of 1913 the evaluation of state records for disposal and authority to permit their destruction were functions of the Commissioner of Education and were administered by the Division of Archives and History. Inasmuch as the 1945 opinion of the Attorney General, referred to above, questioned the Commissioner's power to authorize destruction, chapter 223 of the Laws of 1950 (sec. 186 of the State Finance Law) gave to the Director of the Bureau of the Budget power to authorize or require the disposal of state records; to authorize or require the transfer of non-current state records to designated depositories; to inquire into, and require reports on, "the condition, character, amount and methods of keeping such records"; and to promulgate the necessary rules and regulations to that effect. Chapter 460, Laws of 1960, assigned the program to the Office of General Services, where it is administered by the Bureau of Records Management, Division of Central Operations. Before this transfer the Bureau of the Budget had conducted a survey of the records of all state departments and agencies as part of a statewide management improvement program.[192]

In fiscal 1964 about $28,000 of the total budget of the Office of General Services is earmarked for the records management program. It includes the salaries of two professional employees — the Chief of the Bureau ($11,680–

[191] New York State, Education Department, The State Library, *Organization and Functions* (May, 1958), chart B.

[192] Vernon B. Santen, "The New York State Inventory Project," *American Archivist*, XX (Oct., 1957), 357–67.

$14,774) and a Senior Public Records Analyst ($7,350-$9,513) — and one stenographer ($3,420-$4,063). Maximum salary is received after six years, with longevity increases after five and ten years at the maximum of the grade. Appointments are made in accordance with civil service regulations; that is, the appointee is selected from the first three persons on the list of eligibles. For participation in the entrance-level professional competitive examinations, a Bachelor's or Master's degree or five years of experience in a semi-professional position are required.

To implement the law of 1960, the Commissioner of General Services issued, on May 12, 1961, a set of records management rules that is Part 295 of Title 9 of the *Official Compilation of Codes, Rules and Regulations of the State of New York.* He has also appointed from the state agencies a seven-member State Records Management Advisory Council to advise him and his staff in the formulation of policies and programs in the records management field.

Under article 13, State Finance Law, the Commissioner authorizes the disposal of state records, except that disposal of judicial records is left to the justices of the Appellate Division of the Supreme Court in their geographic areas of jurisdiction (section 89 of the Judiciary Law). Disposition of records is authorized by means of lists or schedules. Agency requests to destroy records are examined by the Director of the Budget, by the Comptroller, by the Commissioner of Education, and by the Commissioner of General Services with consideration of their respective areas of responsibility; and any one of them may stop a proposed destruction within a period of thirty days. The same procedure is followed for both listed and scheduled records. Provision is made for emergency destruction of records that have become a menace to human life or human health and to property. There are also provisions for the loan or lease of records. It was estimated that, by the spring of 1963, 80 per cent of the state's records were scheduled for retention or disposal and that about 90 per cent of the records currently being created were scheduled.

The Commissioner's rules and regulations also spell out the records management responsibilities of heads of state agencies. They must conduct an active and continuing program "for the effective management, preservation and disposition" of their records and must appoint a staff member to serve as the agency's records officer. In setting up and administering the program, agencies receive the advice of the Bureau of Records Management. This office gives about a third of its time to records management advisory service and another third to disposition and retention scheduling. The remaining third of its work is research in these two fields, a function in which it co-operates closely with the Public Records Section of the Division of Archives and History of the State Education Department. The excellent collaboration between the officers responsible for state and local records management, respectively, has created a general awareness among state and local officials that in the total area of records management expert service is available. The two officers have provided technical assistance to the essential records program administered by the State Civil Defense Commission as part of the state's continuity of government program.

The Commissioner of General Services also has authority to require state agencies to transfer non-current state records to depositories designated by him. Careful plans for a records center are now being developed with the participation of the Records Management Advisory Council. Designed for a storage capacity of 210,000 cubic feet and expandable by a further addition to over 300,000 cubic feet, the center will have a receiving area, an office area, an inspection area, and a vault area. The last will have six units, three to be used for the storage of paper records, two for the storage of microfilm, and one for the storage of tapes. The center is expected to cost $1,500,000 including storage equipment but exclusive of operational equipment, which will cost $75,000 more. Material to be destroyed within two years will not be taken into the center. It is estimated that, when ready for occupancy, 80 per cent of the vault space will be used. The yearly turnover of records in the center will amount to 72,000 cubic feet.

THE LOCAL RECORDS PROGRAM [193]

The local records program of the state has its roots in the act of 1913, referred to above. This law provided for the office of the Supervisor of Public Records as part of the newly created Division of Public Records (later combined with the Division of History of the State Department of Education). The act, and consequently the work of the supervisors, emphasized the preservation of records and contributed to that end. It did not furnish a tenable basis for the destruction of useless local records, nor did it give assistance to local units in the management of their ever increasing record holdings.

An act of 1951 (Public Officers Law, sec. 65-b) established a centrally controlled local records disposition program, and subsequently there has been developed an impressive program of records management assistance to local officials, which operates on a request basis and covers such areas as microfilming, filing and indexing, protection and storage, and equipment. The city of New York and its counties subject to the city charter are

---

[193] The history and development of this program is discussed in great detail by Dorothea S. Santen, "New York's Local Records Management Program" (M.A. thesis, Maxwell Graduate School of Citizenship and Public Affairs, 1956), 115 p. See also Howard W. Crocker, "The Local Records Program in New York State," *American Archivist*, XIII (Jan., 1950), 3–14; and "The New York State Local Record Program," *ibid.*, XX (Jan., 1957), 31–40. On the records program of the city of New York, see Jason Horn, "Municipal Archives and Records Center of the City of New York," *American Archivist*, XVI (Oct., 1953), 311–20, and James Katsaros, "Managing the Records of the World's Greatest City," *ibid.*, XXIII (Apr., 1960), 175–80.

exempt from participation in the program. Disposition of the records of all local courts, like that of state courts, is left to the justices of the Appellate Division of the Supreme Court in their geographic areas of jurisdiction (sec. 89, Judiciary Law).

The local records program is administered by the Associate Public Records Analyst ($9,010–$11,572), who reports to the State Historian and Director of the Division of Archives and History in the State Education Department. He is assisted by two Senior Public Records Analysts ($7,350–$9,513), a Public Records Analyst ($5,910–$7,723), and a secretary ($3,420–$4,603). In fiscal 1963–64 the sum of $42,800 was budgeted for the local records program. Staff members are appointed in accordance with civil service regulations and must have college degrees and some management experience. A training program "in the shop" and practical experience are designed to equip them for independent work in the field.

The Division of Archives and History is housed in the Education Building and has no holdings, for at present records remain with the local units. To provide for their storage insofar as they are to be preserved, a plan for regional depositories was suggested in 1944.[194] Now the Public Records Section is experimenting with the construction of local depositories or records centers. In addition to a county archives in Montgomery County and a protected storage facility in Herkimer County for the records of towns and villages, the first county records center was to be in operation in Warren County late in 1963, and a center for Oneida County is being developed. A municipal records center in the town of Oyster Bay has been functioning since 1961. All these are considered test installations, to be appraised before other centers are encouraged.

The local records disposition program, operated on the authority of section 65-b of the Public Officers Law, is the core of the local records management program. Disposition is by list rather than schedule, and the Public Records Section has certain well-warranted doubts about the wisdom of converting the operation to disposition by schedule. Under the present system, records analysts select or local officers request records for disposal; the analysts assess their value by consultation with officials concerned; they check the laws, court decisions, and legal opinions concerning similar records; and, with the aid of the State Historian and others, they set tentative retention periods. The State Historian, for the Commissioner of Education, submits the lists with their tentative retention periods for review by state departments and agencies, which may request an extension of the retention periods or even permanent retention of the records. Besides checking on the continuing value to the state, the State Comptroller also considers possible federal interest in the records listed. Upon completion

[194] Hermann F. Robinton, "A Proposed Regional Public Records Plan for New York State," *New York History*, XXVI (Apr., 1945), 189–207.

of the entire reviewing process, the analyst sets a retention period. "Local Records Disposition Request" forms, listing types of records and records of various local offices for which retention periods have been cleared, are sent to all local officials having such records in their custody; and these lists facilitate their work in obtaining disposal authorization. In applying for consent to destroy, the requesting officer submits the request to the Commissioner of Education, attaching a certification of approval by his governing body; a records analyst checks the request; the Commissioner signs; the State Historian countersigns; and the request is then returned to the local official as consent to destroy. Retention periods have been set for more than 2,000 types of local records, and "Local Records Disposition Request" forms have been developed covering nearly all the disposable records in towns, villages, and school districts and in most county and city offices. Established retention periods are periodically reviewed for possible reduction, and considerable work is being done on the records of offices in which a large proportion requires long-term retention.

Since 1950 the Division of Archives and History, through its Public Records Section, has been extremely active in providing records management services to local government units. It has issued a number of manuals on how to control records, suggesting filing systems for villages, towns, and schools; it has also issued a filing system for historical information, a basic index for minutes, and guide lines for alphabetizing records. Other publications, such as a guide to managing town records and a guide to the operation of a municipal records center, are in various stages of preparation. Drafts of all these documents have been and are being submitted to appropriate associations and individuals for comment and criticism. *A Preliminary Guide for Public Education Records in New York State* reflects an attempt to develop lists of research material for scholars and others interested. Of the enthusiastic acceptance of the entire program there seems to be no doubt.

An integrated program for microfilming records of about 20,000 local offices — at a cost of several million dollars — is considered impossible. Local initiative and appropriations must be relied upon, and some thirty counties are taking steps to microfilm their land records, particularly deed and mortgage records. Should there ever be an active state archives, it might obtain funds to buy copies of the earlier land records.

It is estimated that the Public Records Section gives about 25 per cent of its staff time to records disposition, 50 per cent to records management advisory services, 10–15 per cent to research, and the rest to travel and to maintaining and cultivating contacts with local officials.

COMMENTS

1. New York does not have an archival agency equipped and staffed to receive and administer the state's non-current valuable records.

2. Both the state and the local records management programs are progressing remarkably well. Thanks to constant co-operation and exchange of information between the officials in charge, problems stemming from the division of administrative responsibility have been effectively overcome. A policy decision, however, should be reached to provide an integrated state archival and records management program defined by statute. If more than one agency is involved, the duties and responsibilities of each should be spelled out for administrative guidance.

NORTH CAROLINA

In North Carolina the concept of a historical-archival agency called a department of archives and history, which was first developed in Alabama, has been realized in its full potentiality and with ready adaptation to the changing needs of the time.

BACKGROUNDS

As in other southern states, it was a historical society that gave North Carolina the impetus toward establishing an organization that was to concern itself with the history of the state and its sources.[195] On January 23, 1903, the State Literary and Historical Association requested the general assembly to set up "a commission to preserve the State's history," and accordingly there was passed a bill (North Carolina, Pub. Laws, 1903, ch. 767) setting up in Raleigh the North Carolina Historical Commission of five members. It was "to have collected from files of old newspapers, from court records, church records and elsewhere valuable documents pertaining to the history of the State" and to have them published by the State Printer. The powers of the commission were broadened four years later (Pub. Laws, 1907, ch. 714) by giving it responsibility for marking and preserving historic sites and buildings, diffusing knowledge of the state's history, and encouraging the study of, and research on, that history. Also, and more significantly, state, county, town, and other public officials were authorized "to turn over to said Commission for preservation any official books, records, documents, original papers, newspaper files, printed books or portraits not in current use." The commission's authority was drastically strengthened by the Public Records Act of 1935 (Pub. Laws, 1935, ch. 265), which gave it authority over the disposal of official records, both state and local, and made all public officials responsible for the proper care of their records.

[195] For the following see *The North Carolina Historical Commission: Forty Years of Public Service, 1903–1943* (Raleigh, 1942), 115 p.; *The First Half Century, the North Carolina Department of Archives and History: A Record of Achievement, 1903–1953* (Raleigh, 1953), 26 p. A good summary, including later developments, is in H. G. Jones, "The State Department of Archives and History," *North Carolina Libraries*, XIX (Winter, 1961), 5–15.

Always alert to its task, the Historical Commission initiated and carried out programs for the collection and preservation of records of World Wars I and II, and it participated effectively in the work of the WPA Historical Records Survey. In 1943 the name of the commission, whose size had been increased from five to seven by an act of 1941 (Pub. Laws, 1941, ch. 306), was changed to Department of Archives and History (Pub. Laws, 1943, ch. 237) — hereafter called the department — in order to emphasize its archival activities and to stress the importance and permanence of its work. It operates under an Executive Board of seven members appointed by the Governor and serving overlapping terms of six years each.

In the postwar period the department entered the field of records management. A law of 1945 (Pub. Laws, 1945, ch. 55) gave it basic authority to operate such a program. It lacked the appropriation and facilities for the purpose, until it received the money for a records center in 1947 and until the center could be opened in September, 1953.[196] The department's responsibility for current and semi-current records received final recognition in 1959 by "an act clarifying the authority of the State Department of Archives and History to conduct a records management program for state agencies" (Pub. Laws, 1959, ch. 68), including the operation of records centers and a centralized microfilming program. In the administration of the program, now expanded into the areas of records creation and maintenance, the department is to have the assistance of all public officials.[197]

THE DEPARTMENT OF ARCHIVES AND HISTORY

To discharge its manifold duties, the Department of Archives and History was organized in the 1940's in a number of divisions that operate under the Director's effective yet broad-minded supervision. They are the Division of Archives and Manuscripts, the Division of Historic Sites, the Division of Museums, and the Division of Publications. The Division of Archives and Manuscripts, under the State Archivist, consists of the following sections: Administration, which includes the Microfilm Services Center; Archives; Local Records; and State Records — each administered by an Assistant State Archivist. The State Records Section operates the records management program for state agencies, while the Local Records Section has responsibility for records management on the local level. The latter also processes local records that are transferred to the department and carries on a statewide program of inventorying, scheduling, repairing, and microfilming county and municipal records.

The Historical Commission's first budget (1903) was $500. By 1907 the budget had gone up to $5,000, and in 1931 it reached a pre-depression

[196] Fannie Memory Blackwelder, "The North Carolina Records Management Program," *North Carolina Historical Review*, XXXV (July, 1959), 346.

[197] For the department's legal history see the *Laws Pertaining to the Activities and Functions of the State Department of Archives and History* (Raleigh, 1960), 16 + 3 p.

peak of $30,865. Severely cut during the depression, appropriations began a steep climb after World War II, until they totaled $690,000 in fiscal 1962 for all purposes of the department. In fiscal 1964 the budget dropped to $662,000, but it still includes the impressive sum of $285,000 for the agency's archives and records management program.

The budget of the department originates from consultation by the budget officer with the division heads. After final approval of the various requests by the Director, the division heads participate in defending the estimates before the Budget Division of the Department of Administration and before the Advisory Budget Commission, which is composed of two senators, two representatives, and two other persons appointed by the Governor. After all this screening, the Joint Appropriations Committee and finally the general assembly are likely to look benignly at the amounts budgeted.

The work of the Historical Commission, and later that of the department, has benefited greatly from the stability of its personnel, the result partly of dedication to the work of the agency and partly of enlightened salary arrangements. The first Secretary of the commission (until 1907 one of its members) was R. D. W. Connor, whose appointment as Archivist of the United States has been called "the most significant national recognition that has come to the North Carolina Historical Commission."[198] In 1908 an archivist was added to the commission's paid staff. Increase in personnel was rapid when the activities and responsibilities of the agency expanded after World War II. The total staff of the department now consists of ninety-eight persons, forty-five of whom are employed in the archives and records management program.

The department's staff operates under the State Personnel Act. Excellent job descriptions explaining the nature of the work and acceptable experience and training for all positions have been developed by the State Personnel Department (the professional ones with the assistance of the Department of Archives and History), and these govern the appointment of incoming personnel. Payment is based on a salary schedule that provides increases in a number of steps. Salaries of janitors, clerks, and lower-grade professional personnel are quite adequate, but supervisory positions are difficult to fill at the present pay rates.

In fiscal 1964 some representative salaries were:

Director	$12,000
State Archivist	7,656– $9,744
Assistant State Archivist for State Records (Records Management Consultant II)	6,960– 8,844
Assistant State Archivist for Archives (Archivist III)	6,024– 7,656

[198] Henry S. Stroupe, "The North Carolina Department of Archives and History — the First Half Century," *North Carolina Historical Review*, XXXI (Apr., 1954), 195.

Assistant State Archivist for Local Records
(Archivist III) 6,024– 7,656
Records Management Consultant I 5,748– 7,294
Archivist II 5,220– 6,636
Archivist I 4,752– 6,024
Clerk IV 4,524– 5,748
Clerk III 2,744– 4,752
Photographer I 2,744– 4,752
Stenographer II 3,408– 4,320
Reproduction Equipment Operator II 3,408– 4,320
Clerk II 3,252– 4,116
Janitor-Messenger 2,352– 2,964
Janitor 2,244– 2,832

During the first four years of its existence, neither an office nor staff was available to the commission. From 1907 to 1914 the Secretary occupied a room on the second floor of the Capitol at Raleigh. In 1914 the commission moved to the State Administration (now Library) Building on Morgan Street. Since 1939 the department has had its quarters, now air-conditioned, in the State Office Building, later renamed the Education Building, where it occupies the first floor and half of the ground floor, a total of 48,890 square feet. Space is its most critical problem, so critical that some groups of archives have had to be sent to the records center. The Microfilm Services Center is located in the old YMCA Building (recently purchased by the state), and one employee is stationed in the Capitol. Both the Carolina Charter Tercentenary Commission and the North Carolina Confederate Centennial Commission approved support of the request for a new building as their most important project. In 1963 the general assembly appropriated $3,000,000 to construct a new building for the Department of Archives and History and the State Library and an additional $50,000 to build a security vault for records essential in case of disaster. It is hoped that the building can be completed in 1965.

The department has very effectively made its services known by means of flyers addressed to the general public and to special-interest groups. Information supplied in an eight-page pamphlet, *Services to the Public* (1956), which had been preceded by a similar one (1943), was supplemented and elaborated in *Historical Research in the North Carolina Department of Archives and History* (1957, 8 p.) and *Genealogical Research in the Department of Archives and History* (1962, 8 p.). *Records Management in North Carolina* (1960, 12 p.) is another such publication of the department.

As for more substantial publications, the department's record is most impressive. By 1962 it had "published a total of 518 items, either original material or reprints. These include documentary volumes, finding media of [its] archives and manuscripts, pamphlets, leaflets, maps, charts, biennial reports, the *North Carolina Historical Review,* and *Carolina Com-*

ments." [199] During the last biennium reported on, a total of 187,998 items were distributed. The *North Carolina Historical Review* (40 vols., 1924–63) ranks high among state historical magazines, and the *Biennial Report* is one of the few truly informative reports of state archival agencies. The department is expected to take over and complete the great task of republishing the *Colonial Records of North Carolina*, which has been initiated by the Carolina Charter Tercentenary Commission.

The department's success in administering its archives program undoubtedly profits from its prestige as the historical agency of the state. In 1914 "the Hall of History was transferred from the State Museum to the Historical Commission," a move involving "over 11,000 objects." [200] Under the department's Division of Museums, it has become a showcase to document the principles and ideals upon which the state was founded. Assistance to the Tarheel Junior Historian Association is part of the division's responsibilities. In 1955 the historic sites function was entrusted to the department, and by 1960 nine such projects were under the care of its Division of Historic Sites. Assistance is also given to local and private non-profit organizations engaged in similar work. Furthermore, in 1955 the general assembly affiliated the Tryon Palace Commission, responsible for restoring and managing this palace in New Bern, with the Department of Archives and History. A historical markers program, begun in 1935, is now conducted as part of the historic sites program.

It is characteristic of the department's role in the state's historical activities that its Director serves *ex officio* as Secretary of the executive committees of the Carolina Charter Tercentenary Commission and the North Carolina Confederate Centennial Commission and is a member *ex officio* of many other state commissions in the historical field.

THE ARCHIVES PROGRAM

In accordance with its initial mandate and subsequent legislation, the department has acquired 7,000 cubic feet of permanently valuable records of state agencies, counties, and other governmental units; records of individuals, business firms, churches, labor unions, and other organizations; copies or reproductions of material relating to North Carolina in the possession of the United States and foreign governments; maps; newspapers; pamphlets; and textbooks. When the commission in 1943 reviewed its past activities, the records of the most important state agencies and records from seventy-three of the state's one hundred counties had found their way into its custody.[201] In 1962 the number for counties had grown to ninety-

[199] North Carolina Department of Archives and History, *Twenty-ninth Biennial Report, 1960–1962* (Raleigh, 1962), pp. 67–83.

[200] Stroupe, *loc. cit.*, pp. 190 ff.

[201] See the guide to the holdings of the department in *Forty Years of Public Service*, pp. 62–85. For a more up-to-date summary of the holdings see Philip M. Hamer (ed.),

five. Since 1959 the holdings of the Division of Archives and Manuscripts have been enriched by the results of the newspaper microfilm project, aimed at microfilming all North Carolina newspapers published before 1870 and many later ones. This was an operation of great complexity, since it involved obtaining microfilms of scattered runs or copies from institutions outside the state.[202] On the other hand, miscellaneous printed material, including pamphlets, broadsides, and catalogs, has been turned over to various libraries — a wise step.

From the first, the department has been successful in taking in from state and local agencies and other sources accessions that are reported regularly in its *Biennial Report.* Careful control is kept over accessions, but strangely enough they are not numbered, although numbering is now an almost general practice.

Because there are two other excellent manuscript depositories in the state, the division does not pursue an aggressive policy of acquiring private manuscripts. Substantial amounts of these, however, have come to it since the publication of the North Carolina Historical Records Survey Project's *Guide to the Manuscript Collections in the Archives of the North Carolina Historical Commission* (Raleigh, 1942); therefore, all accessions after 1939 are now being analyzed for the purpose of organizing the manuscript collections into a coherent whole and preparing a new guide.

Arrangement and description of the holdings have suffered from rapid intake and lack of personnel available for these functions. As in many other state archival agencies, there was for some time no up-to-date guide or other over-all finding aid that would help the intelligent research worker to orient himself. Work on unprocessed groups was to be completed in 1963, however, and a guide to the archival holdings was to be published in the same year.

Microfilm operations are not centralized. The department microfilms records of state agencies in its State Records Section, but it carries on other microfilming operations: (1) in the Local Records Section, which microfilms in the counties all records classified as essential and permanent (three cameramen move from county to county in this project); and (2) in the Administration Unit of the Division of Archives and Manuscripts, which microfilms all early North Carolina newspapers and provides microfilming services at a fee for anyone who desires copies of materials in the Archives, and which operates the Microfilm Services Center in the basement of the old YMCA Building in Raleigh. The Microfilm Services Center processes all microfilm produced, makes positive copies, and performs other

---

A Guide to Archives and Manuscripts in the United States (New Haven, 1961), pp. 477–79.

[202] Department of Archives and History, *North Carolina Newspapers on Microfilm* (Raleigh, 1962, proc.), 12 p. (revised, 1963); and H. G. Jones and Julius H. Avant (eds.), *Union List of North Carolina Newspapers, 1751–1900* (Raleigh, 1963, proc.), 152 p.

services relating to microfilm. More than 400,000 linear feet are produced annually. The Division of Archives and Manuscripts has a new continuous model photostat machine and a Xerox 914 copier operated in the Archives Section. Still photography is a function of the Division of Museums.

For repair work, a Barrow laminator has been in operation since 1950. Three employees devote their full time to the restoration of documents, and they laminate currently 100,000 pages a year. Approximately two-thirds of the records being laminated are from the counties; the rest are state records, private manuscripts, and other materials in the Archives. The department has its binding done by commercial contract. The repair equipment is used in off hours for the lamination of materials for libraries and private individuals who pay the operator for his time and reimburse the department for supplies used.

Approximately 2,640 persons consult nearly 6,000 records each year in the divisional research room, where two experienced staff members are on duty. About 30,000 photographic copies and 1,000 feet of negative microfilm are produced for the public. Fill-in form letters are put to good use in answering mail inquiries, furnishing copies as requested, and making certifications from the records. About 4,150 mail and telephone inquiries are handled per year.

As early as 1911 Dr. Connor was able to report "that students are beginning to find their way to . . . [the Commission] and to make use of . . . [its holdings] in their investigations into North Carolina and American history." [203] This trend has continued. During the 1960–62 biennium visitors and mail inquirers from twenty-nine institutions consulted the holdings of the division. Another service to scholarship is the one-semester course in archives administration offered by the department in co-operation with Meredith College.

RECORDS MANAGEMENT AND RECORDS DISPOSITION

For a good many years the department has been dedicated to the idea that "both records administration and archives are part of a larger whole and administratively should not be divided." [204] The present expanded records management program is based on General Statutes, 132-8, as amended by the 1961 general assembly. It requires the department to conduct a program "for the application of efficient and economical management methods to the creation and utilization, maintenance, retention, preservation, and disposal of official records" and "to establish standards, procedures, and techniques for effective management of public records," to make surveys for that purpose, and "to recommend improvements in current records management." The amendment requires the department

[203] North Carolina Historical Commission, *General Information* (Raleigh, 1911), p. 19.
[204] Christopher Crittenden, "The North Carolina Record Center," *American Archivist*, XVIII (Jan., 1955), 56.

also to "establish and maintain a program for the selection and preservation of public records considered essential to the operation of government and to the protection of the rights and interests of persons" and, to the extent necessary and possible, to produce preservation duplicates "of such essential records."

On January 24, 1962, all agency heads were required by Governor Terry Sanford to appoint records officers who will work with the department "in coordinating the records management program." For their assistance, the department published at the same time its *Records Management Handbook: Records Disposition* (21 p., proc.). Funds were obtained in 1961 to expand the program to include supervision over the creation as well as maintenance, disposal, and preservation of public records. The Department of Archives and History has the final disposal authority for state records (G.S., 121-5). Schedules are drawn up by the department in cooperation with agency records officers, the agency heads certify that the respective records no longer have official or administrative value after certain specified dates, and the department specifies that they have no value for research purposes. By 1963 inventories including disposal and retention schedules had been completed for all but one major state agency. Recently the authority of the department has been further strengthened by a memorandum of the Department of Administration (Mar. 19, 1962), according to which that department will approve requests for new filing equipment only after discussion with the Department of Archives and History. A second records management handbook, *Files and Filing*, was published in 1963; a third, *State Records Center*, in 1963; and a fourth, *Essential Records*, will follow in 1964. With considerable thought, the Assistant State Archivist for State Records has projected the work of his section for the next six years.

First established without the participation of the Department of Archives and History and in wholly unsuitable premises, the records center since 1953 has been housed in a new building operated by the State Records Section of the Division of Archives and Manuscripts. In accordance with chapter 68, Session Laws of 1959, the center is under the exclusive control of the department as one of its "mandatory functions." Conversion to the use of shelving and corrugated boxes has increased its storage capacity about 30 per cent to 37,000 cubic feet, and holdings are estimated at 26,750 cubic feet. During the last biennium reported on, 13,484 cubic feet of records were received at the center and 8,211 cubic feet were removed. Generally speaking, turnover at the center seems to be fairly rapid. Agencies refer to their records either by telephone (47,300 calls per year) or by personal visits to the center (200 per year).

A central microfilm project was started by the department in 1951 and, with a steady increase in staff and facilities, has been in successful operation ever since. Upon completion of the new records center, the operation was moved to that building "so as to coordinate the microfilm project with the overall records control program." [205]

LOCAL RECORDS MANAGEMENT

The beginnings of records management service to local government may be traced to North Carolina's early concern with local records. In 1907, "county, town, or other officials" (Pub. Laws, 1907, ch. 714) had been authorized to turn records over to the Historical Commission, and in the following decades records from many counties were transferred to its custody. The first concrete step toward setting up a local records management program was taken in 1957, when funds were appropriated for the position of a public records examiner. He began his activities in 1958. A bill formally authorizing a county records management program and appropriating the necessary funds was passed and was signed on June 19, 1959 (Pub. Laws, 1959, ch. 1162). This made it possible to establish the County Records Section, now called Local Records Section, in the Division of Archives and Manuscripts and to staff and equip it. The section has the following duties: (1) receiving and processing records transferred to the State Archives; (2) inventorying and scheduling county records; (3) repairing those needing attention; (4) microfilming permanently valuable county records; (5) processing and preserving security copies; (6) providing similar service to municipalities and other subdivisions of the state as far as possible.[206]

In carrying forward its work, the Local Records Section has the help of an Advisory Committee on County Records composed of active county officials appointed by the department. This committee assisted in the preparation of the *County Records Manual* (1960, 73 p.), republished as *County Records Manual, 1962*. Similarly, the *Municipal Records Manual* was produced with the help of an Advisory Committee on Municipal Records composed of active municipal officials appointed by the department. Microfilming of permanently valuable municipal records is being undertaken as time and funds permit.

COMMENTS

1. A new building is the department's first *desideratum*.

2. The program of arrangement and description of archives should be intensified, as soon as additional personnel becomes available.

---

[205] Blackwelder, *loc. cit.*, p. 349.

[206] On the work of the Local Records Section, see H. G. Jones, "North Carolina's Local Records Program," *American Archivist*, XXIV (Jan., 1961), 25–41; and John A. McMahon, "The Local Records Program in North Carolina," *North Carolina Historical Review*, XXXIX (Spring, 1962), 165–74; McMahon, "A County Official Looks at a State-Supervised County Records Program," *American Archivist*, XXV (Apr., 1962), 211–18. Records and microfilms acquired are processed by the Records Unit of the Local Records Section in accordance with a detailed *Instruction Manual* (May, 1961), 21 p. + appendix, 11 p. (proc.).

3. Salaries of Assistant State Archivist positions should be adjusted to bring them into line with salaries in other states for positions of comparable responsibility.

NORTH DAKOTA

By established custom, the North Dakota State Historical Society has served as a depository for permanently valuable state records.

BACKGROUNDS

When North and South Dakota became separate states, the territorial records were divided by lot, with North Dakota receiving the papers of the Governors and territorial Secretaries and those pertaining to institutions in the state and with South Dakota supposedly getting the rest.[207] How the records that North Dakota obtained came into the custody of the library of the State Historical Society (founded in 1884) is not clear. In 1914 it was reported that the archives were in a chaotic condition and that efforts to make them accessible were frustrated by the cramped space in the library, then housed in the State Capitol at Bismarck.[208]

THE STATE HISTORICAL SOCIETY

The State Historical Society is governed by a Board of Directors comprising sixteen elected and five *ex officio* members (the Secretary of State, the Governor, the Treasurer, the State Auditor, and the Director of the Game and Fish Commission) and is headed by the Superintendent, who supervises the administration of the society's museum and library and the operation of the State Parks Committee. The 1963–65 budget appropriated $105,250 for the Historical Society and $283,388 for the State Parks Committee. Practically all the society's income is derived from state funds.

The society's librarian, responsible for the library, newspapers, maps, pictorial material, state and federal documents, manuscripts, and archives, receives a salary of $5,220 — after twelve years on the job. There are also a clerk and a microfilm operator. There is no special appropriation for archival purposes.

Originally housed in the State Capitol, the society moved in 1924 into the Liberty Memorial Building, a four-story stone structure, 105 by 61 feet, erected at a cost of $415,000. Of the seven stack levels in wings 50 by 20 feet, five are occupied by the Historical Society and two by the State Library Commission, which has offices in the same building.[209]

[207] For the amusing story, see *Official Report of the Proceedings and Debates of the First Constitutional Convention of North Dakota* . . . (Bismarck, 1889), pp. 862 ff., 887–90, and 926 ff., and Margaret Rose, "The Archives of Dakota Territory," *American Archivist*, XXVI (July, 1963), 307–13.

[208] National Association of State Libraries, *Proceedings and Addresses, 1913–1914* (Washington, 1914), p. 26.

[209] Lewis F. Crawford, "The Liberty Memorial Building," *North Dakota Historical Quarterly*, I (Oct., 1926), 46.

Archival holdings are stored in a basement vault and on the seventh floor of the building. They include the 1885 territorial census, also available on microfilm, the 1915 and 1925 state censuses, federal land records, and papers of the territorial and state Governors, the last kept folded in metal containers as arranged by WPA personnel. In the past there was no regular flow of record material into the library, but during fiscal 1962 the Assistant Administrator for Records Management transferred 199 cubic feet of records to the library.[210]

Archival material can be made available to searchers in the library's research room, but it is apparently little used, except for census records. The state departments most interested in these records — the agencies concerned with vital statistics, social security, and welfare — do their own searching.

A microfilm planetary camera is available and is used chiefly to film newspapers and private papers owned by the society.

RECORDS MANAGEMENT AND RECORDS DISPOSITION

A records management act (Acts, 1961, ch. 33; Pocket Supplement to the Centennial Code, ch. 54, sec. 46.01–46.11), which became effective on July 1, 1961, had its origin in a records management survey completed by Records Engineering, Inc., in 1959 and subsequently presented to the legislature.[211] It provides "for continuing programs for the efficient and economical management of state records." The act takes no cognizance of the role the society has played as an archival depository, nor does it make other provision for the preservation and administration of the state's archives. Under the act, the Secretary of State is designated as State Records Administrator and is charged with establishing and administering a records management program in the executive branch of the state government. To that end, he is to set standards and develop procedures and techniques for effective records management, make surveys of paper-work operations and recommend improved methods of records management, establish standards for the preparation of retention and disposal schedules, and obtain necessary reports from state agencies. Agencies, besides maintaining effective records management programs and making and maintaining adequate documentation of their organization, functions, policies, decisions, procedures, and essential transactions, must submit retention and disposal schedules and lists of their records no longer needed for current business and of no administrative, legal, or fiscal value. Upon request, the State Records Administrator is to provide records manage-

[210] North Dakota, Secretary of State, *Thirty-fourth Biennial Report, July 1, 1960 to June 30, 1962*, p. 7.

[211] Records Engineering, Inc., *Report to Special Study Committee, Thirty-sixth Legislative Assembly, State of North Dakota, I* (Oct. 23, 1959), 67 p., proc. Volumes II and III contain the retention and disposal schedules recommended.

ment assistance to the legislative and judicial branches of the government.

The Administrator, "after consultation with the official or department head concerned," authorizes the destruction of agency records without the concurrence of archivally and historically competent persons, although the librarian of the State Historical Society has been called in sometimes for advice. A bill (S.B. No. 236) that would have provided for the transfer of historically valuable records to the society was killed by the 1963 legislature. The Administrator has no power to initiate records management programs, nor does he have a records center to which records of limited retention value can be transferred. The records management act does not mention the preservation of permanently valuable records.

The program is staffed with one person, the Assistant Administrator for Records Management, who has a good knowledge of the operations of the state government and who draws a salary of $6,300, included in a $20,000 appropriation for records management and the publication of the state "Blue Book." Neither he nor other state employees, except those in offices receiving federal funds, are under a merit system.

The program is solely concerned with records retention and disposal. On the basis of the inventories prepared by Records Engineering, 14,076 cubic feet of records were disposed of immediately,[212] and retention periods have been proposed by the agencies and approved by the State Records Administrator.

Senate Bill No. 236, mentioned above, would have provided the legal authorization for both a records center and a microfilm program. New legislation and appropriations are still needed for the purpose. The question of the allocation of responsibility for permanently valuable records and their custody is still open; for, while the State Historical Society has and receives such records, it is not empowered by statute to take them over.

House Bill No. 829, bringing county records under the records management program of the Secretary of State, was enacted by the 1963 legislature. The same legislature also authorized (H.B. No. 598) the destruction of certain village, town, and township records.

COMMENTS

1. North Dakota has no statute assigning to any agency authority over the preservation and administration of its archives, though the State Historical Society has served as a *de facto* depository for selected archival material. The records management act should be amended to deal with the matter of archives. If the State Historical Society is to be the legally constituted custodian of the state's archives, it needs additional competent staff and adequate appropriations.

2. Under the records management act disposal authority rests with the

[212] North Dakota, Secretary of State, *op. cit.*, p. 7.

[213]

Administrator "after consultation with the official or department head concerned." The head of the state archival agency, assisted by competent professional personnel, should have a voice in the process so that records of permanent value will not be destroyed on the sole basis of administrative judgment. If a records management program including a records center is to be developed, trained personnel must be added to the Administrator's office.

OHIO

The Archives Division of the Ohio Historical Society has been named the archival agency of the state. Records management is under the State Director of Finance.

BACKGROUNDS

The society, founded in 1885 as the Ohio State Archaeological and Historical Society, remained for many years primarily interested in the exploration and development of prehistoric sites and in historical publication. In 1927 the legislature authorized state agencies to transfer their non-current records to the society, with the permission of the Governor to be obtained in each case (Laws, 1927, sec. 154–59). Stored in the stacks of the society's building on the Ohio State University campus in Columbus, the considerable quantities of records taken over remained neglected, since no money, equipment, or personnel was ever made available for their proper care. Finally, in 1958, the old Governor's Mansion on Broad Street was turned over to the society for use as an archives building, and money was appropriated for its support. A year later the society was officially designated as "the archives administration of the state," and its Division of Archives was created (Laws, 1959, pp. 1021 ff., secs. 149.31–149.42).

A bill to strengthen the records management and archives program of the state (S.B. No. 150) was introduced in the 1961–62 session of the general assembly. It stated more clearly the respective roles and duties of the Archives Division of the society, the State Records Commission, and the Department of Finance; and it authorized the last to concern itself, in cooperation with agency heads, with the problems of records creation and maintenance, to establish and operate records centers, to provide microfilming service to state agencies not in need of full-time microfilming equipment and personnel, and to develop and maintain a records management training program. It appears that this bill would have enlisted considerable support. It was withdrawn, however, and a substitute bill was introduced (Sub. S.B. No. 150), which designated the Director of Finance as State Records Administrator, considerably increased his responsibility for paperwork and records management, defined the duties and responsibilities of agency heads in regard to the execution of a statewide records management program, and authorized the State Records Administrator to establish and operate a central microfilm service — a prerogative strongly opposed by departments, such as that of the Secretary of State, that already have well-developed microfilm operations. This bill died in the Rules Committee of the Senate after being reported out favorably by the State Government Committee.

THE HISTORICAL SOCIETY

The Ohio Historical Society, since 1891 a quasi-public body drawing its support both from the state and from membership dues and other private sources, operates under a Board of Trustees composed of nine elected members, six appointed by the Governor, and two *ex officio* — the Governor and the State Superintendent of Public Instruction. The society functions through its six divisions dealing with history and science, library, education and interpretation, business management, properties, and archives. The services it renders in many fields of archeological and historical work are impressive. It publishes *Ohio History* (formerly the *Ohio Historical Quarterly*), the monthly *Echoes*, history books, bibliographies, and other publications. Its museum has exhibits on Ohio history, archeology, and natural history. The society also administers more than fifty historic and archeological sites of the state and collaborates closely with the public schools and other educational institutions. The collecting and care of private manuscripts are functions of the society's library, though under the law the Archives Division may accept and preserve private documents, records, and archives.

Since 1959 the Archives Division has had its own funds, which stem entirely from state appropriations. The budget amounted to $31,380 in 1961 but was reduced to $26,475 in 1962 and to $25,540 in 1964.[213] Before the budget is presented to the Board of Trustees, the Archivist discusses his requests with the Director of the society.

Section 149.31 prescribes that the state's "archives administration shall be headed by a trained archivist" but does not specify qualifications for his staff. In addition to the State Archivist ($6,800–$8,280), there is provision for an Archives Analyst III ($5,760–$6,900), mainly concerned with county records,[214] and since April 15, 1962, a full-time secretary. None of the positions is in the classified service.

Designation in 1957 of the Governor's Mansion as an archives building [215] has been at best a specious solution to the state's archives problem.

[213] The first appropriation of $52,600 was reduced to $40,600 in a state economy move of May, 1958. Appropriations have thus steadily declined.

[214] He is actually classified as Librarian III. The position of Archivist II was abolished in 1963.

[215] It was chosen as the place "for exhibition of historical archives of the state and the political subdivisions thereof."

Except for some wall space in the upper floors, the basement only can be used for storing records. It is poorly ventilated, crowded, and equipped with wooden shelving; and — after two additional small rooms and the "coal bin" have been fitted out — all the storage space will be exhausted. As a gesture to protect the holdings, the large gas furnace in the basement has been enclosed behind a fireproof wall. The upper floors of the building are used mainly for office space and for small displays of archival material. In short, the building is wholly unfit for the purpose it is to serve, and responsible state officials cannot be blamed for their reluctance to give valuable records to the Archives. The surrounding grounds could be used for an expansion of the existing facilities. Apparently, however, prospects for the erection of a new building are dim. If the university were permitted to buy the Historical Society's museum building on its campus, the society might then acquire space adjacent to the campus and erect two or three buildings for its various activities. No such plans, however, will mature in the immediate future. There is no movement of any significance to support better care of the state archives, nor was the Study Director able to discover any strong interest in archives on the part of state officials.[216]

It is not easy to obtain a conspectus of the holdings of the Archives Division. Accessions received before the creation of the division are kept in the society's library stacks and in other less suitable space in its building, known as the Ohio State Museum, where they occupy 9,100 cubic feet of much-needed space. They include official papers of Ohio's Governors, land records, and other valuable groups of records. These holdings should be integrated with those in the so-called Archives Building, the former Governor's Mansion, but that is impossible because practically all the storage area there (3,150 cubic feet of space) is already filled. As a result, often what seem to be components of the same provenance are found in two places; and, if it is not possible to bring them together physically, they should be integrated in finding aids. This will consume much time. As a first step a program has been started to determine what records there are in the museum and what records should be retained. Control of holdings, including those in local depositories, will be by means of five-by-eight-inch cards prepared in triplicate, one card filed under the department of origin, one under the division thereof, and one under the series. The space provided on the card for the description of the contents of series seems inadequate.

The Archives Division may deposit county records, as well as state records and those of other governmental units, in qualified institutions for public use. Depositories are now in operation at Kent State University

[216] Effective March 1, 1963, space amounting to 800 square feet was rented from Hoover Company on West Broad Street, six miles from the Archives Building.

for the archives of Portage County and the immediate area; the Western Reserve Historical Society for Cuyahoga County; the Historical and Philosophical Society of Ohio, Cincinnati, for Hamilton County; Ohio University, Athens, for Southeast Ohio; the Williams County Historical Society, Montpelier, for Williams County; and the Toledo Public Library for Lucas County. The County Archivist believes that at least twelve local depositories will be needed, but one wonders how the small Archives staff can supervise these depositories effectively.

The Archives Division has no facilities for the rehabilitation of records. Those in need of lamination are sent to firms providing this service.

RECORDS MANAGEMENT AND RECORDS DISPOSITION

Insofar as a state records management program exists, it is under the jurisdiction of the State Director of Finance.[217] The preparation of retention and disposal schedules was begun by the Department of Finance in October, 1959. At this time, however, only one person is assigned to the work, and he must give more than two-thirds of his time to forms management and systems analysis. Records officers charged with drafting schedules have been appointed in most agencies, but except in two major departments — Highways and Mental Hygiene and Correction — they have taken on scheduling in addition to their regular duties. Under these conditions, even though the administrative specialist and the Archivist cooperate in working out schedules, progress has been necessarily slow. As a rather incisive measure, an executive order of August 1, 1963, now provides that records retained for six calendar years prior to January 1, 1963, or for six fiscal years prior to July 1, 1963, shall be destroyed before November 30, 1963, unless they "pertain to a pending case, claim, audit, or action; are otherwise retained in accordance with retention schedules approved by the State Records Commission; are judged to be of such significant archival value by the State Archivist to warrant immediate transfer to the Ohio Archives." The State Archivist was to be advised by October 1, 1963, of records considered for disposal under this six-year disposal authorization.

The unhappy fate of Senate Bill No. 150, referred to above, is particularly regrettable, because action on the establishment of a records center has been delayed. It is badly needed. An official in the Auditor's office has estimated that in Columbus alone the state spends $5,000 to $6,000 a month on rented space for records storage. Equally unhappy is the fact that the holdings of both the Museum Building and the Archives Building include much material of limited or no retention value. According to one

---

[217] Sec. 149.34 of the Revised Code states: "The director of finance shall have the authority to promulgate schedules of record retention and destruction with the approval of the state records commission as provided in Section 149.32 of the Revised Code."

estimate, many records now stored in the Archives Building could be transferred to a records center for short-term storage and subsequent destruction. If that were done, it would facilitate at least partial integration of the record holdings in the Museum and in the Archives. Responsible state officials who are also on the State Records Commission seem to feel that money for a records center might be obtained or that possibly a state-owned building might be equipped for that purpose.

Disposal of state records by list or schedule is subject to the authority of the State Records Commission (sec. 149.32 of the Revised Code), composed of the Superintendent of Public Instruction, the Secretary of State, the Director of Finance, the State Auditor, the Attorney General, and the Director of the Ohio Historical Society, or their representatives. The Archivist of the society serves as the commission's secretary, and this is a good arrangement. The commission has final authority to approve or disapprove departmental applications to destroy records, and the Historical Society is given sixty days within which to claim any records it deems to be of historical value. No money is budgeted for the commission, however, and it has no clerical help. Members of the commission also pointed out that all of them have too many other duties to give adequate time to the commission's work.

An executive order of the Governor of July 19, 1960, has made the commission "responsible for actions to promote the preservation of essential public records, for the prescription of principles and policies to be followed by state and local governmental agencies in the conduct of their records preservation plans and for the necessary duplication, reproduction, and safe storage of such records." Only limited action in compliance with this order has been taken thus far.

The situation being what it is, the county records program of the Archives Division offers better opportunities for action. It is administered by the County Archivist and is based on the act of 1959 (sec. 149.38). The act provides for a county records commission in each county (composed of the president of the board of county commissioners as chairman, the prosecuting attorney, the auditor, the recorder, and the clerk of the court of common pleas) and for a records commission in each municipality and township. The commissions are to provide rules and regulations for the retention and disposal of the public records of the counties or towns, to review retention and disposal schedules and disposal lists, and to submit copies of them to the State Auditor's Bureau of Inspection and Supervision of Public Offices. The State Archives then has sixty days within which to claim any records of "continuing historical value."

The County Archivist spends much time on the road, using a state car and assisting, upon request, county and municipal records commissions in establishing records programs, including microfilming and the preparation of disposal lists. A manual on the scheduling of all county records is ready for publication. Most of the counties now have records commissions, but so far they have been established in only two townships. Municipal court records are specifically exempted from the jurisdiction of the Archives Division.

Ohio has no central microfilm service. Some of the state offices and some counties and municipalities have programs over which neither the Historical Society nor any other co-ordinating authority has jurisdicton. The disposal of microfilmed records is subject to the approval or disapproval of the appropriate records commissions, state or local; and, in the case of county and municipal records, such disposal is subject to final approval of the Bureau of Inspection and Supervision of Public Offices of the Auditor of State.

COMMENTS

1. The present Archives Building is wholly unsuitable for its stated purpose. To provide a measure of relief, those records that have no long-term retention value must be removed from the Museum and the Archives Building.

2. Ohio needs, however, a strong and well-supported archives program, including a modern building with the necessary equipment and storage space, where the present scattered holdings can be integrated and controlled.

3. Additions to the professional staff of the Archives Division are required if its holdings are to be effectively controlled and if the increasing number of local repositories are to receive some professional supervision.

4. Ohio needs a strong, centrally directed records management program, including a records center for the storage of records of limited retention value.

OKLAHOMA

In Oklahoma the archives function is administered by the State Librarian and Archivist. Recent legislation, not yet implemented, has designated him also as State Records Administrator and Records Preservation Officer.

BACKGROUNDS

An act of April 24, 1908 (Session Laws, 1907–8, ch. 42, art. 1), empowered officials and other persons within the state "having the custody of any seal, record, original paper or other document not required by laws of this State to be retained as part of the record of such office to transfer the same to the Oklahoma Historical Society." This society had originated as a result of the combination of two historical societies, one organized at Kingfisher at a meeting of the Indian Territory Press Association on May 26, 1893, the other founded at the university at Norman in 1894 and chartered in January, 1895. Soon thereafter the two societies were consolidated under one constitution, and the combined society became a state agency.[218]

While the society, since 1930 housed in a spacious modern building in Oklahoma City, did nothing to obtain records under the act of 1908, its archival services assumed major importance when the Hastings Act (48 U.S. Stat. L. 501) recognized it "as custodian for the United States of America and the Secretary of the Interior" of federal government field records pertaining to Indians of Oklahoma. Under this act, considerable quantities of records of Indian agencies and subagencies have been deposited with the society's Indian Archives Division.

In 1939, at the urging of the State Librarian, specific legislation was enacted to make the Oklahoma State Library a depository for the state's archives.[219] Begun as a Territorial Library in 1889, the library was housed in downtown Oklahoma City until the completion of the State Capitol in 1917. It was given formal archival responsibilities by a statute of 1939, which created the Records Commission (Laws, 1939, pp. 90–91) and authorized it to examine the records on hand in state departments and institutions and "to destroy such records or, at the request of the State Librarian, deposit such records in the State Library, which, in its discretion, are of no further use to said departments and institutions." This law was repealed, and a later act (Laws, 1947, p. 616) created the Archives and Records Commission and strengthened the powers of the State Library. According to the State Librarian, it took him "some time [subsequent to 1938] to convince the legislature that we should have an archival program."

The act under which the State Library now operates its archival program is Title 74, Oklahoma Statutes 1961, sections 564–76. It gives the Archives and Records Commission sole "authority of the disposition for all public records and archives" exclusive of those of the state's political subdivisions; orders state officers to confer with the State Librarian concerning the desirability of depositing in the State Library records deemed unnecessary for current business; requires them to obtain from the commission authorization to destroy records more than five years old or to transfer them to the State Library, or else to transfer them to the State Library for microfilming and later destruction; gives the Secretary of the Archives and Records Commission the right of access to all public records

[218] On the history of the society, see Grant Foreman, *The Oklahoma Historical Society* [Oklahoma City, 1938], [16] p.

[219] See *A Job Analysis and Organization Survey of the Oklahoma State Library* (May, 1952, proc.), 57 p.; and Oklahoma State Library, Legislative Reference Division, *The Oklahoma State Library: Its Services to the Oklahoma State Legislature* (Oklahoma City, 1959, proc.), 7 p., which, by a strange oversight, does not mention the Archives Division.

and archives of the state; and instructs the commission to begin an examination of the records in Oklahoma City.[220]

The basic act has been supplemented by the 1961 "Preservation of Essential Records Act" (H.B. No. 1123; 67 Oklahoma Stats. 1961, secs. 561–68) and a "Records Management Act" (H.B. No. 1124; 67 Okla. Stats. 1961, secs. 201–16). These acts, based on the model acts of the Council of State Governments, designate the "State Librarian as the State Archivist, Records Preservation Officer, and State Records Administrator." Because of opposition from two of the most powerful departments of the state, both acts were weakened by a clause specifying that "No department, office, commission, board, authority, or other agency, however designated, of the state government, shall be subject to the provisions of this act until such agency shall notify the Governor and Records Preservation Officer (Administrator) in writing of its determination to comply with the act's provisions, provided that such resolve may not be rescinded at a later date."

An act of 1949 (19 Okla. Stats., secs. 911–18) has created in each county a county archives and records commission, composed of the county attorney (chairman), the county clerk (secretary), the county treasurer, and the county court clerk. The commission, upon the application of the appropriate county officer, is empowered to authorize outright destruction of records or destruction subsequent to microfilming.

THE OKLAHOMA STATE LIBRARY

The State Library, managed and controlled by the Justices of the Supreme Court as its Board of Directors, is composed of the following divisions: Archives, Law, Legislative Reference and Research, Library Extension, Public Documents, and Special Services and General Reference.

After discussion with the division heads, the State Librarian submits his budget request to the Budget Director for incorporation in the executive budget. Usually reduced in the process, the budget request goes to the appropriations committees of the legislature and thence to the legislature itself. Frequently supported by the Oklahoma Library Association, the State Librarian defends the budget before the appropriations committees. It is not possible to separate, within the budget, archives expenses from general library expenses. According to the State Librarian's estimate, the Archives Division received 18.5 per cent of the 1962 budget of $200,000. Brief reports on activities of the State Library are included in the budget requests, inasmuch as no formal reports are prepared and published.

The State Librarian and Archivist serves at the pleasure of the State

[220] This last clause stems from Laws of 1953, p. 216.

Library's Board of Directors, but the board has ruled that he may not be removed without cause. The staff is under the merit system, has the typical vacation and sick leave privileges, and participates in the Old Age and Survivors Insurance program. Job descriptions are being prepared by the State Personnel Board in consultation with the State Library. A bill to establish a retirement program, which died in committee in 1961, was to be reintroduced in the 1963 session.

THE ARCHIVES DIVISION

The 1961–63 budget provides the following salaries for personnel administering the State Library's archives funtion:

State Librarian and Archivist .... $8,100–$9,000
Archivist 6,000– 6,900
Microfilm Supervisor 3,600– 4,200
Archival Assistants (2) 2,400– 3,300

Since the salaries of the State Library staff are inadequate, the State Librarian and Archivist finds it difficult to fill professional positions. Key posts, including that of the Archivist, have been vacant since 1957. No systematic archives program can develop unless the Archivist's position is filled by an experienced person, to say nothing of the new records management duties of the State Librarian, which, if taken seriously, call for considerably larger appropriations.

The small archival holdings consist of records of the territory and state and include records of the Governor's office, records of the legislature, Confederate pension records, and records of U. S. land offices in Oklahoma and Indian Territories.[221] Two vaults and space in the library basement are used for these records.

The stacks are so badly overcrowded that no large accessions of records can be accommodated. For purposes of storage, the library has a dilapidated building in the outskirts of the city, colloquially called the pesthouse, into which departments have dumped records and books helter-skelter. The contents of this building are virtually uncontrolled. So far as could be determined during a brief visit, the greater part of the records and surplus copies of official publications there can be discarded. With an appropriation of $90,000 from the 1961 legislature, the library has recently obtained a storage building 60 by 150 feet, called the annex although it is at some distance from the State Capitol. Built of corrugated iron, the annex is equipped partly with library stacks, partly with transfer cases piled eight high. Records center equipment might have been more practical, since the building will be used for archives as well as records center purposes.

[221] Papers of Governors and of private citizens and organizations are in the Division of Manuscripts of the University of Oklahoma Libraries. The State Library limits itself to the acquisition of official records.

The library needs, but does not have, the sum of $3,500 to clean out the "pesthouse" and transfer to the annex material not to be discarded immediately. When the annex is in operation, one person will be stationed there. The Archivist, once appointed, will have his office on the library premises.

There is no equipment for the preservation and rehabilitation of archives. An extensive microfilming program started in 1947 is carried forward with one planetary and two rotary cameras. Records of a great many departments have been, and are being, microfilmed. The negatives are kept in the State Library.

For lack of competent personnel, there is no active program of accessioning, arranging, and describing records. No archival reference service statistics are kept, but it is estimated that about a hundred reference questions a year involve the use of archival material.

Under a 1961 act (75 Okla. Stats. 1961, secs. 251–57) the State Librarian and Archivist is directed to publish the rules and regulations of state agencies. Agencies are required to file with the Secretary of State and with the State Librarian and Archivist certified originals and duplicate copies of all their rules and regulations in force on or before the effective date of the act. They must file similar copies of new rules and regulations and of all revisions and amendments within three days of adoption. Since January, 1962, it has been the duty of the State Librarian and Archivist to publish semi-monthly in the *Oklahoma Gazette* all rules and regulations adopted and to distribute copies to "every county clerk, court clerk, and county law library in the State of Oklahoma, to members of the legislature, and appropriate agencies, libraries and officials." Rules and regulations unless filed and published as required by the act shall be void.[222]

RECORDS MANAGEMENT AND DISPOSITION

Control over the disposal of state records is vested in the Archives and Records Commission, composed of the Attorney General (chairman), the State Librarian (vice-chairman), the State Examiner and Inspector, and the State Treasurer. The agenda of the commission, which meets four or five times a year, is prepared by the State Librarian. He also prepares and keeps on file detailed minutes of the meetings.

As stated before, the county records commissions decide on the destruction of county records. According to its section 913, the act of 1949 does not apply "to any real property mortgage records, including mineral deeds or grants, oil and gas leases and other records pertaining to real estate including tax rolls." Such records may be microfilmed as an aid to preservation. The State Librarian as vice-chairman and secretary of the Archives

---

[222] In 1961 the State Librarian and Archivist compiled for the secretary of the State Election Board the *Directory and Manual of the State of Oklahoma*. He will continue to do so.

and Records Commission "is authorized and directed, insofar as possible, to consult with any county archives and records commission in the establishment and operation of the Commission and the discharge of its duties." A few counties have taken advantage of the provision of the act.

The records management and essential records preservation acts await implementation, since no funds were appropriated for the purpose when the acts were passed. In his budget request for 1963–65 the State Librarian is asking for the following new positions under the Archivist as division chief ($6,960–$8,700): an archivist in charge of records preservation (same salary range), two additional microfilm operators, and three clerks. He also wishes to obtain for the division $31,000 for operating expenses and $3,000 for equipment. All these requests would increase the total budget of the State Library to $489,685 for the biennium. Prospects of obtaining this increase from a "hold the line" administration are uncertain, if not dim. As the State Librarian puts it: "The services of the State Library, including the archival and records function, can hardly compete with . . . [more powerful] interests. The laws are enacted, the idea is present, and the will and knowledge to do the job are present. It cannot be done without financial support." The support has indeed been lacking in the past.

COMMENTS

1. For the proper implementation of the State Library's archives function a sizable increase of its appropriation is badly needed.

2. The vacant Archivist position on the staff of the State Library should be filled as soon as possible.

3. The administration of the preservation of essential records act and of the records management act of 1961 calls for a considerable expansion of the State Library's staff.

OREGON

Initiated in 1945, the archival program of the Oregon State Library has made great strides under the leadership of a professionally trained and experienced archivist.

BACKGROUNDS

As in many other states, the Secretary of State of Oregon was designated by the constitution as custodian of the records of the official acts of the executive department and the enrolled laws and resolutions of the legislature, as keeper of its bills, documents, and papers, and as compiler of a register of all commissions issued. Otherwise, state records were retained by the agencies of origin. In 1935 a fire destroyed the Capitol in Salem, and only the records kept in its vaults and those of agencies outside the building escaped destruction.

In 1933 a conference of librarians and social scientists had urged the Oregon State Library to assume archival responsibilities. Confronted with the problem of selecting the records worthy of preservation, the State Librarian, Eleanor Stephens, at the request of the Board of Trustees of the State Library and subsequently of an Archival Committee of the board, undertook a study of the entire archives situation of the state. A report of the committee (September 24, 1943) stressed the need for a constructive program of archival preservation to be administered by the State Librarian. Independently, a Committee on the Conservation of Cultural Resources, organized in December, 1941, under the State Defense Council, had begun to concern itself with the safety of the state's records and had established a subcommittee on archives of which the State Librarian was a member. The subcommittee submitted, on March 8, 1944, a report of recommendations in line with those of the Archival Committee of the Board of Library Trustees. The "Proposed Uniform State Public Records Act" of the Society of American Archivists[223] was presented to the legislature in 1945 as the basis of an appropriation request. When it failed to pass because it was incompatible with existing statutes and when political expediency indicated that only a minimal program could be passed, a special appropriation was obtained that year for the purpose of employing a State Archivist under the State Librarian. He was to advise on records disposal, establish needs for archival storage space, and draft a comprehensive archives bill for submission to the legislature in 1947. A former member of the staff of the National Archives who had had considerable experience in many aspects of archival work was appointed as State Archivist on January 6, 1946.[224]

The 1947 legislature created the office of State Archivist under the State Librarian, authorized the State Archivist to accession and receive public records of value for legal, research, and administrative purposes, and charged him with giving advice and assistance on public records problems (ch. 401). It also extended the authority granted the State Board of Control, composed of the Governor, the Secretary of State, and the State Treasurer (Laws, 1943, ch. 317), in matters of records disposal to all state records (ch. 372); increased the power already granted to county courts (Laws, 1945, ch. 120) in matters of the disposal of county records, subject to the State Archivist's approval; and provided for the photographic reproduction of records (ch. 351). A 1951 revision of chapter 351 directed agencies to file security copies of essential records with the State Archivist and gave the copies the legal force of the originals in case the latter should be destroyed. Disposal legislation was improved in

[223] American Archivist, III (Apr., 1940), 107–15.
[224] L. S. Cressman, "Oregon Archival Program," Oregon Historical Quarterly, XLVI (June, 1945), 170–73; and Oregon State Library, Division of State Archives, First Biennial Report — July 1, 1944–June 30, 1946 (n.p., n.d.), 8 p.

1953 by authorizing the State Board of Control to grant continuing disposal schedules subject to periodic inspection by the State Auditor and the State Archivist. A revolving fund of $13,400 for microfilm service to be rendered by the State Archivist to state agencies and political subdivisions (Laws, 1955, ch. 87) was abolished in 1961.

In the same year, the basic law of 1947 was clarified in its language by House Bill 1273 (Laws, 1961, ch. 160), and House Bill 1289 (Laws, 1961, ch. 150) established machinery for the transfer to the State Archives of legislative records, including committee records, via the Legislative Fiscal Officer.

THE ARCHIVES DIVISION OF THE STATE LIBRARY

The Oregon State Library, governed by the State Library Board and headed by the State Librarian, consists of an Archives Division, a Field Services Division, a Technical Services Division, and a Readers' Services Division. The Archives Division under the State Archivist "Preserves governmental records of value for legal, administrative, research and security purposes. Advises state, county, and other governmental subdivisions on records problems. Recommends destruction of county records. Furnishes microfilm services." [225] For the temporary preservation of records of limited retention value, the Archives Division operates facilities of the records center type. The Archives Division has its separate staff and its own areas for office, storage, work, and public use. It shares the services of the library's administrative and fiscal staff.

For the 1963–65 biennium, the Archives Division's budget provides $101,214 for personnel, materials, and supplies and capital outlay — less than a tenth of the library's total budget of $1,160,284. The State Archivist prepares his own budget, submitting it to the State Librarian. Reviewed by the State Library Board, it undergoes further review in the Budget Division of the Department of Finance and Administration, which makes its recommendations to the Governor. Hearings on the Governor's budget are held before a subcommittee of the Joint Ways and Means Committee of the legislature. At this time the Legislative Fiscal Officer also analyzes the budget and makes his recommendations. The State Archivist attends the hearings with the State Librarian.

The Archives Division has a staff of eight, with salaries and assignments as follows:

State Archivist	$8,220–$10,140
Archival Assistant (Reference)	5,040– 6,300
Archival Assistant (Technical)	5,040– 6,300
Records Examiner	5,520– 6,900
Clerks (three, one at Records Center)	3,000– 3,912
Secretary	3,180– 3,912

[225] Quoted from *Oregon State Library Organizational Chart, 1962.*

Under the state merit system, appointments are made on the basis of competitive examinations. Archival assistants are selected from the administrative trainees' roster with preference given to those with a background in history or government, while the Records Examiner is taken from the administrative analysts' roster. The State Archivist must have five years of professional experience and a Master's degree with specialization in history, political science, or related study; "or any equivalent combination of experience and training."

The staff is covered by the state retirement system and by social security and workmen's compensation insurance. Each member has ten days of annual leave, increased to fifteen after ten years of service, and sick leave of a day per month. Within salary ranges there are six merit increases.

Under an arrangement with Willamette University at Salem, students are used to help with files analysis and inventorying and receive one hour of credit per semester for each three hours of weekly work.

The Archives Division occupies space in four buildings. A reading room, workroom, office, microfilm room, vault (990 cu. ft.), and storage area (1,236 cu. ft.) are located on the third floor of the State Library. Archives are also kept in the penthouse (1,800 cu. ft.) and the basement (3,700 cu. ft.) of the State Library and in a vault of the State Office Building (674 cu. ft.). The records center, on the second floor of the Finance Building, provides space for 5,190 cubic feet of records, some of them archival. Almost inactive records are stored on pallets at the State Hospital (2,500 cu. ft.). One of the clerks is stationed at the records center in the Finance Building. The lack of centralized facilities [226] is extremely inconvenient for communications and costly in staff time.

A fumigation chamber is located at, and shared with, the Oregon State Penitentiary. Though repair work on bound volumes is done by the State Library, a laminator for the treatment of loose records is badly needed.

The central microfilm service, provided under the 1955 Revolving Fund Act and operated in 1956 with eleven full-time and twenty-four part-time employees in departmental programs and three full-time persons in the central program, was discontinued in 1961, when the program was reduced to security microfilming. It now consists of services provided on a cost basis with four cameras, and 183,056 images were rendered in the first six months of 1963.

The biennial reports of the Archives Division are contained in those of the Oregon State Library. The division has published a number of *Bulletins* for the benefit of its clientele, including *Pioneer Families of the*

[226] Figures given indicate records storage capacities, aggregating 16,147 cubic feet, as against the volume of records on hand, which is 12,317 cubic feet. Much of the space still available is at the State Hospital, which has little shelving.

Oregon Territory, 1850 (2d ed., 1961, 64 p.), an index to the 1850 federal census, and *Have You An Oregon Ancestor?* (1962, 16 p.)

THE STATE ARCHIVES

The Oregon State Archives holds 8,150 cubic feet of records, of which the earliest are those of the Willamette Cattle Company, 1837, and the provisional government, 1841. Holdings are especially rich for the territorial period, 1843–59, and for the period following the Capitol fire in 1935. In addition to records of state agencies, there are records from twenty-three of the thirty-six counties and from four cities, records of the Federal Writers Project, and federal census schedules. A few collections of private papers and pictures are kept in the general library.

Procedures governing accessioning, analyzing, and describing archival material are well developed. On the basis of records transmittal lists, used for records center material as well as for permanent records, accession numbers and record group numbers are assigned (for example, RG-C1 Capitol Planning Commission accession 63-10 or RG-C5 Civil Service Commission accession 63-14). While for center material the process stops with the accession record, archival material is described in inventories, consisting of succinct series descriptions that are designed for use in cataloging, and after these have been approved by the State Archivist entries for the catalog are prepared.

The catalog is in two parts, a catalog of surnames and a subject catalog. The subject catalog includes accession entries, series entries, entries for significant documents, and added entries for subject information obtained from the records as well as from other sources. The needed number of slips is produced cheaply by means of a Card Master. According to the State Archivist, the catalog works well as the principal finding aid, while the inventories serve as a "second line of defense." A cataloging manual is being prepared.

Every step of the process of record arrangement and description is recorded on a Processing Control Sheet. The State Archivist had hoped to use the Termatrex Information Retrieval System for content control over certain series of case files and he requested equipment and one extra clerk for that purpose. This would have been the first application of the Termatrex system [227] to archival material, and its outcome would have been watched with great interest. Unfortunately, the budget request was denied by the Department of Finance and Administration.

Archival reference service requests are recorded in the division's reference room. In 1963 during the six months from January through June, 935 requests for service involved the use of 3,974 records in the reference

[227] For a report on its application to manuscripts, see Elizabeth A. Ingerman, "A New Method of Indexing Manuscripts," *American Archivist*, XXV (July, 1962), 331–40.

room. Of the records used, 623 were on microfilm. Oregon is unique in charging a fee of $4.00 per hour to private individuals and organizations if more than half an hour is required for conducting a general search.

RECORDS MANAGEMENT AND RECORDS DISPOSITION

In 1953 the Department of Finance and Administration initiated a records management program, under which most state agencies appointed records officers, training sessions were held, and a manual of procedures for records disposal was issued. Once the program had been inaugurated, the Archives Division of the State Library took over the direction of the destruction process and the administration of records storage facilities. During the past three years, the Department of Finance and Administration has ceased to deal with records management except in connection with general management surveys, and only the Archives Division's program is in operation.

In practice, the division's role is limited to assisting agencies in inventorying and scheduling records, to administering 4,167 cubic feet of records in its center facilities, and to advising state and county officials on problems of records management. An increase in his staff would enable the State Archivist to assume wider responsibilities in the field.

The records center in the Finance Building handled 539 reference requests involving the use of 1,220 records in the first six months of 1963. During the same period 410 cubic feet of records were accessioned in the Finance Building and 131 cubic feet were destroyed, while 618 cubic feet of records were accessioned at the State Hospital.

The Oregon State Civil Defense Agency has used the advice of the State Archivist in planning the preservation of records essential to the continuity of government and to the safeguarding of the rights of the people. Some state agencies and counties have stored microfilm copies of essential records with the State Archivist. The Board of Health keeps copies of vital records in its major field offices, and other state agencies have done the same with regard to their essential records.

Authority over the disposal of state records is vested in the Board of Control. The board authorizes destruction requests and continuing disposal schedules, the State Archivist having the right to requisition any records thus authorized for disposal. In the first six months of 1963, fifty-one schedules were processed by the Archivist.

In accordance with sections 13 and 14 of Oregon Laws, 1961, chapter 160, a revision of the 1947 act (H.B. 483), county officers, departments, boards, and agencies may, with the consent of the district attorney, request the county court or board of county commissioners to approve the destruction of records of no value to the county or to the public in accordance with regulations prescribed by the State Archivist. County courts and boards of county commissioners may also destroy records in accordance with rules and regulations of the State Archivist (Laws, 1961, ch. 160, sec. 15), and fifteen specific authorizations were considered by the Archivist in the first six months of 1963. The Archivist has the right to requisition records authorized for destruction.

COMMENTS

1. A building providing space for the storage of semi-current as well as archival records is the first need of the Archives Division. It will enable the division to consolidate its operations.

2. Inasmuch as the records management program of the Department of Finance and Administration has become inactive, the State Archivist should be given funds and personnel to administer an effective program on both the state and local levels.

PENNSYLVANIA

The Division of Public Records, first established in the State Library at Harrisburg but since 1945 part of the Pennsylvania Historical and Museum Commission, has archival responsibility for the records of the state and those of its subdivisions. Records management is under the Governor's Office of Administration.

BACKGROUNDS

Probably more than any other state, Pennsylvania during the nineteenth and early twentieth centuries [228] emphasized the publication of its public records, to the detriment of their preservation. Its efforts in that direction resulted in the 138 volumes of *Colonial Records* and *Pennsylvania Archives*, published intermittently between 1838 and 1935 and including records as late as 1902. These volumes are uneven in quality and frequently show remarkable liberties taken by the successive editors. Publication also resulted in the actual loss of archival materials when the original documents were used as printer's copy, and those that were returned to proper custody fared little better. In 1851 a select committee of the legislature found records in a deplorable condition, stored in attics, cellars, and nooks and crannies, where they were exposed to fire, rats, damp, dirt, and mutilation by unscrupulous persons. The report led to still more printing, while the archives continued to be neglected. Accordingly, Herman V. Ames and Lewis S. Shimmel reported to the Public Archives Commission in 1900 [229] that records not in current use or considered especially valuable

[228] For the following see "Report on the Public Archives of Pennsylvania," *Annual Report of the American Historical Association for the Year 1900*, II (Washington, 1901), 267–93; and Henry H. Eddy, "The Archival Program of Pennsylvania," *American Archivist*, XII (July, 1949), 255–66.

[229] "Report on the Public Archives of Pennsylvania," *loc. cit.*

were essentially in the same condition as they had been in 1851; that is, they were stored in boxes, bundles, and loose piles on the floors of attics, basements, and cellars; that records had strayed from one office to another until they were quite confused; and that the State Library had a collection of miscellaneous unclassified material.

In 1903 the Division of Public Records was established in the State Library, and the legislature appropriated $10,000 to "clean, classify and bind old manuscripts and deposit them in the State Library." The first Custodian of Public Records, obtaining advice from the Library of Congress and the Historical Society of Pennsylvania, arranged the archives in a number of series according to a basic chronological scheme and had them mounted in bound volumes.

A seven-member Advisory Commission was created in 1907, and in 1911 the restriction limiting the jurisdiction of the Division of Public Records to records dated before 1750 was lifted. Also, county and municipal officials were authorized to transfer inactive records to the division. Very few such records were transferred, however, and during the entire period from 1903 to 1935 the publication of the successive series of *Pennsylvania Archives* remained the principal concern of the division. Between 1936 and 1943 the WPA Historical Records Survey made detailed listings and analyses of county records, and the inventories for about one-third of the counties were later published, along with the integrated results of the entire project.[230]

Finally, Laws of Pennsylvania, 1945, pp. 139 ff., as amended 1947, pp. 605 ff. (P.L. 407), created the Pennsylvania Historical and Museum Commission, incorporated in it the Pennsylvania Historical Commission, the State Museum Commission, and the Division of Public Records of the State Library, and made it an independent agency. The act not only made the commission the legal custodian of such public records as might be turned over to it by any agency of the commonwealth or of a political subdivision thereof but also conferred upon it the right "to examine into the condition of the records, books, pamphlets, documents, manuscripts, archives, maps and papers kept filed or recorded in the several offices of the departments, cities, and boroughs of the state," to recommend action necessary for the safety and preservation of the public records, and specifically to recommend "standards governing the use of paper, ink, and filing procedure" for records "of permanent and ultimate historical importance." Strangely enough, legislation of the same year (Laws, 1947, pp. 407 ff.) gave the Governor authority over filing systems and microfilming for state agencies. In the matter of records disposal, Laws of Pennsylvania, 1937, pp. 1865 ff., as amended in 1947, provided that requests

[230] Sylvester K. Stevens and Donald H. Kent (eds.), Pennsylvania Historical Survey, *County Government and Archives in Pennsylvania* (Harrisburg, 1947), x + 576 p.

for records destruction must be approved by the commission before destruction could be authorized by the Executive Board, consisting of the Governor and six other heads of administrative departments to be designated by him from time to time.

Ever since 1903 there had been recurrent movements for the erection of an adequate building in Harrisburg for the Pennsylvania State Archives, with the Pennsylvania Historical Association and the Pennsylvania Federation of Historical Societies in the leading roles since the 1940's. In 1945 the legislature appropriated funds for a William Penn memorial building, but they were diverted to other uses because of the financial situation of the state. In 1959 a building program was finally launched, this time for a William Penn Memorial Museum and Archives Building to be completed in June, 1964.

Prompted by a report by the Pennsylvania Economy League to the Pennsylvania State Government Survey Committee of the legislature,[231] a records management program was initiated in the Governor's office in 1954. In 1957 department and agency heads were requested to submit a records management plan to the Office of Administration. It was not, however, until 1962 that the comprehensive survey of all state records was started; this survey is now approaching completion. To place the program on a firm basis, the Office of Administration has proposed certain changes in the state's Administrative Code of 1929[232] designed to assign the authority of the Executive Board in matters of records disposition to a State Records Board; to eliminate the requirement that only records four years old or older may be destroyed; and to authorize destruction on a continuing basis through schedules. These changes would be embodied in an act "to provide for continuing programs for the efficient and economical management of state records."

A bill now pending before the legislature (S.B. No. 212) would create a county records committee whose duty would be "to make or revise a schedule setting forth the time when certain papers and records filed in the offices of the prothonotary or the clerk of courts may be destroyed either with or without microfilming."

THE PENNSYLVANIA HISTORICAL AND MUSEUM COMMISSION

In 1956 the commission, an independent agency, was reorganized to comprise the Executive Office under the Executive Director, the Bureau of Historic Sites and Properties, and the Bureau of Research, Publications, and Records.[233] The first bureau operates a Division of Historic Sites and

[231] Pennsylvania Economy League, Inc., *Records Administration of the Commonwealth of Pennsylvania* (Dec., 1952, proc.), 19 p.

[232] Commonwealth of Pennsylvania, Legislative Reference Bureau, *The Administrative Code of 1929* (Harrisburg, 1957), 255 p.

[233] The recent growth and achievements of the commission are summarized in *The*

Properties, of which there are more than twenty, the State Museum, and the Pennsylvania Farm Museum. The Bureau of Research, Publications, and Records consists of a Division of Research and Publications and a Division of Public Records under the Archivist and Chief of the division.

The General Assembly of Pennsylvania has its general sessions in odd-numbered years. Budget requests of the commission, based on those of the bureau directors and division chiefs, are prepared in the commission's executive office, reviewed by the Governor's budget secretary, and submitted to the legislature as part of the Governor's general budget for the operation of the state government. The commission's Executive Director, sometimes accompanied by his staff, explains and defends his budget before the appropriation committees of the House and Senate.

The 1963 budget provided, for all purposes of the commission, a total of $866,145, of which the Division of Public Records received $72,495. Since 1951 the commission has had a revolving fund, the so-called Historical Preservation Fund, which derives its income from admission fees and sales of publications, postcards, and the like. It is used to finance the publication program of the commission and for other purposes which will, generally speaking, return the money to the fund.[234]

The commission staff of more than 120 employees is recruited through the Governor's Personnel Office and the Civil Service Commission. Members of the professional staff are under the executive civil service system and are appointed on the basis of unassembled competitive examinations, while clerical and other personnel need political clearance. The executive civil service, established by the Governor and the Executive Board in 1959, might possibly be abolished, in which case the professional staff would again be placed under patronage. In recent years the commission has been more secure than other agencies and has suffered neither from political appointments nor from political dismissals.

Among the commission's numerous and substantial publications, the 826-page *Bibliography of Pennsylvania History*, compiled by Norman B. Wilkinson (1957), is a particularly outstanding contribution.

THE DIVISION OF PUBLIC RECORDS

The division has a staff of ten employees, of whom five are professional. The Archivist and Chief, Division of Public Records, receives $6,716–$9,011; the Associate Archivist, $5,785–$7,407; three Assistant Archivists, $4,773–$6,390; one clerk, three clerk-typists, and a clerk-stenographer, $2,791–$4,551. Carefully written job descriptions define the duties and the experience and training required of the incumbents.

Pennsylvania Historical and Museum Commission, Report for the Decade 1952–1962 (n.p., n.d., proc.), 50 p.

[234] In 1961, $71,328 was deposited in this fund.

Housed in three rooms of the Education Building, the division now holds 10,000 cubic feet of public records, 3,500 cubic feet of private papers, 1,743 reels of microfilm, and 900 maps. These records are almost exclusively those created by the legislative and executive branches of the government. Thirteen hundred and twenty-four cubic feet of original source material and films and 260 cubic feet of transcripts, formerly in the commission's Division of Research and Publications, have been transferred to the Division of Public Records. Sixty-three hundred cubic feet of records now held by the departments are earmarked for transfer to the new building.

The William Penn Memorial Museum and Archives Building will be a complex consisting of the Memorial Hall and the Archives Tower. The Archives Tower will have offices, work areas, a research room, and a reference library at its base and 17 windowless stack floors above. A basement will provide space for common-use facilities and 10,000 square feet for the records center. Stack floors one through five will be used for general archives storage and floors six through eight for the storage of restricted material, such as Governors' papers. Floors eleven through seventeen are to be equipped for records center use, while floors nine and ten are reserved for future records center purposes. A total of 138,000 cubic feet of storage space will be available, 78,000 cubic feet for archival use and 60,000 cubic feet for the records center. On the ground floor, wings adjacent to the base of the tower provide offices for the Division of Public Records and for the Division of Research and Publications. The main access to these wings will be through the research room of the Division of Public Records, which thus serves as a vestibule for the two divisions, a decidedly poor arrangement.

In the new building, the Division of Public Records will have a fumigator, a humidifier, a big Arbee laminator, and Barrow de-acidification equipment. Besides its present equipment — a reader-printer and six microfilm readers — the division will be equipped with a planetary camera and a photostat machine with an enlarger-printer.

Although the Executive Board, with the approval of the Historical and Museum Commission, may direct that state records be transferred to the Division of Public Records, accessions have customarily reached the division through negotiation with the agency involved. The pertinent documentation is available in an accession file, organized by agencies. No formal accession registers are kept.

The accomplishments of the division in the field of arrangement and description are noteworthy. After it had been established in 1903, holdings were systematized in the following groups, organized either chronologically or by county: provincial papers, 1650–1776; Revolutionary papers, 1776–83; post-Revolutionary papers, 1783–ca. 1793; so-called Governors' papers,

1790–1838; road and turnpike papers, 1790–1839; county documents; military papers; and passenger lists. Begun in 1948, the tremendous task of dismantling about 500 volumes into which the records had been bound, and organizing them into 29 record groups based on the offices of origin, was brought to successful completion in 1961. This, in the history of archives administration, is one of the few cases in which an attempt to reconstitute original provenance has been carried through without bogging down.

Generally speaking, the system of record groups, subgroups, and series is an adaptation to the needs of a state archival agency of the scheme for the organization of the holdings of the National Archives. To the system of record groups, there corresponds a system of manuscript groups. For both systems the control program initiated will provide the following aids: (1) a summary guide, which, for the public records, is now available in revised form (April, 1963); (2) record group and manuscript group inventories; (3) descriptive itemized lists for material with high reference value; and (4) box- or check-lists specifying containers or volumes and designed primarily for internal control or staff use. A "Chronological View of the Pennsylvania State Archives" — in the language of records management called a records continuity profile — indicates for each record group the time span covered by the records. For military service records, 1775–83, an ambitious project of abstracting information from the original records and recording it on cards is about half completed.

The division keeps a visitors' register and uses form letters to answer inquiries and to certify information from certain types of records. During the first six months of 1963 it processed 881 mail requests for information, 560 of which necessitated consultation of finding aids or records; answered 315 telephone requests for information; and furnished 418 photographic copies of records. Visits numbered 187 and called for producing 320 record items and 783 rolls of microfilm in the research room. In addition, 113 certificates of military service were issued. Genealogical inquiries are handled by the State Library. To facilitate the use of its holdings, the division has issued four four-page information leaflets anticipating and answering questions frequently asked.

The former Director of the division was active in historical associations of the state, taught history in the Harrisburg Area Center for Higher Education and at the Whitehill Industrial School, and was in charge of an oral history project for the Historical and Museum Commission.

RECORDS MANAGEMENT AND RECORDS DISPOSITION

The records management program of the state has been set up in the Records Management Division, Bureau of Program and Management, in the Governor's Office of Administration, which is headed by the Secretary of Administration. Inasmuch as the Office of Administration is not authorized by statute, until recently it did not have a budget of its own, and salaries of the Records Management Division were provided partly from the budget of the Historical and Museum Commission and partly from the budgets of other agencies. Effective July 1, 1963, however, expenses for the Office of Administration were included in the Governor's budget.

The Records Management Division has a staff of five, to be reduced to four in fiscal 1964, and uses the time of one clerk in the Office of Administration pool. The professional staff comprises: a Records Management Specialist ($7,772–$10.432), two Management Analysts III ($6,716–$9,011), one Management Analyst II ($5,803–$7,772), and one management trainee. All the staff members are under the state's executive civil service system; and appointments, except for the Records Management Specialist, are made from the management analyst roster.

Though initiated in 1954, the records management work was performed on a limited scale by personnel not highly qualified, until in 1958 an experienced records management specialist joined the staff. An accelerated records management program was launched on August 21, 1962, when Governor David L. Lawrence announced plans for an inventory of state records in the Harrisburg area and asked agencies to designate records co-ordinators who were to be exposed to short training sessions. Inventorying has been, and is being, done by agency personnel selected, trained, and supervised by the records co-ordinators, whose experience is largely in the administrative or general management field rather than in records management. As of February, 1963, out of a total accumulation of 257,824 cubic feet of records, 67 per cent were proposed to be kept in office space, 11 per cent in agency storage, and 12 per cent in the records center; only 10 per cent were scheduled for destruction. Agencies have been warned that the amount of records proposed to be retained in office space is unreasonably high and that the amount of records proposed to be disposed of is too low. The first schedule, covering most of the non-permanent records of the Department of Property and Supplies, has been completed.

Because it was felt that semi-current records should be readied for transfer to the new records center in the Archives Tower, the inventorying and scheduling process has been divided into two phases: the first phase, now in progress, excludes policy material and any records the agency considers of permanent or indefinite value. A second "go-round" will identify material for transfer to the Division of Public Records, with that division participating in the process.

The forms control program of the Records Management Division is not yet in full operation, though it was conceived in 1958 and the plan was established by a directive of the Office of Administration to all state agencies dated February 16, 1962. An inventory of commonly used forms —

those extensively used by two or more agencies essentially in personnel, accounting, budgeting, and general administrative service — was completed in early 1959. Also, forms are reviewed, advisory service in the field is given, and training sessions have been held. Training sessions have also been provided in the fields of filing and correspondence management.

Under the present law, disposal authority is vested in the Executive Board. The division furnishes staff services to the board in regard to approval of disposal requests and requests for microfilming, which is done by the Division of Document Recording. In the past the board has not considered records for disposal until they were seven years old and has not approved disposal by schedules. As mentioned above, a bill replacing the Executive Board with a State Records Board and providing for continuing programs for the efficient and economical management of state records has been introduced in the legislature (S.B. No. 606). The relationships between the commission and the Office of Administration's Records Management Division need clarification, inasmuch as under the law the former is responsible for the safety and protection of public records and the enforcement of laws relating to them and has, in regard to records of permanent and ultimate historical importance, the right to enforce standards governing "the use of paper, ink, and filing procedure."

No measures have been taken by the state to insure the protection of essential records in case of an emergency.

COMMENTS

1. To strengthen the status and authority of the Historical and Museum Commission as the state's archival agency, it is suggested that its name be expanded to Pennsylvania Historical, Archives, and Museum Commission.

2. It is highly desirable that the present Division of Public Records be raised to bureau status.

3. In the needed records management legislation, the respective roles of the Office of Administration and the Historical and Museum Commission should be clarified.

PUERTO RICO

Inasmuch as the General Archives of Puerto Rico at San Juan has been organized with the active help of the National Archives and Records Service, its practices and program reflect to a certain extent those of our national archival agency.

BACKGROUNDS

The General Archives of the Commonwealth of Puerto Rico owes its existence to Law 5 of 1955. It inherited a complex situation: [235] (1) in

[235] Much of the following is based on the National Archives Planning and Control Case 057–101, entitled "Puerto Rican Archives Assistance."

1899–1901, the central archives of the Spanish governors were removed from the Fortaleza (the Governor's palace) to the Library of Congress; (2) several years later about two-thirds of this material was returned to the island's Department of the Interior, and, subsequently, much that was not needed in the department was transferred to the Historical Archives of Puerto Rico, established by Law 64 of 1919; (3) upon the abolition in 1949 of the Historical Archives the holdings, which had been decimated by a fire in 1926, were stored in the Carnegie Library and later were donated to the University of Puerto Rico. There, in 1953, they were joined by the records that had remained in the Department of the Interior (renamed Department of Public Works in 1949); and (4) meanwhile, in 1944, the records retained by the Library of Congress had been transferred to the National Archives.

By 1953, therefore, the university had become the custodian of the most important records of the Spanish government of the island, except for those still in the National Archives. Under the leadership of Arturo Morales Carión, chairman of the department of history, the university began to display a lively interest in the records entrusted to its care. In the meantime, the Puerto Rico Bureau of the Budget had decided to concern itself with the problem of records accumulation in the operating agencies of the government; and in 1950 it engaged the services of the New York management firm of Barrington Associates. Their preliminary report focused upon reducing the bulk of the records in the agencies without any consideration of the need for an archival depository, an omission criticized by Morales Carión (March 13, 1952). Possibly as a result of such criticism a more thorough survey by Barrington, authorized by Law 378 of 1952 and submitted in September, 1953, included a recommendation to create an archives "as a separate agency" of the government, or, if this arrangement would not be compatible with "the organizational concepts" of the commonwealth, to place the archives "under the University of Puerto Rico or possibly the Department of State."

Article 5 of the act "To establish a Program for the Preservation and Disposal of Public Documents" (Law 5 of 1955), "to be known as the Puerto Rico Public Documents Administration Act," established the General Archives of the Commonwealth of Puerto Rico, attached it "administratively" to the University of Puerto Rico, and provided for a General Archivist to be appointed by the chancellor of the university.[236] An Archives Advisory Committee, composed of representatives of the three branches of government and presided over by the chancellor, was to rule

[236] On the act and its implementation, see Luis M. Rodríguez Morales, "Puerto Rico — the Documents Administration Program," *American Archivist*, XXVI (July, 1963), 379–82. This is a somewhat abbreviated translation of the author's "El programa de administración de documentos públicos en Puerto Rico," in his *Ensayos y Conferencias* (Barcelona, 1962), pp. 97–107.

in the matter of "the disposal of documents in the possession of the Archivist." On the other hand, the preparation of disposal lists was left to the three branches of the government. From these lists, the General Archivist could claim any documents of interest to him.

This is still the basic law governing the status and functions of the General Archives of Puerto Rico, except that by executive order dated June 19, 1956, the establishment has been transferred to the Institute of Puerto Rican Culture, created June 21, 1955, by Law 89. To help with the implementation of the law, Oliver W. Holmes of the National Archives went to Puerto Rico in September, 1956. Subsequently, on May 1, 1957, Charles E. Dewing, also of the National Archives, was placed "in active charge of the Commonwealth Archives during the first 12 months of its operation" with the title of Technical Director and the mandate to "supervise and train the local staff, give advice on the plans for an archive building, work with other government agencies on their disposition programs, and establish procedures." [237] During Mr. Dewing's incumbency, the Archivist of the United States visited the newly established Commonwealth Archives in January, 1958. He applauded the arrangements made so far; and, though considering the act of 1955 "inadequate in many respects," he suggested postponing any attempts to obtain its revision. According to this act, therefore, the Advisory Committee provided for in section 9 has been established [238] under the chairmanship of the Executive Director of the Institute of Puerto Rican Culture, with the Director of the General Archives serving as its secretary.

THE GENERAL ARCHIVES OF PUERTO RICO

While the position of the General Archives might be stronger if it were directly under the Governor of the commonwealth, affiliation with the Institute of Puerto Rican Culture, a widely respected and vigorous organization, has been to its advantage. It enables the General Archives to make a significant contribution to the cultural and intellectual life of Puerto Rico, a cause dear to the inhabitants of the island.

The budget of the General Archives constitutes a distinct part of the budget of the institute. Inasmuch as all expenses except those for personal services ($45,000) are gathered together in one item called Other Operating Expenses ($14,400), the Director of the General Archives has considerable freedom in the use of his resources. The budget of the General Archives originates from recommendations of the Director of the General Archives to the Executive Director of the institute. Both officials defend the Archives budget before the Bureau of the Budget. As a matter of practice, however, the Director of the General Archives does not appear before the appropriations committees of the legislature.

[237] *American Archivist*, XX (July, 1957), 269.
[238] *El Mundo* (San Juan, P.R.), Feb. 6, 1962.

The staff of the General Archives, including its Director, is not under the commonwealth's civil service system. Appointments are proposed by the Director to the Executive Director of the institute, who has the *autoridad nominadora*, and nominations are sent by the latter's office for processing by the Office of Personnel. Similarly, members of the Archives staff may be dismissed by the Executive Director of the institute without any appeal to the Office of Personnel. The Director of the General Archives feels that the secretaries and junior archivists should have civil service status.

In the selection of candidates for professional positions, the Director of the General Archives is handicapped by the fact that the Office of Personnel has not established, and is disinclined to provide, an archivist classification. Prospective appointees, who must have a minimum of four years of university study with specialization in history or the social sciences plus experience in the use and handling of historical documents, are brought in under the classification of *investigador histórico*, which mentions archival duties rather incidentally while emphasizing ability to do historical research.

At present there are, under the Director ($8,400), four junior archivists, misleadingly called *investigadores históricos* ($3,780), one lower-grade junior archivist ($3,240), two clerk-typists including one under provisional appointment, and four workers of custodial or laborer rank. Considering the high cost of living in Puerto Rico, their salaries are low but seem to be in line with those of comparable insular agencies and institutions. Ingrade salary increases are given; but they are not automatic and depend on available funds and individual merit.

The present inadequate building of the General Archives is nothing but a *pis aller*: it is almost filled; it is not fireproof; and it is not equipped for safeguarding records from Puerto Rico's deleterious climate and from pests. To guard against the latter, the building is fumigated once a month by an exterminating firm, and four times a year a fogging machine is used to apply an insecticide to the interior of the building. Because of the impending move to the Bacardi Building, future home of the General Archives, the fumigating chamber for records has not been installed.

In spite of present limitations, the General Archives had absorbed by the spring of 1963 a total of 11,700 cubic feet of records. Four thousand ninety-two volumes of "demographic records" — that is, records of births, marriages, and deaths kept by the island's civilian registration system — will go back to the Department of Health, but this will provide only minor relief. Considerable bodies of police records, property tax records, prison records, and other major accessions have been stored in the west wing of the Bacardi Building until the General Archives can occupy its quarters in the east wing.

The holdings accessioned over a period of five years and representing the major agencies of the government cannot be expected to be under complete inventory control. Many of them, for instance those of the *Audiencia* and *Intendencia*, have been brought in completely disarranged and must be analyzed and organized piece by piece. In most cases, accession inventories serve as the principal finding aids. In processing records, the principles of *respect des fonds* and of the sanctity of the original order are observed. An over-all list specifies the bodies of material transferred, with an indication of their quantities. They will be set up in a record group arrangement once their analysis has been sufficiently advanced.

Under the law of 1955 the General Archives has authority to take over records of local government, but the agency does not intend to exercise this authority unless there is evidence that local records are being neglected. Most certainly the well-established archives of San Juan will be left to the care of the municipality. So far records of four municipalities have been accessioned.

Particularly important among the records of local character are the notarial archives. Under the law of 1955 they remained outside the competence of the General Archives, and it seemed unlikely that this situation could be changed. Surprisingly enough, however, Law 77 of 1961 has authorized the present and future transfer to the General Archives of notarial records that are at least sixty years old. Inasmuch as under the notarial law the General Archives cannot issue copies from the records, the Notarial Archivist of the District of San Juan has been charged with this responsibility. Both the Director of the General Archives and the legislature of the commonwealth deserve praise for arriving at this settlement, which makes available to scholars material basic to all research in economic and social history.

Regarding co-operation with the University of Puerto Rico, there is no formal agreement. It would be desirable to provide for some such agreement, particularly since the university is now moving into graduate work. Much has been done, however, to "sell" the Archives to the public. There is a small exhibit, which is also taken to the schools, and the Director of the Archives gives lectures and talks about his institution on television. A motion picture has been prepared to illustrate the activities of the General Archives; and it, too, has been shown on television.

Because the General Archives has been "in business" for only five years and because its holdings are still being analyzed and described, reference service is not extensive. During fiscal 1963, 811 such services were rendered, including 516 by telephone and 21 by mail.

RECORDS MANAGEMENT AND RECORDS DISPOSITION

Under the present law the General Archives is not directly concerned with records management. This function has been allocated to the Office of Administrative Management of the Bureau of the Budget, where it is being "nursed along" until it can be transferred either to a general services agency or possibly to the General Archives. Now limited to the preparation of disposal lists, the program may slowly expand into other areas of records management, probably at first into the area of files operation. The bureau's official in charge of records management is being called in for assistance by agencies that need his advice. Increasing agency concern with the records problem became apparent when some ninety persons attended a seminar on records management held under the auspices of the Bureau of the Budget and the General Archives, March 26–30, 1962.

With the exception of a general schedule for fiscal records, retention and disposal schedules have not been developed. Retirement is effected by means of disposal lists (*informe de disposición*) prepared with the assistance of the records management specialist in the Bureau of the Budget. Lists are subject to examination and evaluation by the Director of the General Archives. For documents selected for preservation, an accession inventory is prepared. An internal memorandum ably establishes the procedures to be followed in the disposition and control of public records. By the spring of 1963 approximately 58,000 cubic feet of extra copies and useless papers had been authorized for destruction.

While the role of the General Archives in the field of records management is still undetermined, a records center is likely to be installed in the Bacardi Building, future home of the General Archives, before the Archives itself will be ready to move in. Suitable quarters for the center are available in a warehouse adjacent to the main building.

COMMENTS

The General Archives will be unable to accomplish its mission before a number of issues have been settled:

1. Plans for adapting and equipping the Bacardi Building are moving too slowly. Not even the basic decision concerning the location of the uprights in the stacks has been made. It is recommended that work on the building be speeded up as much as possible. The role and status of the General Archives will be very much enhanced once satisfactory facilities are available, because then the records of the Spanish regime, which are still in the National Archives, can be returned to Pureto Rico in accordance with 71 U.S. Statutes at Large, 400 (1957).

2. The records management program cannot be carried forward successfully by a single employee of the Bureau of the Budget, the staff agency of the executive branch. Much can be said for charging the General Archives with the records management function, particularly since the records center will be adjacent to its quarters and apparently under its control.

3. Neither records management nor archives work will assume its rightful position until special classifications for records officers and professional archivists are established by the Office of Personnel.

RHODE ISLAND

In the state of Rhode Island and Providence Plantations the responsibility for the care and preservation of records is divided among the Secretary of State, the State Librarian, the Department of Administration, and other departments of the state.

BACKGROUNDS

"The early corporate character of the colony led naturally to the making of the secretary of the corporation, or the 'general recorder,' the custodian of the records, books, and papers of the colony." [239] Consequently his successor, the Secretary of State, has in his custody the acts and resolves of the legislature, the original papers relating to its proceedings, and the records of his own office. He has also taken over some of the older records of other departments of the state government, though most of the departmental records have remained with their agencies of origin.

As in other New England states, the care of local records first engaged the attention of the authorities. In 1896 a State Records Commissioner was appointed to report on the condition, bulk, and location of the public records of the state and its subdivisions. In 1910 the functions of the State Records Commissioner were vested in the State Librarian who, with the consent of the Senate, is appointed by the Secretary of State for a term of three years. A law of 1922 permitted officials of towns and cities to turn their records over to the State Historical Commission, if authorized to do so by their governing bodies.

To cope with the ever increasing bulk of modern records, Public Laws of 1944, chapter 1487, created a legislative Committee on Accounts and Records, composed of the chairmen of the Finance Committees of the Senate and the House and the Director of Finance, and empowered it to approve or disapprove requests for the disposal of records. Subsequently Public Laws of 1951, chapter 2729, established a Department of Administration, under which a Division of Methods, Research and Office Services was to exercise the department's authority over records management.

THE ARCHIVES OF THE SECRETARY OF STATE

Until 1930 the Archives was "an integral part" of the State Library and considered its "manuscript section." Since then it has been housed in the

[239] Clarence S. Brigham, "Report on the Archives of Rhode Island," *Annual Report of the American Historical Association for the Year 1903*, I (Washington, 1904), 547.

State Capitol at Providence, in one room called the central service room and in three storerooms or vaults. It is headed by the Secretary of State's Assistant for Archives, who has neither clerical nor any other help and whose salary is $6,700. The Assistant serves at the pleasure of the Secretary of State but attains permanent status after twenty-five years of service. An amount of $2,500 for rebinding and the salary of the Assistant for Archives constitute the only special appropriation for the Archives. Holdings begin with the year 1638 and include records of the general assembly, the office of the Secretary of State, colonial courts, the 1875 and 1885 state censuses, and the 1870 federal census. Most of them bound, they stand on shelves along the walls and are inadequately protected from fire, even though the archives room is fire-resistant and metal shelving and furniture are used. Small additions to the various series are received at yearly intervals. Since early record-keeping practices in Rhode Island were quite satisfactory, these series run practically without gaps down to the present, and records listed in an inventory of 1761 can still be identified through that inventory. A card catalog and an index to records created before the Civil War serve as finding aids.

The Archives has no technical equipment of its own but uses the Secretary of State's photostat, microfilm, and instant-copy machines. Searchers share the space in the center of the room with the Assistant for Archives. Reference service statistics are not kept, but it is estimated that 140 letters requiring searches are answered each year, 150 telephone inquiries are handled, and 165 researchers mostly use bound volumes for which tables of contents have been prepared.

There is no intention at this time to establish a real State Archives that will hold all the permanently valuable records of the state, many of which have remained with the agencies that created them. Because the state before 1935 was administered by commissions acting directly under the general assembly, the Secretary of State has early records of many of the present departments not responsible to the Governor.

RECORDS MANAGEMENT AND RECORDS DISPOSITION

The program — as of July, 1963, in the Division of Methods, Data Processing and Central Services of the Department of Administration — is headed by a Records Analyst (present salary $7,605) and staffed with three assistants ($4,212–$5,330) and one laborer ($3,302). Funds for personnel services, plus $300–$400 for records center boxes and $165 for the printing of forms, are provided in the budget of the division and amounted to $25,210 in fiscal 1963–64. The National Records Management Council toward the end of 1951 helped to install the program.

The records management unit makes inventories of existing records of all state agencies, prepares and submits retention and disposal schedules for the approval of the Committee on Accounts and Records, operates the records center, and has charge of the final disposition of records. Some assistance (about 15 per cent of one person's time) is given to agencies on space utilization, forms design, filing procedures, and related matters. Since the parent division has control over the purchase of office equipment, enforcement of regulations concerning records management and disposal is relatively simple. All requests for equipment must be initialed by the Records Analyst.

The records center, set up in 1952, is adequately housed in the basement of the Veterans Memorial Building, a few steps from the State Capitol, and has 20,000 cubic feet of storage space, of which 15,444 are in use. Following is a statistical breakdown of records center activity for the years 1958 and 1960 and the first six months of 1963.

	1958	1960	Jan.–June, 1963
Stored in records center	11,517 cu. ft.	12,502 cu. ft.	16,750 cu. ft.
Accruals	2,450 cu. ft.	2,892 cu. ft.	1,161 cu. ft.
Destroyed[240]	803 cu. ft.	2,078 cu. ft.	658 cu. ft.
Reference requests	11,984	13,991	9,403

The forms for records inventory work, records appraisal, control of records in the center, and reference service requests are simple and appropriate for the purpose.

A central microfilm service for state agencies was established in the fall of 1963.

The records management program seems to enjoy the confidence and cooperation of state authorities. The records center is rich in material that ordinarily would be found in a general State Archives, such as records of the Adjutant General, 1800–1945; notary public and justice of the peace commissions of the Secretary of State, 1873–1926; death and marriage records, 1853–1950; state census records, 1865–1935; and records of district courts, 1886–1950.

THE LOCAL RECORDS PROGRAM

Under the law, the State Librarian is in charge of the local records program. In actual practice, this officer has been unable to administer the program. It is not operative.

COMMENTS

1. The records management program of the Department of Administration functions effectively.

2. The local records program should be revitalized.

3. In the absence of a general State Archives, the state records center

---

[240] During the first six months of 1963, about 780 cubic feet of material in office areas were also destroyed.

has holdings of a potentially archival character. With an increase of its professional staff, it could be developed into an archival depository.

SOUTH CAROLINA

Since its move in 1960 into a modern building in Columbia, the South Carolina Archives Department has been able to start the long overdue process of organizing and inventorying its rich holdings. South Carolina, however, lacks a modern records management program.

BACKGROUNDS

In South Carolina interest in the history of the state and its sources developed early, for in 1829 an agent was sent to London to obtain copies of the records of the colonial period; and these, or abstracts from them, began to be published by the South Carolina Historical Society in 1857. Also, in 1849, the Governor recommended appointment of a person to work on the state archives, and in 1850 John S. Green was appointed for this purpose. In general, the records were well cared for until near the end of the Civil War.

A new start was made in 1891, when, at the urging of the South Carolina Historical Society, a temporary body called the Public Record Commission was appointed to continue the task of obtaining material from England and organizing it. This commission, under the name of Historical Commission, was made permanent by an act of 1894 (Acts, No. 559) and was given a much broader authority, "an important step forward" and probably "the first of its kind . . . in any southern State." [241] The material assembled by the Historical Commission was to be kept in the office of the Secretary of State. Shortcomings of the act — linking the commission with another office and leaving it without regular financial support — were corrected by an act of 1905 (Acts, 1905, No. 454). The general assembly that passed this act wanted a full-fledged agency to care for the non-current archives of the state, publish records and other historical material, direct the marking of historic places, and "supervise the exploration of 'historical remains and Indian mounds.' " [242] Undoubtedly this act was influenced by legislation passed in other Southern states.

The mandate of the Historical Commission remained essentially unchanged for more than forty years. In a self-study the commission undertook in 1949, it admitted failure in some of the most important phases of archival administration; for no systematic effort had been made to obtain

[241] J. H. Easterby, "The Archives of South Carolina," *American Archivist*, XV (July, 1952), 242. For the history of the South Carolina Archives Department, see also the *Annual Report of the South Carolina Archives Department, 1954–1955* (Columbia, 1956), pp. 3–8.

[242] Easterby, *loc. cit.*, p. 243.

records from state agencies, virtually no repair work had been done, and, although most of the older records had been arranged and indexed, adequate inventories and guides had not been prepared.[243] Yet the commission decided to concentrate its efforts on publication as it had in the past. Though this may not have been the best decision, it seemed justified by its results, for the publication program "was far more successful than was expected."[244] There was, moreover, no building in which archival work could have been carried on satisfactorily.

The Archives Act of 1954 (Acts and Joint Resolutions, 1954, No. 692) created a new basis for the operations of the state's archival agency. The act abolished the Historical Commission and transferred its functions to the South Carolina Archives Department. It placed the department under the control of the South Carolina Archives Commission as its governing board and seemed to give it a basis for performing two important new duties: the preservation and care of county records, together with those of the state, and the imparting of information "useful in improving the standards for the making, caring for, and administering public records."[245] As another innovation an Archives Council consisting of the Secretary of State, the Attorney General, and the State Auditor was to advise the Archives Commission on matters relating to the transfer of records and was to act upon recommendations that records of "no significance, importance or value" be destroyed.[246] These provisions, which seemed to contemplate a state and county records management program under the Archives Department, were weakened, however, by leaving the agencies of both state and counties altogether free to co-operate or not, as they wished.

THE ARCHIVES DEPARTMENT

The South Carolina Archives Commission, under which the Archives Department operates, consists of seven members: the heads of the history departments of the University of South Carolina, Clemson College, the Citadel, and Winthrop College, who serve *ex officio*, and representatives of the South Carolina Historical Society, the South Carolina Department of the American Legion, and the South Carolina Historical Association,[247] who serve for terms of five years. The Archives Commission supports the Director of the department wholeheartedly.

For many years the Historical Commission lived on a starvation budget; the average annual appropriation from 1905 to 1949 was less than $7,500.[248]

[243] *Ibid.*, p. 244.
[244] *Annual Report, 1954–1955*, p. 6.
[245] *Ibid.*, pp. 7 ff., and Acts and Joint Resolutions, South Carolina, 1954, No. 692, sec. 13.
[246] *Ibid.*, sec. 9.
[247] The commission member from the Historical Association replaced a representative of the Confederate Veterans.
[248] *Annual Report, 1954–1955*, p. 4.

A rather dramatic change for the better came with the 1952–53 budget, which provided $53,427 — an increase for salaries of 33 per cent, for equipment of 2,170 per cent, and for printing of 803 per cent over the amounts available in 1948–49. The 1963–64 budget appropriates $122,782 to the Archives Department, of which sum $107,132 supports its archival work.

Until 1924 the staff of the Historical Commission consisted of one person only — its secretary, A. S. Salley, Jr. In 1925, after many years of clamoring, Salley obtained an appropriation of $1,800 for an assistant secretary. In the course of time, modest appropriations for a stenographer, a clerk, and a porter were added. Salley, who had since 1948 been known as State Historian and Secretary, was succeeded on June 25, 1949, by the late J. H. Easterby. Increasing budgets have made possible a considerable growth of staff. It now consists of the Director ($10,150), with his secretary ($5,000); two staff members and a part-time secretary in charge of the research room; an Assistant Director ($7,350), who handles arrangement and description work with the help of two full-time employees ($2,670 and $2,377); a historical marker and research specialist ($5,000), who also gives as much time as possible to the series *State Records of South Carolina*; a photographer ($3,700), who also accessions microfilm and printed research aids; a Museum Curator, who handles exhibits, tours of the buildings, and publicity; and three persons in the laminating shop ($10,225). One "editorial assistant" ($4,750) works mainly on editing the *Journals of the Commons House of Assembly* but also inventories the legislative journals and serves occasionally as a stenographer. Another "editorial assistant" ($3,957) is serving an apprenticeship as needed in the arrangement and description, the *State Records*, and the historical marker programs. Publication of the *Papers of John C. Calhoun* consumes practically all the time of their editor ($9,794), his clerk, and his assistant. Titles of positions — in some cases set years earlier by the state's detailed appropriation acts — often do not reflect the work done, and most staff members must undertake more than one activity. It would seem that the department is not adequately staffed for its archival functions, still less for an expansion into records management.

Staff members are not under the merit system, nor, except for the Director, do they have to meet established job requirements. Nevertheless, practically all those in responsible positions have the desirable academic background. Salary increases depend on appropriations, as there is no system of within-grade promotion.

From 1891 to 1936 the Historical Commission occupied an office and two storage rooms in the State House. Facilities in the World War Memorial, to which it was transferred in 1936, were equally inadequate, since this building was "designed to serve primarily as a shrine." [249] In January,

[249] *Ibid.*, p. 5.

1960, the Archives Department moved into its new building. This has a storage capacity of about 50,000 cubic feet, of which some 30,000 cubic feet were filled in 1963. Site, construction, and much of the equipment cost $600,000. As a result of legislative action a first-floor room is occupied by the Confederate Museum, which belongs to the United Daughters of the Confederacy.

A report of the Archives Department quotes "an expert" as saying that the department found itself faced with "the biggest job of restoration of seventeenth and eighteenth century manuscripts in the United States." [250] Appropriations in 1952 and 1953 had made it possible to purchase a Barrow laminator, however; and by June 30, 1963, a total of 396,038 pages had been laminated — an estimated 20 per cent of the necessary repair work.

At a remarkably early time, the Historical Commission took an interest in the use of photography for purposes of documentary reproduction. For a time, beginning in 1912, it used the services of Leet Brothers in Washington for the photostat copying of muster rolls in the War Department, and in 1917 the general assembly allowed the commission $250 for the "Purchase of a Photo-Copier." [251] Photocopying was also used by Salley for publishing the journal of the 1788 convention that ratified the Constitution of the United States.

A program for microfilming all state and county records of permanent value was started in 1950. It operates through:

1. the South Carolina Archives Department, which, using its own equipment, gives priority "to records of general research value";

2. the Utah Genealogical Society's well-known program — positive sets remain in the Archives Department;

3. local government, notably the counties, which employ commercial photographers to make security copies, mostly of recent property records, and which usually send the films for safekeeping to the Archives Department;

4. a few departments of the state government, some of which have their own equipment.

Transfer of records to the Archives Department is obligatory in the case of defunct state agencies and permissive in the case of active state agencies. The department may accept such transfers if they are deemed of permanent value. As to county records, the consent of the governing body of the county and that of the county delegation in the general assembly is required (secs. 7 and 8 or the Archives Act). Destruction of munic-

[250] *Annual Report of the South Carolina Archives Department, 1953–1954* (Columbia, 1955), p. 17.
[251] *Report of the Historical Commission of South Carolina at the Regular Session of 1915* (Columbia, 1918), p. 8.

ipal records can apparently be authorized by the governing body of the city.

Since the Archives Department is still engaged in getting organized and bringing its records under control, it cannot pursue an active policy of filling gaps in its holdings. There is no adequate description of these holdings. Most important among them are the legislative records, Governors' letters and papers, Treasurers' and Comptrollers General's records, military service records, and land records of the colony and state from 1671. A vast miscellaneous group of records of the Register and Secretary of the Province and of the Secretary of State, 1675–1899, contains papers of various provenances. Only about 25 per cent of the present holdings are under inventory control; the rest have to be serviced with the help of rough lists. The department sees the need for organizing its holdings into a system of record groups and preparing inventories of them. An excellent inventory of the land records is approaching completion. Subsequently, legislative and Treasurers' records will be inventoried.

Reference service, particularly to genealogists, has been increasing steadily. In fiscal 1962–63 about 3,400 letters were written in response to inquiries and 454 abstracts from Confederate service records were furnished. Visits to the research room amounted to approximately 2,700, while persons visiting in groups to view exhibits, see the building's facilities, and attend lectures on the activity of the Archives Department totaled 4,451.

The publication record of the Historical Commission and of the Archives Department is impressive. The act of 1905 charged the commission with "the preparation for publication of such official records and historical material, as the state may at any time desire to publish" and with "the diffusion of knowledge in reference to the history . . . and research therein," [252] and this was repeated without material change in the Archives Act of 1954. "Production" began in 1906 with one of the legislative journals, followed by four additional volumes. In 1908 the series *Records of the Revolutionary War* and *Records of the Confederate War* began, and thereafter other series were started. "In some respects the record of the Archives Department as a publisher during the years between 1906 and 1949 was not unsatisfactory." Many of the volumes, however, were small, few series were completed, "and less than five percent of the documents intended for publication were in print." [253]

Since 1949–50 an ambitious program of publication in print and on microfilm has been in operation, generously supported by the general assembly. The program includes the new series of the *Journals of the Com-*

[252] *List of Publications of the South Carolina Archives Department, February 1, 1957* (Columbia, [1957]), p. 1. There is a *First Supplement* to this *List*, February 1, 1957–June 30, 1959 (Columbia, 1959).
[253] *Ibid.*, pp. 1 ff.

mons House of Assembly; the new series of *Records Relating to Indian Affairs*; and the new series of *State Records of South Carolina*. Microfilm has been used to good advantage for the publication of federal census schedules for South Carolina and for the reproduction of the copies of records in the Public Record Office in London relating to South Carolina. Bibliographies and special studies have been issued to assist in the teaching of South Carolina history. Though not specifically directed to do so, the Archives Department issues an annual *Checklist of South Carolina State Publications*. Special tribute should be paid to the *Annual Reports* of the agency under the directorship of Harold Easterby. His 1952–53 *Report* has been called "almost unique in its literary quality." [254] At the end of fiscal 1962–63 about 146 publications were in print or forthcoming.

The department participates in the state's historical marker program by approving inscriptions for markers and monuments on state highways and other state property.

RECORDS MANAGEMENT AND RECORDS DISPOSITION

In its very first year of existence the Archives Commission would have liked to concern itself with records management. Its mandate with regard to current records, as stated in section 13 of the Archives Act of 1954, is very limited. The commission is to "assemble and publish [useful] information regarding paper, ink, filing, binding, and any other matter." Also, the Director of the Archives Department "shall examine the records in the custody" of state and county officials "and make recommendations regarding their preservation" but not regarding other phases of records management, and he is to do so upon request only.

Hampered by inadequate statutory authority, too small a staff, and the need to bring the present holdings of the department under control, the Director nevertheless realizes that the state needs a modern program of records management. Supported by the Archives Commission, late in 1962 he requested but failed to receive from the general assembly $20,000 for hiring a skeleton records management staff during fiscal 1963–64. During the winter of 1962–63, however, while the assembly was in session, activities of the department served to dramatize the state's need for records management and made the Director hope for a more favorable hearing during the 1964 session. An old state warehouse, the only significant remaining depository of non-current records outside the Archives, was cleared and records of permanent value were transferred to the Archives. One records retention and disposal schedule, for a minor state agency, has been developed as a model for presentation during the 1964 session of the general assembly, and a systematic inventory of the current holdings

[254] Morris L. Radoff, "Reports of State Archivists," *American Archivist*, XVII (Oct., 1954), 338.

of the Secretary of State has been compiled as a basis for developing a disposal and retention schedule for this major office.

COMMENTS

1. To achieve control over its holdings, the Archives Department needs a larger staff.

2. A disproportionate amount of the funds of the department is absorbed by its publication program.

3. Inventorying and scheduling of state and local records should have high priority in the department's program, and for this purpose legal authorization should be obtained.

4. An effort should be made to integrate microfilming activities into a planned program.

SOUTH DAKOTA

South Dakota has no legally recognized archival depository. Some state records have found their way into the South Dakota State Historical Society, at Pierre, and small accessions are being received as a result of actions taken by the State Board for the Destruction of Public State Records.

BACKGROUNDS

A South Dakota Historical Society received a certificate of incorporation from the Secretary of State on February 18, 1891. Apparently failing to flourish, it was reactivated in 1901 as the South Dakota State Historical Society (Laws, 1901, ch. 135). The charter act requires state agencies to deposit with the society a hundred copies of each item issued by them. It does not require them, however, to transfer to the society records of permanent value. In South Dakota, as in other states, the Secretary of State has custody of the acts, resolutions, and journals of the legislature; the great seal of the state; all books, records, deeds, parchments, maps, and papers required to be kept by law; the state constitution; and the register of official acts of the Governor.[255] The 1939 legislature created the Records Destruction Board, and the 1955 legislature made it the duty of county officials to turn over non-current records to the State Historical Society for microfilming, after which the originals were to be returned to the counties.

THE STATE HISTORICAL SOCIETY

The society is governed by an Executive Committee composed of eleven trustees elected by the membership of the society for overlapping

[255] For the division of territorial archives between North Dakota and South Dakota see under North Dakota. Apparently South Dakota never received its share.

terms of six years and, *ex officio*, the Governor, Secretary of State, State Auditor, and Secretary of the society. The last is elected by the Executive Committee and by law serves as Superintendent of the Department of History and Director of the Census. In other words, the Historical Society administers the "Department of History, State of South Dakota," as stated on the society's publication, the *South Dakota Report and Historical Collections.* Political considerations are said to have no bearing on the selection of the Secretary-Superintendent.

Consulting with the Executive Committee, the Secretary submits his budget to the Secretary of Finance of the state. As part of the Governor's budget, it goes before the legislature, where the Secretary has ample opportunity to defend it. The 1961–62 budget provided $31,800 for all functions of the society; namely, for the administration of its library and museum and for its historic sites, historical markers,[256] publication, and microfilm programs. Of the $7,300 office expenses $5,300 goes into the purchasing and processing of microfilm. Included in the budget is a revolving fund, termed miscellaneous, which supports the publication program. The Secretary-Superintendent hopes to have the annual budget increased to $34,950 for the next biennium.

Salaries of the staff are low. The Secretary-Superintendent receives $6,000, the maximum fixed by law. Present salaries of staff members are as follows: Assistant to the Superintendent, $5,700 (this position is now vacant); a person in charge of controlling and servicing microfilm holdings, $3,420; a microfilm operator, $2,340; and a secretary-bookkeeper-receptionist, $3,480. Staff members have social security benefits and annual leave (fourteen working days per annum, increased to twenty-one days after fifteen years of service); and they may participate in the state hospitalization plan, to which, however, the state does not contribute. Pay increases depend on appropriations.

Since 1953 the Department of History has had its own building, the Soldiers and Sailors World War Memorial, which contains approximately 86,800 cubic feet of usable space. With the exception of the basement and a vault adjacent to the office of the secretary-bookkeeper, however, this space is used for museum exhibits — in the Pioneer Room downstairs and a War Museum and Indian Room on the second floor. As there is no museum curator, displays cannot be expected to conform to modern concepts of museum management.

Publications of the department include the *South Dakota Report and Historical Collections* and the *Wi-Iyohi,* a monthly bulletin issued for the State Historical Society.

[256] The society is responsible for the texts on all historical markers and, over the years, has contributed 13 per cent of the cost of erecting them.

The Department of History has no archival program, nor is there a trained archivist on its staff. It does have certain archival holdings and a considerable accumulation of microfilms of county records.

Holdings of the department now include some papers of state Governors and other officials and papers of individuals prominent in the history of the state. There are also the records of the territorial and state censuses from 1880 (incomplete) to 1945, which are very much in demand. According to the Secretary-Superintendent, not more than five hundred items have been accessioned during the last fifteen years.

A microfilm program has been in operation since July 1, 1953. It involves the reproduction of newspapers,[257] census records, and county records. Among the county records the first books of county commissioners' records from sixty-four counties, the first tax records, the first registers of court actions, and justice courts records were included in the program. Records of registrars of deeds, because considered current and hence susceptible to being microfilmed *in situ* only, have not been filmed.

Microfilming is done with one flatbed camera. A reader-printer and a Kodagraph reader are available. At least 5,000 reels of microfilm are stored in a basement vault.

There is no precise record of reference services rendered. It is conservatively estimated that 900 to 1,000 census inquiries a year have to be dealt with. For furnishing a certificate from the census records, the department charges a fee of $1.00, the proceeds going into the miscellaneous fund.

RECORDS MANAGEMENT AND RECORDS DISPOSITION

Authority to destroy state records rests with the Records Destruction Board, which is composed of the Governor, the State Auditor, the Attorney General, the State Comptroller, and the Secretary of the State Historical Society. Under the 1939 law, destruction required a unanimous vote of the board members. The outspokenly conservative outlook of the Secretary caused concern on the part of the other members of the board, and this was reflected in the report of a Committee on Records of the state's Legislative Research Council.[258] This report recommended the establishment of a central microfilm service in the Division of Administration of the Department of Finance and suggested changes in the destruction law eliminating the unanimity requirement. The committee did not decide to "buy" the records management act developed by the Committee of State Officials on Suggested State Legislation of the Coun-

[257] The originals of newspapers published before 1952 are turned over to local schools, publishers, and others interested after they have been filmed.

[258] Legislative Research Council, *Sixth Biennial Report, 1961–1962, Report to the 1963 South Dakota Legislature*, XI, Records Management (Nov., 1962), p. 21.

cil of State Governments, and hence its report recommended neither the appointment of a state records administrator nor provision for a records center. Also, the report did not go into the problem of what agency, if not the State Historical Society, is to serve as the official repository of the state's archives.[259]

The 1963 legislature did not provide for a central microfilming facility. It enacted Senate Bill 51 (Laws, 1963, ch. 309), amending the 1939 destruction act to the effect that a majority vote of the board now suffices to authorize the destruction of records, "provided, however, that destruction of any said materials which are less than six years old shall be authorized only by vote of four of the five members of said Board."

COMMENTS

1. Plans for the installation of a central microfilm service not related to a records management program must be viewed with considerable misgiving.

2. South Dakota needs both a records management and an archives program.

TENNESSEE

In Tennessee the State Library and the State Archives functions have been combined in one agency at Nashville and are carried on by clearly separate divisions with equal status under heads responsible to the State Librarian and Archivist.

BACKGROUNDS

Article 2, section 17, of the first constitution of Tennessee gave the Secretary of State custody of "a fair register of all the official acts and proceedings of the governor" and of "all papers, minutes, and vouchers relative thereto." Chapter 2, Acts of 1796, made him the keeper of the bills and proceedings of the legislature, recorder of all bonds and commissions, and keeper of the seal. In 1823 the Secretary of State was named land commissioner of West Tennessee and consequently became keeper of the land records. Over the years his office appears to have become the depository for records of other agencies deemed worthy of preservation.[260]

The archives of Tennessee sustained repeated losses occasioned by six relocations of the state capital from 1796 to 1826 and a final move into

[259] In the words of a staff member of the Legislative Research Council, South Dakota has not yet faced the problem of records and archival management.

[260] For a convenient survey of the early history of the Tennessee archives, see Philip M. Hamer, "The Preservation of Tennessee History," *North Carolina Historical Review*, VI (Apr., 1929), 127–39; and a news note in *American Archivist*, I (July, 1938), 155–58. See also St. George Leakin Sioussat, "A Preliminary Report Upon the Archives of Tennessee," *Annual Report of the American Historical Association for the Year 1906*, II (Washington, 1908), 197–238.

the new Capitol at Nashville in 1853; loans of records to Lyman C. Draper, who willed them to the Wisconsin State Historical Society, and to J. G. M. Ramsey, whose house was burned by a federal soldier in 1862 with the records inside; a hasty move of the capital to Memphis for an adjourned session the same year; and the use of the Capitol at Nashville as a federal fort. The archives suffered from neglect and overcrowding, especially after the Civil War until the turn of the century, with records dumped into such out-of-the-way parts of the Capitol as the west crypt of the basement, where they lay in rotting heaps in the damp and dirt. Over 3,000 volumes of old State Bank records were sold as waste paper, and a janitor is alleged to have burned several cartloads of records because they were "wet and nasty and smelled bad."

In complying with a United States government request to return eighty-five chests of quartermaster vouchers, which had been left in Nashville after the Civil War, Robert Thomas Quarles, the Superintendent of the Capitol, became interested in the Tennessee archives. He obtained a storage room in the Armory basement and began to assemble and classify the records.

Following a first appropriation in 1903 of $1,200 for the preservation of the archives of Tennessee, the sum of $4,000 was appropriated for "the Department of History and Archives" in 1907, and Quarles became Archivist of the state of Tennessee. Although the department was never established by an act of the legislature, it was housed in the attic of the Capitol and continued to receive appropriations until 1919. In that year chapter 76 abolished it and transferred its functions, equipment, and papers to the State Library.[261] Senate Joint Resolutions 12 and 76 of 1919 established the Tennessee State Historical Committee, subsequently called Historical Commission, of twenty-five members to collect for the State Library all data concerning Tennessee's part in all wars. Chapter 74 of 1921 enlarged the powers of the commission, gave it an annual appropriation of $10,000, and authorized "any state, county, town or other public official, in custody of public documents" to transfer to the commission those not in current use.

As a result of the Administrative Reorganization Bill of 1923, the functions of both the State Librarian and the Tennessee Historical Commission were turned over to the Division of Library and Archives in the Department of Education. It received an appropriation of $5,000 for historical and archival work, and in 1927 it took over from the Tennessee Historical Society "for permanent preservation and historical research

---

[261] The Tennessee State Library was created in 1854 (Acts of Tennessee, 1853–54, pp. 111–12) and the Secretary of State was named *ex officio* State Librarian. The library was housed in the Capitol opposite the Senate Chamber. Chapter 52, Acts of 1901, established a State Library Commission, which appointed the librarian, thereby taking his election out of the hands of the legislature and out of politics.

and education, its collections of relics, books, newspapers, portraits, and manuscripts." [262]

In 1951 the Division of Library and Archives was removed from the Department of Education and put under the new Tennessee State Library and Archives Commission of seven members, which also administered the state's regional library extension services. However, the Reorganization Act of 1959 (Public Acts, 1959, ch. 9) returned the Division of State Library and Archives to the jurisdiction of the Department of Education. Under the act "the state library and archives commission shall function as an advisory body to the commissioner of education who shall, in general, undertake to carry out the policies and programs of said commission affecting the state libraries and archives." The commission holds quarterly meetings.

Earlier legislation dealing with the reproduction on film and the destruction of records has been superseded by the Records Disposal Act of 1957 (Public Acts, 1957, ch. 107). This provides for a Public Records Commission consisting of the Attorney General, the Comptroller, the Executive Director of the Legislative Council, the State Librarian and Archivist, and, as non-voting members, the president of the Tennessee Historical Society and the head of the agency whose records are under consideration. The commission is empowered to order the disposal of records, to establish disposal schedules, and to issue appropriate rules and regulations. The State Librarian and Archivist serves "as the administrative officer and the secretary of the commission." The commission is to have the co-operation of records officers to be designated by the agencies.

THE STATE LIBRARY AND ARCHIVES

Reporting to the Commissioner of Education, the State Librarian and Archivist heads a complex organization, which embraces an Administrative Division, the State Library, the State Archives, the Public Libraries Division (in charge of the regional library system), the Restoration and Reproduction Division, the Tennessee Historical Commission, and the Civil War Centennial Commission. The Archives Division, under the Director of State Archives, comprises a Preparation Section, a Search Section, a Manuscript Section, and a Land Office Section.

After screening and co-ordinating the requests of his divisional heads, the State Librarian submits his budget proposal to the Commissioner of Education, who forwards it to the Department of Finance and Administration. Consultation with that department results in a revised budget, which becomes part of the Governor's budget and which is normally approved

---

[262] The present Tennessee Historical Society was organized in Nashville in 1849. After languishing in the early 1850's, it was revived in 1857 and again in 1874 and was incorporated in 1875.

by the legislature. There are no formal hearings before the legislature's appropriation committees. The budget for fiscal 1962 provided $277,000 for all purposes of the State Library and Archives. Except for salaries and archival supplies, the expenses for the archives function cannot be identified.

Traditionally the State Library and Archives has been a non-political agency, though Tennessee does not have a merit system and positions are not filled on the basis of competitive examinations. Job qualifications have been established and salary scales have been set by the State Personnel Department. Staff members enjoy the benefits of a combined state retirement and social security plan. To the former both state and employee contribute 3 per cent on amounts up to $4,200 and 5 per cent on salaries in excess of $4,200. The state also provides a combined hospital, medical, and life insurance system, paying half of the premium. Twelve days each of annual and sick leave are granted.

Salaries have been improved considerably. Effective January 1, 1963, those of the staff members responsible for or connected with archival work have been established as follows:

State Librarian and Archivist .... $7,800–$9,480
State Librarian and Archivist Emeritus....................... 8,220
Director of State Archives................................... 6,720– 8,220
Senior Archivists (3) 6,000– 7,440
Junior Archivists (2) 5,040– 6,360
Director, Restoration and Reproduction Division.............. 6,720– 8,220

The salary of the State Librarian and Archivist seems low compared to those of his division heads, who may earn more than the agency head.

The State Library and Archives Building, in Nashville,[263] a memorial to Tennessee's soldiers of World War II, was dedicated in 1953. Constructed at a cost of $2,500,000 and completely air-conditioned, it houses the State Library and Archives and the offices of the Tennessee Historical Society, the Tennessee Historical Commission, and the State Historian. The Restoration and Reproduction Division, which serves the needs of the entire agency, has a Barrow laminator, a photostat, and three planetary cameras. A fumigation vault and darkroom and multilith facilities have also been provided. Work is done by the division only for the State Library and Archives and not for other state or for local agencies.

The State Library and Archives enjoys close working relationships with educational institutions in the state, especially with Vanderbilt University, and plays an important role in historical activities. The State Librarian and Archivist is chairman of the Tennessee Historical Commission, with

[263] Dan M. Robison, "Planning the Tennessee State Library and Archives Building," *American Archivist*, XIX (Apr., 1956), 139–50.

its historical sites, historical markers, and publication programs, and is editor, for the Tennessee Historical Society, of the *Tennessee Historical Quarterly*. The Historical Commission defrays two-thirds of the cost of publishing the quarterly.

THE STATE ARCHIVES

Because Tennessee did not have an effective records disposal act before 1957, great quantities of non-permanent records were moved into the new State Library and Archives Building even before its completion. As a result and in the absence of a records center, the Archives Division holds, in addition to state records of permanent character, considerable accumulations of records of limited retention value, not all of which have been scheduled for disposition. It is estimated that eventually 50 per cent of these records can be destroyed. Since the Archives Division will continue to serve as a records center, it would be desirable to separate archival and center-type holdings and to assign them to different stack areas. This important step must precede any attempt to organize the archival holdings in a coherent pattern.

The first stack level is equipped with six-drawer file cabinets, while on the other stack levels (numbers two, seven, and eight) one finds continuous shelving equipment of the type used in the archives stacks of the Virginia State Library. Permanent holdings include records of the Secretary of State, legislative records, records of the divisions of the Supreme Court, and land-grant records consisting principally of grant books and certificates. Extra-security vaults on the seventh stack level are used for adoption case records, vital statistics, and other confidential material.

In the main, accession inventories serve as finding aids. Card catalogs have been prepared for the case records of the East and Middle Tennessee divisions of the Supreme Court, and one for the West Tennessee Division is now in progress. An alphabetical catalog controls the Confederate pension records, and the land records are serviced with the help of a WPA-prepared catalog. The so-called Archive Visual Aid, which consists of floor diagrams showing the location of individual holdings and of a breakdown by departments indicating the location of their records, meets the immediate needs of over-all control of the holdings.

Private papers are handled by the Manuscript Section of the Archives Division. Started in January, 1958, its impressive program of acquisition, arrangement, and description has progressed rapidly. An accession book (950 entries to date) is maintained. Techniques of the Library of Congress Manuscript Division are used in processing and listing collections. One hundred "registers" for collections of one box or more have been prepared, and five of them have been issued in multilith form. Since Vanderbilt University has given its manuscripts collection to the State

[259]

Library and Archives, the latter has become the only collecting agency in the state.

During the fiscal year ending June 30, 1963, the following services were rendered by the Archives Division:

	In Person	By Mail	Total
Archives Search Section	367	580	947
Manuscript Section	373	162	535
Land Office Section	269	288	557

In addition, the Search Section responded to 3,091 agency requests for records. Since July 1, 1962, four form letters have been used, three of them designed exclusively for handling inquiries about service in the Confederate forces.

The archives staff is in charge of recording the proceedings of the Tennessee legislature. It is believed that the success of this program has provided the State Library and Archives with valuable contacts.[264]

Although the Utah Genealogical Society has done no microfilming as yet in Tennessee, a county microfilm program was started by the State Library and Archives in fiscal 1962, and records of three counties have been filmed to test the program. Records that the counties are willing to send to Nashville are filmed at headquarters, with film and manpower furnished by the State Library and Archives. The county concerned must agree, however, to microfilm on the premises deeds, wills, and mortgage records and must provide the camera and personnel for the purpose, while the State Library and Archives furnishes the film and trains the operators. Eventually the program will cover counties that cannot afford a camera and personnel by sending microfilm teams to them to do the work.

RECORDS MANAGEMENT AND RECORDS DISPOSITION

Tennessee has no records management program. It needs one badly. Also, there has been as yet no discussion of initiating an essential records preservation program.

The Records Disposal Act of 1957 as amended by chapter 223, Public Acts of 1961, gave the Public Records Commission final disposal authority over state records. Requests for disposal may be initiated by the department concerned or by the State Library and Archives, but before the commission can act the head of the department involved must certify that the records are no longer of official or administrative value or that they can be more economically and efficiently preserved by means other than the preservation of the originals. Requests may apply to records either in the agency of origin or in the Archives; at the request of the creating agency and with the unanimous consent of the Public Records

[264] William T. Alderson, "Legislative Recording by the Tennessee Archives," *American Archivist*, XIX (Jan., 1956), 11–17.

Commission, originals of some records may be destroyed before expiration of the statute of limitations.

Since the passage of the act the Public Records Commission, meeting at fairly regular intervals, has issued 53 records disposal authorizations and its Directive No. 1, which regulates procedures concerning requests for, and approval of, scheduled disposition. Since unanimous consent is required for the destruction of records and since the attitude of some of the commission members is quite conservative, only 11,908 cubic feet of records in the Archives and 1,617 cubic feet in the agencies of origin have been destroyed. So far, the State Treasurer has opposed the destruction of several hundred feet of warrants, although they are duplicated in warrant books, and — to give another example — the Department of Finance and Administration has objected to the disposal of more than 3,000 cubic feet of vouchers for payment of purchases.

The Records Disposal Act does not apply to local records. Upon ninety days' notice to the State Library and Archives, records of any court of record may be authorized for destruction by the appropriate county court.

COMMENTS

1. Inasmuch as for many years to come the stacks of the State Library and Archives Building will be used for the housing of non-permanent records as well as archives, the two categories of record material should be stored separately.

2. As legislation and funds permit, the State Library and Archives should attempt to move into the area of records management.

TEXAS

Housed in the new Archives and Library Building in Austin, the Texas State Library administers the archives of the state. It also has responsibilities in the area of records management.

BACKGROUNDS

The unhappy history of the Texas archives began dramatically with Sam Houston's attempt in 1842 to remove them from Austin, seat of the government, to a safe place at Washington-on-the-Brazos.[265] In 1846, after the annexation of Texas to the United States, early records of land offices around the state were assembled in an agency that later became the

[265] On the early history of the Texas archives, particularly the "Archives War" of 1842, see Dorman H. Winfrey, "The Texan Archive War of 1842," *Southwestern Historical Quarterly*, LXIV (Oct., 1960), 171–84; his "The Archive Wars in Texas," *American Archivist*, XXIII (Oct., 1960), 431–37; and his "The Texas State Archives," *West Texas Historical Association Year Book*, XXXVI (Oct., 1960), 41–50. See also Charles W. Ramsdell, "The Preservation of Texas History," *North Carolina Historical Review*, VI (Jan., 1929), 1–16.

General Land Office. Further attempts at concentrating the records of the earlier regimes of Texas were made in the 1850's, when the Nacogdoches Archives and records of the departments of the Republic were transferred to the custody of the Secretary of State, who in 1848 had been designated as keeper of "all books, maps, charts or publications, the same to constitute a State Library." By an act of 1876 (Laws, 1876, p. 225) the State Library was assigned to a new Department of Insurance, Statistics and History. The act made the State Library the legal archival depository of the state and ordered the Commissioner of the department to

demand and receive from the Secretary of State, the Comptroller of Public Accounts, the Commissioner of the General Land Office, and from such other departments as may have them in charge, all books, maps, papers, documents, memoranda, and data not connected with or necessary to the current duties of said departments or offices, as relate to the history of Texas as a Province, Colony, Republic, and State, and carefully to classify, catalogue, number and preserve same.

Under this provision, the concentration of archives in the State Library went forward. A fire destroyed the State Capitol in 1881, but since most of the records were either in vaults there or in the General Land Office Building, no great losses occurred. In 1891, three years after the completion of the present Capitol, the office of historical clerk as a *de facto* State Librarian was created, and two years later a Spanish translator and classifier took over the function of archivist on his staff. The Archives as a division of the State Library was established in 1907 (Laws, 1907, p. 283).

As a result of work of the Texas Library Association, organized in 1902, the legislature in 1909 divorced the State Library from the Department of Insurance, Statistics and History and put it under the jurisdiction of the newly created Texas Library and Historical Commission (Laws, 1909, p. 122). The commission was named custodian of the state's non-current records, but it was housed in the Capitol with insufficient space; and the Archivist, appointed in 1911, reported that, with the transfer of 1,149 file boxes of records from the basement of the Comptroller's office, available space for manuscript material was completely exhausted and that records remained in the departments of origin tucked away in any places that could be found for them.

From its inception until the late 1950's the commission complained in its biennial reports that it had neither room to carry out its legal duties nor funds sufficient to obtain adequate personnel. The entire first half of the twentieth century could have been summed up in the bitter statement of the commission in its 1944–46 *Report*: "The Commission has no hesitancy in agreeing that conditions are bad. It takes no pride in the fact that the Texas State Library is one of the poorest State Libraries in the country." [266] As records became inactive and space was needed for other purposes, records were moved to the basement of the Capitol, then when that was full to other basements or warehouses, and finally to the "cowbarn" and its annex, where they were piled from the floor to the rafters.[267] The "cowbarn" was also used to store government-owned grain and was the home of very large well-fed rats, which used the records for nest-making.

The 1947 legislature created a Records Administration Division in the State Library (Laws, 1947, p. 945) and made it the custodian of non-current state records but did not appropriate funds for it.

In 1951 the demand for space in the Capitol forced the removal of the archives to the basement of the Highway Building; and, when the Highway Department needed this space in 1956, the archives again were displaced, this time to a quonset hut at Camp Hubbard amid the department's equipment shops and to warehouses south of the Colorado River — disposed of, in the words of J. Frank Dobie, "about as lovingly as a lead mine disposes of slag." [268] Public indignation was aroused by this last shunting of the archives to another dangerous and inappropriate location, and the second archives war of Texas was under way.

In the meantime Senate Concurrent Resolution No. 44 of 1953 had authorized the Governor to appoint a committee of eighteen persons to study what was being done and what should be done concerning Texas' historical heritage and to form, if needed, a statewide non-profit historical foundation to encourage and stimulate historical activities in the state. The Texas State Historical Survey Committee formed eight subcommittees on areas to be embraced by the survey. Its report,[269] which was submitted to the legislature in 1955, made the following recommendations concerning the care and use of archives and manuscripts: that they be housed in at least semi-fireproof buildings and be made available to qualified scholars; that manuscript collections be maintained separately from library materials; that a survey be made of county records with the aim of microfilming them up to about 1910; that another survey be made of methods of maintaining manuscript material in other state libraries; that the National Archives be asked to help in conducting a survey of Texas material at the National Archives with the aim of obtaining copies; and that immediate construction of an archives building be undertaken.

[266] *Texas State Library, Legislative Reference, Historical Archives, Books and Libraries for Texans; Biennial Report of the Texas Library and Historical Commission for the Nineteenth Biennium, September 1, 1944–August 31, 1946*, p. 4.

[267] These records were transferred to the records center when it became available in 1950.

[268] J. Frank Dobie, *The Archives Wars of Texas* (n.p., [1957]), [p. 4].

[269] Texas State Historical Survey Committee, *Report to the Governor and the Fifty-fourth Legislature* (Austin, Tex., n.d.), pp. 27 ff.

The Texas State Historical Association, the oldest historical society in the state, organized the public outcry against the removal of the archives to the quonset hut and led in the demand for the construction of a building for the Texas archives. In its efforts it was joined by the Texas Historical Foundation, a non-profit body organized by the Texas State Historical Survey Committee, and by the Sons and Daughters of the Republic of Texas. The resulting pressure moved the legislature to authorize the construction of the building (Rev. Civil Stats., 1925, as amended through 1962, art. 678m-2, sec. 1, 2). This building, occupied in 1961,[270] stands as a monument to the sympathetic understanding of Governor Price Daniel.

THE STATE LIBRARY

The State Library is under the Texas Library and Historical Commission of six members who, with the approval of the Senate, are appointed by the Governor for overlapping terms of six years. The Director and Librarian serves as the Executive and Administrative Officer of the commission. In addition to its standard library functions, the State Library operates an Archives Division under the Director of State Archives, a Records Administration Division under the Records Chief, a Legislative Reference Division, and a Rural Library Service Division. The Archives Division is the legal depository for the permanently valuable records of the state and also accepts private papers pertaining to the history of Texas. The Records Administration Division is in charge of a records center, though the act of 1947 assigns it much broader responsibility.

On the basis of divisional proposals, the Director and Librarian prepares the agency budget, submits it to the Library and Historical Commission for approval, and forwards it to the directors of the Legislative and Executive Budget Boards. Each of the two boards sends its separate recommendations to a conference committee of the two houses of the legislature. Reviewed by the committee, the budget request then goes to the two houses. Of a total appropriation of $476,082 for the fiscal year ending August 31, 1963, for the Library and Historical Commission, the Archives Division received $31,081.42 and the Records Administration Division $40,368.

The State Library has sixty-eight employees. Under the classification system established in 1961 and administered by the State Classification Office, job descriptions stating educational and other requirements for the various positions have been developed and serve as guides in making appointments. The Director and Librarian serves at the will of the commission and must have "two years training in library science or the

[270] The legislation pertaining to the State Library has been conveniently assembled in its *The State of Texas, Library Laws* (Oct., 1962, proc.), 21 p.

equivalent thereof in library, teaching or research experience" and "at least two years of administrative experience in library, research or related fields." He appoints his assistants and employees subject to the approval of the commission. The Director of State Archives must "present satisfactory evidence of one year's advanced work in American or Southwestern History" and must be able to read French and Spanish easily (Rev. Civil Stats., 1925, as amended through 1962, art. 5445).

The staff salaries are below those for comparable positions at the University of Texas. There is a system of five in-grade steps within salary ranges. Employees have the usual leave benefits — ten days in any one fiscal year, increased to thirteen after fifteen years of continuous service, and one day of sick leave per month — and they participate in the state retirement system, for which the employee's contribution of 4.5 per cent is matched by the state.

The new Texas State Archives and Library Building,[271] dedicated on April 10, 1962, is a $2,500,000 structure of red granite. It consists of the main building with a ground level and four floors (257 by 67 feet) and a seven-story stack area (111 by 48 feet). The third and fourth floors of the main building and the sixth stack level are used by the General Land Office.

THE ARCHIVES DIVISION

The Archives Division, under the Director of State Archives ($7,080–$8,628), has one professional employee ($4,176–$5,088), a documents librarian in charge of the Texas Documents Section [272] ($4,176–$5,088), three half-time clerks (University of Texas students who receive an hourly wage of $1.15), a clerical supervisor, a stenographer, a clerk-typist, and a janitor. The division occupies well-planned quarters in the south wing of the building, where its research room, offices, microfilm room, and map room are located, and uses stack areas number two and four (each 48 by 111 by 8 feet), affording storage space for 21,816 cubic feet of records. All of stack area four and half of stack area two are equipped with shelving.

The Archives Division holds records of the provisional government of Texas, 1835–36; records of the Republic, 1836–45; the Nacogdoches Archives, 1733–1836; and records of the state, including legislative records, Governors' papers, and records of practically all important state agencies to 1961. Included are 400 cubic feet of General Land Office records, 1836–1900, and transcripts of Mexican, British, and Spanish archives, 1755–1846.

[271] Dorman H. Winfrey, "The Texas State Library," *Texas Library Journal*, XXXVIII (Dec., 1962), 101 ff.

[272] The section receives and distributes specified numbers of legislative documents, reports, and publications of all state agencies (Vernon's Annotated Texas Statutes, art. 5442).

Since the move into the new building, accessions totaling 1,055 cubic feet of records, 5,902 books, and 303 reels of microfilm have been taken over. Because the Archives Division competes with the University of Texas and the Southwest Collection, Texas Technological College, in acquiring private material, it has important collections of the papers of prominent Texans. The division is also in charge of the library's very rich Texana Book Collection.

Loose-leaf binders containing pertinent correspondence and transfer lists and, since 1961, an accession register control incoming accessions. In arranging records, the principle of provenance is to be followed. No arrangement and description work is going on now, however, because of the obvious lack of trained personnel. Seymour V. Connor's *Preliminary Guide to the Archives of Texas* (n.p., 1956, 90 p.), a wholly admirable achievement considering the circumstances under which it was prepared, still serves well as an over-all finding aid. Access to manuscript holdings is through a general index, on cards. Maps are well described in James M. Day and Ann B. Dunlap (comps.), *The Map Collection of the Texas State Archives* (1962, 156 p.).

The division has no laminating equipment, and silking is still employed for repairing damaged items. During the 1962 calendar year, 240 yards of silking material was used. A fumigating vault holding 350 cubic feet of records has been installed in the basement of the building.

Since the move into the new building, use of the division's holdings has risen steeply. In the course of twelve months, there were 3,942 visits by persons doing research: 3,287 written inquiries had to be dealt with; and an average of 250 telephone requests per month were handled.

A considerable number of documentary publications have been issued by, or under the auspices of, the Archives Division. To its older publications — such as the *Papers of Mirabeau Buonaparte Lamar* (6 vols., 1920–27), *Journals of the Fourth Congress of the Republic of Texas, 1839–1840* (3 vols., 1929), *Journals of the Sixth Congress of the Republic of Texas 1841–1842* (3 vols., 1940–45), and *Texas Treasury Papers . . . , 1836–1846* (3 vols., 1955) — there have been added the *Letters of Antonio Martinez, Last Spanish Governor of Texas, 1817–1822* (1957) and the *Texas Indian Papers, 1825–1916* (4 vols., 1958–61).

THE RECORDS ADMINISTRATION DIVISION

Headed by the Director of Records ($5,808–$7,080), the division's staff consists of a Clerical Supervisor III ($4,646–$5,436), a Clerical Supervisor I ($3,660–$4,464), a File Clerk II, a watchman, and four half-time file clerks, who are students at the University of Texas.

Chapter 403, Added Acts, 1947 (Rev. Civil Stats., 1925, as amended through 1962), authorized the establishment within the State Library of a Records Administration Division "to manage all public records of the state with the consent and cooperation of the departments and institutions in charge of such records" and to "conduct a photographic laboratory for the purpose of making photographs, microphotographs, or reproduction on film" of records [273] or to have all or part of this work done commercially. A 1963 amendment directs the heads of departments to establish and maintain active, continuing programs for the economical and efficient management of their records, to make and maintain records containing adequate and proper documentation of their organization and functions, and to submit to the Director of the Records Administration Division schedules proposing the length of time during which each series of state records should be kept.

The Records Administration Division started operations in 1951.[274] Although it occasionally gives advice to government agencies on matters pertaining to records management, its main functions are to survey agency records, administer the records center, and service records to government agencies. In co-operation with representatives of the departments, it has undertaken an extensive examination of the records deposited, with the aim of determining their retention value. Records are transferred to the Records Administration Division with a form "Transmittal of State Records," made out by the agency of origin. Forms are reviewed by the Director of the division, "and in conjunction with a representative of the agency" retention periods are set.

Since 1950 the division has had the use of three utility-type structures built at Willow Spring Road (six miles from the Capitol) as records centers, of which one is a quarter of a mile away from the other two.[275] There are 180,700 cubic feet of space available, but since not all of it is equipped with shelving, only 143,000 cubic feet of records can be stored. The performance of the center appears from the following statistics:

	Cubic Feet	Volumes
Records received: 1960–61	6,564	687
Records received: 1961–62	7,928	594
Records destroyed: 1960–61	4,178	183
Records destroyed: 1961–62	2,624	14
	Requests	Items Serviced
Circulation of records: 1960–61	1,900	9,262
Circulation of records: 1961–62	1,886	7,658

[273] At the present time no microfilming is done as provided for in article 5441a, Texas Revised Civil Statutes. Equipment and funds for the purpose have now been requested.

[274] William Carlton, "Records Management in Texas Government," *Texas Libraries,* XXIII (May–June, 1961), 72–76.

[275] Two of the buildings are constructed of corrugated asbestos siding with steel pipes for support. The third building is also of asbestos siding but with wood timbers and boards for support.

Under chapter 494, Laws of 1959 (Rev. Civil Stats., 1925, as amended through 1962, art. 5441b), the State Librarian may, with the approval of the State Comptroller, the State Auditor, and the Attorney General, "transfer, destroy or otherwise dispose of any records of the State of Texas consigned by law to his custody that are more than ten (10) years old" and that he considers valueless. As for records in agency custody, heads of departments and institutions may destroy those lacking legal, administrative, or historical value with the approval of the Librarian. For the destruction of fiscal or financial records, the consent of the State Auditor is also required.

Local archives may be deposited in the Archives Division, but none have been accessioned so far. County records may be disposed of with the consent of the commissioners court after microfilming, after the statute of limitations is reached or the record is five years old, and after notice has been given to the State Librarian, who may take records with historical value (Rev. Civil Stats., art. 6576). Municipal records may be destroyed with the consent of the city council (art. 1015, sec. 33).

COMMENTS

1. Though now very adequately housed, the Archives Division cannot organize and describe its holdings because of the lack of professional staff.

2. The Records Administration Division should be equipped to carry out the broad responsibilities assigned to it by the 1947 act.

3. Management and preservation of local government records have not received adequate attention.

UTAH

Under legislation initiated in 1917 and strengthened during the 1950's, the Utah State Historical Society at Salt Lake City serves as the archival and records management agency of the state.

BACKGROUNDS

The Utah State Historical Society was organized around the turn of the century to disseminate "correct" historical information to the public, to collect material illustrative of the development of Utah, to preserve papers, journals, and reports of explorers and pioneers, and to establish a reference library.[276] Made a state institution in 1917, the society was instructed to hold its "present and future" collections for the state and to serve as custodian of "all records, documents, relics and other material of historical value . . . in charge of any state, county or other official not

[276] Utah State Historical Society, *Report*, 1937-38, p. 1.

required by law to be kept as part of the public records." [277] These last were to be transferred to the society after they had not been in current use for ten years, or earlier at the discretion of the agency head. However, the legislature made no provision for housing the archives.[278]

The role of the society as custodian of the state archives was strengthened by chapter 110, Laws of 1951. It provided for records disposition, authorized the society to appoint an archivist, and outlined his duties. Under a 1954 deficit appropriation by the Board of Examiners — composed of the Governor, the Secretary of State, and the Attorney General — the employment of a State Archivist and of one other person was formally authorized. In 1955, chapter 135 transferred the Governor's mansion to the society and made an appropriation of $20,000 for its upkeep during the 1956–57 biennium.

The society now operates under chapter 141, Laws of 1957 (Pocket Supp. to 1953 Utah Code Ann., Replacement, Title 63-18-1-17). This law defines the duties and objectives of the society, establishes its Division of State Archives, defines public records, names a State Records Committee, establishes standards for microfilming, and gives to films the legal force of the originals. It also instructs the State Archivist to consult with the purchasing agent concerning the quality of materials used in records creation, gives him reasonable access to all public records, and grants the Attorney General the power of replevin. Chapter 140 of the laws of the same year transferred to the Historical Society the Graves Registration and Marking Division of the Adjutant General's office, making it the Military Records Section of the Division of State Archives. Chapter 154, Laws of 1963, designated the State Archivist as State Records Administrator and instructed him to conduct a records management program in the executive branch of the state government.

THE DIVISION OF STATE ARCHIVES

The Utah State Historical Society operates a reference library and the Division of State Archives. It is governed by a Board of Trustees, consisting of the Secretary of State and ten members appointed by the Governor. The board appoints the Director, who must be a person with training and experience in historical work. He serves as secretary to the board and appoints all other personnel of the society.

The budget of the society, formulated by the Director, is first submitted to the society's board — normally a formality — and subsequently to the Budget Office of the Governor, to become part of his budget. After hearings before a joint House-Senate subcommittee, where the Director has an

[277] *American Archivist*, XI (Apr., 1948), 190.
[278] The "relics" are now scattered among various institutions.

opportunity to present and defend his budget, it goes to the whole Budget Committee and then to the legislature.

The society's income for the 1963–65 biennium consists of $213,500 of appropriated funds plus income from sales of publications and from private sources, which gives it a total of $233,500. Of this amount the Archives Division receives $86,500, of which $21,500 is for operation of the Military Records Section. Some administrative expenses connected with the archives operations are taken from the society's budget. Much of the 41 per cent increase in the total society budget over the 1961–63 biennium will be needed to meet new expenses, such as maintenance and care of the former Governor's mansion, employment of an archivist, and payment of the employer's share of the state retirement system.

During its first three years the Division of State Archives concentrated on building the archives program. A temporary change of emphasis from archives to records management took place in 1960. In fiscal 1961 the archives received $10,000 and records management $8,900, but in 1962 the archives received only $7,600 and records management $10,900. The budget for 1963, however, shows a reversal of this trend, with the archives receiving $18,200 and records management $13,700. The "crash program" for records management helped to interest the Governor and legislature in the archives program. This is reflected in the 1963–65 budget of $65,000 as compared with $37,000 for 1961–63.

As of July, 1963, Utah instituted a merit system for state employees; and all persons who were employed as of that date, except the Director of the society, are covered by the system. Job descriptions define the duties of the nineteen professional, clerical, and custodial members of the staff of the society. The position of Historian is vacant and will not be filled during the 1963–65 biennium. Under the Director ($9,800–$12,732) the following constitute the staff of the Archives Division: the State Archivist ($8,280–$11,580), the Records Manager ($6,216–$8,700), an Archivist in charge of the Military Records Section ($5,136–$7,188), two archives assistants in the Archives ($4,248–$5,928 and $2,904–$4,668, respectively), one archives assistant in charge of the records center ($4,248–$5,928), a part-time records clerk ($1,200–$2,400), and a clerk-stenographer ($3,192–$4,452). Salary increases on a merit basis are granted according to an eight-step system but depend upon the budget. After the last step, longevity payments (5 per cent every three years) are automatic.

THE ARCHIVES PROGRAM

For many years housed in the sub-basement of the State Capitol, the State Historical Society in 1957 moved into the magnificent mansion of Utah's "Silver King" Thomas Kearns, which in 1937 had become the

Governor's mansion. It is now used for the society's editorial and other offices, research library, and state archives, and is being preserved as "a show place of the genteel life that Utah's mineral resources produced for one of the state's foremost families." [279]

Except for office space and the collections of the Military Records Section on the third floor, little of the pretentious building can serve archival needs. A basement vault, the former wine cellar, houses the papers of the territorial Governors; a first floor silverware vault houses the legislative papers; the "jewelry vault" on the second floor contains the society's manuscript collections. The bulk of its archival holdings, however, must be satisfied with basement space. There is a fire-alarm system tied in with the nearest fire station. Of 1,300 cubic feet of storage space available, 1,000 cubic feet are now in use. Because the building is not fireproof some archival materials, such as records of the Tax Commission prior to statehood, are kept in the records center.

The basement storage consists of the "Governors' Room," containing papers of the state Governors to 1960 and the records of the Utah Commission, 1882–96; a room for county records, which are not actively solicited; [280] and a third room that holds records of the various state departments organized in record groups. The former bowling alley is used for the library and for WPA material of the Utah Writers Project. Military records, 1849–1900, are in the Military Records Section on the third floor.

Plans are being made for a three-story archives vault,[281] which the 1963 legislature placed on the four-year building program. The vault is to be erected adjacent to the mansion. An architect has been engaged for the project, but the actual construction must wait for an appropriation of a quarter of a million dollars, probably in 1965. It is hoped that eventually the former coach-house, now occupied by the State Library, can be obtained for use as a records center.

A so-called labeling code tantamount to a record group system assigns their place to records accessioned as well as to records to be accessioned. Control is by means of a card catalog consisting of entries for departments of the executive branch, for the legislature and courts, and for subjects. A *Preliminary Inventory of the Records of the Executive Departments in the Utah State Archives* (1959, proc., 33 p.), actually in the nature of a guide, lists the records on hand alphabetically by department.

[279] *Mansion of the Utah Historical Society* [n.d.], p. 2.

[280] Under the law, local records of historical value may be transferred to the Archives Division, but few have been.

[281] On the basis of a records survey completed in March, 1962, there are now in the state 48,262 cubic feet of public records that deserve archival protection and preservation; and, for future growth during the next twenty years, an additional 25,000 square feet should be provided. The basic figure of 48,262 cubic feet, however, was obtained from incomplete reponses of officials circularized and may be too high.

There are no preservation and rehabilitation facilities, but plastic envelopes are used to protect fragile material pending the acquisition of a laminator.

The Archives Division has a flatbed portable microfilm camera and two rotary cameras. Many agencies do their own microfilming — including the offices of the Secretary of State and the State Engineer, the State Road Commission, and the Department of Public Health. Programs are not uniform, for some agencies own and some rent cameras, some make both negatives and positives and some only negatives, and most house their own film or use commercial storage. Chapter 154, Laws of 1963, requires the State Records Administrator (State Archivist) to establish a centralized microfilming program for state agencies. Since no additional funds were appropriated for this purpose, agencies will be charged for this service. The newly appointed State Archivist has had years of experience as director of the vast microfilming program of the Utah Genealogical Society and may be expected to institute many changes in the use of microfilm.

In addition to the Historical Society's rich publication program — which includes the *Utah Historical Quarterly* (2,000 copies printed), reports, works on Utah history, and a bimonthly *Newsletter* — the Archives Division has published the technical manuals referred to below and pamphlets such as *What You Should Know About the Utah State Archives* and *You and Public Records*.

RECORDS MANAGEMENT AND RECORDS DISPOSITION

Since 1960 the Archives Division has offered records management services to state agencies and counties in matters of filing procedures, preparation of inventories, space use, and the like. Now headed by the Records Manager, appointed in September, 1961 — a professional with much experience in federal records management — the program includes training sessions for records officers of state agencies who are to be appointed in accordance with instructions of the Governor. For the benefit of public officials there have been published in processed form a *Records Management Manual* covering records disposition (1960), a *Microfilm Guide* (rev. 1960), and a *County Records Manual* (1960).

The records management act (Laws, 1963, ch. 154), effective on May 14, 1963, makes the State Archivist the State Records Administrator and instructs him to establish standards, procedures, and techniques for effective management of records, to make continuing surveys of paper-work operations, and to recommend improvements in current records management practices, establish standards for the preparation of retention and disposal schedules, and establish and operate a records center and a central microfilm service for state agencies. It outlines the duties of the agency heads in respect to this program and extends it to local governmental units.

The State Records Center, in the basement of the State Capitol, has a storage capacity of 7,000 cubic feet, of which 5,569 cubic feet were in use on July 1, 1963. During the period beginning September, 1961, and ending June 30, 1963, the center processed 3,339 requests for records or for information from the records and destroyed 2,540 cubic feet of records. For the fiscal year ending June 30, 1964, the projection was for 3,000 services and the destruction of 1,500 cubic feet of records. Because of the lack of a drainage system, a flood six inches deep caused by bursting pipes in the summer of 1962 did considerable damage to the center holdings and particularly to a series of letter books. Since that time the more valuable records have been located in the safest places in the records center. The center is fairly well ventilated and is practically fireproof. Once it is in full operation, records will not be received unless controlled by disposition schedules.

For lack of time, the Records Manager has not been able to give records management advice to counties. He has assisted Utah County in setting up a satisfactory records center, and Weber County is setting up an effective records management program.

Though a manual on the preservation of records essential to the continuity of government has been prepared, a program to that effect cannot be said to exist. A proposed law on essential records has been drafted but has not yet been submitted for legislative action.

Final authority over the disposal of all public records is in the hands of the State Records Committee (Pocket Supp. to Utah Code Ann., Replacement, Title 63-18-11, 12), which consists of the State Auditor, the Attorney General, the State Archivist, and the head of the agency concerned. Inventories, disposal lists, and schedules are prepared with the assistance of the Records Manager and circulated among the members of the committee for their approval or disapproval, inasmuch as the committee does not hold any meetings.

Local agencies submit lists of records to be destroyed, keeping one copy and depositing one each with the State Auditor, the Attorney General, and the Archives Division. Authority to approve destruction rests with the State Records Committee.

COMMENTS

The potentially notable archives program of the Utah State Historical Society cannot unfold unless the society receives adequate funds for an archives building, for which plans are now being drawn.

VERMONT

In Vermont the records management and archives functions have been consolidated at Montpelier under the Department of Administration. This is the result of a development that began in 1937 and culminated in a law of 1959 creating a Public Records Division in the department.

BACKGROUNDS

When, in 1915, Augustus H. Shearer surveyed the archives of the state for the Public Archives Commission of the American Historical Association [282] he found them in danger and confusion, with many gaps, some resulting from a fire of 1857 in the State House. Even at the time of the survey many officers of the state still had their offices and records not in Montpelier but wherever they happened to live. Only the records of the Secretary of State were relatively well protected in the Capitol in Montpelier.

As in other New England states, the legislature became concerned first about the local records, quite understandably because in Vermont land records are kept by the towns. Using the results of the WPA Historical Records Survey and working with its staff, a commission appointed in 1935 found that most of the local records were kept in private houses, stores, and barns and were in danger from fire, flood, vermin, and general neglect. To make matters worse, town and city clerks had no guidance whatever with regard to their record-keeping duties and no practical means of finding out about them, because of the numerous and scattered references to the subject in the statutes — more than a thousand of them.[283]

Prompted by the recommendations of the commission, the legislature passed Act 229 of 1937, which created a Public Records Commission. According to an amendment passed in 1943 (Act 166), the commission was to consist of the Director and the chairman of the Board of Directors of the Vermont Historical Society, the State Librarian, the Secretary of State, and one other person appointed by the Governor. The commission enlisted the services of Harold S. Burt, Examiner of Public Records of the state of Connecticut, and Henry H. Eddy, of the Franklin D. Roosevelt Library, as consultants. In its first report, submitted in 1944, which embodied the reports of the two consultants, the commission made recommendations for a state records program, including provision for a new building. Under an appropriation of $10,000 to the commission, a records management program was initiated in early 1952. For years, however, the commission tried in vain to obtain adequate quarters. Finally, in 1957, the legislature created a commission to study the state government. Its recommendations led to the passage in 1959 of Title 3, Vermont Statutes Annotated, chapter 10, which consolidated a number of already existing agencies under a Department of Administration. These were the Divisions

[282] "Report on the Archives of the State of Vermont," *Annual Report of the American Historical Association for the Year 1915* (Washington, 1917), pp. 311–55.

[283] Vermont, Commission To Make a Survey of Early Records of Counties, Towns, and Villages of the State, *Report* (Montpelier, 1936, proc.), 17 p. + 2 appendixes.

of Budget and Management, Finance, Personnel, State Buildings, Public Records, and Purchasing. The Public Records Commission became the Division of Public Records under the Public Records Director, and in 1960 it was able to move into quarters adjacent to those of the Vermont Historical Society on the first floor and in the basement of the recently acquired National Life Insurance Company building, now the State Administration Building. A Public Records Advisory Board is appointed by the Governor with the consent of the Senate.

THE ARCHIVES OF THE SECRETARY OF STATE

The greatest concentration of permanently valuable and historically important Vermont state records is in the archives of the Secretary of State. These records are administered by the State Historian (present salary $110.50 per week!), who reports to the Secretary. Both he and his part-time assistant are under the state's merit system. The State Historian gives about three-fifths of his time to the publication of the *State Papers of Vermont*; one-fifth to arranging, inventorying, and preserving the records in his custody; and one-fifth to assisting visitors and answering requests for information (the number of visitors and reference letters is estimated at about 500 per year).

Holdings include the so-called Vermont State Papers, 1777–1884; legislative records, 1778–1955; Surveyor-General's papers, 1763–1820; laws of Vermont, 1779 to date; certificates and canvasses of votes for federal, state, and county officers, 1800 to date; correspondence and papers of Governors, 1859 to date; corporation records, 1860 to date; and vital statistics, 1760 to date.

This collection of precious material is rather poorly housed in an upper and a lower vault in the State Capitol. The lower vault particularly is not adequately ventilated. A *List of the Major Records in the Vault of the Secretary of State's Office* (Nov. 4, 1952, proc., 6 p.) gives an overview of all the material on hand and notes a number of special indexes. No technical equipment for the restoration or reproduction of records is available.

THE DIVISION OF PUBLIC RECORDS

The division is charged with records management and archival functions. Under the law, its Director is to aid, advise, and inform all or any custodians of public records; to have access to all public records at reasonable times; to recover public records not in the possession of the rightful custodian; to investigate the adequacy of the protection provided for the public records; to plan, and advise agencies on, systems of record-keeping, except where regulated by law; to receive non-current records on request of the agency; to copy, index, repair, edit, or publish public records or lists, inventories, guides, catalogs, or indexes thereof; to co-operate with federal agencies to these ends; to make, with the approval of the Governor, regulations necessary to preserve the records; to maintain a records center; and to administer a central microfilm program.

The division's 1964 budget provides $26,197 for personal services, $500 for supplies, $2,120 for contractual services, $3,000 for equipment, and $996 for social security and related purposes — a total of $32,813. Budgets are prepared by the Director, taken up with the department head, reviewed by his Budget and Management Division, and discussed with the Governor, who makes the budget recommendations. The Director appears before the Appropriations Committee of the House and sometimes before that of the Senate.

The personnel of the division consists of the Public Records Director (present salary $9,544), an administrative assistant ($4,000–$5,174), two photocopy machine operators ($3,224–$4,212), and the records clerk ($3,042–$4,004), who is in charge of the records center. With the exception of the Director, who is appointed for a two-year term by the Governor with the approval of the Senate, all staff members are covered by the state's merit system. This provides a five-step pay increase plus longevity pay; annual and sick leave (one day per month during the first five years of service, one and a quarter days after five years, and one and a half days after ten years); a contributory retirement system; group life insurance, to which the state contributes; a group hospital-medical-surgical program, with the state paying 50 per cent of the "employee-only" premium; and eligibility for a major-medical-expenses group plan.

The archival function of the Division of Public Records is not yet fully developed. One hundred thirty-eight cubic feet of permanent records are kept in center-type boxes in an archives vault adjacent to the records center area, which has a capacity of 364 cubic feet.

RECORDS MANAGEMENT

The records management program began in a modest way in early 1952. Microfilming was done with one rotary camera, inventories were started in the larger state agencies, disposal requests were processed, and, as an interim solution to the housing problem, semi-active records were stored wherever a niche could be found for them. The program now operates on both state and local levels. Records of state agencies have been and are being inventoried by the Director, and disposal schedules have been prepared and approved for about 70 per cent of them. Some advice and assistance is given in regard to space utilization and filing procedures, and court forms are being revised. A section in the Department of Administration develops the highly technical area of data processing.

The operation of the program has been accelerated since the installation of the records center in the basement of the Administration Building.

The area, formerly used for records storage by the insurance company, is well suited to the purpose. It has a storage capacity of 6,718 cubic feet, approximately 64 per cent of which is used. Since the frames of the storage equipment were part of the building, only the shelving had to be acquired.

A *Records Center Procedures Manual* (Jan. 1, 1961, proc.) deals with identification, survey, and analysis of record series; packing and listing them for transfer to the center; reference service on the records; and the disposition of valueless records.

The following figures show the recent activities of the records center:

Fiscal Year	1961	1962	1963
Agencies using the center	7	14	16
Record series analyzed	131	127	34
Boxes (or packages) received	2,768	1,261	749
Boxes removed for destruction	0	3	145
References to state records on microfilm	0	493	963
References to state records in paper form ..	3,449	3,879	5,818
Boxes (packages) housed as of June 30			4,639
Reels of state records housed as of June 30 ..			1,311

Equipped with two photostat copying machines, two rotary microfilm cameras, one flatbed microfilm camera, and one microfilm enlarger, the Public Records Division provides a central microfilm service except for birth, marriage, and death records, which are microfilmed in the Department of Health. Microfilming is used to produce security copies and retention copies of records covered by destruction orders. Production has run as follows:

	1961	1962	1963
Reels of 35-mm. film	137	168	125
Reels of 16-mm. film	58	143	108
Enlargements		105	61
Large photostat prints	1,673	1,455	1,574
Small photostat prints	1,108	815	531

Records management service to local government consumes much of the Director's time. During the last nine years he has visited all 246 town and city clerks' offices, giving aid and advice. He also calls on all newly appointed town and city clerks during their first years in office to acquaint them with the laws governing the administration of their records.[284] Particular attention is given to the housing of these records in safes or vaults. Monthly bulletins are sent to clerks and treasurers to suggest improvement, acquaint them with statute changes, and supply them with perti-

[284] During fiscal 1962 the Director made 94 personal inspection and assistance calls, traveling approximately 5,500 miles by car. Of 138 towns surveyed in 1935, three had fireproof buildings and 38 had safes or vaults of some kind. As of July 1, 1962, only 41 of the 246 towns and cities lacked any fire protection for their records.

nent news items. The Director also participates in the programs of the town officers' educational conferences. There are as yet no plans for microfilming local records except by private microfilm service companies at local expense. In 1951–52, however, the Utah Genealogical Society microfilmed all town records to 1850, and the division hopes to extend the microfilming beyond that date. Positive copies of the microfilms of local records are kept in the Division of Public Records and account for the high rate of reference service — 785 reels produced for 189 searchers in fiscal 1963.

Biennial reports of the division are included in those of the Department of Administration.

DISPOSAL OF STATE AND LOCAL RECORDS

The Public Records Advisory Board has final authority over the disposal of all public records, including local records. Since agencies are not required to have records officers, destruction schedules are normally prepared by the Director. He presents requests to the advisory board for its approval within sixty days after receipt, and he issues the necessary destruction orders once approval has been obtained. During fiscal 1963 twenty-three destruction orders, covering 108 items, were issued to custodians of records of state agencies. Five tons of records were sold to scrap dealers.

Chiefly as a result of group meetings and personal visits by the Director to towns, 792 destruction orders were issued during fiscal 1963 for the destruction of local records. No estimate of the number of cubic feet of local records destroyed is available.

COMMENTS

1. The records management program of the Division of Public Records is well under way.

2. If the division is to carry out the functions of a central archival depository of the state, it will need both expanded facilities and additional professional staff.

VIRGINIA

Both archives and records management functions are carried forward by the Virginia State Library in Richmond, and the respective programs have developed slowly but steadily during the last forty years, thanks to increasing support by the legislature and the people of the state.

BACKGROUNDS

The records of colonial Virginia and those of the state prior to 1865 sustained greater losses than the records of any other state along the eastern seaboard. In fact, they were practically annihilated as a result of frequent fires and relocations of the capital, destruction during the Revolutionary War, and finally the burning of Richmond by the Confederates before their evacuation and the pillage of the city by Union troops at the end of the Civil War. Many of the oldest county records, too, which for their protection had been taken to Richmond from the Chesapeake Bay and River areas, shared the fate of the colonial and early state records in 1865.

Between the Civil War and the turn of the century very little was done to care for Virginia's records; for poverty, indifference, and a lingering defeatist attitude combined to retard both archival development and historical endeavor.[285] Lester J. Cappon has stated that the one institution in the state that before 1920 pointed the way toward historical scholarship was the Virginia State Library.[286] It had been created in 1828, when the Clerk of the Executive Council, successor to the old Privy Council, was named Public Librarian and when the council was instructed to formulate rules and regulations for the operation of the library. Between 1830 and 1903 the library was under the control of the general assembly's Joint Committee on the Library, with the Secretary of the Commonwealth acting as State Librarian from 1832. It was the Library Committee which, in the 1870's, contracted with W. Noel Sainsbury in England to obtain copies of some of the official records there, a first effort to get from English repositories substitutes for some of Virginia's lost records. A State Library Building, already too small when it was occupied, was constructed in 1895.[287] By the time William G. Stanard reported to the Public Archives Commission on "The Virginia Archives," [288] almost 2,000 boxes of records and 900 bundles and packages of unboxed papers had found their way into the State Library.

The new constitution of 1902 created the State Library Board to have charge of the State Library. Inspired by the activities of the Public Archives Commission, the general assembly passed an act (Acts, 1902, ch. 253), defining the board's responsibility. This law was revised and amplified in 1904. An act of 1918 (ch. 231) authorized localities to transfer to the institution records not in current use. Furthermore, in 1926 the State Library was given the right to take custody of pre-1790 court records that were not properly cared for, except will books and deeds; and in 1926 also it was authorized to borrow and photostat pre-1800 court records (later advanced

[285] Lester J. Cappon, "Two Decades of Historical Activity in Virginia," *Journal of Southern History*, VI (May, 1940), 189–200.
[286] *Ibid.*, pp. 192 ff.
[287] The archives annex, also too small when built, was added in 1920.
[288] *Annual Report of the American Historical Association for the Year 1903*, I (Washington, 1904), 645–64.

to pre-1865), to keep one set of the photostats, and to give one set, together with the originals, to the local authority, unless the appropriate judge ordered the originals to remain in the State Library.

The WPA Historical Records Survey proved a "most constructive factor in Virginia . . . in arousing public interest and producing concrete results in the field of local archives."[289] In 1941 the survey was brought under the central supervision of the State Archivist, and when it was discontinued its unpublished materials were deposited in the State Library. By the time this happened, the State Library had occupied its new building, which is described below, a move that prompted legislation to strengthen the authority of the State Library in matters archival.

A law of 1940 (ch. 216) provided that records of state agencies might be deposited in the State Library and might be removed only by the head of the depositing agency, and that records might be destroyed with the consent of the State Librarian and the State Comptroller or their deputies, except that no land or personal property books could be destroyed. An act of the same year (ch. 239) empowered the heads of agencies, with the approval of the Governor, to have records reproduced and the originals destroyed. Before the Governor gave consent to such destruction, however, he was to consult with the State Librarian concerning the records' historical value, and the latter could have any of them transferred to the State Library for permanent preservation. This section also gave certified copies the legal force of the originals. In 1962 the power of approval for microfilming and destruction was transferred to the State Librarian.

THE VIRGINIA STATE LIBRARY

The Virginia State Library is governed by the State Library Board of seven members, six appointed by the Governor for terms of five years, and the seventh, the Superintendent of Public Instruction, *ex officio*. The board appoints the State Librarian, who must have professional training. The library is organized in a number of divisions: the Administration Division, the General Library Division, the Historical Publications Division, the Extension Division, the Archives Division, and the Records Management Division.

Total appropriations for the library amounted to $907,310 in fiscal 1962. After a discussion with his division heads, the State Librarian prepares his budget request. First approved by the State Library Board and then reviewed by the Division of the Budget, it is forwarded to the Governor's Advisory Committee, which is composed of legislators. With the advice of the committee, the Governor makes his recommendations to the general assembly.

The State Library is under the state merit system. Professional librarians

[289] Cappon, *loc. cit.*, p. 198.

are certified by the State Board for the Certification of Librarians, of which the State Librarian is secretary. The State Librarian's office is the personnel office for the library. There is no political patronage, and promotions are authorized by the State Librarian on the basis of merit, with ratings being made annually and salaries reviewed about every two years. For the certification of archival personnel, a Master's degree in history or political science is normally required, although those lacking the degree may receive scholarship help to complete the requirements. "Fringe" benefits include life insurance, social security annuities, and professional and other types of leave.

The work of the Historical Publications Division, which has a staff of five classified as historians, is closely related to that of the Archives Division. The Virginia State Library has published in the past *Journals of the House of Burgesses, Legislative Journals of the Council of Colonial Virginia, Minutes of the Council and General Court, Executive Journals of the Council of Colonial Virginia* (the fifth and final volume of this work is now being edited), *Journals of the Council of State* (it is planned to continue this series), *Letters of Governors* (3 volumes only), vestry books, publications relating to the history of Virginia in World War II, fifty-six annual reports, some containing supplemental material of historical value, and twenty-five volumes of a bulletin series, largely bibliographical. The *Bulletin* of the library was discontinued in 1956 and a new series, *Virginia State Library Publications*, was begun. Nineteen numbers of the latter have been issued, covering a variety of historical and bibliographical subjects. The bibliography of official publications of the state, found in the *Bulletin* and *Publications* series, is one of the few complete state bibliographies. In 1951 the library began to publish a popular illustrated historical magazine, *Virginia Cavalcade*, which still continues.

The Virginia State Library is housed in a steel and concrete building, constructed in 1941 at a cost of $1,838,000. The facilities provided for the Archives Division there are still among the best in the United States.

THE ARCHIVES DIVISION

The Archives Division has a staff of twenty employees, of whom ten are professional in their educational preparation and the work assigned them. The professional salaries are: the State Archivist, $8,784–$10,992; Archivist C, $7,344–$9,168; Archivist B, $6,432–$8,040; five Archivists A, $5,640–$7,032; and two archival assistants, $4,320–$5,400. The head of the photographic laboratory receives $4,704–$5,880.

In 1962 the division had in its custody 62,802 volumes; 11,517,016 record items; 6,078 reference reels of microfilm; and 39,358 maps; these materials cover three and a half centuries and consist of non-current public records and other papers relating to Virginia and the South. They fall into the following categories: colonial records, 1607–1776; executive records; legislative records; judicial (county) records; and non-archival papers. Governor's papers and the executive papers held by the Secretary of the Commonwealth are received two years after a change in the administration. Legislative records include early petitions received from the counties; these, in fact, are requests for legislation.

The Archives Division occupies the west end of the first floor of the State Library; has separate stack areas, a catalog room, and a well-designed reading room; houses the rare books in its "treasure room"; and has an extensive area for photographic, fumigating, and cleaning facilities, which are available to the library as a whole. Twelve- and eighteen-inch steel shelving is used to store archival material in a mixed system in which manuscript material and large volumes are filed flat and smaller bound volumes are filed upright. For flat filing, clam-shell type boxes are used; these can be placed on shelves of either width, since they are twelve by eighteen inches. Of the 27,500 cubic feet of space available for archival storage, 25,000 feet are used.

Through the years different patriotic societies of Virginia have paid for the restoration and repair of pre-1865 county court records. W. J. Barrow, inventor of the Barrow laminating machine, has had his workshop in the State Library since 1941 and has done all the laminating work for the Archives Division on a contract basis at relatively low cost.

Ample photographic equipment enables the division to provide service to the entire library. It has one photostat recorder, one single-face machine (18 to 24 inches), two Recordak Model D flatbed cameras, three projection printers, one film processor, one Depue positive printer, dryers, eight MPE micro-readers for the use of the public, and five readers, including two flow readers, for the use of the staff. Film is stored in forty-three film cabinets. All photographic work is done on the premises by four persons. Xerox prints of frequently used archival material are being produced in order to avoid the purchase of another reader. Photoreproduction is used to preserve badly worn and often consulted material.[290]

The control and handling of incoming accessions are carefully regulated. On the basis of receipts issued, the Archivist C keeps a short handwritten accession record, with an indication of the inclusive dates of the records received and the control number assigned, and subsequently he drafts a more elaborate document consisting of an entry and additional data, called an accession analysis sheet. Analyses may run to fifteen pages. The entries are also placed on cards to be filed in a public catalog of the dictionary type and are then recorded in the formal accession register. The catalog is the initial finding aid. From this, for more detailed information,

[290] The division's program for the photostating of county court records antedating 1865 has been referred to on pp. 279 ff. It is in connection with this project that the patriotic societies support the restoration of documents in need of repair.

staff and searchers can turn to the accession analyses to which the cards refer. Inasmuch as the accession analysis technique is of recent origin, documents of this kind are being prepared for all records received earlier. The Archivist C, working backward through the years, is now processing the accessions of 1951.

Besides these finding aids, there is a two-volume "Inventory of Holdings," in which the departments and other agencies appear in alphanumeric order. Each lot of records received is listed under the agency of origin, with its accession number, an indication of its volume, and some additional information. This is considered a principal means of controlling the growth of the division's holdings and reporting them in the State Library's annual *Reports*.

Because routine operations take up practically all the time of the Archives Division's staff, there is no opportunity for more refined arranging and analyzing of records. The photocopying of marriage bonds, which are first arranged chronologically and later indexed in each volume of the bound copies, and a similar project for loose wills and deeds are happy exceptions to this situation.

The research room is extremely well planned to control entrance and exit and the supervision of searchers. Elevators are so located that records asked for are directly delivered to the charge-out desk. The A Archivists alternate in taking charge of the research room. Open from 8:15 A.M. to 5:00 P.M., Monday through Saturday, this room was used in 17,186 visits in fiscal 1962. The researchers consulted 14,053 manuscript items,[291] 30,224 reels of microfilm, and 753 maps. Most frequently used are the microfilm copies of Virginia county records that were filmed by the Utah Genealogical Society through 1865, records from family Bibles, Revolutionary War records, Confederate service records, and Land Office records. Demand for microfilm material is so heavy that a searcher is allowed to use a reader for only two hours if other clients are waiting. It is estimated that 50 to 75 per cent of the constant visitors are genealogists, though biographers and historians are coming to the archives in increasing numbers. About a hundred letters requesting information are answered each week, and ten thousand photoprints are supplied in accordance with order forms returned to the division. Form letters are used, and there are standard texts for answers to individual requests.

In addition to the systematic program of providing bound photoprints of county court records mentioned above, the Archives Division may accept county court records for deposit when the local clerk's office is inadequate for safe storage. The division does not favor centralized storage for local records, remembering what happened in 1865, when local records were concentrated in Richmond for safety.

[291] Every unit is counted as an item, be it a single document, a folder, or a box.

The leading role of the library and of the Archives Division in particular is well illustrated by their effective participation in the Virgina Colonial Records Project. This project was initiated in connection with the 350th anniversary of the founding of Jamestown, after a 1952 survey had revealed that Virginia's colonial records could be largely reconstituted with photographic copies of public records and other Virginia-related material in English depositories. The project, originally financed by the federal government, is now continued by the State Library and other Virginia libraries, and the general assembly has underwritten it by appropriations to the State Library to the extent of $17,500 in 1963–64. The State Archivist acts as the chairman of the committee in charge of the project, and so far more than 5,000 survey reports and 400 reels of film have been forwarded to Richmond by the agent in charge of the operation in England. This extensive program [292] will enrich the holdings of the Archives Division most significantly.

THE RECORDS MANAGEMENT DIVISION

Evidently based on the Governor's statutory power to authorize the photoreproduction and the destruction of records, a records management program was launched in the Division of the Budget of the Governor's office in 1949. The *Records Management Program Manual of Procedures* issued by the division (Richmond, 1949) as the first such manual prepared at the state level and based on the survey reports of Records Engineering, Inc., contained regulations governing records disposition, proffered advice on filing methods and forms control, and proposed a filing scheme for the records of the division. In 1959 the program was transferred to the State Library, where a Records Management Division was created to operate it. The division consists of the State Records Administrator ($7,680–$9,600), a Records Examiner ($6,432–$8,040), a duplicating service supervisor ($3,936–$4,920), two photographers, and two clerks. In 1962 an effort was made to obtain passage of a model records management law, including authority to establish records centers, but this was not approved by the Advisory Legislative Council. The State Library Board was authorized, however, to conduct the records management program (Acts, 1962, ch. 256).

Most of the present schedules were prepared from 1949 to 1953 and must now be replaced by new ones. Since this requires all the attention of the division, other aspects of records management are minimized at this time. Inventorying is done in the state agencies by *de facto* records officers, though in sluggish areas the Records Examiner may do the job. In the

[292] Edward M. Riley, "The Virginia Colonial Records Project," *Legal Historian*, I (Dec., 1962), 3–5. See also Virginia State Library, *The Public Record Office: History, Description, Record Groups, Finding Aids, and Materials for American History With Special Reference to Virginia* (Richmond, 1960), 188 p.

process, examples of forms are assembled for future use in a forms control program. In fiscal 1962 agency records that had filled 2,537 file drawers were destroyed under schedules, and in the same year the contents of 461 file drawers were destroyed after microfilming.

The microfilm program of the Records Management Division does not constitute a centralized service. It serves the needs of small agencies only, for an agency that can justify a program of its own is permitted to establish an installation for the purpose. Requests for microfilming by the Records Management Division and for permission to set up separate programs must be approved by the State Librarian. The amount of microfilming now going on could probably be reduced if there were a records center.

On request, the Records Management Division may give advice and assistance to local units. Apparently, however, such service is rarely requested. Similarly, little is done for the preservation of records essential to the continuity of government.

Under the Virginia Code, sections 42–59, the State Librarian or his deputy and the State Comptroller have the final disposal authority. While the use of schedules for the continuing destruction of records is not specifically authorized, the law is broad enough to permit it. A number of specific acts provide for the disposal of county records. Except for court and other records in which the state has an interest, city councils have jurisdiction over the disposal of municipal records.

COMMENTS

1. Legislation allowing the establishing of records centers and their control by the State Library would improve the present records management service.

2. The professional archives staff should be increased to permit more constructive arrangement and description work.

3. Once a larger staff is available, consolidation of the present accession analyses into complete inventories should be considered.

WASHINGTON

Since 1957, records management and archival administration in the state have been under the Division of Archives and Records Management of the Department of General Administration. Housed since the spring of 1963 in a new records center and archives building at Olympia, the division is now in a better position to carry out its functions.

BACKGROUNDS

Until 1909 Washington had made no provision for the care of its archives. Consequently, Jacob N. Bowman, reporting to the Public Archives

Commission of the American Historical Association,[293] found them in lamentable condition, housed in poor and insufficient space, and victims of indifference on the part of the responsible officials. A law of 1909 (Session Laws, ch. 38) attempted to improve this deplorable situation by creating a Public Archives Commission composed of the Governor, the Secretary of State, and the State Auditor; making it the official custodian of all public documents, records, and archives; and empowering state, county, and other officials to transfer their non-current records to the commission. For twenty years thereafter the State Librarian acted as archivist, always hampered by lack of funds and facilities in which to keep the archives. Upon the abolition of the Public Archives Commission and a successor agency, the archives in 1929 were put in the care of the Department of Finance, Budget and Business; and in 1938 they were housed in the basement of the new Social Security and Public Lands Building, in 13,000 square feet of space poorly adapted to archival use. In 1954 the archives were transferred to the Department of Public Institutions and in 1955 to the new Department of General Administration.

Committees established in 1941 and 1951 and given authority over the destruction of useless records remained ineffective. In 1951, however, the first Archivist with professional qualifications was appointed in the person of Robert W. Nesbit. Serving as secretary to the destruction committee, he was able to speed up the disposal of great quantities of valueless papers and to establish a measure of control over those retained as permanent or semi-permanent records. At the 1956 meeting of the Society of American Archivists he received valuable suggestions that assisted him in drawing up a comprehensive archives and records management bill that embodied the most advanced thinking in the field. The bill, approved by the Governor on March 23, 1957, became chapter 246, Session Laws of 1957, and laid the groundwork for the present program of records and archival management in Washington. The act declares all public records to be the property of the state, creates a Division of Archives and Records Management in the Department of General Administration, and defines the duties of the State Archivist, who is in charge of the division. These duties are to centralize and manage the archives of the state, to inventory and develop retention and disposal schedules for the records of all state agencies, to establish and operate records centers, to gather and disseminate information on all phases of records management, to operate a central microfilming bureau, and to approve microfilm projects undertaken by other agencies of the government. The act also establishes a small State

[293] "Report on the Archives of the State of Washington," *Annual Report of the American Historical Association for the Year 1908*, I (Washington, 1909), 365–98. For subsequent developments, see Robert W. Nesbit, "The State Archives of Washington," *Pacific Northwest Quarterly*, XLVIII (Apr., 1957), 44–46.

Records Committee, of which the State Archivist is a member, to pass on disposal requests and schedules.

THE DIVISION OF ARCHIVES AND RECORDS MANAGEMENT

The division is headed by the State Archivist, who also has the title of Administrator of the Division of Archives and Records Management. His biennial budget request is reviewed by the Budget Officer of the Department of General Administration and by the responsible budget examiner in the central budget agency. As part of the Governor's budget, it is submitted to the legislature. In the past the State Archivist has been in attendance at the hearings before the Appropriations Committees of the two houses. The 1962 budget provided $23,720 for the needs of the division.

The staff of the division is small, and the salary scale is not impressive. Present salaries are:

State Archivist	$7,524–$8,964
Assistant State Archivist	5,088– 6,048
Records Clerk III	4,104– 4,884
Records Clerk III	3,468– 4,104
Clerk Stenographer II	3,936– 4,680

The State Archivist lacks professional archival help, since the Assistant State Archivist's time goes almost wholly into records management. This means that archival work has practically come to a standstill.

All personnel of the division are under the state's merit system, administered by the State Personnel Board. A system of merit increases provides four steps within salary ranges after completion of a six-month probation period. "Fringe" benefits include twelve days of annual leave, increased to fifteen and eighteen days after prescribed periods of service; twelve days of sick leave per year; a state retirement system to which both state and employee contribute 5 per cent of the latter's salary; and social security coverage.

Until the spring of 1963 the division's facilities were totally inadequate. It had some odd-shaped basement space in the Public Land Building, where a cubbyhole had been partitioned off as "office" for the State Archivist, basement space in the General Administration Building for records of agencies housed in that building, and similar space in the Public Health Building — making a total capacity of 45,000 cubic feet. Three thousand cubic feet of material housed in the legislative garage were transferred to the new building while it was still under construction.

The 1961 legislature authorized the construction of an archives and records center building, to be financed by the sale of state-owned shorelands located within incorporated cities, and appropriated $571,000 for the purpose. The building, part of the Capitol Building group and ready for occupancy in the spring of 1963, provides on three levels 49,200 square feet of storage space. Except for 4,000 square feet of space for offices, workroom, and storage of supplies, the entire facility is below ground. On each level there is a large room for records center use and a smaller one for archives, with a respective storage capacity of approximately 130,000 and 13,000 cubic feet. The records center space is humidity-controlled, while the archives rooms have humidity and temperature control. A fumigating vault, a microfilm room with a darkroom attached, and a small exhibit display case have been provided, and space has been set aside for installing a laminator. Unfortunately one room will have to serve both as workroom and as research room for archival users.

The decision to place practically the entire facility underground was prompted by a number of considerations: the desire not to disturb the aesthetic unity of the Capitol Building group by a storage-type structure, the necessity to save on building costs, and the advantage of providing additional fall-out shelter space in the Capitol area.

The following discussion is based on conditions antedating the division's move into its present quarters.

ARCHIVAL ACTIVITIES

The division has in its custody territorial and state records, 1854–1920. They consist chiefly of the official correspondence of the Governors from 1854 (fairly complete only for 1890–1920) and records of the Supreme Court, the Department of Education, the Office of the Secretary of State, and the Highway Department. Because of space limitations, archival holdings hitherto were not physically separated from records center holdings, and no distinction was made between the two in regard to their servicing. A total of 3,464 cubic feet of records was accessioned during the 1962 calendar year. In the absence of an accession register, which was to be started on April 1, 1963, file copies of transmittal sheets were used for control.

There has been practically no arrangement and description work. With the move into the new building, a record group system will be instituted that will cover both records center and archival holdings. Because of the lack of a clear distinction between center and archival material, reference service statistics refer to both types of records. During the 1962 calendar year, 6,867 requests for service were answered with the help of records in the Public Land Building, where the division was then housed. Statistics for the records center in the General Administration Building — 19,136 services — are not wholly reliable because the center was of the "self-service" type; that is, agency representatives walked in, helped themselves, and supposedly signed a log. All this will change with the move into the new building. It should be clear, however, that any attempt to establish arrangement and descriptive control over the archives will have to wait until the division is given a second Assistant State Archivist.

Under the 1957 act, local records designated by the Archivist as of primarily historical value can be transferred to a depository selected by him. This matter is now being considered by an *ad hoc* committee composed of representatives of the State Library, the three major historical societies, and the five institutions of higher learning of the state, with the State Archivist as chairman. The committee is working on an agreement under which the ten co-operating institutions will serve as depositories for local records of permanent value.

RECORDS MANAGEMENT AND RECORDS DISPOSITION

In the area of records management, emphasis so far has been on inventorying and scheduling and on providing records center service. Though records officers have been appointed in the agencies, inventorying and scheduling are done by the Division of Archives and Records Management, principally by the Assistant State Archivist. Some of the larger agencies — such as the Departments of Agriculture, General Administration, and Vocational Education — and the Governor's Office have been completely covered. Inventorying will be resumed with greater vigor once the division is able to accept transfers for temporary storage in the new records center. Occasionally the State Archivist advises agencies on files management. Otherwise, full implementation of the 1957 law depends on a considerable expansion of the division's staff, which is not to be expected in the near future.

Advice and assistance to local units are also hampered by the lack of personnel. The State Archivist sometimes goes to larger cities to assist them when they are setting up comprehensive records programs or are submitting large lists and schedules of records for disposal.

The Central Microfilming Bureau provided for in the 1957 act has not been established. Lacking a full-time operator, the division did a limited amount of microfilming (116 reels) in 1962, using one planetary and one rotary camera, mainly to save storage space. In the next fiscal year the division expected to have a full-time operator and the additional help of operators from two major departments — Highways and Labor and Industries.

The State Archivist and one appointee each of the State Auditor and the Attorney General constitute the State Records Committee, which must meet at least once every quarter. The State Archivist acts as chairman of the committee and also keeps the minutes. The committee approves, modifies, or disapproves transfer and retention schedules prepared by the State Archivist in co-operation with agency records officers and acts upon

[289]

requests to destroy any public records. According to the State Archivist, the same persons have served for many years as appointees of the Attorney General and the Auditor, have demonstrated genuine interest in the work of the committee, and have given him excellent co-operation. During the 1962 calendar year, 3,759 cubic feet of records were approved for destruction, 453 of them after microfilming.

The State Records Committee is hampered in its decisions by section 6 of the 1957 act, according to which "official public records" not photographically reproduced cannot be destroyed unless they are ten years old or unless the department of origin shows to the satisfaction of the committee that retention for ten years is both unnecessary and uneconomical. Furthermore, any shorter retention period must have the approval of the Director of the Budget, the State Auditor, and the Attorney General. In the case of "office files and memoranda" the State Records Committee is not bound by the above limitations.

County, municipal, and other local government records, provided that they have been photographically reproduced or are ten years old, may be destroyed with the approval of the State Archivist, the Chief Examiner of the Division of Municipal Corporations of the State Auditor's office, and a representative of the Attorney General.

In 1963 the legislature passed House Bill 33 (Laws, 1963, ch. 241), which enjoins all officers of the state to designate the essential records of their offices and transmit them or copies of them to the State Archivist for reproduction by microfilm or other miniature photographic process. The Archivist is directed to co-operate in the storing and safeguarding of the reproductions in a place recommended by the State Director of Civil Defense. House Bill 34, which made similar provision for the records of the political subdivisions and municipal corporations of the state, was vetoed by the Governor. Both bills were drafted by the civil defense agency in co-operation with the State Archivist.

COMMENTS

1. To assist him in organizing and analyzing the archival holdings of the division, the State Archivist needs the help of at least one more Assistant State Archivist.

2. In the area of records management, the full intent of the act of 1957 cannot be carried out unless additional trained personnel are added to the division's staff.

WEST VIRGINIA

In West Virginia, the care and preservation of public records is far from unified. The Department of Archives and History at Charleston is the official archival agency of the state but, for reasons to be explained later, it is not operative; the West Virginia Collection of the University of West Virginia at Morgantown has been extremely active in acquiring county, local, and some state records; and the Commissioner of Finance, in his capacity of State Records Administrator, is in charge of administering the Public Records Management and Preservation Act of 1961, which takes no cognizance of the existence of the two archival institutions in Charleston and Morgantown.

THE DEPARTMENT OF ARCHIVES AND HISTORY

The Department of Archives and History, created by chapter 64, West Virginia Acts of 1905, is under the Board of Public Works,[294] and the Governor as chairman of the board appoints the State Historian and Archivist, who heads the department. Taking over the collections of the West Virginia Historical and Antiquarian Society, a quasi-public organization that had been chartered by the state in 1890,[295] the department was given the following mandate: to publish materials provided by the legislature, to receive copies of all state publications and reports, to collect all kinds of pertinent historical materials, and to adopt a system of preserving and classifying them. In due course the department, with headquarters in the State Capitol, established its library and museum sections. It also acquired archival and manuscript material, but it never provided an archives section to service and systematically expand its holdings.

The department's budget for fiscal 1964 provides $35,300 for personal services, $7,205 for current expenses, and $8,000 for equipment, all of which serves the library and museum functions of the department. The budget is prepared by the Director for submission to the Governor and the Board of Public Works.

The Director of the department is a political appointee of the Governor. The agency enjoyed a period of stability when Mrs. Roy Bird Cook was in charge (1946–53). Since she left, a new Director has been appointed with each change in the administration. The present Director was appointed in 1961. A former professor of education and dean of students at West Virginia Wesleyan College and a past president of the West Virginia Historical Society, he understandably has been unable to cope with the archival responsibilities of the department and to organize the means to discharge them. Staff members are not necessarily affected

[294] The board consists of the Governor, the Secretary of State, the Auditor, the Treasurer, the State Superintendent of Free Schools, the Attorney General, and the Commissioner of Agriculture.

[295] First Biennial Report of the Department of Archives and History of the State of West Virginia (Charleston, W. Va., 1906), pp. 19 ff.

by a change in administration, though the curator of the museum was dismissed after such a change in 1961.

Salaries are low, as exemplified by that of the Director, which is $7,000. The three librarians working under him receive $5,604, $4,308, and $3,480, respectively, while the museum curator is paid $3,732.

The department has been deprived of its office space and now operates in the library, which is located on the fourth floor of the State Capitol. The museum, housed in the basement of the Capitol, has not been able to profit significantly from modern trends in museum administration for lack of adequate space, but it still uses some of its space for German machine guns of World War I.

In recent years the department has not received any sizable accessions to its archival holdings.[296] They include a good collection of Governors' papers, 1861–1936, minutes of the legislative assembly of 1863, Civil War records of various kinds, court records, records of a few organizations and churches, and a number of collections of private papers. These materials are stored in a few bays in the library stacks that are protected by iron grilles.

Finding aids in the department consist of Innis C. Davis' *A Bibliography of West Virginia: Legislative Hand Book and Manual*, from 1916 on; and various calendars of the individual collections. Equipment includes three microfilm readers, one Verifax, and a small laminating machine. This is a table model and seems to be used mainly to laminate non-archival material.

The department issues an annual *Short Title Checklist of West Virginia State Publications* (proc.).

THE WEST VIRGINIA COLLECTION

The West Virginia Collection of the West Virginia University Library in Morgantown owes its existence to the untiring efforts of Charles H. Ambler, who as head of the university's history department in 1933 prevailed upon the university's Board of Governors to authorize a Division of Documents in the university library. In spite of the lack of staff and proper financing, the division embarked on an active acquisition program, which continued until World War II terminated its existence. Reactivated as the West Virginia Collection in 1950, it has made remarkable progress under the leadership of its present curator and with the interest and support of the university authorities, especially the university librarian.

The West Virginia Collection consists of a Manuscripts Section, the West Virginia Room book collection, and a Photoduplication Section. Its 1962–63 budget provides the following salaries: $9,400 for the Curator

---

[296] They seem to be essentially those listed on pp. 116 ff. of the *Biennial Report of the Department of Archives and History for the Period Ending June 30, 1938*.

of the West Virginia Collection, $8,200 for the Associate Curator of the Manuscripts Section, and $3,600 for an assistant. The West Virginia Room book collection is under an Assistant Curator, who receives $5,100. Professional salaries are set by the university librarian, and annual increases have been given in the past decade.

Archival and manuscript holdings are safely housed on the ninth and tenth stack levels of the library building, although the library stack equipment is not very satisfactory for the shelving of archives boxes. The Photoduplication Section has a planetary microfilm camera, a Xerox reproducer, and a photostat machine. Microfilm readers and a reader-printer are also available. A comprehensive newspaper microfilming program is in progress (394,929 exposures on 35-mm. film made in fiscal 1962–63).

In 1933 the West Virginia legislature sanctioned the transfer to the university of non-current public records in state, county, and local offices.[297] The Division of Documents and the successor West Virginia Collection have made good use of the authority thus conferred on them. Operating in a vacuum much of the time, they have acquired the records of some state agencies (files of the Commissioner of Agriculture and books of the State Treasurer) and considerable quantities of records of about eighteen counties, including records of county court cases, vital statistics, land records, and tax records. The West Virginia Collection, not the Department of Archives and History, has also co-operated with the microfilming project of the Utah Genealogical Society and has made student assistants available for preparing its county records and manuscript holdings for microfilming. It now preserves the copies of all films produced (713 reels of Virginia county records and about 1,400 reels of West Virginia county records in 1961).

Besides public archives, including those of the university, the West Virginia Collection has a very large number of archives of churches, institutions of all kinds, and business firms. It has also acquired numerous collections of papers of Governors, political leaders, and other individuals prominent in the history of the state. Total archival and manuscript holdings comprised 1,678 collections, about three million items, at the end of fiscal 1962–63.[298]

Materials are shelved in the order of their accession and are controlled by the *Guide to Manuscripts and Archives in the West Virginia Collection*, compiled by Charles Shetler (Morgantown, 1958), with a supplement

[297] Chapter 92, Acts of the West Virginia Legislature, 2d extraordinary sess., 1933. See also the *First Report of the Archivist of the Division of Documents of the West Virginia University for the Year 1935–1936* (Morgantown, n.d.), p. 5.

[298] They consist of 1,156 archival type boxes; 783 volumes; 678 folders; 916 microfilm reels of archival material, including records of state agencies and West Virginia University; and 3,126 boxes and 4,443 manuscript volumes of county court records.

due in 1963; by a shelf-list of thirteen drawers; and by other finding aids, such as a name index to the correspondence files in the major nineteenth-century collections. A monthly accessions list has been published since January, 1961.

THE RECORDS MANAGEMENT PROGRAM

The records management program of the state is based on the Public Records Management and Preservation Act of 1961 (West Virginia Code, 1931, as amended by ch. 5, art. 8). The program is directed by the Commissioner of Finance, who is designated State Records Administrator and is advised by the Records Management and Preservation Committee. This advisory committee comprises the Governor, the Auditor, the Attorney General, the President of the Senate and Speaker of the House of Delegates, the President of the Supreme Court of Appeals, a judge of a circuit court, and the State Director of Civil and Defense Mobilization, or their respective representatives. No historian or archivist serves on the committee.

Under the act, which was inspired by the model legislation recommended by the Council of State Governments, the State Records Administrator is directed, with the advice of the Records Management and Preservation Advisory Committee, to establish standards, procedures, and techniques for the effective management of records; to survey continuously the practices of the agencies in connection with the creation, maintenance, storage, and servicing of records; to set up standards for the preparation of retention and disposal schedules; to determine the categories of records essential for the operation of government in time of disaster and for the preservation of the rights of citizens; and to properly maintain them or preservation duplicates of them. Also:

No record shall be destroyed or otherwise disposed of by any agency of the state, unless it is determined by the administrator that the record has no further administrative, legal, fiscal, research or historical value.[299]

Agency heads are instructed to establish and maintain programs for the economical and efficient management of their records, to make and maintain records that adequately document their activities and that will protect the state and its citizens, to conduct inventories, to submit retention and disposal schedules to the Administrator, and to co-operate with the Administrator in conducting surveys and in complying with the regulations issued by him.

The records administration program is now staffed with one employee, an attorney, and it received $10,000 in the 1962–63 budget. The State Records Administrator has issued, for the use of state agencies, a *Manual of Procedures* (Nov. 2, 1961). Besides stating the statutory requirements and

[299] West Virginia Code, 1931, as amended; ch. 5, art. 8, sec. 17.

defining terms used, it spells out the policies for the disposition of records, the standards for determining retention periods for state records, and the respective responsibilities of the State Records Administrator and of the agency heads. It also explains records retirement procedures and the forms to be used in the process.

Although the Department of Archives and History is mentioned neither in the act nor in the text of the *Manual,* the "Request for and Authorization of Records Retirement" (Form RM-2) [300] calls for approval of such authorizations by the State Auditor and by "Archives and History." On the other hand, no reference is made to the keeping of permanently valuable records by the Department of Archives and History; and it can be tacitly assumed that these, together with records authorized for later disposal, are to be in the custody of the State Records Administrator. He seems to be impressed by the idea of a combined records center and archives facility such as exists in the state of Michigan and, if possible, wants to provide the same arrangement in West Virginia.

So far, the Department of Archives and History has made no attempt to obtain a working arrangement with the State Records Administrator. In fact, the value of such an arrangement might be questioned, since the department has no personnel trained and experienced in the appraisal of records. That judgment is available at the West Virginia Collection of the West Virginia University Library, but this institution is 210 miles from the state capital and is not authorized to participate in the disposal procedure.

COMMENTS

1. As matters now stand, the state of West Virginia has no archival program. If the Department of Archives and History is to serve as the state's archival agency, it must: (*a*) receive legal recognition as such, which it is denied in the Public Records Management and Preservation Act of 1961; (*b*) obtain adequate quarters and equipment; (*c*) be staffed with trained personnel; and (*d*) be protected against the removal of personnel because of changes in the state's administration.

2. Once the department is properly staffed, its participation in the disposal process must be formalized.

3. There should be a clear understanding in regard to the role of the West Virginia Collection in the care and preservation of local records.

4. Unless the status of the Department of Archives and History can be changed in accordance with paragraph 1, above, it would be preferable to place the state's permanently valuable records under a new archival unit subject to the authority of the State Records Administrator. In this case, too, adequate facilities, a trained staff, and protection from political influence would be indispensable.

[300] It is reproduced on p. 12 of the *Manual.*

WISCONSIN

The State Historical Society of Wisconsin, in Madison, with its long and distinguished record in all fields of historical endeavor, serves as the archival agency of the state. Responsibility for the management of state records rests with the Department of Administration.

BACKGROUNDS

Founded in 1849, chartered by the state in 1853, and granted state funds in 1854, the society was made a permissive depository for state records in 1907, when the legislature authorized state officials to turn over to it, for permanent storage and "expert indexing," records no longer needed for the conduct of their business. A more effective archival program was initiated by chapter 316 of the Laws of 1947. It designated the society as the official and "ultimate depository of the archives of the state" and created a Committee on Public Records, which was to have authority over the disposition of public records.[301]

Legislation enacted in 1957 and 1959 removed the archives staff first to the Executive Department, Bureau of Purchases, and then to the Department of Administration, Bureau of Management; but the archival holdings remained in the society's building. In 1960, however, the archives staff was placed under the society again, and most recently the Division of Archives and the so-called "manuscript library" of the society were combined into the Division of Archives and Manuscripts.

THE STATE HISTORICAL SOCIETY

The State Historical Society of Wisconsin is an official state agency but has a private membership and is governed by a Board of Curators elected by the membership except for the *ex officio* members — the Governor, the Secretary of State, the State Treasurer, the President of the University of Wisconsin, and the Superintendent of Public Instruction. The board appoints the Director of the society. Administratively the society is responsible to the Governor and fiscally to the legislature. The society operates a Library; a Museum; a Division of Publications; a Division of Administrative Services; a Division of Research; offices of Field Services, Sites and Markers, School Services, Local History, and Public Information; and a Division of Archives and Manuscripts, which is responsible for the archives program of the state.

While the State Historical Society derives considerable income from its large private endowments, membership dues, sales of publications, and fees for admission to historic sites, as an official agency of the state it receives most of its funds from appropriations authorized by the legislature.

[301] Clifford L. Lord, "The Archival Program of Wisconsin," *American Archivist*, XII (July, 1949), 243–52.

From a modest $500 in 1854 they have increased to $607,099 in 1963. Inasmuch as most of the needs of the Division of Archives and Manuscripts, such as heat and light, general supplies, and office equipment, are included in lump sums in the society's budget, only items such as personal services, archival supplies and equipment, and purchase of manuscripts can be identified as expenses for the combined archives-manuscripts function. In fiscal 1963 for the Manuscripts Section salaries were $37,401 and other expenditures were $37,503, while for the Archives Section salaries were $13,691 and expenditures for archival supplies and equipment were $17,620.

The society's budget is prepared by the Director on the basis of divisional budget requests, reviewed by the society's Board of Curators and submitted to the Department of Administration, which prepares the Governor's budget recommendations to the legislature. The Joint Finance Committee of the legislature reviews the Governor's budget and frequently makes significant changes before the budget is approved by the legislature. The Director of the society defends his requests first before the Governor and subsequently before the Joint Finance Committee.

With the exception of the posts of Director, Associate Director, and Assistant Director of the society, all the positions on the society's staff are in the classified service, administered by the Bureau of Personnel in the Department of Administration. Positions are filled by competitive civil service examinations based on task statements and performance standards. Patronage and political sponsorship are conspicuously absent.

The physical facilities of the society hardly suffice for its manifold activities and are particularly inadequate for the archives-manuscripts operation. As long ago as 1918 Theodore C. Blegen recommended solving the space problem "by the construction of a plain, inexpensive, though dignified and adequate, building near the present Historical Library. This building would be used for the housing and administration of the non-current state archives, and for the public document, newspaper and periodical divisions of the Historical Library." [302]

Co-operation between the society and the University of Wisconsin has always been very close. Graduate students are used to good advantage as part-time workers in the Division of Archives and Manuscripts as well as in other units of the society. Also, the society offers through the university accredited courses in historical agency work, which give some attention to the care of archives and manuscripts.

Little need be said here about the extensive publication program of the society, since, with the exception of the manuscript guide referred to later, it does not serve directly the purposes of the Division of Archives and Manuscripts. The program includes books on Wisconsin and United States history, the *Wisconsin Magazine of History*, historical magazines

[302] *Report on the Public Archives* (Madison, 1918), p. 99.

[297]

for children of high-school and elementary-school age, and a monthly "newsletter" type of publication for members of the society.

THE DIVISION OF ARCHIVES AND MANUSCRIPTS

The combined Division of Archives and Manuscripts has eight professional staff members, two in the Archives Section and four in the Manuscripts Section, all of them well qualified by training or long experience in historical work. In addition, one person each is in charge of the Mass Communications History Center and the McCormick Collection. Salaries range from $8,136 to $10,536 for the position of State Archivist and head of the division, and from $4,524 to $8,724 for assistant archivists and assistant manuscripts librarians in the Manuscripts Section. Considering its responsibility for the area research centers, the Archives Section seems very much understaffed.

Holdings of the division are kept in certain library stack areas, in the basement of the society's building (the so-called north compression chamber), in a walled-off space in its entrance hall, in the records center in the State Office Building, and in the basement of the Capitol.[303] The total space occupied amounts to about 23,000 cubic feet; and, for all practical purposes, it is filled. Conditions will improve only if the society acquires the new or added facilities that it is trying to obtain.

To make its services more readily available to the people of the state, the society, as early as 1949,[304] began to experiment with the concept of regional archival depositories. These depositories, now renamed area research centers, are located at various state colleges and function in accordance with agreements that spell out the respective responsibilities of the centers and the society. Holdings, which consist of the permanently valuable records of county and local government units, the archives of the college at which the center is located, and private papers of preponderantly local interest, are processed and described by the division, while the college provides the space and the reference service. As a novel feature, there is provided a carefully regulated loan service between the division and the centers, under which material in the division can be made available at the center and records and papers in a center can be used at the Madison headquarters. In addition to alleviating pressure on space in the division's stacks, the arrangement is primarily designed to make available for college faculties and graduate students primary source materials for research in local history. Title to the county and local records in area research centers is retained by the society.

Notwithstanding the decentralization of materials resulting from setting up the area research centers, the holdings of the present Division of Ar-

[303] The division pays a rental of $2,500 a year for storage space in the records center.
[304] *American Archivist*, XII (Oct., 1949), 443.

chives and Manuscripts constitute an impressive assemblage of primary source material. Records stem from eighty-five state agencies and certain local government units and span the years from 1812 to 1961.[305] Under regular annual disposal authorizations from 1947 to 1960 and under retention and disposal schedules since 1960, sizable accessions have found their way into the custody of the division. The annual accumulation will require increased storage capacity. Present archival holdings are organized in record groups and controlled by means of a Kardex file, consisting of cards that for each series furnish about six lines of descriptive data. More detailed finding aids exist for the Governors' papers, for the plat books, and for the society's own archives. The draft of a "Guide to the State Archives of Wisconsin," prepared by the late Howard A. Merritt, Jr. (35 p., typed), should be brought up to date and published.

The holdings of the division's Manuscripts Section — the former "manuscript library" — are known as one of the richest collections of the country. Originally focused on material on Wisconsin and the old Northwest, recent collecting policy has assumed nationwide responsibility for certain categories of material, such as records of the labor movement and papers pertaining to the history of American science, mass communication, race relations, business, and urban history. The acquisition by the society of the famous McCormick Collection has led to collecting agricultural material on a national scale. The Manuscripts Section conducts, mostly through the society's Field Service, an active collecting program, but as a matter of policy it accepts practically no collections on deposit. Whenever possible, papers are kept in their original arrangement. They are controlled by means of a card catalog consisting of collection cards, donor cards, and subject cards, and — for collections of some size — by inventories. The *Guide to the Manuscripts of the Wisconsin Historical Society*, by Alice E. Smith (Madison, 1944), and its *Supplement Number One*, by Josephine L. Harper and Sharon C. Smith (Madison, 1957), need yet another supplement listing later accessions, for which cards have been and are being prepared.

The holdings of the Mass Communications History Center,[306] originating from H. V. Kaltenborn's gift of his papers to the society, are physically in, and processed by, the Manuscripts Section; but they are controlled separately. The center has begun to collect in the areas of journalism, public relations, and advertising, in addition to radio and television. The Wisconsin Center for Theatre Research, a collection of papers consisting primarily of those of playwrights but including also those of some actors and

[305] These amount to about 15,000 cubic feet.
[306] See State Historical Society, Mass Communication History Center, *The H. V. Kaltenborn Collection* (Madison, 1961), 32 p.; and a flyer entitled *Mass Communication History Center* (n.d.), stating briefly the center's collecting program in the fields of the press, radio and television, public relations, advertising, and theater and cinema.

production companies, is a joint enterprise of the society and the speech department of the university, which does the necessary field work.

In 1951 the McCormick Collection, which is now housed separately in offices adjacent to the general reading room, was taken over by the society. A processed guide to its holdings is available, and an item-by-item catalog of the Cyrus Hall McCormick personal and family papers (1809–84) has been prepared.

The materials of the Manuscripts Section are far more extensively used than those of the Archives Section. In 1962–63 the latter filled 614 reference requests, of which 231 came from state agencies and 383 from private persons, including 192 from scholars. Four hundred fifty-five of these requests involved use of archival material on the premises. During the same period the Manuscripts Section had 2,913 registrations of researchers and wrote 591 reference letters — a total of 3,504 reference services. Archival and manuscript users are accommodated in the divisional research room under the supervision of staff members of the Manuscripts Section, who do processing work as best they can while glued to their desks.

Inasmuch as the Division of Archives and Manuscripts has no facilities for repairing documents, those needing rehabilitation are sent out to be repaired. Photoreproduction for other state agencies is centralized under the State Board of Health, Bureau of Vital Statistics. The State Historical Society, however, does its own microfilming with one camera. It also has on the premises a photostat machine and a Verifax copying machine, and a microfilm reader-printer is available in the research room of the Division of Archives and Manuscripts.

As might be expected, the division takes considerable interest in the records of the state-supported colleges. It gave assistance to the Archives of the University of Wisconsin — now well housed, organized, and staffed — in the Memorial Library, and through its Area Research Centers at Oshkosh, Stevens Point, River Falls, Eau Claire, and Whitewater (with others to be established) it contributes materially to the preservation of college archives. In the general area of educational history, a project financed by the Fund for the Advancement of Education has enabled the State Archivist to assemble information about the records of educational institutions and about the papers of persons and organizations that concerned themselves with, or attempted to influence, education in the state. The ultimate aim is to bring into the society's custody source material useful to research in the history of education in Wisconsin. A similar project is now under way to collect material on the history of natural resources and conservation.

RECORDS MANAGEMENT

The records management program of the state, which was started in the State Historical Society in 1947, was formally established in 1959 with the creation of the Department of Administration. Headed by the Records Management Supervisor in the department's Bureau of Management, the ambitious program is concerned with the preparation of retention and disposal schedules; correspondence, forms, and files management; systems analysis; and space utilization. Scheduling was begun in 1960 and now covers about a third of the existing 10,000 records series in all state agencies. An agency training program in the management of forms, files, correspondence, and directives has been prosecuted vigorously.

The staff consists of the Records Management Supervisor ($9,816–$12,756), a Systems and Procedures Analyst III ($8,316–$10,836) in charge of forms and files management, two Systems and Procedures Analysts II ($7,116–$9,216) in charge of space management and records retirement, a Systems and Procedures Analyst I ($6,036–$7,896) in charge of current records, a Records Center Supervisor ($4,056–$5,256), a records center clerk ($4,176–$4,836), an office clerk ($4,056–$5,256), and part-time student assistants. All positions are in the state's classified service, and the duties of their incumbents are defined in job descriptions and "task and performance standards," documents prepared jointly by the employee and his immediate supervisor.

As noted below, the Records Management Supervisor serves as the secretary of the Committee on Public Records. He has developed an administrative practices manual, which covers agency records management responsibilities, microfilming projects, forms design standards, forms program review, filing equipment and supplies, records center storage, records disposal procedures, and the destruction of confidential records.

The records center is operated by the Records Center Supervisor with the assistance of a clerk and has a storage capacity of 23,748 cubic feet in the basement of the State Office Building and the Capitol, of which some 17,902 cubic feet are now occupied. Capacity will be increased in 1964 to 34,250 cubic feet. In order to be acceptable for storage, records must be covered by retention and disposal schedules unless special permission is obtained from the Records Management Supervisor. Depositing agencies, which retain legal custody over the records they deposit, make out the customary transmittal sheets, box and list the records in accordance with center methods, and pay a charge of sixty cents per cubic foot occupied. In 1962–63 there were 14,419 references to center holdings. Of the 17,145 cubic feet of state records destroyed in 1962–63, about 2,500 were accessioned and destroyed by the records center staff.

A 1959 act charges the Committee on Public Records, referred to above, with establishing a system to protect and preserve essential state records necessary for the continuity of government. The records management staff has sent a report on a system to the state Civil Defense Office.

The records management staff controls the microfilming service of the

Board of Health by reviewing all microfilm projects to see that the expenditures are justified and to fulfill the requirement that the Committee on Public Records must approve any microfilming application when retention of the film is a condition of destruction of the originals.

RECORDS DISPOSITION

In accordance with section 16.80 of the Wisconsin Statutes, authority over the disposition of state records is vested in the Committee on Public Records, composed of the Governor, the Attorney General, the State Auditor, and the Director of the State Historical Society. The Records Management Supervisor of the Department of Administration acts as the committee's executive secretary and submits to it requests for authorization of records disposal after having obtained the approval of the State Archivist.

County records are destroyed under statutory records disposal schedules. Municipalities may adopt records disposal schedules by ordinance. The Committee on Public Records may reduce the minimum retention periods for municipal records, which is fixed by section 18.01 of the Statutes (Assembly Bill 377A, 1963). Local officials on all levels who wish to dispose of records must notify the State Historical Society so that, within a period of sixty days, the State Archivist may claim any he deems of long-term value. Only an increase in his staff would enable him to work more effectively with local officials and to prevent unauthorized destruction, which occasionally seems to occur.

COMMENTS

1. The facilities of the Division of Archives and Manuscripts of the State Historical Society of Wisconsin are inadequate. A separate building for the division, or space in a new second building for the society, is urgently needed.[307]

2. The Archives Section of the division is understaffed, particularly since it must concern itself with the area research centers.

3. Wisconsin needs a local records act to provide for better management of current records, for the microfilming of valuable records, and for controlled destruction of non-current records. An effective local records program will also demand an increase in the division's staff.

WYOMING

The Wyoming State Archives and Historical Department, in Cheyenne, is the historical, archival, and records management agency of the state.

[307] In August, 1963, the Wisconsin legislature appropriated $2,400,000 for an addition to the State Historical Society Building, to be devoted primarily to stacks for archives and manuscripts.

The Wyoming Historical Society was created in 1895 to collect and protect the artifacts of Wyoming's past in a historical museum. The secretary of the society was to serve as State Historian, and the State Librarian had custody of the society's property. From 1895 to 1919 the state granted the society $250 per year, but the facilities were so poor and the society was moved around the State Capitol so frequently that much of the museum collection disappeared. In 1919 the Historical Society was reactivated as the State Historical Board, which appointed a State Historian. From 1932 to 1951 the State Librarian served *ex officio* as State Historian.

The first archives law to be passed in Wyoming was chapter 106, Session Laws of Wyoming, 1943. It made the State Historical Board custodian of the public archives of the state and its political subdivisions, provided for records disposal on both state and local levels, and gave replevin power to the Attorney General. This law was not implemented, however, and an act of 1951 created the State Library, Archives and Historical Board with jurisdiction over the State Archives and Historical Department and the State Library.[308] Repeated almost word for word in chapter 143, sections 2 and 10–14, Session Laws, 1953, the act defined the functions of the board; created the State Archives and Historical Department under a Director who was to be *ex officio* the State Historian, State Archivist, and Museum Curator; and regulated the transfer of records to the department.

A 1955 law (ch. 147) established the State Centralized Microfilm Department for the purpose of reducing storage space needed and for security purposes. A reorganization act of 1959 (ch. 77) redefined the duties of the Director of the State Archives and Historical Department; conferred upon the Director certain records management duties, including the operation of records centers; and authorized the Director to establish a Central Microfilm Division "deemed and considered a continuance of and successor to the Centralized Microfilm Department heretofore established by chapter 147, Session Laws of Wyoming, 1955 as amended by chapter 106, Sessions Laws of Wyoming, 1957." The records, machinery, supplies, and furniture of the latter were to become the property of the State Archives and Historical Department. The act also called for the designation of records officers in all state agencies and gave disposal authority to a Records Committee composed of the department's Director as chairman and secretary, the Attorney General, and the State Examiner or their respective appointees.

THE STATE ARCHIVES AND HISTORICAL DEPARTMENT

The department is governed by the State Library, Archives and Historical Board, composed of one person each from the state's seven judicial

[308] Lola M. Homsher, "Wyoming State Archives and Historical Department," *American Archivist*, XXII (July, 1959), 323–29.

districts, one member at large, and the Attorney General. Members appointed by the Governor serve for overlapping terms of six years. The State Archives and Historical Department consists of three divisions: the Historical Division; the Archives and Records Division, under which the archives, centralized microfilm, and records center programs are operated; and the Museum Division. Funds requested in the 1963–65 budget proposal for a fourth division, to be in charge of historical sites, were not granted.

The budget for the 1963–65 biennium appropriated $304,220 to the department, a little more than $152,000 per fiscal year, of which the Archives and Records Division received $90,000. In consultation with the division heads, the Director drafts the budget; submits it to the State Library, Archives and Historical Board for approval; and prepares the necessary copies for the Governor. The Director may defend the budget before the Governor and the Ways and Means Committee of the legislature. In 1963 the committee reduced the department's budget request by about $20,000.

The Director of the department receives a statutory salary of $9,000. There are nineteen other employees, eight of whom are in the Archives and Records Division. Their salaries are: Chief of the Archives and Records Division, $5,700–$7,140; three Assistant Archivists, $4,440–$5,880; one Archives-Records Clerk, $3,840–$5,280; three microfilm operators, $2,940–$4,980; and one clerk-typist, $2,760–$4,020. In-grade annual increases are granted on a merit basis if they are approved by the board and provided for in the budget. Appointments, made on the basis of job descriptions that have been prepared by the Director, must have the approval of the State Personnel Commission.

The department is housed in the modern State Office Building, which it shares with a number of other agencies. It has outgrown its facilities in every respect. It needs more space for its museum, for its offices, and for its Historical Division — and it has practically no space for the state's archives. It serves as headquarters for the Historical Society, of which the Director is the executive secretary, and for the society's chapters in sixteen of the state's twenty-three counties.

The publications of the department's Historical Division include the *Annals of Wyoming* (a much-respected journal), a newsletter entitled *History News*, historical booklets, brochures, and general historical material. The Director writes a weekly column carried by many newspapers in the state and also prepares for the State Library, Archives and Historical Board a detailed quarterly report (processed), a model of good administrative "bookkeeping." A *Biennial Report* in printed form is submitted to the Governor.

There are two state museums under the Museums Division: the State

Museum in the State Office Building in Cheyenne and, since 1959, the Fort Bridger Museum at Fort Bridger. Before 1963 the department was further burdened with the administration of a great number of historic sites, a task for which it did not have the necessary technical and custodial staff. Its function in regard to historic sites is now limited to planning the restoration of sites to be developed and to administering any museums established on them (ch. 117, Laws of 1963).

THE ARCHIVES PROGRAM

Because of the shortage of storage space, the department is unable to carry out its mission as the depository for the permanently valuable records of the state and its subdivisions. Some office space has been partitioned off for storage and has been equipped with steel shelving; but it amounts to only 1,270 cubic feet and is almost filled. At this time no further accessions can be accepted. The microfilm holdings are kept in a vault adjacent to the office of the Director. The Historical Division has private papers amounting to about 1,000 cubic feet, 182,158 micro-images of material borrowed for the purpose of preserving it on microfilm, and 2,945,060 micro-images of newspapers.

Although the Archives and Records Division is not in a position to receive accessions, it has developed a system of inventory control over the records of state agencies and of counties that, when completed, will make it possible to locate any record desired. These inventories for state agencies, counties, and municipalities furnish historical data for the respective offices; and list, office by office, the records *in situ*, those transferred to the Archives or records center, and those microfilmed. For counties and municipalities, however, the program is still in its initial stages.[309] A master index consists of cards of different colors for the names of records officers, for records on film, for records in the records center, and for records in the archives. A second set of the master index is available for consultation in the Historical Division.

The department's request for a laminating machine was refused by the 1963 legislature, but funds for the purpose will be asked for again in 1965. The department has a great array of photographic equipment, most of which it inherited from the Centralized Microfilm Department: two 16-mm. rotary cameras, three 35-mm. planetary cameras, one 35-mm. planetary camera that is used in the counties, and three Recordak viewers. Three other readers and a reader-printer are available in the Historical Division. The microfilm program is operated in one large room on the department's premises. During the 1961–63 biennium 997 reels of 16-mm. film and 2,411 of 35-mm. were produced. Film is commercially developed.

[309] Only the records of Laramie County — except for the county clerk's office and for certain municipal offices of Cheyenne and Laramie — have been inventoried.

State agencies that desire copies of microfilm receive them free of charge if their requests are approved by the State Records Committee, but local authorities must pay for them. Originals are either returned to the agency of origin or destroyed under procedures described below. A darkroom adjacent to the microfilm room is used mainly for the processing of glass plates and for copy work.

During the 1961–63 biennium, 33 departments were served and 2,172 archival searches were made. In addition, 1,191 records center searches were conducted, and 1,084 facsimile copies were furnished from microfilm.

RECORDS MANAGEMENT AND RECORDS DISPOSITION

Although authorized by the 1959 act to "disseminate to interested agencies information on all phases of records management," the department so far has not been able to conduct any such comprehensive program. Records officers have been appointed in the state agencies, and inventories and schedules are prepared by the staff of the Archives and Records Division for submission to the State Records Committee.

In the Supreme Court Building adjacent to the State Library, the division operates a records center with a storage capacity of 5,000 cubic feet. Although the center was almost filled during the 1958–60 biennium with 4,386 cubic feet of records, it has been able to take in 1,522 more cubic feet, thanks to the destruction of useless material. Total holdings as of July, 1963, were 4,828 cubic feet. Except for some shelving that separates the center from the State Library, records are stored in transfer cases and center-type boxes placed one on top of another. It is believed to be unwise to install shelving, for sooner or later the space will have to be relinquished to the State Library.

Wyoming participates actively in the program to preserve records essential to the continuity of government: by the end of the 1961–63 biennium, 17,459,475 state records and 2,643,883 county records [310] had been microfilmed. The state's civil defense organization is planning a blast-proof shelter in Cheyenne that will provide storage for security copies. Pending construction of the shelter, on which no action has as yet been taken by the legislature, the copies are kept in the State Archives and Historical Department.

Disposal procedures, which were first created by chapter 106, Session Laws of 1943, are now prescribed by sections 6 and 7, chapter 77, Laws of 1959, under which the State Records Committee has authority over records disposal. The committee consists of the Director of the Archives and Historical Department (as chairman and secretary), the Attorney General, and the State Examiner or their respective representatives; it holds regular

[310] These are from fourteen of the twenty-three county clerks' offices. Property records in Wyoming are in the offices of county clerks.

meetings, which last from thirty minutes to three hours. The Chief of the Archives and Records Division, who serves as recording secretary, assembles the so-called "Analysis of Records Forms," with the recommendations of the originating department, prepares and circulates the agenda, calls the meetings, and prepares and circulates the minutes. Occasionally the agenda may take up two or three meetings of the very co-operative committee. During the 1961–63 biennium, the committee acted on 143 requests from 47 departments, agencies, and counties; and as a result of its action 2,716 cubic feet of records were disposed of, while an additional 1,132 cubic feet of records were disposed of after microfilming. The committee approves lists as well as schedules. State agencies, counties, and municipalities must, however, present individual requests for the destruction of scheduled records.

COMMENTS

1. Wyoming needs a combined records center and archives building so that its successful program can develop its full potentiality.

2. The Director of the State Archives and Historical Department is heavily burdened with supervising the activities of three (and potentially four) divisions and with serving as executive secretary of the Historical Society. In addition to the Assistant Director in charge of administration, there is needed an assistant to whom some of the professional responsibilities can be delegated.

CHAPTER III

⊓⊔⊓⊔⊓

A Summary of Findings

This summary derives, from the information furnished in Chapter II, some general conclusions on the present legal basis, organization, and programs of state archival agencies. These conclusions are offered in regard to the following: the authority, status, and staff of the archival agency; its archives program; its role in records management; and its other activities.

Needless to say, it would be neither useful nor possible to deal in summary with the great variety of arrangements for archival service that exist throughout the nation. These are set forth seriatim in Chapter II. The aim here is rather to give a synthesis of the conditions prevailing in state archives and of the thinking and practices of state archivists. To sustain the generalizations, reference has been made to specific situations, operations, and performances that, positively or negatively, support them.

The great diversity in state archival organization and service also militates against the presentation of nationwide data in tabular form. Three such tabulations, however, are included as appendixes to this report. They are designed to bring together, for comparative purposes, data pertaining to budgets and total expenses for professional salaries of archival agencies (Appendix B); salaries of agency heads and senior archivists (Appendix C); and the record holdings of archival agencies (Appendix D).

For specific information about events, facts, and conditions referred to in this chapter, the reader should consult the pertinent state essays in Chapter II.

THE STATE ARCHIVAL AGENCY

Legal Authority of Archival Agencies

Legislation governing the status, organization, and functions of archival agencies varies greatly from state to state. Because of "the proverbial reluctance of American Commonwealths to profit by example," the Public Archives Commission refrained from developing and suggesting "a specific and detailed plan for public record keeping," although the commission and later the Conference of American Archivists and the Public Archives Committee of the National Association of State Libraries paid constant attention to legislation pertaining to archives of individual states.[1]

Once a national association of archivists had been established in 1936, the time seemed more propitious to promote "Uniform or similar state archival legislation" as "the most direct course to a general improvement in the administration of state and local archives."[2] Neither the "Proposed Uniform State Public Records Act," developed by the Committee on Uniform State Archival Legislation of the Society of American Archivists, nor later model bills to create a state department of archives and history or a state archives department had, however, any large-scale effect on archival legislation in the states. Federal archival legislation, including the Records Disposal Act of 1943 and the Federal Records Act of 1950 with its emphasis on the records management function, exercised far greater influence. Helpful also was the exchange of experience among practicing archivists, facilitated by the activities of the society's Committee on State and Local Records. In recent years the records management act included in the suggested legislation of the Council of State Governments for 1960 has served as a model for legislation in a number of states, particularly those in which the archival agency had not been authorized to concern itself with the management of current and semi-current records. The council's preservation of essential records act, however, has not been widely accepted as a model.[3]

This chapter will not consider the legislation of states with antiquated laws. Discussion will be focused on the legislation of states that have fully developed archival programs, particularly those that combine archival and records management functions in the same agency (Colorado, Delaware, Illinois, Kentucky, Louisiana, Maryland, Minnesota, New Hampshire, New Jersey, New Mexico, North Carolina, Oklahoma,[4] Texas, Utah, Vermont, Virginia, Washington, and Wyoming).

Modern archives laws offer definitions of the term public records. Characteristically these definitions distinguish between record and non-record material — the latter including, for instance, duplicate copies of processed documents and stocks of publications — and define as records documentary materials regardless of their physical form, hence including maps, photographs, books, and other documents that have been made or received "in pursuance of law or in connection with the transaction of public business"

[1] See pp. 19, 24, and 26.
[2] Albert R. Newsome, "Uniform State Archival Legislation," *American Archivist*, II (Jan., 1939), 2. See also p. 31.
[3] See pp. 341 f.
[4] The Oklahoma State Library has no funds to administer a records management program. In most of the other states named, the records management function is far from being fully developed.

and "preserved or appropriate for preservation" because of their evidential or informational value. The Public Records Act of Washington of 1957 and a Wyoming act of 1959 divide public records into official public records and other public records, the latter designated as office files and memoranda. According to the definition given in the Washington act, official public records consist solely of documents relating to the receipt, use, and disposition of public property and income, agreements involving the state or any of its agencies, claims filed against the state or any of its agencies, and "all records or documents required by law to be filed with or kept by any agency of the state of Washington. . . ." Similarly the Illinois State Records Act of 1957 distinguishes between records in general and "public records." [5] The latter are "All records of the expenditure or receipt of public funds," and they are to "be open to public inspection . . . at all reasonable times." Such attempts to differentiate between records in general and "public records" reflect a limited and now superseded interpretation of "public records" as those open for public inspection.

Most acts agree that public records are the property of the state and must not be alienated or mutilated, that their custodians are responsible for their safekeeping, and that the custodians must turn the records over to their successors in office. Earlier acts prescribed that for the making of records of permanent value, inks, typewriter ribbons, and paper of durable quality must be used. Recent laws that embody the concept of records management state the duties of agencies in regard to record-making and record-keeping more comprehensively: agencies must establish and maintain programs for the economical and efficient management of their records. These agency programs are expected to establish controls over the creation, maintenance, and use of records; to result in adequate documentation of the agency's functions, policies, organization, and essential transactions; and to provide co-operation with the agency in charge of the state's records management program.

Laws that assign statewide records management responsibility to the archival agency define that agency's authority in matters of records management. It is to establish standards and procedures for the effective management of agency records and especially for the preparation of retention and disposal schedules; to survey agency records operations and recommend improvements; and to provide low-cost storage space in records centers for records of more than short-term value but not of permanent legal, administrative, or research value. The archives–records management agency is normally authorized to extend records management service to the local subdivisions of the state and, if requested to do so, to the legislative and judicial branches of the state government.

[5] In the Illinois Local Records Act of 1961 this distinction has been dropped.

Except in states in which the head of the archival agency is subordinate to a government department, a state library, or a historical society, legislation usually sets forth the professional qualifications he should have and the mode of his appointment and empowers him to select his assistants. It also designates the officers or committee that will share, with the archivist and the head of the agency who has custody of records, authority to dispose of valueless records, and it may settle procedures in regard to their destruction. As a minimum, legislation gives the archivist the right to ascertain whether records to be disposed of have research or historical value and, on this basis, to select those that must be transferred to the archives.

Legislation also deals with the transfer to the archives of records no longer needed for the transaction of current business but deemed to be of permanent value. In the matter of transfer, Louisiana and Delaware laws give unusual authority to the archival agency.[6] With the use of disposal and retention schedules, which stipulate at what time records must be released to the state archives, the problem of their transfer has become largely academic. Records of a discontinued agency must always be turned over to the archives unless that agency's functions are taken over by one or more successor agencies.

In regard to the operation of the archival agency, legislation imposes upon the agency's head the duty to preserve, repair, arrange, and describe the records in his custody and to grant reasonable access to them to scholars, students, and other qualified persons. Legislation also authorizes the agency head to furnish copies of any of the documents in the archives and to certify such copies with his signature and official seal, whereupon they will be admitted as evidence as if they were the original documents.

Legislation often also makes provision for the recovery of public records that have been removed from official custody. Where such provision is made, replevin authority is normally vested in the attorney general of the state. In New Jersey, however, the Bureau of Archives and History is authorized "to demand and receive from any person any public records in private custody."

States still lacking adequate legislation can find examples of good laws in other states. Among recent laws, that of Louisiana deserves attention in spite of the fact that its implementation leaves much to be desired.

Status and Functions of State Archival Agencies

The organization for archival service and the functions of state archival agencies vary considerably from state to state. It could not be otherwise because, in establishing an archival agency, each state was free to make arrangements suitable to its governmental structure and also because these

[6] See pp. 327 ff.

arrangements inevitably reflected changing attitudes toward the nature and uses of archives, as these attitudes developed among those interested in archival preservation.

Early in the century archival materials were considered preponderantly as materials for historical research; hence in many Southern states, where agencies to care for them were being established at that time, these agencies were called historical commissions or departments of archives and history and were put in charge of both archival administration and historical activities worthy of state support. In other states, chiefly in the Midwest, where strong, publicly supported state historical societies already existed, this same attitude resulted in entrusting the archives function to these societies. A change of outlook took place in the 1920's and 1930's, when the nature of archives as the essential documentation of government and their use for administrative and legal purposes began to be emphasized. This broadened concept led to the establishment of agencies concerned exclusively with the administration of the state archives. Still later, when the need for the effective and economical management of current and semi-current records was realized, the concept of the archives–records management agency responsible for the entire life span of records developed and was put into practice.

By now, archival depositories of one kind or another exist in all but three states — Alaska, Maine, and Missouri. In Montana and in the Dakotas the state historical societies have been used as depositories for archival material, although they have not been legally charged with the archives function. In the other forty-four states, the administrative setup is as follows:

Five states — Colorado, Louisiana, Maryland, Minnesota, and New Mexico — have independent archives–records management agencies.

In eleven states — Arizona, Connecticut, Florida, Indiana, New Jersey, New York, Oklahoma, Oregon, Tennessee, Texas, and Virginia — the archival agency is a component of the state library.

In five states — Hawaii, Kentucky, New Hampshire, Vermont, and Washington — archival responsibility has been entrusted to a division of the fiscal or general services department.

In five states — California, Georgia, Illinois, Massachusetts, and Rhode Island — archives administration is under the office of the Secretary of State.

Eleven states — Alabama, Arkansas, Delaware, Iowa, Michigan, Mississippi, North Carolina, Pennsylvania, South Carolina, West Virginia, and Wyoming — have agencies variously called departments of archives and history, historical commissions, public archives commissions, and the like.

Seven states — Idaho, Kansas, Nebraska, Nevada, Ohio, Utah, and Wisconsin — use the state historical society as an archival agency.

A number of recent changes are worthy of note. In four states the historical society has lost the archives function to other agencies — to the Division of State Archives and Public Records in Colorado, to the State Archives and Records Service in Minnesota, to the Commission on Public Records in New Mexico, and to the State Library in Oklahoma. It is even more significant that some states have set up agencies in charge of both archives and records management within fiscal or general services departments. This was first done in Washington State. More recently New Hampshire established its Division of Records Management and Archives in the Department of Administration and Control, and in a number of states archival and records management operations have lost independent status to become units of fiscal or general administrative departments. In Vermont the former Public Records Commission has become the Division of Public Records (headed by the Public Records Director) of the Department of Administration; the Kentucky State Archives and Records Service has been placed as "an administrative unit" under the Commissioner of Finance, although the State Archives and Records Commission under which the service had been operating has retained its disposal authority; and in Hawaii the Board of Commissioners of Public Archives was abolished and its functions were transferred to the Department of Accounting and General Services when the constitution of the state and the Reorganization Act of 1959 cut the number of departments down to twenty in addition to the Governor's and Lieutenant Governor's offices.

As the changes in Hawaii, Kentucky, and Vermont and the recent action in New Hampshire seem to indicate, there is a definite trend to absorb into administrative or fiscal departments formerly independent agencies that are responsible for both archival and records management activities. From the viewpoint of both the archivist and the user of archives this trend must be looked upon with considerable misgiving. If the head of the archives–records management division is a key officer of an executive department, he may be appointed as a reward for political services and hence may be subject to dismissal when a change in state administration occurs. It is also to be feared that in such an organization records management will be stressed to the detriment of archival preservation.

Functions of state archival agencies differ as widely as does their status. The historical-archival agencies — the departments of archives and history, the historical commissions, and the historical societies — administer various historical activities in addition to their archives function, and some of them have also taken charge of records management programs. Charging one and the same agency with historical and archival responsiblities may have beneficial results in that these responsibilities, if impartially supported, supplement and strengthen each other. It may, however, lead to the agency's emphasizing the more popular historical activities to the detriment of its archival duties. Archives–records management agencies combine responsibility for the fields of both current and semi-current records and archives. Finally, pending further development, a state archival agency may be concerned solely with the administration of public archives. This is true of the archives divisions of some state libraries.

Although the archival agency, for a variety of reasons, is involved in historical activities even if not administratively in charge of them, it is necessarily interested in the creation and maintenance of records while they are current and semi-current and also in the process of disposing of those of no permanent value. In a number of states, mostly those with a solid tradition of archival administration, the state archival agency or its parent agency has been able to assume responsibility for records management. This has happened in Colorado, Delaware, Hawaii, Illinois, Maryland, North Carolina, Oklahoma, Texas, Utah, Virginia, and Washington. In six states — Kentucky, Louisiana, Minnesota, New Hampshire, New Mexico, and Vermont — agencies newly established were put in charge of both archives and records management. Separate records management programs exist or have been authorized in Alaska, California, Indiana, Massachusetts, Michigan, Montana, Nebraska, New York, North Dakota, Ohio, Oregon, Pennsylvania, Rhode Island, West Virginia, Wisconsin, and Puerto Rico. Whether or not such programs are in the archival agency or in another agency of the government, many of them are underdeveloped or indeed embryonic. No funds have been appropriated for records management in Nebraska and Oklahoma though records management legislation has been enacted; in Alaska records management work has ceased; and other programs are of such recent origin or are so seriously understaffed that not much has been accomplished.

Budgets and Budgetary Procedures

The status of the archival agency has considerable bearing on the way in which its budget requests are formulated, presented, and approved. Heads of independent agencies are obviously in a better position to defend their requests before state budget agencies and legislative committees than are their colleagues who operate within a parent agency, be it a state library, a state historical society, or some other state agency. Independent status may also permit the state archivist to have personal contacts with legislators and to win friends among them who will understand and support archival interests.

Heads of independent agencies formulate their budget requests in consultation with their program heads, submit them for administrative review to the budget officer or agency of the executive branch, and defend them before the appropriations committees or the joint appropriations committee of the legislature. Before the budget is submitted for administrative review it may be reviewed by the independent agency's governing board, and the chairman or members of the board sometimes attend administrative and legislative hearings to support the agency's requests.

Where the archival service is part of another agency or organization, its role in the budgetary process is usually quite limited. The opportunity for its head to justify his requests may in fact end after his budgetary requests have been presented and reviewed by the head of the parent agency. In one state this superior does not even inform the archivist of the cuts that have been made in the various items of his request. There are, however, a number of states in which the archivist is in attendance when administrative and legislative hearings on the parent agency's requests are held and hence is in a position to defend his part of the budget.

In most states, agency requests are reduced at the stage of executive budget review, although a few archival agencies have established such a reputation for honest budgeting that their requests are normally granted. Most agencies, whether independent or part of a parent agency, find it difficult to obtain increased appropriations in spite of justifiable need. In Ohio, for instance, appropriations have actually decreased during the last three years, and in Oklahoma it has been impossible to implement the records management and essential records preservation act because the State Librarian and Archivist was denied appropriations for the purpose.

Success or failure to obtain appropriations for an adequate archives program depends on several factors (some of them imponderable). Prominent among them is the tradition of the state in caring for its historical resources and the extent to which archival and general historical activities enjoy the support of legislators, state officials, patriotic societies, and the public. Concern about local records and about making them available has undoubtedly contributed to building up "grass-roots" support for the archives. Much, of course, depends on the personality of the state archivist and his ability to "sell" his program. He may do so with particular success if, as state records administrator, he can demonstrate to legislators and fiscal officers that an integrated program of records management and archives administration not only serves the intelligence needs of the government and the research interests of the citizen but also reduces government expenses. At this time the number of states that support an adequate archival program is still small — probably not more than four or five.

It is extremely difficult to obtain, for purposes of comparison, reliable and meaningful figures in regard to appropriations for archival purposes. Disregarding the differences in general salary levels between states like New York and California on the one hand and most of the Southern states on the other hand, archival expenditures are not always clearly separable from those for related purposes; for they depend on the scope of the duties of the archival agency, which, for instance, may or may not include the

[315]

collection and processing of private papers. In addition, expenditures of the independent archival agency normally include those for general supplies, light, heat, and the like, which in the case of a subordinate archival agency are absorbed into the budget of the parent organization. Appendix B to this report represents an attempt to tabulate, state by state, the latest budget figures available for the operation of archival and records management units insofar as they are reasonably separable. In addition, total salary figures are given for professional and records management positions. Salaries of clerks, laborers, and microfilm machine operators are not included in these figures.

State Archives Personnel

In practically all states that have archival agencies worthy of the name, staffs are too small to carry out all essential archival functions. As a result, arrangement and description of holdings must be neglected and, because of the lack of guides and other finding aids, reference services consume an unduly large amount of time — a vicious circle from which there is apparently no escape. Lack of staff also keeps archivists from productive participation in research activities one of the hallmarks of their professional status. Furthermore, where archival administration and records management are the responsibility of one and the same agency, the urgent demands of the latter may make the archives the Cinderella of the operation. Unsatisfactory salary arrangements and lack of job security, too, contribute to deterring highly qualified persons from accepting archival posts and make it difficult to fill vacant positions.

Procedure for appointment to archival posts differs greatly. Agency heads are appointed by the agencies' governing boards or, where the archival agency is part of a larger organization, by that organization's board. If the archival agency functions within a government department, its head is nominated by the head of the department and appointed in accordance with the state's appointment procedures. In only a few cases is the head of the archival agency under the state's classified civil service. In fact, there has been a noticeable trend to deprive heads of archival agencies of civil service status, as has recently happened in Hawaii and in Kentucky.

In twenty-three states subordinate professional personnel is in the classified service. In most of these states applicants for positions must pass competitive examinations, and appointments must be made from among the top candidates on the lists of eligible persons. Where there is no merit system or where it does not apply to the archives staff, subordinate professional staff members are selected by the head of the archival agency and appointed with the approval of the agency's governing board or the head of the department or organization of which the archival agency is a part.

[316]

The archivist's work is not simply that of a custodian of records. He cannot carry out his most important functions — those of selecting the records of permanent value, of providing access to them through arrangement and description, and of making them available to government, scholars, and other users — unless, in addition to practical experience, he has certain prerequisites that are acquired through academic study. These prerequisites include: a good knowledge of history, especially of the history of the United States, and of its sources; experience in the techniques of historical research; familiarity with the organization and workings of government on its various levels; and mastery of the theory and methods of archives administration and of the essentials of records management. Archives work is professional work and demands an academic preparation largely comparable to that for college teaching.

All archival agencies are confronted with the problem of finding professionally trained candidates for positions to be filled, for there is as yet in this country no academic curriculum leading to a degree in archives administration comparable to a Master's degree in library science. Some courses in archives administration and records management have been introduced into the curricula of a few universities as part of academic programs in history or public administration, but these programs do not confer upon their graduates degrees that identify them as professional archivists. Qualification for professional service is certified by a professional degree, and so long as there are no programs leading to the degree of Master of Arts or Master of Science in Archives Administration,[7] the prospects of building up a corps of professionally qualified archivists remain dim.

In the absence of adequate academic programs, archival agencies select their staffs from among men and women with Bachelor's or, preferably, Master's degrees in history or political science, subject them to a period of "learning by doing," and perhaps send them to one of the short-term training courses offered in Washington, D.C., in Denver, Colorado, and occasionally in other cities, where they have an opportunity to acquire or increase their knowledge of the theory and techniques of archival work. This substitute for a regular academic program including theory and practice works particularly well in the case of appointees who formerly served in archival institutions as part-time helpers, while studying as college seniors or graduate students.

If archival agencies find it difficult to attract suitable applicants for professional positions, they may soon find it equally difficult to retain experienced personnel. In years past there has been relatively little turn-

[7] So far no university has established such a program. As the demand for archival personnel increases in the states, in churches and universities, and in business, schools of public administration and library schools may consider offering programs to confer upon successful candidates a professional degree in the field.

over in the staffs of archival agencies. Recently, however, salary scales of academic institutions have been improved and positions in newly established or expanded colleges have become available. As a result of these new opportunities, several experienced and promising archivists have accepted college teaching positions for which undoubtedly they are well qualified and which offer them better pay and complete freedom during the summer vacation.

Still other difficulties may hamper successful recruitment for archival positions. In the first place, appointment procedures in several states are so "informal" that appointees do not even receive letters of appointment, and they are therefore subject to dismissal with no appeal to higher authority. In at least one state, staff members are subject to embarrassing and costly solicitation for the benefit of a political party, and in another state the fully qualified and highly respected archivist was abruptly dismissed so that an unqualified but deserving party worker might have the post. In West Virginia it has become a tradition to replace the head of the archival agency — and sometimes members of his staff — whenever the administration changes. Finally, as has been pointed out, salaries are low in most states; and in many of them, because there is no provision for merit increases in accordance with a general classification and pay plan, increases in salary depend wholly on appropriations and hence are uncertain. In almost all states, however, "fringe benefits" provide paid annual and sick leave and participation in old age and survivors' insurance and state retirement systems.

A chart showing salaries of heads of archival programs and their senior professional assistants is provided as Appendix C. Where no organized program exists, the person in charge of archives has been indicated as senior archivist. Salaries of staff members who give only part of their time to the archives function have been disregarded, as have been those of heads of historical societies, historical departments, state libraries, and other governmental organizations of which the archival agency may be a part.

THE ARCHIVES FUNCTION

Holdings of State Archival Agencies

The extent to which state archival agencies have been able to build up their holdings depends on a number of factors. Prominent among them are: the effectiveness of the state archives and/or records management laws; authority over the archives of the political subdivisions of the state; availability of storage space for accessions; and, finally, an active policy of acquisition on the part of the archival agency. In many states — Mississippi, Ohio, and Wyoming, for instance — lack of storage facilities has made it impossible to concentrate material of recent origin in archival custody.

Generally speaking, archival agencies have acquired the records of the colonial or territorial periods of their respective states, though in Idaho the records of the territorial legislature are still held by the Secretary of State. In a number of states a constitutional provision makes the Secretary of State responsible for the constitution itself and for certain other types of records, and this prevents the transfer of these records to the state archives. Normally the laws and the journals of the legislative assembly are in the archival agency. In most states, however, the records of legislative committees — including petitions and communications from private persons — have been retained by the legislature or have been destroyed.

Archival agencies, being part of the executive branch, have been better able to concentrate the records of that branch, and those of the Governor have been of particular concern to them. Colorado's, Kansas', Maryland's, and North Carolina's archival agencies have been successful in obtaining the Governors' records and in making their transfer a tradition. That Michigan's Governor G. Mennen Williams gave his official records, together with his private papers, to the Michigan Historical Collections and not to the state archives is a regrettable exception to prevailing practice.

Except in six states — Florida, Hawaii, Indiana, Massachusetts, Oklahoma, and Washington — the archival agency is authorized to take over the permanently valuable records of the political subdivisions of the state.[8] Only the archival agencies of Delaware, Maryland, and North Carolina, however, have been willing or able to make use of their prerogatives by bringing in considerable quantities of original records. Elsewhere, the volume of such records in state archival custody is small, and new solutions to the problem of preserving them are being sought.[9]

Many archival agencies include among their holdings papers of individuals, institutions, and families. Inasmuch as the acquisition of such non-official material is not necessarily a function of the state archives, it is discussed below in a separate section under the heading "Acquisition and Administration of Private Papers."

Although obviously the holdings of state archival agencies are only an inaccurate measure of their performance, an attempt has been made to assemble all available figures on record holdings in tabular form (see Appendix D).

Physical Facilities

During the last twenty-five years much progress has been made in providing state archival agencies with modern, functional, and fire-resistive facilities either in separate buildings or in those of the parent agency or in combination with the records center.[10]

[8] In Washington the State Archivist may select depositories to which local records designated "as of primarily historical interest" may be transferred.
[9] See pp. 323 and 336 ff.
[10] Records center buildings are discussed on pp. 339 ff.

In Hawaii, Illinois, Maryland, and South Carolina the state archival agency enjoys the exclusive use of a modern building and so will the State Archives of Georgia when it occupies its impressive new structure. State library and state archives share new accommodations in Massachusetts, New Jersey, Tennessee, Texas, and Virginia, and the same plan will be followed in North Carolina. In New Hampshire and in Washington new buildings provide space for both records center and state archives, and in Pennsylvania the Archives Tower will also accommodate the records center in several of its seventeen stories.

In other states existing facilities have been expanded in one way or another. The Colorado Division of State Archives and Public Records is assigned a historical building with a modern annex while retaining its archives vaults in the building of the Historical Society and its records center in the State Services Building; in Oklahoma a utilitarian structure provides additional space for the archival and library holdings of the state library; and in Arkansas a modern annex to the Old Capitol adds some space to the facilities of the Historical Commission.

There seems to be a trend to combine records center and archives in the same structure. This can be observed in the new buildings of New Hampshire, Pennsylvania, and Washington and in existing structures in Minnesota, New Mexico, and Puerto Rico, where older buildings have been or are being adapted to this dual purpose. In Michigan the Archives Division is nothing but a tenant in the records center building, which is under the Department of Administration; and the same may be said of the California archives, which are housed in the Central Records Depository.

From the professional point of view, the use of war memorial buildings for housing archival material has provided little satisfaction. In the war memorial buildings of Alabama, Mississippi, and South Dakota all available space for archives has been exhausted — small wonder, when so much of the buildings must serve to display museum materials! Nor have archives in the care of historical societies fared much better. While they are reasonably well housed in Kansas and Nebraska, the Archives and Manuscripts Division of the Wisconsin State Historical Society has suffered acutely from inadequate accommodations. In Ohio and in Utah the state historical societies have inherited the former mansions of the state Governors. In Ohio the mansion is supposed to serve as an archives building, a purpose for which it is wholly unsuitable. The Utah building, headquarters of the society, will at least be supplemented by an archives vault, for which plans are now under way.

Though some states have been willing to appropriate funds for new buildings, in many others archival agencies cannot carry out their functions because they are hampered by inadequate facilities. New York, for instance, has been without the services of an archival agency because, for a long time, the responsible unit of the State Library has been unable to take in any major accessions. Nevertheless, the general picture of archival facilities in the states has become brighter during the past few decades.

Preservation and Rehabilitation of Holdings

Before records are placed on the shelves, they must be cleaned; and vacuum cleaning equipment for this purpose is available in most archival agencies. Cleaning, however, will not protect the records from decay unless vermin, fungi, and other pests are also removed. To meet this need, fumigating equipment of the kind first installed in the National Archives has been provided in Colorado, Hawaii, Maryland, Minnesota, North Carolina, Tennessee, Texas, and Washington; and it is also included in the plans for the new buildings of Georgia, New Jersey, Pennsylvania, and Puerto Rico. Oregon has its accessions fumigated in the state penitentiary.

For the restoration of documents, embedding them between sheets of tissue and acetate foil, preceded by deacidification, has become the accepted method. Nine archival agencies — in Delaware, Georgia, Illinois, Maryland, Minnesota, North Carolina, Puerto Rico, South Carolina, and Tennessee — now own equipment for this purpose. Virginia uses the services of a firm with facilities in the State Library, while others send documents to commercial firms to have them laminated.

The older nineteenth-century processes of restoring documents have been abandoned, except in Connecticut, where the Emery method of silking is still practiced with considerable skill, and in Texas, where silking is also used.

In its new archives building, Pennsylvania will use a "pettifogger" to humidify folded documents before they are flattened to prevent their breaking along the creases when they are unfolded.

Photoreproduction

Photoreproduction of records has become an indispensable tool of records management and archives administration.[11] All archival agencies have, or have access to, photographic equipment. Independent agencies have their own facilities for photographic reproduction, while those that are under larger agencies either do photographic work for all units of the agencies or rely on the services of their photographic laboratories.

Photographic reproduction serves in the first place the internal needs of the archival agency. It is used for producing security copies of holdings of particular value or of such fragility that copies rather than the originals should be made available to the searcher. The archival agency also furn-

[11] For a discussion of microfilming, state by state, see Dorothy K. Taylor, "State Microfilming Programs," *American Archivist*, XXII (Jan., 1959), 59–82.

ishes its clients with photographic copies of records on photostat or microfilm, upon payment of a fee. For lack of personnel an agency may find it difficult, however, to reproduce on microfilm whole series of records, though as a matter of principle this may be desirable. Microfilm publication programs of the kind initiated by the National Archives and Records Service, though on a more limited scale, have been undertaken in a few states. Negative microfilm in storage should be carefully inspected at intervals.[12]

Aside from using microfilm for strictly archival purposes, the archival agency charged with records management functions — or, where separate, the records management agency of the state — may operate a centralized microfilm program for the state and possibly for its subdivisions. The advantage of such centralization is a lower cost per unit, resulting from better use of equipment and from the work of highly skilled operators, and this advantage has been realized in a number of states. Strong centralized programs are in progress in Colorado, Delaware, Hawaii, Illinois, Michigan, Maryland, North Carolina, Vermont, Virginia, and Wyoming.[13] Those of Delaware, Maryland, and North Carolina extend to units of local government, and that of Colorado offers service to them on a selective basis. Most of the states having centralized programs also permit independent microfilming in agencies whose needs justify the setting-up of separate operations, as for instance a highway department or a bureau of vital statistics. All such independent programs, however, should be approved by the state archival or records management agency.

Whether or not microfilming is centralized, it must be related to and anchored in a records control system under which it is handled as a phase of records disposition. In at least two states the decision to microfilm any series of records is incorporated in the records disposal and retention schedule, a very commendable practice. Because microfilming ungoverned by a records control system cannot be considered sound practice, microfilm projects — though condoned and possibly even carried out by the archival agency, as for instance in Arizona, Iowa, and Oklahoma — should be discontinued until a records management program has been set up. A centralized microfilm service administered by an agency other than the archives or records management agency is particularly objectionable. Happily where such independent programs were authorized they have have been discontinued (in Kentucky, Mississippi, and Nebraska) or

[12] Recently the formation of microscopic spots on some rolls of processed negative microfilm has been discovered. According to its news release TRG-6301 W of September 25, 1963 (1 p., proc.), the National Bureau of Standards has been investigating the cause and nature of these defects for the past year. See also R. W. Henn and D. G. Wiest, "Microscopic Spots in Processed Microfilm: Their Nature and Prevention," *Photographic Science Engineering*, VII (Sept.–Oct., 1963), 253–61.

[13] In Utah and Washington centralized microfilming by the state's archival agency has been authorized by law but has not yet been set up.

transferred to the state archival agency (in Wyoming); or else funds for setting them up have not been made available.

Centralized microfilm service, where offered by the state archival or records management agency, involves certain arrangements in regard to the cost of labor, material, and processing. These differ a great deal. Agencies may be charged the cost of the film, as in Delaware; or the cost of film and processing, as in Michigan; or the cost of film, labor, and processing, as in New Jersey. In North Carolina microfilming is done at no cost to the agency requesting the service, and in Colorado agencies are charged cost plus 2 per cent.

In several states the microfilming of local records has been adopted as the ideal means of both insuring their preservation and making them available at state archival headquarters. Such work was encouraged by the large-scale microfilm project of the Utah Genealogical Society.[14] This undertaking, begun in 1938, was intended to reproduce on film, for the use of members of the church, wills and probate records, deeds and land records, marriage bonds and licenses, vital statistics, and other records of genealogical interest to 1850. In Georgia the program is still in progress under the supervision of the County Archivist of the Department of Archives and History; among other states Delaware and North Carolina are continuing it with a view to producing also security copies of permanent records. North Carolina, at the same time, films for research purposes unofficial records of historical importance. In Maryland the county land and probate record project of the Hall of Records is designed to microfilm all land records from 1850 to 1949.

There is no commonly accepted rationale that underlies the selection of records for microfilming. Generally speaking, the purposes are to promote economy, insure security, and serve research needs. Microfilming as a security measure has become particularly important in connection with the program to safeguard against disaster the records essential to the continuity of government and to the rights and privileges of citizens.[15]

Disposal of Useless Records

A. STATE RECORDS.

Long before the advent of mechanical methods of making records it had become apparent to archivists in this country and abroad that not all public records could or should be preserved for posterity; and, as a result, the destruction of those of ephemeral value and the selection of those with long-term value had become major concerns of the archivist. To eliminate records not worth preserving, use was made of

[14] Archibald F. Bennett, "The Record Copying Program of the Utah Genealogical Society," *American Archivist*, XVI (July, 1953), 227–32.

[15] This phase of the application of microfilming is discussed on pp. 341 ff.

the disposal list, a document specifying the records that an agency considered to be of no future value. Such a list, however, was not necessarily the most expeditious device to achieve the elimination of valueless records. Under existing laws agencies were responsible for taking the initiative in asking for permission to destroy records, and frequently they did not do so until all their available space for records had been exhausted and an emergency had developed. Use of the disposal list also made it necessary for archivists and other officials authorized to approve destruction of records to deal time and again with records of a repetitive kind, records that could have been disposed of at regular intervals once they had been evaluated as only of ephemeral use.

The Federal Records Disposal Act of July 7, 1943 (57 Stat. 380), sanctioned, for the disposal of such repetitive records, the use of the disposal schedule. This concept, discussed at the 1942 and 1943 meetings of the Society of American Archivists,[16] could not fail to interest state archivists, who were also faced with the problem of expediting the disposal of useless records.

Illinois was the first state to authorize, in a 1943 law, the use of the disposal schedule. By now, this device has been sanctioned in the legislation of twenty-nine states and Puerto Rico. It is not used in Delaware. Other states in which scheduling for periodic destruction of identical records is not practiced are those that have no records management programs and two states (Nebraska and Oklahoma) that have records management legislation but no means for implementing it. It goes without saying that, for records of the non-repetitive kind, the disposal list is still used and that in many states scheduling for disposal has just begun.

Scheduling must be preceded by inventorying the records series on hand in the agencies and by appraising their retention values. Inventory-taking may be planned as a government-wide process and carried out simultaneously in all agencies under the guidance of the records management agency, as was done in New York,[17] to be followed by appraisal and scheduling; or — and this is the normal procedure — record holdings may be inventoried, appraised, and scheduled agency by agency.

Inventorying, appraising, and scheduling records may be undertaken by the staff of the records management agency or else by government agencies in co-operation with records management personnel. In the opinion of the state records management agencies, members of their staffs are best equipped to do the job, and they are doing it in Kentucky, Maryland, Minnesota, North Carolina, Rhode Island, Vermont, Washington,

[16] Robert H. Bahmer, "Scheduling the Disposition of Records," *American Archivist*, VI (July, 1943), 169–75; and Christopher Crittenden and Nell Hines, "The Disposal of Useless State Archives," *ibid.*, VII (July, 1944), 165–73.

[17] Vernon B. Santen, "The New York State Inventory Project," *American Archivist*, XX (Oct., 1957), 357–67. See also p. 197 of the present report.

Wisconsin, and Wyoming. In most states the records management staffs assist personnel of other agencies in inventorying, appraising, and scheduling records. This process could not be centralized in such large states as California and New York.

Great differences are manifest in regard to machinery for the approval of records destruction, be it by list or schedule, and in regard to the participation of the state archivist in the process. For the final approval of lists and schedules, some one of the following arrangements is made:

1. Authority rests with the archival agency's governing body, as in Arkansas, Iowa, Louisiana, and Minnesota.

2. In twenty-two states *ad hoc* committees, commissions, or boards, frequently called state records commissions, approve schedules and lists. Their composition varies from state to state. Typical members are the attorney general, the state auditor, the state comptroller, and the state treasurer, and as a rule these officials may appoint subordinates to represent them. In a number of states in this group, representatives of historical interests and state archivists are included in the membership of the commission or board.

3. Key officials of the state individually approve requests without acting as a committee or commission. In New York, for instance, the Commissioner of General Services, the Comptroller, the Commissioner of Education, and the Director of the Budget separately examine and pass on disposal lists and schedules, and any one of them may stop a proposed destruction.

4. An existing board or commission, such as a state board of examiners or a board of control or public works may be assigned responsibility for passing on requests for the approval of lists or schedules.

5. In Rhode Island the function is carried out by the Legislative Committee on Accounts and Records. As far as can be determined, Rhode Island is now the only state [18] in which the legislative branch of the government makes the final disposal decision (as is the case in the federal government).

6. In a few states, the approval function is vested in a non-archival official of the state — the Secretary of State in Georgia, the Comptroller in Hawaii, the head of the Division of Audits in California. The State Records Administrator in West Virginia decides upon the "administrative, legal, fiscal, research, and historical value" of records to be disposed of.

7. In Colorado disposal requests are reviewed by the State Archivist's Advisory Board, but final decision rests with the State Archivist and the Attorney General.

8. In Delaware and North Carolina, the head of the archival agency has exclusive authority in the matter of records disposal.

[18] Until 1957, the Kansas legislature approved the destruction of records. See p. 119.

As a rule, approval of disposal lists or schedules is subject to unanimous agreement of whatever committee or group of officials has disposal authority. A 1963 South Dakota act, however, rules that a majority vote suffices for the destruction of records, and a Montana act of the same year gives the Comptroller an overriding vote.

Regardless of where the final authority rests, no records are listed or scheduled for destruction without the consent of the agency of origin. It is axiomatic also that the archivist must have a voice in the destruction process, that in fact no records may be destroyed that he considers of permanent value. Except in a few states this prerequisite has been safeguarded in one of the following ways:

1. The archivist or the head of his parent agency serves as chairman, secretary, or a member of the committee, commission, or board that is entrusted with disposal authority.

2. The archivist or the head of his parent agency is one of the officials whose approval is required for permission to destroy records.

3. The archivist examines requests for the approval of lists and schedules and designates the records he deems worthy of preservation in the archives before the legally constituted authority takes action. This is done, to give but two examples, in California and in Maryland. In the latter state, records may be destroyed with the written approval of the Board of Public Works once the State Archivist and Records Administrator has declined to accept them for permanent preservation. After a disposal schedule has been approved by the board, however, its consent is no longer needed for the continuing destruction of the records scheduled.

4. Even in states that have no legally authorized state archives, the head of the institution that serves *de facto* as an archival depository is given an opportunity to select from records to be destroyed those that he wishes to take over.

Opinions are divided on the best procedure for the disposal of records. Leading archivists maintain that the decision on what records to keep and what records to destroy should be both the duty and the prerogative of a responsible archivist and that, although he may find it wise to consult with other officials of the state, the full responsibility should be his. They particularly question the value of decisions made by committees or boards, pointing out that such decisions tend to be perfunctory. Much depends on whether the membership of these groups is stable and on the extent to which the archivist is able to arouse their interest in the job to be done. When the Director of this Study attended meetings of the Minnesota Archives Commission, of the New Jersey State Records Committee, and of the Advisory Committee of the Colorado State Archivist, he felt that the members took their duties seriously and that discussions were both thorough and based on a good deal of previous experience.

B. LOCAL RECORDS.

Arrangements for the disposal of local government records differ widely. In a good many states pertinent legislation deals with both state and local records, though in effect little may be done to control the destruction of local records. Among these states are Arizona, Colorado, Delaware, Georgia, Kentucky, Louisiana, Maryland, Minnesota, New Jersey, North Carolina, North Dakota, Utah, Vermont, Virginia, and Wyoming. In Illinois two local records commissions, one for "upstate" and one for "downstate," have been authorized; and county records commissions have been established or provided for by law in Alabama, Indiana, Ohio, and Oklahoma. In other states the boards of county commissioners or supervisors or the county courts have been given power to permit the destruction of records, frequently with the obligation first to notify the archival agency, which may select those worthy of preservation.

The device of the disposal schedule is beginning to be used for expediting the destruction of useless local records. To facilitate its application, states have begun to develop manuals that suggest retention periods for typical kinds of records, but such manuals do not relieve responsible local officials from obtaining the approval of their governing body and that of the archival agency.

Understandably, archival agencies have given primary attention to the disposal of county records. In due time they will have to concern themselves with the disposal of the records of the municipalities (should they have such power) and of other subdivisions of the state. Some agencies have done so already.

Since disposal of local records is so closely related to records management, it is also discussed below, in the section "Records Management Assistance to Local Government."

Accessioning of Public Records

If the archival agency is to render effective service to the state government and to private searchers, it must have in its custody the permanently valuable records of the state that are no longer needed for current business.

Older legislation governing the transfer of records from agency to archival custody authorized the agency alone to decide when records of permanent value should be released for transfer to the archives. Recent legislation, however, indicates a trend toward obligating agencies to transfer non-current records to archival custody. Under the Louisiana Public Records Act of 1956, records more than fifty years old must be turned over to the Archives and Records Commission unless the agency having such records certifies in writing that they are needed for the dispatch of current business.[19] Going even further, Delaware law empowers the Public Ar-

[19] In 1945 the Maryland Hall of Records became a mandatory repository for court-house records predating April 28, 1788.

chives Commission of the state to select and transfer to the Hall of Records non-current records that the commission "deems to be of an historical or public interest" and imposes penalties on public officials who refuse to relinquish such records. It should be added that so far the Louisiana law has not taken effect because the commission has no archives building, and that in Delaware, as in other states, the archival agency relies on persuasion rather than on the letter of the law.

In a number of states the accessioning of records has practically ceased because the archival agencies have nowhere to put new accessions — as in the New York State Library and in the Mississippi Department of Archives and History — and therefore discourage transfers. In other states, in which a historical society serves as a depository *de facto* rather than as one legally authorized, accessions are taken in only rarely and without reference to any plan.

A great improvement of the accessioning process has taken place, or is to be expected, in states in which the device of the retention and disposal schedule has been legalized and governs the disposition of records. Where schedules have been prepared and are enforced, accessions of permanently valuable records reach the archival agency in a steady and regulated flow that facilitates the process of integrating them with the records previously received.

The archival agency, however, must keep a careful record of its accessions. In many places, the practice is to put pertinent correspondence and letters of transmittal in "agency folders," each of which contains all documents relating to transfers from a given agency. Although this may suffice as a record of transactions, it does not readily furnish the data needed for statistical purposes. If information of this kind is desired, all accessions should be entered in an accession register — be it a bound book or a loose-leaf binder — under consecutive numbers and with an indication of their origin, quantity, inclusive dates, and the disposition made of them in the archival agency. Separate accession registers should be kept for official records and for private papers, if the latter are also accepted by the archival agency.

It is a duty of the archival agency to bring new accessions to the attention of the interested public. The Delaware Public Archives Commission does so by distributing processed accession lists, and a few archival agencies list accessions in their annual or biennial reports. Too many archival establishments, however, neglect this simple means of giving information to scholars and arousing public interest in their holdings.

Arrangement and Description

Arrangement and description of archival material serve the dual purpose of maintaining its integrity and completeness and of making its contents readily accessible for use by government agencies and private searchers.

A modern program of arrangement and description may be expected to meet the following requirements: the body of records of an agency or institution that has been transferred to archival custody must be maintained as an entity, variously called *fonds*, record group, or archive group; the different record series constituting this body of records must, so far as possible, be retained in their original structure; the relationship of these series to each other must be determined; and a comprehensive plan for the organization of the *fonds*, record groups, or archive groups should be adopted. To perpetuate the order established and to facilitate the use of the records, a finding aid program should provide the following: a general guide to the holdings of the archival agency; inventories or checklists for individual *fonds* or record groups; and detailed finding aids, such as calendars and indexes, for series of high reference value.

Arrangement and description suffer, however, from the shortage of professional personnel that plagues most state archival agencies. In California the Historian, States Archives, presides singlehanded over the archives of the state and must content himself with the "irreducible minimum of records control," and the archives of Minnesota have remained practically untouched since their transfer from the State Historical Society to the State Archives and Records Service. Other factors too have hampered arrangement and description work. In Georgia and until recently in South Carolina the available space has been so inadequate that the processing of archives proved impossible.

In some archival agencies the first order of business has to be expiating the sins of the past. The Public Records Division of Pennsylvania, during many years of hard work, has dismantled and reorganized into record groups about five hundred volumes of records that had been forced into a subject arrangement. Similar tasks of reconstituting original provenances must still be done in Georgia and in South Carolina. In Massachusetts, however, where the so-called Massachusetts Archives will have to be kept in the subject arrangement they were given in the 1830's, they are being made more easily accessible through a calendar on cards that has been in progress for a good many years.

Few states carry forward any planned and sustained programs of archival arrangement and description, and their procedures vary a great deal. Nevertheless, all archival agencies now follow the principle of provenance, under which the records of an agency or institution are kept together as a body and under which also, within that body, records are maintained in their original order. The same principle begins to be followed, so far as possible, in the arrangement of private papers.

The National Archives uses for the organization of its holdings the

[329]

concept of the record group, which denotes the records of an agency of the government or, in the case of a large agency, those of a constituent part of it. A number of state archival agencies have adopted this concept and some of them have established systems of record groups under which definite places are assigned to the records of departments and agencies and also to those of counties, municipalities, and other subdivisions of the state that have been accessioned or may be accessioned in the future. Colorado, Idaho, Oregon, Pennsylvania, Utah, and Wisconsin are using or developing a system of this kind for the organization of their holdings. Within provenances, whether they are called record groups or not, individual series are kept in the arrangement they had in the agencies of origin whenever such an arrangement can be discovered.

If work on arranging records has suffered from lack of professional personnel, the preparation of finding aids has fared little better. This is particularly true of general guides that undoubtedly are needed by the scholar, for they enable him to obtain a conspectus of the archival agency's holdings and to chart his course without undue reliance on the help of the archivist. Dunbar Rowland published his *Official Guide to the Historical Materials in the Mississippi Department of Archives and History* as early as 1914, but his example was not followed until in 1942 the Maryland Hall of Records printed its guide called a *Catalogue of Archival Material*. A new edition of this is in progress. Seymour V. Connor's *Preliminary Guide to the Archives of Texas* (1956) was a particularly remarkable achievement because it was compiled at a time when the records were difficult of access. In recent years the guide as a general finding aid has been gaining ground. A processed guide to the Pennsylvania Archives is available in a second edition, a shorter guide lists the records of the executive departments in the Utah Archives, and soon a guide to the archives in the North Carolina Department of Archives and History will be forthcoming.

Few archival agencies now use a card catalog as a general finding aid. Illinois was the first state to do so, and the techniques on which its catalog is based are closely related to those of library cataloging. The card catalogs of Oregon and Virginia are less elaborate and seem to serve archival reference needs quite well. Also, their preparation is less time consuming than that of the Illinois card catalog. Most state archivists seem to feel that cataloging does not lend itself easily to use in an archival establishment.

For record holdings of normal interest, checklists or inventories are prepared. The former furnish only the title of the records series together with its inclusive dates and the quantity of the records, while the latter describe their contents in greater or less detail. Inventories are compiled in Colorado, Michigan, North Carolina, Oregon, Pennsylvania, and South Carolina. In New York the state inventory project has described the holdings of the Manuscripts and History Section of the State Library. In many states, however, neither checklists nor inventories are compiled, and accession lists have to serve instead. It is probably true that the descriptive techniques of the National Archives have not been widely accepted by state archivists because their application consumes much time and also because at least the early series of state records can be serviced without elaborate finding aids.

Because of the shortage of trained personnel that in general prevents archival agencies from doing much arrangement and description of records, detailed finding aids cannot be prepared except for material exposed to heavy reference use. Some archival agencies have inherited indexes compiled by the WPA Historical Records Survey; in some Southern states card catalogs afford access to Confederate pension records; in Tennessee card catalogs have been prepared for the case records of the East and Middle Tennessee divisions of the Supreme Court and one for the West Tennessee Division is still in progress; and the numerous indexes available to genealogists in the Maryland Hall of Records are listed and explained in that agency's *Bulletins*.

The calendar, consisting of abstracts of individual documents, chronologically arranged, is especially useful to searchers because it acquaints them with the contents of each document without their having to consult the originals. If printed, it enables the student at a distance to send for copies of the items that are of interest to him. Preparation of a calendar, however, calls for a great expenditure of experienced staff time, and hence calendars must be limited to small holdings of high reference value that because of faulty arrangement are difficult to use or that because of age and fragility should not be exposed to heavy wear and tear. Calendars in card form are still in progress to facilitate the use of the so-called Massachusetts Archives and the Oregon Provisional Government records. The printed calendars of the "Rainbow Series" of the Maryland Hall of Records are the fruit of many years of devoted labor by the staff of that agency.

Reference Service

Archival agencies provide reference service in a number of ways: they lend records to government agencies; they furnish information from records and photographic copies of records to government agencies and private persons; and they make the originals available for use in their research rooms.[20]

It is an accepted axiom that service to government must take precedence over service to private persons. To what extent the former makes demands on the staff of the archival agency depends, of course, on the amount of permanently valuable records of recent origin that are accessioned by the

[20] For reference service to college and high-school students, see also pp. 343 ff.

state archives. The Archives–Records Management Division in Illinois handles more requests from state agencies (13,877 in 1960–62) than from private persons (12,426), while the Massachusetts Archives Division — with its almost exclusively historical holdings — renders most of its services to researchers. The demands of such scholars are particularly heavy if, in addition to official records, the archival agency has collections of private papers. In 1962–63 the Archives Section of the Wisconsin Division of Archives and Manuscripts handled 614 reference requests, as against 3,504 services provided during the same period by the Manuscripts Section.

Reference requests of private persons are particularly numerous and time consuming if the archival agency has census records, the originals or microfilm copies of land records, probate records, and other types of material that are of paramount interest to genealogists. Thanks to its extensive indexes to probate records, testamentary proceedings, and similiar series, the Maryland Hall of Records is able to service this material with relatively little effort. Undoubtedly the time and effort spent in preparing detailed finding aids of this kind is an investment from which the archival agency as well as its clients will benefit.

There is no generally accepted policy in regard to the amount of time that archival agencies will spend on answering written requests for information. Understandably, they try to be as helpful as possible to scholars, though they cannot be expected to undertake major research in the records. Agencies may decide to satisfy requests for information only when the desired information can be obtained from finding aids, for "To spend less time in providing information from records and to spend more time in providing information about records," [21] including the preparation of finding aids to them, is a policy that should be generally adopted. As a matter of public relations, however, the archival agency may find it difficult to restrict its information service. The reference activities of the Mississippi Department of Archives and History as reported for 1961–63 (11,029 written replies to information requested, besides 11,183 research room visits) are certainly out of proportion to the number of its professional personnel and have reduced its usefulness as the state's archival agency.

It is not customary for archival agencies to charge for time spent on answering requests for information except that searches in census records are frequently subject to a fee that varies from twenty-five cents to a dollar. The Oregon State Archives, however, demands a fee of three dollars for census searches and four dollars an hour for general searches that require more than a half-hour of staff time.

For the consultation of archival material on the premises, archival agen-

[21] Frank B. Evans, "The State Archivist and the Academic Researcher — 'Stable Companionship,'" *American Archivist*, XXVI (July, 1963), p. 320.

cies provide research rooms. Examples of good research rooms are found in the new buildings of Virginia, Tennessee, and Texas. The increasing availability at archival headquarters of rich microfilm holdings of local records and of federal and other records on microfilm has begun to pose a special problem, for the number of visitors has made it necessary for some agencies to limit the time when any one person may use a reader. In future buildings — or perhaps even in existing buildings — special microfilm reading rooms with adequate numbers of readers will be necessary.

Comparative statistics of the reference activities of archival agencies might be expected to furnish a yardstick by which to measure their services to their states and to the public. For two reasons, however, such statistics would be useless. First, the services rendered depend on the types of material serviced, which differ from state to state and which in some cases include large holdings of personal papers and even of newspapers. Second, there is no uniformity in the compiling of statistical information.[22] Some agencies, for instance, count an archival user only once, when he receives permission to consult records, while others count him every time he visits the research room. Furthermore, few agencies distinguish between types of users — government personnel, scholars, and other private persons. It is small comfort to note that librarians, too, are confronted with the problem of statistical information, for only recently the American Library Association has initiated a project "to establish a national system of library data collection for administrative use and research needs."[23]

Publications

For obvious reasons the general publication activities of historical societies, departments of archives and history, and state libraries to which state archival agencies may be subordinate do not fall within the scope of our discussion. It will be limited to archival publications and to other publications that an archival agency may undertake.

As a professional agency of the government and as an institution dedicated to the service of the research worker, the archival agency must publish annual or biennial reports. Regrettably, not all archival agencies prepare such reports, others prepare but do not publish them, and still others are allowed so little space in the reports of their parent agencies that their reports are practically useless. Some good examples of informative reporting, however, may be cited. The annual reports of the Maryland Hall of Records rank high among them, and since these often consider general problems of the field, they constitute a real service to the archival

[22] The Director of the Study was authorized by his Advisory Committee to suggest a tentative system of data collection to state archival agencies, and he did so late in 1962. Only a few agencies were able to furnish data in accordance with his scheme for the six-month period beginning January 1, 1963.

[23] Library of Congress, *Information Bulletin*, XXII (Aug. 12, 1963), 434 ff.

profession of the country. Other useful reports are those of the North Carolina Department of Archives and History and of the Illinois Archives–Records Management Division. Replies to the questionnaires annually sent to state archival agencies by the Committee on State and Local Records of the Society of American Archivists and published in condensed form [24] are no substitutes for full reports. Indeed, the society might well encourage state archival agencies that do not publish reports to send to it typed reports, so that at its headquarters full and up-to-date information on state archival activities would be available.

In the publication of finding aids,[25] the record of our state archival agencies is far from impressive. In the first place, published guides to their holdings are conspicuously lacking. Maryland's Hall of Records is getting ready to reissue, under a different title, its *Catalogue of Archival Material*, long out of print, and the second volume of its *County Courthouses and Records of Maryland* will be a general description and history of these records. The North Carolina Department of Archives and History will soon publish its archives guide, and that of the Public Records Division of Pennsylvania is available in processed form. For general information on the holdings of other archival agencies, one must turn to Philip M. Hamer's *Guide to Archives and Manuscripts in the United States*, which, though eminently useful for collections of private papers, is not sufficiently informative and detailed for the prospective searcher of archives.

Published finding aids for individual record groups or series are few indeed. Maryland's *Land Office and Prerogative Court Records of Colonial Maryland*, the seven volumes of its *Calendars of Maryland State Papers*, and Delaware's calendars of the *Ridgely Family Letters* and of the *Kent County, Delaware, Probate Records* stand out as noteworthy achievements. Inventories of record groups have been and are being produced in near-print by the Michigan Archives Division, and the Archives Division of the Tennessee State Library and Archives has available for distribution "regiters" of some of its manuscript collections. New York's *Preliminary Guide for Public Education Records* is an interesting attempt to list, on a state-wide basis, records relating to a major subject.

Articles about the holdings and services of state archival agencies are a means of bringing them to the attention of prospective users. They are useful if published in the *American Archivist*, as many of them are, but far more useful if published in learned journals for the benefit of persons outside the archival pale. Archival agencies have done too little of this kind of legitimate "advertising." Many archival agencies have tried, however, to "enlighten" the general public by issuing short brochures and flyers.

[24] See p. 35.
[25] See also pp. 361 ff.

State archival agencies also responsible for records management have issued manuals and guides for the use of agency personnel. These documents deal with topics such as files maintenance, inventorying of records, preparation of retention and disposal schedules, and administration of a records center. Among such publications, North Carolina's *County Records Manual* and *Municipal Records Manual* are of particular interest.

Archivists are particularly well fitted to compile the state's manual or year book, for they are necessarily concerned with the history and organization of the state's government. In Georgia and Maryland the State Archivist publishes the state manual, and in Oklahoma the State Librarian and Archivist issues the manual and also the *Oklahoma Gazette*.[26]

Publication, by archival agencies, of historical works, monographs, and journals is referred to in a later section on historical activities.

Exhibits

The idea that exhibits should be used to explain to the general public the nature of archives and the archival function, and to encourage interest in the history of the state, has become generally accepted.

Archival exhibits vary greatly in size. That of the Massachusetts Archives Division is a veritable museum viewed annually by thousands of visitors and necessitating the maintenance of a regular guide service. Most other state exhibits, however, are of modest size and are installed in the entrance hall of the building, where a receptionist or some other close-by staff member can exercise the necessary supervision. Often charters of the colonial era or the constitution of the state are kept in display cases within special vaults that can be opened to permit inspection of these precious and impressive documents.

Archival documents can be displayed with particular effectiveness as part of the general exhibit or museum of a department of archives and history or a historical society, but this is rarely done. As a corollary, archival agencies not responsible for historical activities might enhance the attractiveness of their exhibits by obtaining, for display purposes, artifacts substantively related to the documents on exhibit; but this, again, is rarely done. The Texas State Library shows interesting specimens of its archival holdings together with recent books for which they have been used — a fine device to demonstrate to the public one of the purposes for which an archival establishment is maintained.

Local Archives Programs

The records of local government are sources of prime importance to the social scientist, to the student of legal history, and to the genealogist;

[26] Publication of checklists of State publications is dealt with on p. 34.

hence their preservation and accessibility have been a matter of concern to archivists ever since the Public Archives Commission of the American Historical Association started its investigations. At various times, the problem of providing for the safekeeping of local archives was also debated at the Conference of American Archivists.[27]

Historically speaking, some of the New England states and New York were the first to adopt measures aimed at safeguarding local archives. These measures included: the preservation of local records in so-called fireproof buildings; the use of approved paper, inks, and typewriter ribbons in record-making; the repair and rebinding of damaged records and volumes; and the orderly transfer of records from the outgoing to the succeeding officeholder. Not all these preservation programs have survived, and only that of New York has been modernized to include, in addition to records preservation, effective guidance to local government units in matters of records management. The program of Rhode Island withered away after its transfer in 1910 to the State Library, and in Massachusetts it lost momentum when it became a function of the office of the Secretary of State.

The full value of local government archives was revealed, and an important step toward their control was taken, when the WPA Historical Records Survey embarked on its vast project of inventorying local records. This contributed to their becoming known but did not solve the question of how to preserve them. Legally, almost all state archival agencies are empowered to take local archives into their custody. In actual practice, only a few — Delaware, Maryland, and North Carolina — believing that concentration of local archives was the best guarantee of their safekeeping and was also in the interest of researchers, initiated programs of taking over original local records.

The problem of preserving local records and of making them accessible lost much of its complexity when microfilming became available as a means of cheap photographic reproduction, for microfilming makes it possible to leave local archives *in situ* and to assemble security and reference copies at the state archives. Large-scale microfilming of important local series had its beginnings in the microfilm project of the Utah Genealogical Society. In exchange for facilitating the project, state archival agencies have received second negatives or positives of the records reproduced. In Georgia the project is still going forward under archival control. Other states, notably Maryland and North Carolina, are continuing it on their own beyond its cut-off date — about 1850. Tennessee has pilot microfilm projects under way in three counties.

In other states, however, the cost of a program of microfilming local records is thought to be prohibitive; and another device, that of the re-

[27] See p. 29, n. 80.

[336]

gional depository for local records, is being tried to preserve them and to facilitate their use. In Wisconsin, depositories called area research centers have been established at a number of state colleges; Illinois conservatively plans to have three regional depositories at major universities of the state; a few centers are projected in Washington and about half a dozen in Michigan; Ohio already has depositories at six institutions and a historical society; and Kentucky uses regional "holding areas" at the Universities of Kentucky, Louisville, and Southern Kentucky.

Present experience does not permit evaluating the usefulness of the regional depository plan. If it is to be sound, depositories must be subject to supervision from state archival headquarters, arrangement and description of holdings must be the duty of state archival staffs, the depository must clearly separate records on deposit from whatever manuscript collections it may have, and the archival agency must reserve the right to discontinue depository agreements if they prove unsatisfactory. Certainly, only substantial institutions with competent and adequate staffs should be selected as depositories, and the state archival agency should have enough personnel to make its supervision effective.

THE RECORDS MANAGEMENT FUNCTION

Records Management

The boundaries of the area called records management or paperwork management have not been clearly defined. "Records management" assumes responsibility for mail, correspondence, files, and forms management; for office equipment and supplies; for records storage and records disposition; for documentation; and for surveys and audits of agency records operations. "Paperwork management" is supposed to include also paperwork quality control, directives management, reports management, and clerical work measurement.

Long an administrative no man's land, records management in the early 1940's became a concern of the National Archives and somewhat later of the states.[28] In those with a strong tradition in the archives field the need for a program of records management and the benefits that such a program would reap for both the government and the archival agency were readily understood, and state archivists took the initiative in promoting legislation on records management that assigned to them responsibility for its administration. State archival agencies have taken either full or partial charge of records management in the following states: Colorado, Delaware, Hawaii, Illinois, Kansas, Maryland, New Jersey, North Carolina, Oklahoma, Texas, Utah, Virginia, Washington, and Wyoming. In Kentucky, Louisiana, Minnesota, New Hampshire, New Mexico, and

[28] See Rex Beach and John T. Caton, "State and Local Government Records Programs," *American Archivist*, XXIV (July, 1961), 289–95.

Vermont newly established dual-purpose agencies are to discharge both the records management and the archives functions.

In a number of states, however, records management is assigned to another department of the state government. It is, or is supposed to be, a function of the Secretary of State in Nebraska and in North Dakota. Elsewhere it has been taken on by a department of finance, a department of administration, or a department of general services. This has happened in California, Indiana, Michigan, New York, Ohio, Oregon, West Virginia, and Wisconsin. In Pennsylvania the records management program is in the Governor's Office of Administration; in Connecticut the State Records Management Committee has been made responsible for carrying out a records management program; and in Puerto Rico the Bureau of the Budget is responsible.

Assignment of records management responsibility to an archival or other agency of the state, however, does not necessarily mean that a program is actually under way, for in Nebraska and Oklahoma records management acts have been passed but are, so far, only "scraps of paper." In many states, as for instance in Ohio and Massachusetts, one person gives part of his time to records management work. Among the states that have adequately staffed programs are California, Colorado, Illinois, Maryland, Michigan, New York, North Carolina, Pennsylvania, and Wisconsin. Because the programs in most of these states are in their early stages, they emphasize the inventorying and scheduling of records for disposition.[29] In a number of states, however, workshop sessions have been arranged for agency personnel; and, for their benefit, handbooks on files and filing, the use and services of the records center, and records disposition have been published.

In practically all states whose records management programs show promise, records officers or liaison officers in the agencies co-operate with the state records management authority. Success or failure of the program depends largely on whether these officers can give enough time to their records management duties and on whether they have been properly indoctrinated in regard to their functions. A one-time training session of a few hours cannot adequately acquaint them with the techniques of inventorying their records for scheduling. Conferences and training courses for agency records officers and, in general, close working relationships between the state's records management authority and agency records officers are an important phase of a successful records management program.

As a rule, records management service is limited to agencies of the executive branch of the government of the state. Upon request, the agency in charge of records management may make its services available to the two other branches of government, but such services seem to be rarely requested. Where an administrative agency other than the archival agency

[29] See pp. 366 ff.

is responsible for records management, assistance with the records of local government units is normally left to the archival agency. Naturally this is the case where the records management function has been assigned to the archival agency or a newly created archives–records management agency.

The functions and operations of the records center and records management assistance to local government are discussed below in this chapter.

The Records Center

Profiting from the experience of the federal government, many states have established records centers for the administration of records of limited retention value. A facility of this kind is generally considered necessary in a fully developed records management program.

Where both archives administration and records management are under the same agency, it naturally is responsible for the records center. In those states, however, that have separate archives and records management agencies, the center is usually under the records management agency. It is under the archival agency or its parent agency in Connecticut, Indiana, Oregon, and Texas. Effective January 1, 1967, the California Central Records Depository will be transferred from the office of the Secretary of State to the newly established Department of General Services.

Much can be said for housing state archives and records centers in the same buildings, as was first done in Michigan, where the Archives Division operates as a "tenant" in the records center. The new buildings of New Hampshire and Washington provide combined facilities, and in New Mexico an existing structure has been adapted to accommodate both the records center and the archives. In Pennsylvania part of the Archives Tower will serve as a records center.

Practices with regard to the location of the records center vary considerably. The centers of Rhode Island, Illinois, and North Carolina are in or near the area of government buildings in the heart of the capital, and the two Maryland centers in Annapolis and Baltimore and the Wisconsin center are in the basements of general administration or state office buildings. If centers are located at the outskirts of the capital city or at a considerable distance from it, as they are in Connecticut, Michigan, New Jersey, and Texas, messenger service has to be provided between the centers and government agencies.

In states in which a concentration of business and industry in cities other than the capital has necessitated decentralization of state services, branch records centers have had to be established. California has two such centers, one in Los Angeles and one in San Francisco; and, as noted above, Maryland has a center in Baltimore in addition to its Annapolis center.

Experience in records center administration proves that optimum utilization of space is achieved if the records center is housed in a structure designed for records storage, as are the records centers of Maryland, Michigan, and North Carolina and the combination buildings in New Hampshire and Washington. Unfortunately, many centers are housed in space not planned for records center use; and few such centers are as satisfactory as that of Rhode Island, which is in the Veterans Memorial Building in Providence. As a minimum requirement, records centers should be in fire-resistive buildings. In this respect those of Connecticut and Iowa leave much to be desired.

In the matter of records center administration, states have learned much from the federal government and from each other. There are a number of useful manuals in which transfer to and procedures of a state records center have been regulated. As a matter of general practice, only records scheduled for disposition are admitted to the records center. Indeed, the very purpose of the center is defeated if it is used mainly for storing unscheduled records, as it has been in Massachusetts.

Records centers are still lacking in a number of states. In Kansas it is believed that there is no need for a records center (although one has been authorized), for disposal of records in accordance with schedules is said to proceed expeditiously from agency premises. In other states, however, the absence of a records center is keenly felt. Ohio and Mississippi have to rent space for storing records; and in Alabama and Arizona records that, because of their limited retention value, should be in records centers occupy much-needed space in the buildings of the archival agencies.

Records Management Assistance to Local Government

From the early days of settlement, colonial legislatures were concerned with the preservation of local records, more often than not without tangible results. Late in the nineteenth century, concrete measures toward that end were taken in New England, especially in Massachusetts and Connecticut.[30] New York acted similarly early in the twentieth century. In these states supervisors or examiners of public records were appointed and legislation was enacted to enforce the use of suitable materials in record-making, the proper maintenance of records (including provision for "fireproof" vaults), and the transfer of records from the incumbent of an office to his successor. These measures were aimed at the preservation of records rather than at an improvement of record-making practices — the principal objective of the records management programs that developed during the 1940's in the federal government and in some of the states.

Few of the programs developed enter effectively into the areas of local records creation and maintenance. Outstanding among them is that of the Public Records Section of the New York Division of Archives and History

[30] See pp. 15 ff.

with its manuals on records control and filing systems and similar useful publications. In most other states that have authorized records management assistance to local government — they number about twelve — the emphasis so far has been on the inventorying and scheduling of records for disposition. In North Carolina a *County Records Manual* and a *Municipal Records Manual* have been developed to suggest retention periods to local government units; a Michigan *Local Records Manual* is to assist them in inventorying and scheduling records; and a similar manual of New Jersey explains regulations governing the destruction of local records, deals with standards for photographing records and — like the North Carolina manuals — offers records retention schedules that municipal and county officers may use as guides to records retention.[31]

Substantial programs to microfilm local records for security and research purposes have been initiated in Delaware, Maryland, North Carolina, and Wyoming. In some other states (Colorado, Oregon, Virginia) microfilming for local agencies is done on a limited basis.

Preservation of Essential Records

As a supplement to its *Suggested State Legislation Program for 1960*, the Council of State Governments published a "Preservation of Essential Records Act." It was designed as a model of legislation to insure the preservation, in times of disaster, of records essential to the continuity of government and to the rights and privileges of citizens. This piece of suggested legislation has not met with wide acceptance. It has been enacted in Oklahoma and, in combination with the council's records management act, in Nebraska and West Virginia. In these three states, however, no steps have been taken so far to implement the acts. In other states an essential records preservation bill was introduced but not passed. It failed twice in Hawaii, it was held up in three sessions of the Michigan legislature, and it is still pending in committee in New Jersey. In Connecticut a records management bill that included provision for the protection of essential records was twice defeated.

Action to meet the intent of the legislation proposed by the Council of State Governments has fared better in those states that already have records management programs. In Illinois, Minnesota, and North Carolina legislation on the books has been amended to authorize programs for the preservation of essential records. Such programs in Minnesota and North Carolina are well under way, while in Illinois an "inventory of records essential to emergency operation of state government" is now being taken by the State Archives–Records Management Division of the Secretary of State. A California act of 1963 includes responsibility for essential records protection among the functions of the new Department of General Serv-

---

[31] The disposition of local government records is discussed on p. 327.

[341]

ices. In Ohio and Wisconsin the State Records Commission and the Committee on Public Records, respectively, are to establish suitable programs.

Taking the initiative in some other states, civil defense agencies, archivists, and records managers have started essential records programs. In Louisiana the civil defense agency is supporting a "pilot project" of microfilming by the State Archives and Records Commission; in Maryland, at the request of the Board of Public Works, the microfilming of county records has been accelerated; in Delaware the Public Archives Commission has filmed practically all pertinent records of the state; in Oregon the civil defense agency and the State Archivist have co-operated in planning a preservation program; and in Wyoming, by the end of the 1961–63 biennium, 17,459,475 pages of state records and 2,643,883 pages of county records had been filmed. In many other states, government agencies and counties independently have done a considerable amount of microfilming for security purposes.

To serve this end, security copies must be stored in places where they are adequately protected from destruction. Little has been done, however, to provide such central storage facilities. California's Secretary of State accepts from agencies security microfilm for storage in space that he has rented from a commercial firm, and other states are contemplating rental arrangements of this kind. In the absence of such arrangements, many state agencies use their field offices for storing security copies of their essential records. Funds for a state-owned security vault have now been appropriated in North Carolina.

RELATED FUNCTIONS

Co-operation With Educational Institutions

The movement to preserve and care for archives developed under the auspices and with the strong support of American scholarship;[32] and ever since then co-operation between archival agencies and institutions of higher learning has been growing. In this respect the situation resembles that in European countries, where archival institutions came into existence at a much earlier time.

Needless to say, relations are particularly close in states in which archival activity is part of the functions of an archival-historical agency or organization. Co-operation is extremely effective in Wisconsin, where a relationship approaching a common purpose results in many a joint effort of the State Historical Society and the department of history of the university. There are, however, some other states — including Colorado, Kansas, Nebraska, North Carolina, and South Carolina — in which universities and archival agencies maintain close working arrangements.

A particularly useful opportunity for co-operation can be found in the

[32] See Chapter I.

field of archival administration treated as an academic subject. Courses of this kind, combined with internships, are offered by the North Carolina Department of Archives and History in co-operation with Meredith College and by the Colorado Division of Archives and Public Records in co-operation with the University of Denver. Colorado also provides an intensive summer course, similar to that of The American University in which the Maryland Hall of Records, the National Archives, and the Library of Congress have participated for almost twenty years. In Wisconsin staff members of the State Historical Society teach in the "historical agencies course" of the university. Though not providing formal instruction, some archival agencies — for instance that of Oregon — arrange internships for advanced history students to acquaint them with archival techniques and thus to prepare them for archival positions.

In addition to offering courses in their professional field, archivists, because of their backgrounds and training, are well equipped to teach part-time in academic institutions. Many of them do so. To give an example, the Assistant Secretary and the Archivist of the Kansas Historical Society are connected with academic institutions as instructors. The Archivist teaches the course in the history of Kansas. Wherever courses in the history of the state are part of the curriculum, archivists would indeed be particularly competent to take charge of them.

Archival agencies also collaborate with universities and colleges by furnishing material for the writing of Master's theses and doctoral dissertations and for the research interests and the needs of faculty members. Much, it seems, might be done to expand and intensify this type of co-operation. On the one hand, professors should consult more frequently with archival agencies in regard to subjects deserving investigation, and they should certainly not assign to candidates for higher degrees topics calling for the use of archival material before archivists have explored their feasibility. On the other hand, archivists have done too little to bring important accessions to the attention of social science departments, and lack of guides to archival holdings has also kept students and professors from exploiting them. Archivists should seek and obtain opportunities to acquaint graduate seminars with the nature and importance of archival material and with the techniques of using it.

Bonds between educators and state archivists are understandably strongest in states where a major academic institution is located in or near the state capital — always the seat of the state archival agency — and where archival holdings are well arranged and described. No fruitful co-operation, however, can develop where important parts of the state's archives have not been transferred to the archival agency or where holdings have not been arranged and described and hence are not easily accessible.

Except in special cases, the archival agency denies access to its holdings to high-school students, though it may be willing to answer their inquiries. Permanent and temporary exhibits will adequately accomplish the purpose of acquainting this group with the *raison d'être* and services of a state archives.

Historical Activities

Historical-archival agencies — such as departments of archives and history, historical societies, and state libraries of which the archival unit is a constituent part — are enjoined by law to engage in one or more of the following historical activities: publication of official and non-official records, of a state historical journal, and of a history of the state or of monographs on phases and aspects of the history of the state and its subdivisions; archeological research and excavation; establishment and administration of a state historical or archeological museum; assistance to local historical societies and museums; formulation of texts for historical markers and erecting and maintaining such markers; restoration of historic sites and buildings and explaining their significance; and preparation for, and participation in, the commemoration of historic events.

Many such agencies, even without specific legal direction, maintain museums, historic buildings, and historic sites; erect, or prepare the texts for, historical markers; and publish the historical journals of their states [33] and possibly also newsletters for their members and for members of regional and local historical societies in their states. Important archeological programs are administered by the historical societies of Kansas, Nebraska, and Ohio. A considerable number of these agencies also publish historical monographs and collections of original source material. Although evaluation of these activities does not fall within the scope of this study, two comments are in order here: (1) such related operations must have a separate and competent staff; and (2) the archives function must not be condemned to play Cinderella while historical activities that are more spectacular and popular are more generously supported by the legislature.

A number of states, of course, have archival agencies that are responsible solely for archives and records management. The Archives–Records Management Division in Illinois has no historical functions, and the same holds true of the archival agencies of California, Colorado, Georgia, Hawaii, Indiana, Kentucky, Louisiana, Massachusetts, Minnesota, New Hampshire, New Mexico, Oklahoma, Vermont, and Washington, and to a degree of the Maryland Hall of Records, though some of its publications, while *prima facie* related to its archival program, are also valuable contributions to the legal, administrative, and architectural history of the state.

Although the archival agency may not have been given any historical

[33] This is the case in Alabama, Idaho, Iowa, Kansas, Michigan, Montana, Nebraska, Nevada, North Carolina, South Dakota, Utah, Wisconsin, and Wyoming.

responsibilities by law, state archivists everywhere are involved in them in various ways. Many of them are members of Civil War centennial and other commemorative commissions, many belong to historical markers committees, and several serve as members or secretaries of the boards of historical societies. With their archival exhibits — of which the archival "museum" in Massachusetts is the most impressive example — archivists help to arouse the interest of the people in the history of their state. The General Archives of Puerto Rico uses a motion picture film for this purpose, and the New Jersey Bureau of Archives and History has contributed exhibits to the "Historymobile" of the state.

Regardless of the role of the archival agency in historical activities, as the custodian of the state's records from colonial and territorial times it is bound to have an important place in the historical interests of the state and its citizens. In fact, its status and its support depend largely on the contributions of its staff to historical studies, either by facilitating the use of its holdings or by actively participating in historical work through the publication of articles and monographs.

Acquisition and Administration of Private Papers

Private papers, frequently referred to as historical manuscripts, are the records of non-official bodies such as institutions and organizations of all kinds, the records of business and industrial enterprise, and those of families and individuals. As long as official records were considered primarily as materials for historical research, there was an understandable tendency to treat bodies of official records like private papers, to disregard their organic character, to disrupt their arrangement, and to describe them item by item. As the nature of archival material began to be grasped, however, and as its significance for governmental purposes began to be realized, the two types of material — archives on the one hand and private papers on the other — were clearly distinguished, with the result that now the administration of archives and the collection and administration of private papers are considered separate though related tasks.

Growing awareness of the difference in origin and nature between the two types of documentary material is reflected by the more recent laws governing archival agencies as well as by agency practice. In certain states the archival agency is responsible exclusively for public records and does not accept any private papers. This is particularly true of states in which a historical society or major university library has become the traditional center for collecting and administering private papers, as, for instance, the Minnesota or the Massachusetts Historical Society.

In other states the archival agency may accept only collections of papers related in subject matter to its official holdings. That of California has brought together collections of papers of Congressmen from the state.

The Division of State Archives and Public Records of Colorado takes a special interest in the papers of state officials that are intermingled with public records. Similarly the newly established State Commission of Public Records in New Mexico has acquired mixed collections of private papers and public records formerly in the hands of the New Mexico Historical Society.[34]

In the majority of the states, archival agencies or their parent agencies are in the "private papers business." A good many of them accept private papers if they happen to be offered but do not pursue an active program of acquisition. To be effective, however, a collecting program needs the services of an employee who will go out into the "field," and, since few agencies can afford field representatives, their collecting activities are likely to remain haphazard.

Organizationally speaking, the care of private papers may be assigned to the archival agency, even when such responsibility is by law assigned to the parent agency; or it may be carried out by a different unit of the parent agency. The latter arrangement is found in Indiana, where the Indiana Division of the State Library is responsible for private papers; in Ohio, where the Library of the Historical Society is in charge of them; and in Wyoming, where they are kept in the Historical Division of the Archives and Historical Department.

In many states, however, the care of private papers is organizationally consolidated with the archives function. The table of organization of a small archival agency may not mention private papers at all, though a member of the archives staff may be assigned to care for them or to give them some of his time. Where private paper holdings are of considerable size and importance, as in Wisconsin and in Kansas, a division of archives and manuscripts consisting of an archives and a manuscript section may be established, or a separate manuscript section may be part of the archives division, as is the case in Tennessee.

In the techniques of processing private papers, a rather remarkable change has taken place. Chronological arrangement of papers as the only acceptable method of organization has been abandoned and replaced by the precept of maintaining them in their original order, wherever a meaningful order can be found or can be restored if it has been disturbed. For the description of private papers, the so-called register used in the Manuscript Division of the Library of Congress, corresponding to the inventory of archivists, is beginning to be adopted. Many registers of private papers have been compiled by the Tennessee Manuscript Section, referred to above, and some of them have been published, a very laudable practice. In most archival agencies, control of collections of private papers is by

[34] The South Carolina Archives Department is not to solicit private papers, though it may accept them if its services are needed to prevent their destruction.

means of a card catalog. For the same purpose, guides have been prepared in a number of agencies. Among them, those of the Manuscripts Section of the Wisconsin Historical Society and of the West Virginia Collection are particularly noteworthy.

Responsibility for Printed Government Documents

Record sets of state publications are part of the permanently valuable documentation of the state; hence these sets, together with the unpublished records, should be preserved in the state archival agency, where they should be protected from the wear and tear resulting from frequent use.

In relatively few states, however, has the archival agency been made legally responsible for assembling this type of material. In Delaware all state agencies, boards, and commissions and all counties and municipalities must deposit with the Public Archives Commission two copies each of their publications; in Maryland the Hall of Records has been declared a depository for all annual reports and publications of state agencies and for all local codes; and in Hawaii the Archives Division receives all state government publications. Designated as one of four depositories for Kentucky state publications, the Kentucky State Archives and Records Service published in 1963 the first such list for Kentucky. Though not declared depositories for all state publications, the departments of history and archives of South Carolina and West Virginia publish checklists of such publications of their respective states. The Archives Division in Hawaii and the Alabama Department of Archives and History receive and issue copies of the slip laws of their states.

The acquisition, storage, and control of all printed government documents is a time- and space-consuming activity, and hence state archival agencies have refrained from undertaking it of their own initiative. Instead they have relied on the state library, a law library, or the library of the legislative reference service to perform this task. If some other such agency does preserve state publications, the archival agency should make sure that, in addition to copies exposed to staff and public use and therefore subject to eventual damage or loss, a complete set of government documents is assembled and kept intact as a record set.[35]

Registration and Publication of State Authoritative Issuances

Under federal law the Office of the Federal Register of the National Archives and Records Service files and publishes in the *Federal Register*

[35] Paul Lewinson, "The Preservation of Government Publications," *American Archivist*, XXII (Apr., 1959), 188, proposes "that archivists, as members of the intellectual community and as persons specially charged with responsibility for official documentation, should take the initiative in efforts to provide for the nonarchival preservation of published government documents that it is not practical for archival agencies to preserve."

presidential proclamations and executive orders; federal administrative regulations, orders, and notices that affect a class of the public; and other pertinent issuances. Filing and publication of comparable state issuances is not a function of state archival agencies, except in Oklahoma. According to 75 Oklahoma Statutes, sections 251–57 (S. B. No. 266, approved June 21, 1961), agencies must file with the Secretary of State and with the State Librarian and Archivist certified originals and duplicate copies of their rules and regulations that were in force on or before the effective date of the act and similar copies of all new rules and regulations. Those issued after January 2, 1962, are published by the State Librarian and Archivist in the semi-monthly *Oklahoma Gazette*.[36]

In the opinion of some leading archivists, there is in other states a great need for a system of registering and publishing state official issuances. It certainly is a task that the archival agency would be well qualified to carry out if it were given the authority and the necessary funds.

[36] See p. 223.

CHAPTER IV

꜀꜀꜀꜀꜀꜀

Standards for State Archival Agencies

INTRODUCTION

Concern for the records of the states and of subordinate units of local government is not of recent origin, for it goes back to colonial times and received further impetus when interest in state history began to manifest itself in the nineteenth century. This interest, however, expressed itself mainly in acquiring copies of pertinent source materials from abroad and in documentary publication of such material as well as certain key series of a state's records. It was not until the end of the last century that the necessity of preserving and making accessible the original records was fully realized and that historians and others concerned urged the establishment of institutions to take charge of assembling and administering records of value to them. Recent decades have seen increasing awareness of the importance of sound archival arrangements for the protection of those records that are a reservoir of previous governmental experience, that are indispensable for historical and other research, and that safeguard the rights and privileges of the citizen and enable him to trace the history of his family, a wholly legitimate desire.

Many states have recognized their obligation to establish and maintain archival agencies equipped and staffed to discharge these manifold duties. They have recognized that, in providing archival establishments, they are not merely satisfying the needs of the scholar engaged in esoteric endeavor from which only a few will benefit, but on the contrary are providing service that, in the first place, makes available to leaders and officials of the government previous policies and decisions on which enlightened and consistent action must be based and, in the second place, is a service to which the citizen is entitled no matter what his research interests may be. Care and preservation of archival documents is a duty *par excellence* of statesmen in the United States, for the very existence and governmental arrangements of the nation stem from three great federal documents—

[349]

the Declaration of Independence, the Constitution, and the Bill of Rights — and from the constitution and bill of rights of each state.

Services to be expected of archival agencies, however, are no longer limited to the preservation and administration of the permanently valuable records of the government they serve. Expansion of government into new fields of action, growth and complexity of the administrative apparatus, co-operation of governmental agencies in discharging the same function, and — probably more than anything else — new techniques for the production and multiplication of documents have so increased the volume of records, on hand and constantly being created, that their appraisal and the wise selection of those worthy of preservation have become a major function of the archivist. It is he who, with the assistance of qualified government officials and scholars, must face the awesome task of selecting from mountains of record material the small core that will constitute for posterity the essential documentation of the state.

In order to discharge this duty, the archivist must not only have access to the far-flung record holdings of his government, and he must not only have a decisive voice in determining what portion of them should be preserved. He must also help to make sure that the "right" records are created and that they are created in such a fashion that those among them of permanent value can be easily segregated for transfer to his custody. He may discharge this responsibility by maintaining liaison with the record-creating agencies of the state and giving them advice when asked, or he may be charged with assisting them in the creation of records and in the management of records while current, and with administering a records center, a storage facility in which semi-current records are kept while awaiting destruction after stated periods of time. Sound records management and records center service result in substantial savings; therefore, states that do not provide for them are ill advised and oblivious of an important means to reduce the cost of government and thus to ease the citizen's tax burden.

In the federal government and in states with a great tradition in archives administration the archivist also serves as records administrator. Where, on the other hand, records management has been made the task of the general management and services agency of a state, that agency must seek the co-operation of the archivist, because the effectiveness of his operation is largely determined by the way records are created, by the kind of records that are created, and by the procedures for maintaining them during the current and semi-current phases of their existence.

A look at the archival map of the United States discloses a diversity of state archival arrangements that approaches incomparability with regard to control over the archival agency and its location in the government, functions entrusted and funds available to it, philosophy and techniques of work, and many other facets of its personality. In the same region there may be found establishments that meet or approach the highest standards of the archival profession, while in neighboring states no archival program exists, or, where it exists, it is undeveloped and undernourished. Maturity and effectiveness of archival arrangements have little relationship to the duration of the state's history and the time span of its archives. Archivally underdeveloped states are found in the areas of first settlement as well as in the interior of the country, and, as a corollary, some western states have praiseworthy programs that are well under way.

Provision of archival service is so basic a prerequisite of the modern state, so rightful a demand of its citizens, and so essential a component of its governmental and cultural affairs that no state can afford to be without it. Furthermore, it requires so small a portion of the state revenue that no state has an excuse for not providing it. It is for the guidance of legislators and responsible state officials that, for a long time, the Society of American Archivists, now in the twenty-eighth year of its existence, has wanted to make its experience available. This experience is embodied in the statement of standards for state archival agencies that follows. Given the diversification in the structure of state governments and the different backgrounds that have shaped existing state archival administration, the set of standards developed must be of a general nature, and their application must depend on what beginnings and foundations there are to build on. It is hoped, however, that from the experience now on hand there have been abstracted the essentials that deserve consideration on the part of legislators and government officials who wish to have the record of their state preserved for generations to come.

The needs are basically the same everywhere and the means of meeting them have much in common. An effective state archives in every state — that is the goal toward which this statement of standards is directed.

ORGANIZATION FOR ARCHIVAL SERVICE

Legal Authority

1. Each state of the United States should establish and support an archival agency organized either as an independent agency or as a constituent but separate part of a parent agency.

2. The authority of the state archival agency should rest on statutory or constitutional provisions that clearly set forth the functions it is to perform.

3. The authority conferred should extend to the records of all branches of the government of the state and to those of its political subdivisions.

4. Inasmuch as the management of records, while current and semi-current, and the preservation of those with permanent or long-term value

[351]

are essentially one task, responsibility for both is best vested in the same agency.

5. Accordingly, the basic act establishing the archival agency should deal with both archival and records management service, including the safeguarding of records essential to the continuity of government and to the protection of the rights of its citizens in times of disaster.

6. The basic act should include legal provision for the replevin of public records that have been illegally removed from official custody.

7. The archival agency should have an official seal and authority to certify copies of its records.

8. Qualifications and mode of appointment and dismissal of the head of the archival service should be stated in the basic act.

Status and Location in the Government of the Archival Agency

1. Inasmuch as the archival agency serves all branches and agencies of the government, and inasmuch as it should be professionally staffed and directed on a nonpartisan basis, it is best given the status of an independent agency, governed by a board or commission.

> The governing body may be composed of key officials of the state serving *ex officio* or of citizens actively interested in the objectives of the archival agency and appointed by the Governor for overlapping terms, or it may be a mixed body including both key officials of the state and appointed members. Boards or commissions governing agencies or organizations of which the archival service may be a part may be similarly constituted.

2. If the archival service is not to be an independent agency, its ideal status is that of an agency directly reporting to the Governor. This gives it a place of greatest prestige and enables it to discharge its functions unhampered by departmental sympathies and antipathies.

3. Where the archival function has been assigned to the state library, this function should have co-equal status with the library function, and the equality of status should be expressed in the title of the combined agency, as in the Tennessee State Library and Archives. As a minimum, the archives unit should have division status directly under the state librarian and archivist.

> The United States is one of the few countries in which libraries have sometimes been made responsible for the administration of official records. Archives administration and library administration are intrinsically different tasks in regard to materials handled and techniques, and while the state library may be charged with the archives function, its dual role as the state's archival agency and library should be recognized in its organization as well as in its title.

4. Where the archival function has been assigned to a historical agency or organization, that function should enjoy equal status with its historical or other divisions. Also, the archival responsibility should be stated in

the name of the historical agency or organization, as in the North Carolina Department of Archives and History.

> In many states one agency has been charged with both archival and historical functions; and, given their significant relationship, this combination of responsibilities has often been mutually beneficial. It should, however, be expressed in the title of the agency.

5. Departments to which the archives function has been or may be assigned are the Department of Education, the Department of Finance, the Department of Administration or General Services, and the Office of the Secretary of State. The Secretary of State has been by tradition the custodian of the most important categories of records; and, if located in his office, the archival agency will profit from that tradition, provided that the Secretary of State has retained his ancient position of prestige and influence.

> A combined archives and records management agency may be able to discharge its records management function effectively if it is in the Department of Administration or in a Department of Finance that provides general management service to the state.

6. If the archival agency is in a department headed by an elected official or an official appointed by an elected official of the state, statutory provisions governing the qualifications of the head of the archival agency and the mode of his appointment and dismissal are especially essential.

Budgetary Requirements

1. Whether an independent agency or part of a parent agency, the archival agency should have a separate budget.

> The budget should be formulated by the head of the archival agency. The budget of an archival agency subordinate to a parent agency should include all items related to the archives function, such as archival salaries and specifically archival supplies and equipment.

2. The head of the archival agency should be permitted to defend his requests before the head of the parent agency, if part of such an agency; before the budget officer, commission, or other body of the executive branch; and before the legislature.

Internal Organization

1. The archival agency should be organized around its major programs, depending on the scope of its functions, such as preservation and administration of state archives, care of local archives, records management, administration of records centers, and various historical activities.

2. Excellence of performance is encouraged by the delegation of responsibility to program heads.

3. The head of the archival agency, while responsible for developing

policies and supervising the execution of programs, should be free to represent his agency effectively in its relations with officers and legislators of the state and with libraries, institutions of higher learning, the National Archives and Records Service, the Society of American Archivists and other professional societies, sister agencies in other states, and the general public.

State Archives Personnel

1. To achieve the highest professional standards, state archives staffs should meet in every respect the requirements of the positions to which they are appointed.

> The following categories of personnel should be provided:
> *a*) Professional
> *b*) Technical
> *c*) Clerical
> *d*) Maintenance and custodial

2. For professional positions, academic as well as professional-archival qualifications should be required.

> The head of a state archival agency should have a Ph.D. degree in the social sciences or humanities or, as a minimum, a Master's degree in one of these fields or equivalent earned degrees in jurisprudence. Professional staff members should normally have Master's degrees. Academic experience of the head of the archival agency and his professional staff members should be in the areas of American history; American government with emphasis on state and local government; public law; organization and management, including records management; historiography; and methods and materials of research. It should be supplemented by the study of other social sciences, such as economics and sociology.

3. Professional staff members should not be expected to engage in routine activities that can be carried out by other personnel.

> The processing and servicing of modern records can frequently be accomplished by technical personnel under professional supervision.

4. For technical personnel, successful completion of a high-school education should be required.

5. Appointment to professional and technical positions should be solely on the basis of merit, and dismissal should be for cause only. Staff members to be dismissed should be entitled, upon appeal, to a hearing before the governing body of the archival agency or other legally constituted authority.

> Each appointee should receive a letter of appointment giving the terms of the appointment and a job description. The job description should state that, in addition to the duties specified, further duties may be assigned by the head of the archival agency.

6. Professional and technical positions should be open to all qualified applicants (see 2 and 4, above) without a residence requirement.

A rigid residence requirement limits the head of the archival agency in selecting the applicants best qualified for jobs to be filled. It also militates against a healthy exchange of experience between states. Though a good knowledge of the history of the state and its government is an essential part of the archivist's equipment, it can be acquired on the job.

7. Types and levels of employment and the salaries attached to them should be stated in a classification and pay plan.

In the absence of pertinent civil service regulations, staff members should be entitled to annual and sick leave, insurance, retirement, and other benefits enjoyed by other employees of the state. Also, there should be provision for salary increments for meritorious service.

8. Professional qualifications for archival service are similar to those for teaching in institutions of higher learning, and hence professonal archival salaries should be on a level with those paid by such institutions. Otherwise, archival agencies are likely to lose experienced personnel to colleges and universities.

9. Staff members should be made to feel that they are engaged in work that is basic to the pursuit of scholarly research, and they should be encouraged to undertake research projects of their own. In the interest of maintaining professional contacts and morale, professional staff members should be enabled to attend the meetings of learned societies, particularly those of representative professional organizations such as the Society of American Archivists, and adequate funds for this purpose should be included in the budget. Service as an officer of a learned society should constitute an acceptable part of the workload of a professional archivist.

Physical Facilities

1. Because of its responsibility for irreplaceable documentary material, the archival agency must be housed in a fire-resistive building, which should comply with the standards of the National Fire Protection Association. The premises it occupies must be safe from floods, steam and water pipes, and other possible hazards to the holdings, and they must be structurally adequate to support the required weight loads.

2. The building should be planned and equipped to meet all demands of archival preservation and service. Its temperature and humdity should be controlled in all areas where records are stored or used.

In the building the following facilities should be provided: an entrance hall, which may also serve for exhibits; offices easily accessible to visitors; a research room also easily accessible and designed for effective supervision of searchers; photographic and document repair laboratories; a receiving area with cleaning facilities and a fumigating vault; and stack areas and vaults specially equipped and protected for archival storage. The following are among desirable facilities to be provided: an exhibition hall, a conference room. an auditorium.

3. While such an arrangement is not ideal, the archival agency may share its building with a functionally related agency or organization, provided that it occupies separate premises and that the entire building is fire-resistive.

If the archival agency shares the building with the state library or the state historical society, or is part of one of these, it need not build up a strong historical library (though it must have its own collection of technical and reference publications), for its users will have easy access to the library and manuscript collections of the historical society or state library. In a number of states the archival agency and the records center have been housed in the same building; this has advantages from the standpoint of centralized reference service, particularly to government agencies.

FUNCTIONS OF STATE ARCHIVAL AGENCIES

Administration of Permanently Valuable Records

1. Assembling, preserving, and servicing the permanently valuable records of the state is the central and primary responsibility of the state archival agency.

This mandate of the state archival agency includes responsibility for the records of the judicial and legislative branches of the government as well as those of the executive branch.

2. Responsibility of the archival agency for the public records of the state should extend to the records of the state's political subdivisions, even if they are not physically concentrated in the agency.

Responsibility for Records Management

1. In most of the states known to lead in archival administration, the administration of the records management and archives functions has been combined in the hands of one official, frequently designated as state archivist and records administrator.

This is the most desirable arrangement because the effectiveness of the archivist's work depends to a considerable extent on the way records are created and maintained in the agencies of origin.

2. If the records management function is administered by or in an agency other than the state archives, close co-operation between the state archivist and the records administrator is essential.

3. For standards that should apply to the archivist's role in records management, see under "The Archival Agency and Records Management," below.

[356]

Historical Activities

1. As the legal custodian of the state's permanent records, the state archival agency should occupy an important place in the historical activities of the state.

> Historical activities that might be undertaken or assisted by the archival agency include: the collection and preservation of non-official records, private papers, and other documentary material; the publication of official and non-official records and of other documentary material (see also under "Publication," below); archeological research and excavations; the formulation of texts for historical markers and erecting and maintaining them; the restoration, maintenance, and interpretation of historic sites and buildings; the establishment and administration of a state historical or archeological museum; the publication of the state historical journal; assistance to local historical societies and museums; the publication of histories of the state and of monographs pertaining to phases and aspects of the history of the state and its subdivisions; and preparation for, and participation in, the commemoration of historical events.

2. While none of these activities is incompatible with the basic mandate of the archival agency, they should be undertaken only if discharging them does not interfere with the agency's primary archival responsibility.

3. Where they are undertaken, they should have a separate budget, and a separate and competent staff should be assigned to them.

Collecting of Non-official Records and Private Papers

1. It is in the interest of historical and other serious research if, in addition to public records, non-official records and private papers are assembled and accessible in the state archival agency.

> As a corollary, the state archival agency should limit itself strictly to official records unless assigned responsibility for collecting non-official records and private papers. If assigned such responsibility, the archival agency should emphasize the acquiring of papers of residents of the state who have been prominent in the public affairs of the United States and of the state and its subdivisions.

2. The collecting, processing, and describing of private papers is a time-consuming activity and should not be undertaken by the archival agency unless a special staff, including a field representative, can be assigned to it.

3. Where in a given state there exist one or more institutions actively pursuing the acquisition of non-official and private papers, such as a state historical society or the manuscript division of a state library or of a major university library, the field should be left to them.

> As an exception to this rule, a state archival agency might continue its collecting activities if traditionally it has been a depository for non-official records and private papers.

[357]

4. Mixed bodies of materials — that is, collections consisting of both public records and private papers — should under all circumstances be taken over by the state archival agency rather than be divided with the components going to different establishments.

Responsibility for Printed Government Documents

1. Responsibility for assembling and preserving a complete record set of published state documents normally rests with the state archivist.

> Inasmuch as these documents constitute part of the records of state agencies and institutions, the record set should normally be preserved in the state archives together with the unpublished records. This responsibility may be discharged by arrangement with the state library or other appropriate state institution. Also, unless close at hand, complete sets of the laws, legislative proceedings, and other governmental publications should be available in the state archives for the convenience of staff and searchers.

2. If there is no other agency to undertake the task, the state archival agency should prepare and issue annual or biennial lists of all state publications.

THE ARCHIVES FUNCTION

Control Over the Disposal of Public Records

1. Official records of the state must not be destroyed or scheduled for destruction without the approval of the state archivist.

> Disposal authority may be vested in the state archivist, a committee, or a board composed of state officials. Where it rests with a committee or board the archivist should be a member, and his affirmative vote should be required for disposal approval.

2. Inventorying of records in agency custody, as a first step toward preparing retention and disposal schedules, and scheduling of records are best handled by state archives personnel, unless there are available the services of a separate records management agency or an agency records officer. (See also under "The Archival Agency and Records Management," below.)

> In states in which disposal lists and schedules are prepared by the records manager of the state, the archivist should have ample opportunity to examine the series specified for either retention or destruction and should be a member of the committee that has authority in the matter.

3. Disposal of local records should similarly be subject to the approval of the state archivist.

Assembling the State's Archives

1. There should be a program for the orderly accessioning of the state's records of permanent or long-term value.

Ideally, accessions should reach the archival agency in a steady flow through the operation of approved retention and disposal schedules. Where schedules are not yet in effect, records should be accessioned in blocks of a size likely to facilitate the process of integrating them with existing holdings. Piecemeal transfer of records from agency to archival custody should be discouraged.

2. A concerted effort should be made to acquire records unduly retained by agencies or in danger of physical deterioration. This will be facilitated by a legal provision to the effect that state agencies should not keep records more than 50 years old unless the head of the agency certifies in writing that they are needed for the dispatch of the agency's current business.

3. With regard to the accessioning of local records, see under "Care and Preservation of Local Archives," below.

Preservation and Rehabilitation of Records

1. The archival agency is responsible for protecting from physical deterioration the records entrusted to it.

Before being placed on the shelves, accessions should be fumigated to free them of vermin and other pests and should be cleaned.

2. Lamination of records, preceded by deacidification, has become the accepted method of rehabilitating paper records in need of repair.

Lamination is needed for the rehabilitation not merely of the older documents. Records of the "wood pulp age" (beginning about 1850) often need protection against decay, and hence lamination equipment should be on hand in every state.

Arrangement of Holdings

1. Archival holdings must be arranged in accordance with the universally accepted principle of provenance, according to which records of different origin must not be intermingled. They should be retained in their original order unless exceptional circumstances dictate otherwise.

Normally, the permanently valuable records of one agency will be set up as a record group. Records of small agencies, boards, commissions, and committees may be considered subgroups of a collective record group, particularly if they pertain to the same or similar functions.

2. Organization of record groups in accordance with a preconceived scheme that assigns a place to the records of each agency that has transferred records, or will do so in the future, has much to recommend it.

3. Private papers normally should be organized in accordance with archival principles of arrangement.

Where a collection of private papers does not have a discernible pattern of arrangement that can be followed, the different modes of arrangement —

chronological, by name of correspondent, and by subject — should be carefully considered before one is chosen.

Description of Records

1. A finding aid program should determine the types of finding aids to be produced and assign priorities to meet the needs of government agencies, research workers, and others.

> The inventory is generally considered the basic archival finding aid. It normally describes a record group, series by series. Additional finding aids, such as itemized lists, calendars, and indexes, might be considered for groups with high reference value.

2. A general guide to the holdings should be published, and whenever necessary it should be revised and republished.

> An archival agency cannot fulfill its mission unless there is available a finding aid of this kind that enables users, particularly those at a distance, to acquaint themselves in a general way with the holdings of the agency. (See also 3 under "Publication," below.)

3. The all-inclusive dictionary type of catalog organized along library catalog lines, including index entries, can provide a practical device for the description of archival holdings, if — but only if — experienced staff and time can be devoted to preparing main and secondary entries and to keeping the catalog up to date.

Reference Service

1. Rendering reference service to agencies of the state government and to private persons engaged in research is one of the fundamental duties of the state archival agency.

2. Reference service to government and its various units and subdivisions must take precedence over all other types of reference service.

3. For reference service on the premises, a properly equipped research room within easy reach of the stacks is necessary. Searchers, of course, should not be permitted to enter the stacks.

> Access to the research room should be controlled, and precautionary measures must be adopted to prevent searchers from damaging, disarranging, or removing documents from the files. Rules for the use of records in a research room should be clearly stated and posted or published, and a staff member should be present at all times to assist and supervise searchers. There should be no fee for making records available in the research room.

4. There should be a definite policy governing the extent of research that may be done for persons at a distance.

> Normally the archival agency should supply data that can be obtained from finding aids but should not conduct extensive searches in the records themselves.

5. Users should be provided with photographic copies and other reproductions of documents at a reasonable cost, if the staff time required to locate such documents is not excessive.

Extensive orders for whole runs or series of records should be filled to the extent that there are available, beyond normal demands, sufficient funds and staff time for preparing the records for microfilming; and generally a master negative should be retained so that the originals need not be filmed again.

6. Preparation of reference statistics should receive careful attention, for it is mainly through such statistics that the archival agency can demonstrate to state fiscal authorities its value and its needs.

Photographic Reproduction

1. An archival agency without photographic equipment and staff and funds to operate such equipment has become unthinkable.

2. In the interest of economy and efficiency the archival agency (or, if separate, the records management agency of the state) should administer a centralized microfilm program for all state agencies and departments.

Where no such centralized microfilm program is authorized, the setting up of agency microfilm operations and the purchase of equipment for this purpose should be subject to the approval of the archivist or the records administrator.

3. Microfilming for preservation purposes, when the original records are to be destroyed, should be limited to records of long-term value that for reasons of bulk are more economically preserved on film; to records of high research value; and, for security purposes, to records essential for the continuity of the government of the state and the protection of the rights of the citizens.

4. Indiscriminate microfilming not related to and controlled by a retention and disposal program is wasteful. Where uncontrolled programs are in progress they should be suspended until a records control system has been installed.

Publication

1. An archival agency should have a well-considered publication program to make its services and holdings known, to help the scholar at a distance prepare for and use these services and holdings, to give public officials advice on records management, and to insure and enhance its status as an effective agency of government.

A publication program should include or envisage the following publications: annual or biennial reports; guides, inventories, and other finding aids; records management guides, reports, and manuals; documentary publications; articles by staff members in learned journals, the state manual or yearbook; an official gazette; information leaflets and bulletins for the general public; and catalogs of permanent and temporary exhibits.

2. Every archival agency should publish an annual or biennial report.

Publication of a report is needed for a variety of purposes: it serves as an account to the government and the citizens of the state of the use that has been made of the funds appropriated; it acquaints both with the services the archives can render and thus prompts them to use its resources; and it facilitates the exchange of experience among state archivists, helps to create among them a common philosophy, and fosters the application of common techniques.

3. Publication of a guide to its holdings is a duty of the state archives.

The guide is a general finding aid that the searcher should be able to consult before he turns to the archival agency for information or plans to use its holdings, and it will spare the archival agency many unnecessary inquiries. Unless such guides are published, scholars will not be educated to consult archival material as they have learned to use the collections of the great manuscript depositories of the country.

4. Inventories and other finding aids should be published for groups of records and private papers subject to frequent consultation.

For disorganized groups or physically dispersed series of high reference value the publication of calendars should be considered. Calendars might also be considered for the purpose of bringing together abstracts of documents in different series relating to a subject, person, or place.

5. Articles and news notes for learned journals should be prepared to acquaint scholars with the services of the archival agency in general, its holdings and recent accessions.

Articles might also be used to point out themes, subjects, and new approaches that could be successfully developed on the basis of the holdings of the archival agency.

6. Records management manuals and guides should be issued to acquaint public officials with the essentials of good record-making and record-keeping.

If these documents are prepared and issued by a separate records management agency, the state archivist should have the opportunity to contribute to them regarding the discussion of proper storage methods, documentation of essential state functions, and filing systems that will facilitate the selection of records of enduring value.

7. The archival agency should undertake, or arrange for, the full-text letterpress publication, with appropriate editorial treatment, of archival documents of important value for scholarly research or of wide public interest.

Publication is merely an extension of reference service in that it is the normal way an archivist makes documents available for widest use. Letterpress publication, because of its expense, should be conservatively used and carefully planned. Scholars not on the staff may be invited to edit such documents under various arrangements, but if publication is sponsored by the archival agency the archivist should establish standards and approve the manuscript. Editing and publishing projects that may be privately initiated and privately financed should also be encouraged and generously assisted when they are properly planned and executed.

8. Publication on microfilm should be considered primarily for the complete publication of series. Uniform standards of editing microfilm publications should be developed.

9. The archivist is ideally fitted to prepare and publish the annual or biennial yearbook or manual of the state.

Not only are he and his staff familiar with the legal background, organization, and functioning of the state government, but also they will profit from this task, because it will enable them to stay in constant touch with the workings of state agencies and with administrative changes. Publication of the yearbook should be an item specifically recognized in the budget, and it should be handled by an editor under the supervision of the archivist.

10. Leaflets describing the archival institution, its holdings, and its services should be made available to the general public.

Such leaflets should include a statement of the hours when the building is open and other information useful to the searcher at a distance.

11. The archival agency charged with general historical functions should issue a periodical newsletter for the benefit of local historical societies, their members, and the general public.

Exhibits

1. Provision should be made for both permanent and temporary exhibits of archival material. The state's constitution and key documents of its colonial or territorial period might be displayed in a permanent exhibit. Temporary exhibits should be planned to commemorate significant events in the state's history and the services and contributions of its outstanding citizens.

2. Exhibits should be located in space that can be kept under effective control, and documents on exhibit should be especially protected from damage by light and heat.

Care and Preservation of Local Archives

1. Whether or not it is charged with this function by law, the state archival agency cannot escape responsibility for the care and protection of local archives.

Local archives contain "grass-roots" information pertaining to the history of the state and data of the highest importance for research purposes.

2. Preservation of local archives is best achieved by concentrating them, whenever practicable, in the custody of the state archival agency.

> Where wholesale concentration of local archives is not possible or practical, at least records of the colonial, territorial, and early statehood periods should be concentrated in the state archives.

3. Insofar as physical concentration of local archives proves impractical, their preservation can be safeguarded by one of two measures: (*a*) the microfilming of records of permanent value, the storing of security copies, and the making available of reference copies in the state archival agency; or (*b*) the establishment of regional depositories for the preservation and administration of the originals.

> Microfilming of local records and concentration of copies in the state archives not only provide security copies of the records but also enable the searcher to use local records in one central spot, where pertinent state agency records and other local records are also accessible to him. Next to physical concentration of the records, a microfilming program of this kind is the best protective device and is superior to the use of regional depositories. The latter should be established only in connection with the libraries of large state institutions of higher learning, where there are fully adequate facilities and where records will be serviced by competent staffs. The number of regional depositories should be kept to a minimum, legal custody of the records should be vested in the state archival agency, and processing — including the preparation of finding aids — must remain the task of the state archives staff.

THE ARCHIVAL AGENCY AND RECORDS MANAGEMENT

General Considerations

1. The interests of the state in the proper selection and preservation of its archives are served best if the records management and archival functions are administered by the same agency.

> If the two functions are assigned to different agencies, however, there should be close co-operation between them as well as a clear demarkation of their respective responsibilities.

2. The combined archival–records management agency must have qualified staffs to administer both functions.

> The records management program calls for the services of specialists competent to handle all phases of this rapidly expanding field. Responsibility for the archives function must be assigned to staff members who, in addition to technical knowledge, have the necessary academic experience in history and other social sciences.

3. Where records management and archives administration are assigned to different agencies, the archivist should have an opportunity to partici-

[364]

pate in the inventorying of records for appraisal and scheduling purposes.

> Working together with the records management team in conducting the inventory of records, the archivist will obtain a conspectus of the state's entire documentation process and its residues. He will also detect gaps and inadequacies that exist in the state's documentation of essential functions, a situation that must concern him as the custodian and administrator of the permanently valuable records of the state.

4. The appraisal of records is essentially a function of the archivist.

5. No matter where the records management function is located, there are a number of "musts" on which the operation and success of the archival agency normally depends: (*a*) the total record holdings of the state must be under inventory control; (*b*) their disposition must be regulated by means of retention and disposal schedules; (*c*) there must be machinery for keeping these schedules up to date and for co-ordinating common records management problems of state and local agencies; (*d*) there must be a fire-resistive records center in which semi-current records will be held for stated periods of time before their final disposition; (*e*) there must be records management service available to local government units; (*f*) there must be a program and appropriate facilities to preserve records essential to the continuity of government and to the protection of the rights of citizens.

Records Creation

1. Official records serve the purposes of perpetuating the memory of legislative, judicial, and executive action; of expediting and checking upon the execution of the administrative process; and of guaranteeing the rights and privileges of the state and its citizens. The creation of records is a concomitant of, and subordinate to, the governmental process.

2. To participate in the process of records creation in a given agency, the archivist should be able to work effectively with responsible agency personnel, unless as state records administrator he already has a share of the responsibility.

3. The archivist should have a voice in determining whether or not there are being created the records needed to document the organization, functions, and programs of the state so that the administrative and legal needs of the state and the needs of governmental, historical, and other research are adequately provided for.

> Technological progress has revolutionized the process of records creation. With a view to insuring the creation of records of permanent value and significance in accessible form, the archivist should be thoroughly conversant with the newer processes of records creation and thus able to proffer competent advice.

[365]

Current Records Maintenance

1. Current records maintenance involves the organization and storing of records through the application of proper processing and filing systems and the efficient use of space and appropriate equipment.

2. The modes of organizing and keeping records while in current use are of vital concern to the archivist, for they have a decisive effect on their accessibility when transferred to his custody.

> Experienced in servicing records organized according to various patterns, the archivist is competent to advise agencies in matters of records maintenance and standards even when he is not charged with records management duties. As an adviser, he should insist on the separation of records of presumably permanent value from those likely to be disposed of at regular intervals and should identify classes of records ultimately to be transferred to his custody.

3. The archivist should assist in planning agency finding aids that will facilitate the servicing of records after he has taken them over.

The Records Center

1. States should provide inexpensive facilities for housing, administering, and disposing of semi-current records, whenever such facilities effect economy and efficiency.

> Records centers should be located in or close to the center of government, or else messenger service should be provided between the center and the governmental offices so that agency service requests may be met expeditiously.

2. Careful service statistics should be kept to document the center's activities and to test the appropriateness of the retention periods set.

3. In states providing separate records management and archival agencies, the records center should be administered by the archival agency. Optimum reference service is achieved where records center holdings and archival holdings are both administered as part of the archival program.

Inventorying, Appraisal, and Scheduling

1. The total record holdings of the state should be under inventory control.

> In the inventory, series should be carefully described with regard to their content and the purpose they serve so that their significance may be properly assessed.

2. In order to be useful, inventories are best prepared by the staff of the agency charged with administering the records management function on a statewide basis, be it the state archival agency or a separate records management agency.

[366]

If inventorying is to be done by agency records officers, they must be thoroughly trained, instructed, and advised by the staff of the agency in charge of records management for the state.

3. Appraisal of records for their value to the agency of origin, to the government in general, and to researchers must precede retention and disposal judgment and decisions.

Appraisal of records for their value to the agency of origin is primarily the task of agency records officers.

Appraisal of records for their value to the government in general is primarily the task of the state records administrator and the archivist.

Appraisal of records for their value to researchers of all kinds is a function of the archivist.

4. The retention and disposal schedule as an instrument to govern the disposition of records should as soon as possible supersede the use of disposal lists prepared for the purpose of destroying accumulations of records.

5. Inasmuch as the archivist is the state's professional expert and arbiter in all matters regarding records of lasting value, records must not be destroyed without his approval. Accordingly, control over the disposal of records is dealt with under "The Archives Function," above.

APPENDIX A

ЛЛЛЛ

A Selective Glossary of Terms

NOTE: In preparing this glossary, the author has made extensive use of the draft *Glossary of Records Terminology* of the National Archives and Records Service (Jan., 1956, proc.), 31 p.; and of the *Glossary of Archival and Records Administration Terms Applicable to the Work of the Departmental Records Branch*, compiled by Ken Munden (The Adjutant General's Office, Departmental Records Branch, *Standing Operating Procedures, Section 10*; Washington, 1957, proc.), 495 p.

Accession — (1, *vb.*) To take into the custody of an archival agency records from their creating or former custodial agency; (2, *n.*) an accumulation of records so transferred.

Appraisal — The process of determining the retention value of records, based on a study of their content, their arrangement, and their relationships to other records. Also termed "evaluation."

Archival Agency — An agency charged with identifying, appraising, assembling, preserving, arranging, describing, and providing reference service on archives (*q.v.*) and with authorizing the destruction of records of transitory value.

Archival-Historical Agency — An agency responsible both for the administration of archives and for historical activities such as the administration of historic sites and buildings, the publication of historical works and periodicals, and the maintenance of a historical museum.

Archives — Records of a government agency or other organization or institution having enduring values because of the information they contain. The term is also applied to the records of families and individuals, especially if consciously organized for preservation.

Archives Box — A container, usually of high-grade cardboard with pH neutral, for the packing and shelving of archives.

Archives–Records Management Agency — An agency responsible for both the administration of archives and the management of current records.

[368]

Arrangement — The organization of the holdings of an archival agency in accordance with the principle of provenance (*q.v.*).

Calendar — A finding aid consisting of abstracts of individual documents chronologically arranged. Calendars may be so detailed that reference to the originals is unnecessary.

Catalog — A finding aid, usually in the form of cards, describing library and archival items in alphabetical or some other predetermined order.

Classification — The process of assigning records to their places in an established "scheme of classes" in which they are normally retained after their transfer to the archival agency.

Description — The preparation of finding aids (*q.v.*) in the archival agency.

Disposal List — A document listing records proposed for destruction that, because they are not repetitive, are not suitable for periodic disposition by means of a retention and disposal schedule (*q.v.*).

Disposition Schedule — See *Retention and Disposal Schedule*.

Documents — Instruments (regardless of their physical form or characteristics) that contain information. The term "documents" includes writings, printed materials, maps, sound recordings, and motion pictures.

Evaluation — See *Appraisal*.

File — An accumulation of records created and kept in a predetermined order or sequence.

Finding Aids — The descriptive media prepared by the archival agency for the dual purpose of controlling its holdings and facilitating the finding of records or of information in the records. Finding aids include guides, inventories, shelf-lists, and calendars (*q.v.*).

Fonds — A term widely used on the continent of Europe to designate the archives of an agency, institution, or organization, and corresponding in general to the concept of the record group (*q.v.*) evolved in the United States.

Guide — A finding aid describing briefly all or part of the holdings of an archival agency.

Historical Manuscripts — This term may cover "(1) bodies or groups of papers with organic unity, in the nature of archives, personal or institutional; (2) artificial collections of manuscripts acquired by a private collector from various sources, usually gathered according to plan but without regard for *respect des fonds*; (3) individual manuscripts acquired by the repository for their special importance to research and comprising a collection of what, for want of a better term, are sometimes called 'miscellaneous manuscripts.'" [1] For unorganized papers of a personal nature the term historical manuscripts is now being super-

[1] Lester J. Cappon, "Historical Manuscripts as Archives: Some Definitions and Their Application," *American Archivist*, XIX (Apr., 1956), 104–5.

seded by the term "private papers." For "bodies or groups of papers with organic unity" the term "archives" is preferred.

Inventory — A descriptive list, usually by series, of the records, or part of the records, of an agency, institution, or organization.

Lamination — A process, normally preceded by de-acidification, of reinforcing a fragile or damaged document by enclosing it between sheets of transparent material, such as cellulose acetate foil, and bonding it to the material by the application of heat and pressure.

Microfilming — The photographic technique of producing on film miniature copies of documents.

Non-record Material — Material not included within the definition of records (*q.v.*), such as extra copies of documents and stocks of publications and processed documents.

Paperwork Management — This term includes, in addition to the area of records management (*q.v.*), the quality control of paperwork, directives management, reports management, and clerical work measurement. Frequently, however, the terms "records management" and "paperwork management" are used interchangeably.

Parent Agency — A government agency, organization, or institution of which the archival agency is a constituent part.

Provenance — The office origin of an archival unit (record group, series, folder, etc.).

Record Group — This concept, as first used in the National Archives and subsequently adopted by many state archival agencies, designates "a major archival unit established somewhat arbitrarily with due regard to the principle of provenance and to the desirability of making the unit of convenient size and character for the work of arrangement and description and for the publication of inventories." Normally the unit consists of the permanently valuable records of an agency, institution, or organization and is made up of a number of series (*q.v.*).

Records — The papers, maps, photographs, or other documentary materials, regardless of physical form or characteristics, made or received by any government agency or private institution or organization in pursuance of its legal obligations or in connection with the transaction of its business and preserved or appropriate for preservation by that agency, institution, or organization or its legitimate successor as evidence of its organization, functions, policies, decisions, procedures, operations, or other activities or because of the informational value of data contained therein.[2]

Records Center — A facility, sometimes called a record center, for the storing, servicing, and processing of records that need not be retained in

[2] This definition is based on the definition of records in the act of July 7, 1943, concerning the disposal of federal records (57 Stat. 380).

office space but must be kept for varying periods of time before their ultimate disposition (see *Records Disposition*).

Records Center Box — A container of standard dimensions, ordinarily of corrugated cardboard, used for records storage in a records center.

Records Disposal — A form of records disposition (*q.v.*) that involves the outright destruction of records.

Records Disposition — Actions taken to deal with records that are no longer needed for the current business of an agency, institution, or organization. These actions include: destruction, transfer to a records center for temporary storage, reproduction on microfilm and subsequent destruction, and transfer to an archival agency for permanent preservation.

Records Management — The ensemble of practices designed to achieve efficient and economical creation, maintenance, and disposition of records. It involves developing standards, procedures, and techniques for managing correspondence, forms, mail, and files and includes control of office filing equipment and supplies, scheduling records for disposition and administering their storage, documenting agency activities, and undertaking surveys and audits of records operations.

Records Survey — A comprehensive study of the records of one or more agencies for the purpose of "taking stock," often made as a basis for the preparation of retention and disposal schedules (*q.v.*) and for the formulation and institution of a records management program.

Retention and Disposal Schedule — A document (also called records control schedule) that, for the series of repetitive records of an agency, institution, or organization, states the periods of time for which they are to be retained in agency space; the periods of time for which they must be retained in a records center; and the periods of time or the events after which they shall be destroyed or, if of permanent value, microfilmed as a means of reducing their bulk or transferred to the archival agency.

Series — A sequence of records classified and filed in accordance with a filing system.

Shelf list — A listing of records, normally series by series, in the order in which they are kept on the shelves.

Silking — The process of reinforcing or repairing documents by pasting light, coarsely woven silk fabric on each side of the paper; sometimes called "crepelining," the "Vatican method," or the "Emery method."

APPENDIX B

꙼ꓶꓶꓶꓶ

Budgets and Professional Salaries
of State Archival Agencies

EXPLANATORY REMARKS

In the following table an attempt has been made to assemble, for comparative purposes, data pertaining to the budgets of archival and records management agencies and to their expenses for professional services. Under both budgets and professional salaries, expenses for an archival, a records management, and a combined archives and records management agency, unit, or operation have been entered in the appropriate columns.

Budget figures in themselves, however, do not give a truly reliable picture of actual costs of operation. Even in the case of an independent agency, expenses for maintenance, guard and janitor service, light, heat, and ordinary supplies may or may not be included in these costs. In the case of an archival agency that is part of a government department — a state library, a state department of archives and history, or a state historical society — the expenses reported for the archives operation normally include solely those for personnel and for specifically archival supplies.

Professional salaries paid probably give a more nearly accurate picture of what the states are spending for archival and records management purposes; and these are therefore entered in the table. The totals given do not include the salaries of technical, clerical, and janitorial personnel. In regard to professional salaries, those of the last steps within salary ranges have been used for all states that have classification and pay plans, because in such states the salaries now paid depend on each incumbent's length of service and do not lend themselves to determining how much a given state provides for professional service. Where no classification and pay plans are in effect, however, salary figures are based on present salaries. Furthermore, salaries of staff members who give only part of their time

[372]

to archival and records management duties have been disregarded, as have those of heads of state libraries, departments of archives and history, and so on, who devote some time to supervising archival and records management operations.

APPENDIX C

ЛЛЛЛЛ

Salaries of Heads of State Programs and of Responsible or Senior Archivists[1]

SALARY RANGE	ARCHIVAL AGENCY	RECORDS MANGEMENT AGENCY	COMBINED AGENCY	RESPONSIBLE OR SENIOR ARCHIVISTS
$3,000– $4,000				1
$4,000– $5,000	1			1
$5,000– $6,000				4
$6,000– $7,000	1			10
$7,000– $8,000		3	2	9
$8,000– $9,000	6	2	1	7
$9,000– $10,000	4	2	3	3
$10,000– $11,000	7	1	2	
$11,000– $12,000	1		2	
$12,000– $13,000	1	1	2	
$13,000– $14,000				
$14,000– $15,000		2	1	

[1] Within each salary range, the number of persons earning that salary has been indicated.

[374]

ⅬⅬⅬⅬⅬ

Record Holdings of State Archival Agencies

STATE	HOLDINGS	REMARKS
Alabama	192,000 cu. ft	Includes material ordinarily kept in records centers.
Alaska		Alaska has no archival agency.
Arizona	3,000 cu. ft.	
Arkansas	1,200 vols.	
California	18,000 cu. ft	
Colorado	8,000 cu. ft.	
Connecticut	7,000 cu. ft.	Holdings dispersed among 20 vaults of various sizes.
Delaware	15,285 cu. ft.	Includes records center holdings.
Florida	200 cu. ft.	
Georgia	1,350 cu. ft. 60,000 vols.	
Hawaii	4,450 cu. ft.	
Idaho	2,000 cu. ft.	
Illinois	80,000 cu. ft.	
Indiana	3,000 cu. ft. 15,000 vols.	
Iowa	24,000 cu. ft.	
Kansas	5,700 cu. ft.	
Kentucky		Archival holdings not yet concentrated.
Louisiana	120 cu. ft.	Department of Archives of the Louisiana State University has 1,055,000 items of state and parish archives.
Maine		Maine has no archival agency.
Maryland	1,000 cu. ft. 15,000 vols.	
Massachusetts	38,500 cu. ft.	
Michigan	3,200 cu. ft.	
Minnesota	15,000 cu. ft.	
Mississippi	9,000 cu. ft. 5,000 vols.	
Missouri		Missouri has no archival agency.

STATE	HOLDINGS	REMARKS
Montana	990 cu. ft.	
Nebraska	6,000 cu. ft.	
Nevada	Insignificant holdings	
New Hampshire	200 cu. ft.	About 225 cu. ft. of official records and church records are held by the New Hampshire Historical Society.
New Jersey	10,000 cu. ft.	Includes records center holdings.
New Mexico	764 cu. ft.	
New York	40,000 cu. ft.	
North Carolina	7,000 cu. ft.	
North Dakota	520 cu. ft.	
Ohio	12,250 cu. ft.	
Oklahoma	Not determined	
Oregon	8,400 cu. ft.	
Pennsylvania	13,500 cu. ft.	
Puerto Rico	11,700 cu. ft.	
Rhode Island	350 cu. ft. 870 vols.	
South Carolina	20,000 cu. ft.	
South Dakota	Small holdings	
Tennessee	60,000 cu. ft.	Includes material ordinarily kept in records centers.
Texas	30,000 cu. ft.	
Utah	1,000 cu. ft.	
Vermont	500 cu. ft.	
Virginia	4,000 cu. ft. 63,000 vols.	
Washington	45,000 cu. ft.	Includes records center holdings.
West Virginia	3,500 cu. ft.	This figure refers to the West Virginia Collection.
Wisconsin	23,500 cu. ft.	Does not include the rich holdings of the Manuscripts Section.
Wyoming	1,250 cu. ft.	Does not include 1,000 cu. ft. of private papers in the Historical Division of the Archives and Historical Department.

ЛЛЛЛ

Basic Bibliography of Writings on Public Archives Administration in the United States

INTRODUCTORY NOTE

Because this report is intended to contribute to good archives-keeping throughout the nation, it is appropriate to include a short bibliography of writings on public archives administration. This will enable government officials, legislators, and others interested to explore those aspects and phases of archival organization and administration that may be of concern to them.

The bibliography has been limited to general works and articles, except for some items dealing with practices of the federal government and of individual states that are of general significance, and only a few particularly important works in foreign languages have been entered. Publications of state archival agencies and articles pertaining to the development, status, and functions of these agencies will be found in the appropriate sections of Chapter II. In the items below the symbol *AA* represents the *American Archivist*, and NA is used for the National Archives.

A. THE EVOLUTION AND STATUS OF PUBLIC ARCHIVES ADMINISTRATION
IN THE UNITED STATES

European Backgrounds

BAUTIER, ROBERT-HENRI. "Les Archives," in Charles Samaran (ed.), *L'Histoire et ses méthodes*, pp. 1120–66. Paris: Librairie Gallimard, 1961. Excellent survey of archival development.

BLEGEN, THEODORE C. "Archives and Their Administration: A Study of European and American Practices," in his *A Report on the Public Archives* ("State Historical Society of Wisconsin Bulletins of Information," No. 94), pp. 13–62. Madison: The Society, 1918.

BRENNEKE, ADOLF. *Archivkunde: Ein Beitrag zur Theorie und Geschichte des europäischen Archivwesens*, ed. Wolfgang Leesch. Leipzig: Koehler & Amelang, 1953.

POSNER, ERNST. "Some Aspects of Archival Development Since the French Revolution," *AA*, III (July, 1940), 159–72.

Archival Developments in the United States in General

BAUER, G. PHILIP. "Public Archives in the United States," in William B. Hesseltine and Donald R. McNeil (eds.), *In Support of Clio: Essays in Memory of Herbert A. Kellar*, pp. 49–76. Madison: State Historical Society of Wisconsin, 1958.

BUTTERFIELD, LYMAN H. "Archival and Editorial Enterprise in 1850 and 1950; Some Comparisons and Contrasts," American Philosophical Society, *Proceedings*, XCVIII (1954), 159–70.

HAMER, PHILIP M. (ed.). *A Guide to Archives and Manuscripts in the United States*, compiled for the National Historical Publications Commission. New Haven: Yale University Press, 1961.

LELAND, WALDO G. "The First Conference of Archivists, December 1909: The Beginnings of a Profession," *AA*, XIII (Apr., 1950), 109–20.

The National Union Catalog of Manuscript Collections, 1959–1961 — 1962. 3 vols. Ann Arbor, Mich.: J. W. Edwards; Hamden, Conn.: Shoe String Press; 1962–64. "Compiled by the Library of Congress . . . from reports provided by American repositories of manuscripts." *Index 1959–1962.*

WHITEHILL, WALTER M. *Independent Historical Societies: An Enquiry Into Their Research and Publication Functions and Their Financial Future.* Boston: Athenæum, 1962.

Federal Archival Developments

BAHMER, ROBERT H. "The National Archives After 20 Years," *AA*, XVIII (July, 1955), 195–205.

BUCK, ELIZABETH H. "The National Archives and Records Service of the United States," *Archivum*, XI (1961), 121–35.

GROVER, WAYNE C. "Federal Government Archives," *Library Trends*, V (Jan., 1957), 390–96.

———. "The National Archives at Age 20," *AA*, XVII (Apr., 1954), 99–107.

KAHN, HERMAN. "The Presidential Library — a New Institution," *Special Libraries*, L (Mar., 1959), 106–13.

KRAUSKOPF, ROBERT W. "The Hoover Commissions and Federal Record-keeping," *AA*, XXI (Oct., 1958), 371–99.

SHELLEY, FRED. "The Interest of J. Franklin Jameson in the National Archives: 1908–1934," *AA*, XII (Apr., 1949), 99–130.

ALDERSON, WILLIAM T. (comp.). *Directory of State and Provincial Archivists and Records Administrators, 1963.* Nashville, Tenn.: Society of American Archivists, 1963, proc. The first such directory was prepared by the society's Committee on State Archives in 1951, updated by the editor of the *AA*, and published in Vol. XVII (July, 1954), 209–19. Directories were also published in 1959 and 1961 (H. G. Jones, ed.) and in 1962 (William T. Alderson, ed.).

BAHMER, ROBERT H. "The Archival Function in the States," *AA*, XXII (Apr., 1959), 203–9.

BRYAN, MARY GIVENS (comp.). *Comparative Study of State and U.S. Territorial Laws Governing Archives.* 2 vols. N.p.: Society of American Archivists, 1955, 1956, proc.

———. "Trends of Organization in State Archives," *AA*, XXI (Jan., 1958), 31–42.

GATES, CHARLES M. "The Administration of State Archives," *AA*, I (July, 1938), 130–41. Also *Pacific Northwest Quarterly*, XXIX (Jan., 1938), 27–39.

"How Can the States Be Persuaded To Take Care of Their Historical Archives?" *Annual Report of the American Historical Association for the Year 1922*, I, 120–51. Includes reports by R. D. W. Connor (North Carolina), Cassius C. Stiles (Iowa), and George S. Godard (Connecticut)

JONES, H. C. (ed.). *Guide to State and Provincial Archival Agencies, 1961.* [Raleigh, N.C.]: Society of American Archivists, 1961, proc.

———. "State Archival–Records Management Programs in the United States," *Archivum*, XI (1961), 135–42.

NEWSOME, ALBERT R. "Uniform State Archival Legislation," *AA*, II (Jan., 1939), 1–16.

NORTON, MARGARET C. "The Archives Department as an Administrative Unit in Government," National Association of State Libraries, *Papers and Proceedings, 1930*, pp. 44–48. Also in American Library Association, *Bulletin*, XXIV (Sept., 1930), 563–67.

———. "Organizing a New State Archives Department," *Illinois Libraries*, XXVIII (Dec., 1946), 496–503.

———. "The Place of Archives in Government," *ibid.*, XXXIV (Apr., 1952), 153–60.

———. "Scope and Functions of a State Archives Department," National Association of State Libraries, *Proceedings and Papers, 1936–37*, pp. 15–20. Also in Society of American Archivists, *Proceedings, 1936–37*, proc., pp. 75–82, and in American Library Association, *Public Documents, 1937*, pp. 262–75.

PALTSITS, VICTOR H. "An Historical Résumé of the Public Archives Commission from 1899 to 1921," *Annual Report of the American Historical Association for the Year 1922*, I, 152–60.

SMILEY, DAVID L. "The W.P.A. Historical Records Survey," *In Support of Clio*, pp. 3–28. Madison: State Historical Society of Wisconsin, 1958.

SOCIETY OF AMERICAN ARCHIVISTS. State Archives (Records) Committee. *Reports*. N.p.: Society of American Archivists, 1956, proc. Includes reports on records disposal policies (Robert M. Brown), microphotography (Lola M. Homsher), and salaries (Gust Skordas).

——. State Records Committee. *Reports*. N.p.: Society of American Archivists, 1957, proc. Includes continuation reports on state and U.S. territorial laws (Mary Givens Bryan, comp.) and records disposal policies (Robert M. Brown, comp.), and a report on the replevin of public records (Philip P. Mason, comp.).

Local Archives

DEVALINGER, LEON, JR. "The Place of County Records in the State Archival System," with discussion by Albert C. Corey, *AA*, XI (Jan., 1948), 37–41.

McMAHON, JOHN A. "A County Official Looks at a State-Supervised County Records Program," *AA*, XXV (Apr., 1962), 211–18.

RENZE, DOLORES C. "Colorado's County Records—the Syncretic Approach," *AA*, XXV (Apr., 1962), 207–10.

RUDDELL, RICHARD. "Recent Developments in Municipal Records," *AA*, XVIII (July, 1955), 255–66.

SCAMMELL, J. M. "Local Archives and the Study of Government," *AA*, II (Oct., 1939), 225–43.

SKORDAS, GUST. "Maryland's County Records — the Eclectic Approach," *AA*, XXV (Apr., 1962), 199–206.

B. PRINCIPLES AND TECHNIQUES OF ARCHIVES ADMINISTRATION

General: Books

ENDERS, GERHART. *Archivverwaltungslehre*. Berlin: Rütten & Loening, 1962.

JENKINSON, HILARY. *A Manual of Archive Administration*. Rev. ed., London: Lund, Humphries, 1937.

MULLER, SAMUEL, J. A. FEITH, and R. FRUIN. *Manual for the Arrangement and Description of Archives*, trans. from the 2d Dutch ed. of 1920 by ARTHUR H. LEAVITT. New York: H. W. Wilson, 1940.

SCHATZ, RUDOLPH. *Behördenschriftgut — Aktenbildung, Aktenverwaltung, Archivierung*. ("Schriften des Bundesarchivs," No. 8.) Boppard a. Rh.: Boldt, 1961.

SCHELLENBERG, T. R. *Modern Archives: Principles and Techniques*. Chicago: University of Chicago Press, 1956.

General: Articles

BORN, LESTER K. "Archives," *Encyclopædia Britannica*, II (Chicago, 1962), 288–92.

BUCK, SOLON J. " 'Let's Look at the Record,' " *AA*, VIII (Apr., 1945), 109–14.

CAPPON, LESTER J. "Historical Manuscripts as Archives: Some Definitions and Their Application," *AA*, XIX (Apr., 1956), 101–10.

HOLMES, OLIVER W. " 'Public Records' — Who Knows What They Are?" *AA*, XXIII (Jan., 1960), 3–26.

LEAVITT, ARTHUR H. "What Are Archives?" *AA*, XXIV (Apr., 1961), 175–78.

NORTON, MARGARET C. "Archives and Libraries, a Comparison Drawn," *Blue Book of the State of Illinois*, 1939–40, pp. 427–43. N.p., n.d.

——. "Some Legal Aspects of Archives," *AA*, VIII (Jan., 1945), 1–11.

POSNER, ERNST. "Archives," *Collier's Enclyclopedia*, II (New York, 1962), 556–57.

U. S. NATIONAL ARCHIVES. *Archival Principles: Selections from the Writings of Waldo Gifford Leland*. ("Staff Information Papers," No. 20.) Washington, 1955, proc.

The Archivist and Records Management

ALLDREDGE, EVERETT O. "Total Paperwork Management," *NOMA Management Quarterly*, II (June, 1962), 10–22.

BEACH, REX, and JOHN T. CATON. "State and Local Government Records Programs," *AA*, XXIV (July, 1961), 289–95.

BROOKS, PHILIP C. *Public Records Management*. Chicago: Public Administration Service, 1961.

CANADA. Royal Commission on Government Organization. *Management of the Public Service*. Vol. I. Ottawa: The Commission, 1962. Part IV deals with "Paperwork and Systems Management."

JOHNSON, EDWARD N. "Trends in County Records Management," *AA*, XXIV (July, 1961), 297–301.

LEAHY, EMMETT J. *Records Management in the United States Government; a Report with Recommendations Prepared for the Commission on Organization of the Executive Branch of the Government*. Washington, 1948.

MACLEAN, IAN. "Modern Public Records Administration and the Relations of Records Officers and Archivists," *Archives — Techniques and Functions in a Modern Society; Proceedings at the Summer School in Archives Held at the University of Sidney, March 1957*, pp. 6–19. Sydney: New Century Press, 1957.

McCOOL, OLLON. "The Metes and Bounds of Records Management," *AA*, XXVII (Jan., 1964), 87–93.

Norton, Margaret C. "The Archivist Looks at Records Management," *Illinois Libraries*, XXXVIII (Sept., 1956), 222–33.

Radoff, Morris L. "What Should Bind Us Together," *AA*, XIX (Jan., 1956), 3–9. The work of the records manager and that of the archivist constitute essentially one task for which the archivist should assume responsibility.

Ross, H. John. *Paperwork Management: A Manual of Workload Reduction Techniques.* South Miami, Fla.: Office Research Institute, 1961.

The Records Center

Alldredge, Everett O. "Archival Training in a Record Center," *AA*, XXI (Oct., 1958), 401–7.

Campbell, Edward G. "Buildings and Equipment of Federal Record Centers in the United States," *Archivum*, VII (1957), 21–25.

Crittenden, Christopher. "The North Carolina Record Center," *AA*, XVIII (Jan., 1955), 53–57.

Denny, J. H. "New-Type Storage for Records," *AA*, XXIV (July, 1961), 309–12.

U.S. General Services Administration. National Archives and Records Service. *Federal Records Centers.* Rev. ed., Washington, 1963.

Training and Status of Archivists

Grover, Wayne C. "Archives: Society and Profession," *AA*, XVIII (Jan., 1955), 3–10.

Kahn, Herman. "Librarians and Archivists — Some Aspects of Their Partnership," *AA*, VII (Oct., 1944), 243–51.

Posner, Ernst. "Archival Training in the United States," *Archivum*, IV (1954), 35–47.

Schellenberg, T. R. "The Future of the Archival Profession," *AA*, XXII (Jan., 1959), 49–58.

Buildings and Equipment

Gondos, Victor, Jr. "American Archival Architecture," American Institute of Architects, *Bulletin*, I (Sept., 1947), 27–32.

National Fire Protection Association. *Protection of Records.* (Standard No. 232, rev.) Boston: National Fire Protection Association, 1963.

U.S. National Archives. *Buildings and Equipment for Archives.* ("Bulletins," No. 6.) Washington: Government Printing Office, 1944.

Preservation and Rehabilitation of Archives

Bahmer, Robert H. *Recent American Developments in Archival Repairs, Preservation and Photography.* (Report [to the] IVᵉ Congrès International des Archives, 17–20 août 1960.) Stockholm: Almqvist & Wiksell, 1960.

BARROW, WILLIAM J. *Manuscripts and Documents: Their Deterioration and Restoration.* Charlottesville: University of Virginia Press, 1955.

KATHPALIA, Y. P. "Hand Lamination with Cellulose Acetate," with comment by JAMES L. GEAR, *AA*, XXI (July, 1958), 271–76.

LANGWELL, W. H. *The Conservation of Books and Documents.* London: Pitman & Sons, 1957.

MINOGUE, ADELAIDE E. *The Repair and Preservation of Records.* ("NA Bulletins," No. 5.) Washington: Government Printing Office, 1943.

PAPRITZ, JOHANNES. *New Methods, New Materials and New Results in the Restoration and Conservation of Archives and in Documentary Phototechnique Since 1950.* (Report [to the] IVᵉ Congrès International des Archives, 17–20 août 1960.) Stockholm: Almqvist & Wiksell, 1960.

TURNER, ROBERT W. S. "To Repair or Despair?" with comment by JAMES L. GEAR, *AA*, XX (Oct., 1957), 319–34.

U.S. NATIONAL ARCHIVES. *The Rehabilitation of Paper Records.* ("Staff Information Papers," No. 16.) Washington, 1950, proc.

WILSON, WILLIAM K., and B. W. FORSHEE. *Preservation of Documents by Lamination.* ("National Bureau of Standards Monographs," No. 5.) Washington: Government Printing Office, 1959.

Photoreproduction of Archives

HALE, RICHARD W., JR. (comp.). *Guide to Photocopied Historical Materials in the United States and Canada.* Ithaca, N.Y.: Cornell University Press, 1961.

LUTHER, FREDERIC. "The Language of Lilliput: A Thesaurus for Users of Microfilm," *Library Journal,* LXXXVI (Mar., July, Oct., and Nov., 1961), 929–32, 2425–30, 3238–41, 3743–46; LXXXVII (Jan., 1962), 48–54.

McDONALD, JERRY. "The Case Against Microfilming," *AA*, XX (Oct., 1957), 345–56.

NORTON, MARGARET C. "Photography for State Records," *Illinois Libraries,* XXVIII (Feb. and Mar., 1946), 151–55 and 180–87.

TAYLOR, DOROTHY K. "State Microfilming Programs," *AA*, XXII (Jan., 1959), 59–82.

U.S. DEPARTMENT OF THE ARMY. *Microfilming of Records.* ("Technical Manuals," No. 12-257.) Rev. ed., Washington, 1955.

U.S. NATIONAL ARCHIVES. *The Preparation of Records for Publication on Microfilm.* ("Staff Information Papers," No. 19.) Washington, 1951, proc.

WEIS, MARGARET M. "The Case *for* Microfilming," *AA*, XXII (Jan., 1959), 15–24.

Disposition of Records

BAHMER, ROBERT H. "Scheduling the Disposition of Records," *AA*, VI (July, 1943), 169–75.

BAUER, G. PHILIP. *The Appraisal of Current and Recent Records*. ("NA Staff Information Circulars," No. 13.) Washington, 1946, proc.

CALKIN, HOMER L. "Inventorying Files," *Public Administration Review*, XI (Autumn, 1951), 242–52.

LAMB, W. KAYE. "The Fine Art of Destruction," in Albert E. J. Hollaender (ed.), *Essays in Memory of Sir Hilary Jenkinson*, pp. 50–56. Society of Archivists, 1962.

SCHELLENBERG, T. R. *The Appraisal of Modern Public Records*. ("NA Bulletins," No. 8.) Washington: Government Printing Office, 1956.

U. S. DEPARTMENT OF THE NAVY. Office of the Secretary. *Disposal of Navy and Marine Corps Records*. Washington: Department of the Navy, 1961, proc. An excellent example of an agency manual.

U. S. GENERAL SERVICES ADMINISTRATION. National Archives and Records Service. *Applying Records Schedules*. Rev. ed., Washington: Government Printing Office, 1961.

Arrangement and Description of Records

HAMER, PHILIP M. "Finding Mediums in the National Archives: An Appraisal of Six Years' Experience," *AA*, V (Apr., 1942), 82–92.

HOLMES, OLIVER W. "Archival Arrangement — Five Different Operations at Five Different Levels," *AA*, XXVII (Jan., 1964), 21–41.

MUNDEN, KENNETH. "The Identification and Description of the Records Series," *AA*, XIII (July, 1950), 213–27.

RADOFF, MORRIS L. "A Guide to Practical Calendaring" and "A Practical Guide to Calendaring," *AA*, XI (Apr. and July, 1948), 123–40 and 203–22.

U.S. NATIONAL ARCHIVES. *The Control of Records at the Record Group Level*. ("Staff Information Circulars," No. 15.) Washington, 1950, proc.

———. *The Preparation of Lists of Record Items*. ("Staff Information Papers," No. 17, Rev.) Washington, 1960, proc.

———. *The Preparation of Preliminary Inventories*. ("Staff Information Circulars," No. 14.) Washington, 1950, proc.

———. *Principles of Arrangement*. ("Staff Information Papers," No. 18.) Washington, 1951, proc.

VAN SCHREEVEN, WILLIAM J. "Information Please: Findings Aids in State and Local Archival Depositories," *AA*, V (July, 1942), 169–78.

Special Types of Archives

BAUMHOFER, HERMINE M. "Film Records Management," *AA*, XIX (July, 1956), 235–48.

FRIIS, HERMAN R. "Cartographic and Related Records: What Are They, How Have They Been Produced and What Are Problems of Their Administration?" *AA*, XIII (Apr., 1950), 135–55.

McCAMY, C. S. *Inspection of Processed Photographic Record Films for Aging Blemishes.* ("National Bureau of Standards Handbooks," No 96.) Washington: Government Printing Office, 1964.

NOLL, DANIEL F. "The Maintenance of Microfilm Files," *AA*, XIII (Apr., 1950), 129–34.

U. S. LIBRARY OF CONGRESS. Reference Department. Map Division. *Maps: Their Care, Repair and Preservation in Libraries.* Rev. ed. by CLARA EGLI LE GEAR. Washington, 1956.

VANDERBILT, PAUL. *Notes on Care and Arrangement of Picture Collections.* Madison: State Historical Society, 1955, proc.

Reference Service

CONNOR, SEYMOUR V. "The Problem of Literary Property in Archival Depositories," *AA*, XXI (Apr., 1958), 143–52.

CROSS, HAROLD L. *The People's Right to Know: Legal Access to Public Records and Proceedings.* New York: Columbia University Press, 1953.

EVANS, FRANK B. "The State Archivist and the Academic Researcher — 'Stable Companionship'," *AA*, XXVI (July, 1963), 319–21.

LAMB, W. KAYE. "The Archivist and the Historian," *American Historical Review*, LXVIII (Jan., 1963), 385–91.

LAND, ROBERT H. "Defense of Archives Against Human Foes," with comments by LUCILE KANE and RICHARD D. HIGGINS, *AA*, XIX (Apr., 1956), 121–38.

PARKER, WYMAN W. "How Can the Archivist Aid the Researcher?" *AA*, XVI (July, 1953), 233–40.

RICHARDS, KENNETH W. "The State Archivist and the Amateur Researcher," *AA*, XXVI (July, 1963), 323–26.

RUBINCAM, MILTON. "What the Genealogist Expects of an Archival Agency or Historical Society," *AA*, XII (Oct., 1949), 333–38.

Exhibits and Publications

CARTER, CLARENCE E. *Historical Editing.* ("NA Bulletins," No. 7.) Washington: Government Printing Office, 1952.

CRITTENDEN, C. C. "Publication Policies for Archival and Historical Agencies," *AA*, III (Oct., 1940), 245–50.

HAMER, PHILIP M. "'. . . authentic Documents tending to elucidate our History'," *AA*, XXV (Jan., 1962), 3–13.

LEISINGER, ALBERT H., JR. "The Exhibit of Documents," *AA*, XXVI (Jan., 1963), 75–86.

SANBORN, HERBERT J., and NELSON R. BURR. "Exhibition Catalogs," *AA*, XVII (July, 1954), 265–71.

Protection of Records Essential to Government Continuity

COUNCIL OF STATE GOVERNMENTS. Committee of State Officials on Suggested State Legislation. *Continuity of Government: Records Management and Preservation.* N.d., n.p. Reprinted from *Suggested State Legislation, Program for 1961.*

MUNDEN, KEN. "Records Essential to Continuity of State and Local Government," *AA*, XXII (Jan., 1959), 25–37.

NATIONAL ASSOCIATION OF COUNTIES RESEARCH FOUNDATION, INC. *Records Management and Preservation for National Survival.* ("Information and Education Service Reports," No. 22.) Washington, 1962.

U. S. GENERAL SERVICES ADMINISTRATION. National Archives and Records Service. *Protecting Vital Operating Records.* Washington, 1958.

Administration of Private Papers

BOYD, JULIAN P. "The Function of State and Local Historical Societies with Respect to Manuscripts," American Library Association, *Archives and Libraries*, 1940, pp. 127–36.

BRAND, KATHERINE E. "Developments in the Handling of Recent Manuscripts in the Library of Congress," *AA*, XVI (Apr., 1953), 99–104.

——. "The Place of the Register in the Manuscripts Division of the Library of Congress," *AA*, XVIII (Jan., 1955), 59–67.

GORDON, ROBERT S. "Suggestions for Organization and Description of Archival Holdings of Local Historical Societies," *AA*, XXVI (Jan., 1963), 19–39.

JACKSON, ELLEN. "Manuscript Collections in the General Library," *Library Quarterly*, XII (Apr., 1942), 275–83.

KANE, LUCILE M. *A Guide to the Care and Administration of Manuscripts.* ("American Association for State and Local History Bulletins," Vol. II, No. 11.) Madison, Wis.: The Association, 1960.

SCHELLENBERG, T. R. "Arrangement of Private Papers," *Archives and Manuscripts*, [I] (Aug., 1957), 1–20.

——. "Description of Private Papers," *Archives and Manuscripts*, I (Aug., 1958), 1–19.

WILSON, WILLIAM J. "Manuscript Cataloging," *Traditio*, XII (1956), 458–555.

INDEX

ЛЛЛЛЛ

NOTE: Because of the nature and purpose of this study and the presence of an analytical table of contents, the index deviates somewhat from standard practice. The introduction and Chapters I, III, and IV have been indexed in depth. For Chapter II, which contains the essays on the development and status of archives administration in the states, the following entries only have been provided under the name of each state: the name of the state archival agency and, if different, that of the state records management agency; and a standard entry directing the reader to the section dealing with the state. To these inclusive entries for Chapter II have been added the numbers of all pages elsewhere in the book that refer to the state or agency. It has been considered unnecessary to index the names of agencies predecessor to the present archival agencies and the names of other state agencies, legislative bodies, and institutions that have been connected with, or now play some role in, the archival and records management activities of the states. All such names, however, are covered by inclusive pages under the state names. Place names irrelevant to the main theme of the study are not indexed, but personal and corporation names have been indexed throughout the book.

Archivists, Conference of (A.H.A.), 24, 25, 26, 33, 336
Archivists, Society of American. *See* Society of American Archivists.
Arizona: archival development and legislation, organization for archival service, the archives function, records management and records disposition, care of local records, 45–49. *See also* 4, 327, 340, 375, *and Appendix B.*
Arizona Department of Library and Archives, 45–49, 312, 322. *See also Appendix B.*
Arkansas: archival development and legislation, organization for archival service, the archives function, records management and records disposition, care of local records, 49–53. *See also* 4, 320, 375, *and Appendix B.*
Arkansas History Commission, 21, 49–53, 312, 325. *See also Appendix B.*
Arrangement, 14, 34, 328–31; defined, 369; standards, 359. *See also Chapter II under state names.*

Bahmer, Robert H., 3, 5
Bancroft, George, 16
Barbour, Col. Lucius C., 15
Barrington Associates, 238
Barrow, W. J., 282
Bartlett, Richard, 14
Benedon, William, 184
Berkeley, John, Lord, 183
Bevan, Joseph V., 11, 84
Binkley, Robert C., 28
Blegen, Theodore C., 297
Boell, Jesse E., 29
Bond, Carroll T., 136
Bowman, Jacob N., 57, 285
Bray, Mayfield, 3
British Record Commissions, 11, 12
Brodhead, J. Romeyn, 12
Brown, Robert M., 3
Bryan, Mary G., 36
Buck, Elizabeth H., 5
Buck, Solon J., 2, 26–29 *passim,* 154, 195
Budgets, 314–16; standards for, 353. *See also Chapter II under state names and Appendix B.*
Buildings, archival, 30, 319–21; standards for, 355–56. *See also Chapter II under state names.*
Burgess, John W., 16
Burnett, Edmund C., 18
Burrage, Henry S., 132
Burt, Harold S., 73, 274

Calendars, 331, 334; defined, 369
California: archival development and legislation, organization for archival service, the archives function, records management and records disposition, care of local records, 53–60. *See also* 4, 315, 320, 325, 326, 375, *and Appendix B.*
California Department of General Services, Management Research Section, 57–60, 314, 338, 341. *See also Appendix B.*
California Secretary of State, Archives and Central Record Depository, 32, 53–60, 312, 329, 339, 342, 344, 345. *See also Appendix B.*
Cappon, Lester J., 27, 29, 35, 279
Carnegie Institution of Washington, 2
Carteret, Sir George, 183
Catalogs, 330, 331, 347; defined, 369
Chatelain, Verne E., 28
Checklists, 330
Child, Sargent B., 28
Civil and Defense Mobilization, Office of, 34, 35. *See also* Essential records.
Civil Works Authority, 28
Clapp, Verner W., 6
Clark, Thomas D., 120, 121
Classification, defined, 369
Cogswell, Joseph G., 16
Colonies, record-keeping in, 7–10
Colorado: archival development and legislation, organization for archival service, the archives function, records management and records disposition, care of local records, 60–68. *See also* 4, 22, 309, 321, 322, 323, 325, 326, 327, 330, 338, 341, 375, *and Appendix B.*
Colorado Executive Department, Division of State Archives and Public Records, 60–68, 312, 313, 314, 319, 320, 337, 342–46 *passim. See also Appendix B.*
Conference of Archivists (A.H.A.), 24, 25, 26, 33, 336
Connecticut: archival development and legislation, organization for archival service, the archives function, records management and records disposition, care of local records, 68–74; colonial records, 10. *See also* 4, 15, 19, 274, 312, 321, 339, 340, 341, 375, *and Appendix B.*
Connecticut State Library, 24, 32, 68–74. *See also Appendix B.*
Connor, R. D. W., 29, 30, 204, 208
Continental Congress, 11
Continuity of government, records essen-

tial to, 34, 323, 341–42, 365. *See also Chapter II under state names.*

Cook, Mrs. Roy B., 291

Copying of records, 11, 12, 13. *See also* Microfilming.

Council of State Governments, suggested legislation, 35, 254, 309, 341

Council on Library Resources, 3–6 *passim*, 79

County records. *See* Local archives.

Court records, local, 15, 34, 35

Crittenden, Christopher, 3, 9, 29

Cromwell, Emma G., 120

Current records, 366. *See also* Records management *and* Schedules.

Daniel, Gov. Price, 264

Davis, Edwin A., 126, 127

Dawson, Edgar, 74

Definitions of terms used, 368–71

Delaware: archival development and legislation, organization for archival service, the archives function, records management and records disposition, care of local records, 74–81. *See also* 4, 33, 309, 321–25 *passim*, 327, 334, 336, 341, 342, 347, 375, *and Appendix B.*

Delaware Public Archives Commission, 21, 32, 74–81, 311, 312, 314, 319, 328, 337. *See also Appendix B.*

Description of records, 18, 21, 34, 328–31; defined, 369; standards for, 360. *See also* Finding aids *and Chapter II under state names.*

deValinger, Leon, Jr., 6, 78

Dewing, Charles E., 239

Directories of archival agencies, 35, 36

Disposal list, defined, 369. *See also* Records disposal.

Dobie, J. Frank, 263

Document, defined, 369

Documentary publication, 10–13 *passim*, 27, 31

Documents issued by state, printed, 347, 358

Draper, Lyman C., 256

Duniway, David C., 2, 3, 35

Dupont Co., 73

Duties of archival agencies. *See* Functions of archival agencies *and Chapter II under state names.*

Easterby, J. H., 248, 251

Eddy, Henry H., 29, 274

Educational institutions, co-operation with, 342–44. *See also Chapter II under state names.*

Emery Record Preserving Co., 71, 145, 321

England, 10, 11, 12, 18

Essential records, 34, 323, 341–42, 365. *See also Chapter II under state names.*

Europe, 29; archives in, 1, 2, 7, 10, 16. *See also individual nations.*

Evans, Luther H., 28, 195

Everett, Edward, 16

Exhibits, 335, 363. *See also Chapter II under state names.*

Federal Emergency Relief Administration, 28, 176

Federal-State Relations, S.A.A. Committee on, 36

Felt, Joseph B., 14, 143

File, defined, 369

Finding aids, defined, 369. *See also* Calendars, Guides, Indexes, *and* Inventories.

Fire Protection Association, National, 355

Fire resistance. *See* Physical facilities.

Fish, Carl R., 22

Florida: archival development and legislation, organization for archival service, the archives function, records management and records disposition, care of local records, 81–84. *See also* 4, 375, *and Appendix B.*

Florida State Library and Historical Archives, 81–84, 312, 319. *See also Appendix B.*

Fonds, defined, 369

Force, Peter, 11

Ford, Worthington C., 89

France, 7, 10, 12, 23

Fumigation, 321. *See also* Physical facilities.

Functions of archival agencies, 31, 313–14; non-archival, 342–48; standards for, 356–64. *See also Chapter II under state names.*

Garrison, Curtis W., 29

Genealogical Society of the Church of Jesus Christ of Latter-day Saints. *See* Utah Genealogical Society.

Georgia: archival development and legislation, organization for archival service, the archives function, records management and records disposition, care of local records, 84–89. *See also* 4, 11, 321, 323, 325, 327, 329, 335, 336, 375, *and Appendix B.*

Georgia Secretary of State: Department of Archives and History, 21, 84–89, 312, 320, 344; Microfilm Division, 88. *See also Appendix B.*

[389]

Germany, 12, 16, 17, 23
Gillis, J. L., 24
Glossary of archival and records management terms, 368–71
Godard, George S., 71
Godfrey, Carlos E., 184
Green, John S., 246
Guides, 21, 330, 334, 343, 347, 362; defined, 369. *See also Chapter II under state names.*

Hamer, Philip M., 3
Harlow, George H., 23
Hawaii: archival development and legislation, organization for archival service, the archives function, records management and records disposition, care of local records, 89–94. *See also 4, 321, 322, 341, 375, and Appendix B.*
Hawaii Department of Accounting and General Services, Archives Division, 89–94, 312, 313, 314, 316, 319, 320, 337, 344, 347. *See also Appendix B.*
Hazard, Ebenezer, 11, 13
Head, Edwin L., 53
Hill, Olney W., 4
Historical manuscripts, defined, 369. *See also Papers, private.*
Historical Manuscripts Commission (A.H.A.), 18
Historical Publications Commission, National, 4
Historical Records Survey, 25–29, 61, 126, 274, 280, 331, 336
Historical societies, 2, 14, 20–23 *passim*, 34. *See also Chapter II under state names.*
Hitt, John M., 25
Holdings of archival agencies, 318–19, 321, 375–76; standards for administering, 358–63. *See also Chapter II under state names.*
Holmes, Oliver W., 4, 239
Hoover Commission, first, 32, 54
Hopkins, Harry, 28
Houston, Sam, 261
Hunt, Gaillard, 24

Idaho: archival development and legislation, organization for archival service, the archives function, records management and records disposition, care of local records, 94–98. *See also 4, 330, 375, and Appendix B.*
Idaho State Historical Society, 22, 94–98, 312. *See also Appendix B.*
Illinois: archival development and legislation, organization for archival service,

ice, the archives function, records management and records disposition, care of local records, 98–105. *See also 4, 22, 34, 309, 310, 321, 322, 324, 327, 330, 338, 339, 341, 375, and Appendix B.*
Illinois Secretary of State, Archives–Records Management Division, 23, 30, 32, 98–105, 312, 314, 320, 332, 334, 337, 344. *See also Appendix B.*
Indexes, 14, 23, 331, 332
Indian Territory Press Association, 219
Indiana: archival development and legislation, organization for archival service, the archives function, records management and records disposition, care of local records, 105–11. *See also 4, 19, 327, 338, 346, 375, and Appendix B.*
Indiana Department of Administration, General Services Division, 108–10. *See also Appendix B.*
Indiana State Library, Archives Division, 105–11, 312, 314, 319, 344. *See also Appendix B.*
Institutional history, 16, 17
Interior, U.S. Department of the, 189, 220, 238
Inventories, 29, 330, 362; defined, 370. *See also Guides and Chapter II under state names.*
Iowa: archival development and legislation, organization for archival service, the archives function, records management and records disposition, care of local records, 111–14. *See also 4, 19, 150, 322, 325, 340, 375, and Appendix B.*
Iowa Department of History and Archives, 22, 23, 111–14, 312. *See also Appendix B.*

Jameson, J. Franklin, 17, 18
Jefferson, Thomas, 12
Johns Hopkins University, The, 16, 17
Joint Committee on Materials for Research, 26, 28

Kaltenborn, H. V., 299
Kansas: archival development and legislation, organization for archival service, the archives function, records management and records disposition, care of local records, 114–19. *See also 4, 21, 22, 166, 320, 342, 343, 344, 346, 375, and Appendix B.*
Kansas Editors and Publishers Association, 115

Kansas State Historical Society, 114–19, 312, 319, 337, 375. See also Appendix B.

Kearns, Thomas, 270

Kellar, Herbert A., 22, 154

Kentucky: archival development and legislation, organization for archival service, the archives function, records management and records disposition, care of local records, 120–25. See also 4, 33, 34, 309, 322, 324, 327, 347, 375, and Appendix B.

Kentucky Department of Finance, State Archives and Records Service, 120–25, 312, 313, 314, 316, 337, 344. See also Appendix B.

King, Grace, 126

Lamination, 321; defined, 370. See also Repair and Chapter II under state names.

Lawrence, Gov. David L., 236

Lawrence-Leiter and Co., 167

Leahy and Co., 145, 167, 180, 181

Legislation, Archival, S.A.A. Committee on, 31

Legislation, Uniform State, S.A.A. Committee on, 31

Legislation on records and archives, 9, 10, 14–16, 22, 31, 35, 36, 308–14, 324, 359; standards for, 351–53; suggested, 35, 254, 309, 341. See also Chapter II under state names.

Leland, Waldo G., 23, 24, 98

Libraries. See State libraries.

Library-archival agencies, 2, 14, 22–25 passim, 30, 312. See also Chapter II under state names.

Library Functions of the States, Survey of, 4

Library of Congress, 24, 89, 189, 191, 238, 259, 343, 346

Library Resources, Council on, 3–6 passim, 79

Littleton Griswold Committee (A.H.A.), 138

Local archives and records, 14, 15, 20, 27–29, 33–35, 327, 331, 332, 334, 335–37, 340–41; standards for care, 363–64. See also Essential records and Chapter II under state names.

Long, Gov. Earl K., 127

Louisiana: archival development and legislation, organization for archival service, the archives function, records management and records disposition, care of local records, 125–31. See also 4, 309, 311, 325, 327, 328, 375, and Appendix B.

Louisiana Archives and Records Commission, Archives and Records Service, 125–31, 312, 314, 337, 342, 344. See also Appendix B.

Louisiana State University Library, Department of Archives and Manuscripts, 126, 129–30

McCain, William D., 160, 161

McIlwaine, H. R., 24

McNitt, Esther V., 106

Maine: archival development and legislation, organization for archival service, the archives function, records management and records disposition, care of local records, 131–34. See also 4, 312, 375, and Appendix B.

Maine Secretary of State, 131–34

Manuals, records management, 335, 340, 341, 362

Manuscript Collections, National Union Catalog of, 97

Manuscripts, historical, defined, 369. See also Papers, private.

Martin, James W., 120

Martin, Wade O., 127

Maryland: archival development and legislation, organization for archival service, the archives function, records management and records disposition, care of local records, 134–42; colonial records, 8, 9. See also 4, 30, 309, 321–27 passim, 330–41 passim, 375, and Appendix B.

Maryland Hall of Records, 32, 134–42, 312, 314, 319, 320, 333, 337, 342, 343, 344, 347. See also Appendix B.

Massachusetts: archival development and legislation, organization for archival service, the archives function, records management and records disposition, care of local records, 142–48; colonial records, 9. See also 4, 14, 15, 19, 20, 329, 331, 335, 336, 338, 340, 345, 375, and Appendix B.

Massachusetts Secretary of the Commonwealth, Archives Division, 142–48, 312, 314, 319, 320, 332, 344. See also Appendix B.

Materials for Research, Joint Committee on, 26, 28

Mayer, Col. Brantz, 135

Michigan: archival development and legislation, organization for archival service, the archives function, records management and records disposition, care of local records, 148–54. See also

4, 19, 34, 109, 314, 322, 323, 334, 337–41 *passim*, 375, *and Appendix B.*
Michigan Department of Administration, Office Services Division, 149, 151–53. *See also Appendix B.*
Michigan Historical Commission, Archives Division, 148–54, 312, 320. *See also Appendix B.*
Microfilming, 25, 33, 34, 35, 321–23, 336, 341; defined, 370; standards, 361, 363. *See also Chapter II under state names.*
Microfilming, S.A.A. Committee on, 34
Middle West, 21–23, 33, 312. *See also state names.*
Minnesota: archival development and legislation, organization for archival service, the archives function, records management and records disposition, care of local records, 154–59. *See also* 4, 22, 309, 321, 324–29 *passim*, 341, 345, 375, *and Appendix B.*
Minnesota State Archives and Records Service, 154–59, 312, 313, 314, 320, 337, 344. *See also Appendix B.*
Mississippi: archival development and legislation, organization for archival service, the archives function, records management and records disposition, care of local records, 159–64. *See also* 4, 318, 322, 328, 332, 340, 375, *and Appendix B.*
Mississippi Department of Archives and History, 21, 159–64, 312, 320. *See also Appendix B.*
Missouri: archival development and legislation, organization for archival service, the archives function, records management and records disposition, care of local records, 164–68. *See also* 4, 115, 375, *and Appendix B.*
Missouri Press Association, 166
Missouri State Historical Society, 164–68, 312
Montana: archival development and legislation, organization for archival service, the archives function, records management and records disposition, care of local records, 168–71. *See also* 4, 314, 326, 376, *and Appendix B.*
Montana Historical Society, 168–71, 312. *See also Appendix B.*
Montgomery, T. L., 24
Monypenny, Philip, 4
Morales Carión, Arturo, 238
Mormon microfilm program. *See* Utah Genealogical Society.

Munden, Ken, 5, 34
Myers, Irene T., 120

National Archives, 2, 3, 28–32 *passim*, 129, 150, 235, 238, 239, 263, 321, 322, 329, 331, 337, 343
National Archives and Records Service, 2, 32, 43, 44, 97, 167, 347
National Association of State Libraries, 24, 25, 309
National Historical Publications Commission, 4
National Park Service, 28, 173
National Records Management Council, 244
Nebraska: archival development and legislation, organization for archival service, the archives function, records management and records disposition, care of local records, 171–76. *See also* 4, 19, 314, 322, 324, 338, 341, 342, 344, 376, *and Appendix B.*
Nebraska Secretary of State, 172, 175–76, 338
Nebraska State Historical Society, Division of Library and Archives, 21, 22, 171–76, 312, 320, 344. *See also Appendix B.*
Nelson, William, 183
Nesbit, Robert W., 286
Nevada: archival development and legislation, organization for archival service, the archives function, records management and records disposition, care of local records, 176–79. *See also* 4, 26, 376, *and Appendix B.*
Nevada Secretary of State, 178–79
Nevada State Historical Society, 22, 176–79, 312. *See also Appendix B.*
New England, 15, 29, 33, 336, 340. *See also state names.*
New Hampshire: archival development and legislation, organization for archival service, the archives function, records management and records disposition, care of local records, 179–82. *See also* 4, 14, 26, 309, 320, 339, 340, 376, *and Appendix B.*
New Hampshire Department of Administration and Control, Division of Records Management and Archives, 33, 179–82, 312, 313, 314, 337, 344. *See also Appendix B.*
New Hampshire Historical Society, 14, 376
New Jersey: archival development and legislation, organization for archival service, the archives function, records

management and records disposition, care of local records, 183–88. See also 4, 320, 321, 323, 326, 327, 339, 341, 376, and Appendix B.

New Jersey State Library, Bureau of Archives and History, 183–88, 309, 311, 312, 337, 345. See also Appendix B.

New Mexico: archival development and legislation, organization for archival service, the archives function, records management and records disposition, care of local records, 188–93. See also 4, 22, 309, 339, 376, and Appendix B.

New Mexico State Records Center and Archives, 33, 188–93, 312, 313, 314, 320, 337, 344, 346. See also Appendix B.

New York: archival development and legislation for archival service, the archives function, records management and records disposition, care of local records, 193–202. See also 4, 12–15 passim, 19, 29, 33, 314, 315, 324, 325, 330, 334, 336, 338, 340, 376, and Appendix B.

New York Commissioner of Education, Division of Archives and History, Public Records Section, 199–202. See also Appendix B.

New York Office of General Services, Bureau of Records Management, 197–99, 202. See also Appendix B.

New York State Library, 14, 193–97, 312, 320, 328. See also Appendix B.

Newsome, A. R., 27, 28, 29

Non-record material, defined, 370

North Carolina: archival development and legislation, organization for archival service, the archives function, records management and records disposition, care of local records, 202–11; colonial records, 8, 9. See also 4, 14, 19, 33, 34, 309, 321–27 passim, 330, 334, 335, 336, 338–42 passim, 376, and Appendix B.

North Carolina Department of Archives and History, 21, 32, 202–11, 312, 314, 319, 320, 337, 342, 343. See also Appendix B.

North Dakota: archival development and legislation, organization for archival service, the archives function, records management and records disposition, care of local records, 211–14. See also 4, 26, 314, 327, 338, 376, and Appendix B.

North Dakota Secretary of State, 212–14, 338. See also Appendix B.

North Dakota State Historical Society, 211–14, 312. See also Appendix B.

Norton, Margaret C., 25, 27, 30, 101, 195

Ohio: archival development and legislation, organization for archival service, the archives function, records management and records disposition, care of local records, 214–19. See also 4, 34, 105, 314, 315, 318, 320, 327, 337, 338, 340, 346, 376, and Appendix B.

Ohio Department of Finance, 217

Ohio Historical Society, Archives Division, 22, 214–19, 312, 344. See also Appendix B.

Oklahoma: archival development and legislation, organization for archival service, the archives function, records management and records disposition, care of local records, 219–24. See also 4, 26, 115, 166, 309, 315, 319, 322, 324, 327, 335, 341, 348, 376, and Appendix B.

Oklahoma Historical Society, Indian Archives Division, 220

Oklahoma Library Association, 221

Oklahoma State Library, 22, 219–24, 312, 313, 314, 320, 337, 338, 344. See also Appendix B.

Oregon: archival development and legislation, organization for archival service, the archives function, records management and records disposition, care of local records, 224–30. See also 4, 32, 314, 321, 330, 331, 332, 338, 339, 376, and Appendix B.

Oregon State Library, Archives Division, 224–30, 312, 342, 343. See also Appendix B.

Organization of archival agencies, 19–24; standards for, 351–56. See also Administration of archives and Chapter II under state names.

Osgood, Herbert L., 19

Overman, William D., 29

Owen, Marie Bankhead, 40

Owen, Thomas M., Sr., 20, 38

Paltsits, Victor H., 26

Paper Chemistry, Institute of, 79

Papers, private, 20, 27, 28, 30, 345–47, 357–58, 359, 370. See also Chapters II under state names.

Paperwork management, defined, 370. See also Records management.

Parent agency, defined, 370

Rhode Island: archival development and legislation, organization for archival service, the archives function, records management and records disposition, care of local records, 243–46. *See also* 4, 314, 325, 336, 339, 340, 376, *and Appendix B.*

Rhode Island Department of Administration, Division of Methods, Data Processing and Central Services, 244–46, 324. *See also Appendix B.*

Rhode Island Secretary of State, 243–46, 312. *See also Appendix B.*

Ridgely, David, 134

Riley, Franklin L., 21, 159

Robertson, James A., 136

Rockefeller Foundation, 166

Rowland, Dunbar, 21, 159, 160, 163; and Mrs. Rowland, 161

Sainsbury, W. Noel, 279

Salaries, 35, 315, 318, 374. *See also Chapter II under state names and Appendix B.*

Salley, A. S., Jr., 248, 249

Sanford, Gov. Terry, 209

Schedules, disposal and retention, 31–34 *passim*, 322, 328, 338, 339, 341, 365, 366. *See also* Records management.

Schellenberg, T. R., 28

Scientific school of history, 16–17

Scroggs, William O., 125

Seattle, Wash., Federal Records Center, 43, 44

Security copies of records, 33, 35. *See also* Essential records.

Series, defined, 371

Shambaugh, Benjamin F., 22, 111, 113

Shearer, Augustus H., 274

Sheldon, A. E., 171

Shelf list, defined, 371

Shimmel, Lewis S., 230

Silking, 71, 145, 321; defined, 371

Social Science Research Council, 26

Society of American Archivists, 30, 286, 324, 351; activities on behalf of study, 2–6 *passim*; committees, 3–6 *passim*, 31, 34–36, 309, 334; founding and activities, 29–32

South, 19–21, 31, 312, 314, 331. *See also* state names.

South Carolina: archival development and legislation, organization for archival service, the archives function, records management and records disposition, care of local records, 246–52; colonial records, 10. *See also* 4, 14, 26, 321, 329, 330, 347, 376, *and Appendix B.*

South Carolina Archives Department, 21, 246–52, 312, 320, 342. *See also Appendix B.*

South Dakota: archival development and legislation, organization for archival service, the archives function, records management and records disposition, care of local records, 252–55. *See also* 4, 26, 211, 376, *and Appendix B.*

South Dakota State Historical Society, 252–55, 312, 320, 326. *See also Appendix B.*

Southern Historical Society, 81

Sparks, Jared, 13, 16

Stanard, William G., 279

Standards, National Bureau of, 62, 97

Standards for archival agencies, 5, 6, 15, 31, 35, 349–67

State historical societies, 2, 22, 23, 30. *See also Chapter II under state names.*

State libraries, 2, 12, 14, 15, 22, 23; National Association of State Libraries, 24, 25, 30. *See also Chapter II under state names.*

State Records Committee, S.A.A., 3, 4, 31, 34–36

Status of archival agencies, 311–13, 352–53. *See also Chapter II under state names.*

Steiner, Lewis H., 135

Stephens, Eleanor, 225

Stiles, Cassius C., 23, 113, 150

Surveys of archives, 18, 19, 25–29, 35. *See also* Historical Records Survey.

Swan, Robert T., 15

Tennessee: archival development and legislation, organization for archival service, the archives function, records management and records disposition, care of local records, 255–61. *See also* 4, 321, 333, 334, 346, 376, *and Appendix B.*

Tennessee State Library and Archives, 21, 255–61, 312, 320. *See also Appendix B.*

Texas: archival development and legislation, organization for archival service, the archives function, records management and records disposition, care of local records, 261–68. *See also* 4, 309, 321, 330, 333, 335, 339, 376, *and Appendix B.*

Texas State Library: Archives Division, 261–68, 312, 314, 320, 337; Records Administration Division, 266–68. *See also Appendix B.*

Ticknor, George, 16
Tilton, Asa C., 24
Town records, 15, 29, 200. *See also* Local archives *and names of New England states.*
Training: for professional archives work, 29, 317, 343; for records management, 338
Turner, Frederick J., 22

Uniform State Legislation, S.A.A. Committee on, 31
Utah: archival development and legislation, organization for archival service, the archives function, records management and records disposition, care of local records, 268–73. *See also* 4, 26, 309, 327, 330, 376, *and Appendix B.*
Utah Genealogical Society, 33, 74, 80, 87, 133, 139, 249, 260, 272, 278, 293, 323, 336
Utah State Historical Society, Division of State Archives, 22, 268–73, 312, 314, 320, 337. *See also Appendix B.*

Value of archives, 1, 32
van Lear, Arnold J. F., 194
Vaughan, John H., 189
Vaults, 14, 35. *See also* Buildings, archival, *and* Physical facilities.
Vermont: archival development and legislation, organization for archival service, the archives function, records management and records disposition, care of local records, 273–78. *See also* 4, 309, 322, 324, 327, 376, *and Appendix B.*
Vermont Department of Administration, Division of Public Records, 273–78, 312, 313, 314, 338, 344. *See also Appendix B.*
Vermont Secretary of State, 275. *See also Appendix B.*
Viles, Jonas, 165
Virginia: archival development and legislation, organization for archival service, the archives function, records management and records disposition, care of local records, 278–85; colonial records, 9. *See also* 4, 259, 309, 321, 322, 327, 330, 333, 341, 376, *and Appendix B.*
Virginia State Library: Archives Division, 21, 278–85, 312, 314, 320, 337; Records Management Division, 284–85. *See also Appendix B.*

Washington: archival development and legislation, organization for archival service, the archives function, records management and records disposition, care of local records, 285–90. *See also* 4, 34, 309, 310, 321, 324, 339, 340, 376, *and Appendix B.*
Washington Department of General Administration, Division of Archives and Records Management, 285–90, 312, 313, 314, 319, 320, 337, 344. *See also Appendix B.*
West Virginia: archival development and legislation, organization for archival service, the archives function, records management and records disposition, care of local records, 290–95. *See also* 4, 314, 325, 338, 341, 347, *and Appendix B.*
West Virginia Collection, 291–95, 347, 376. *See also Appendix B.*
West Virginia Commissioner of Finance, 294–95. *See also Appendix B.*
West Virginia Department of Archives and History, 21, 290–95, 312, 318, 347. *See also Appendix B.*
Western Historical Manuscripts Collection, 166
Western State Atomic Vaults, Inc., 60
Whitehill, Walter M., 115
Wier, Jeanne E., 177, 179
Williams, Gov. G. Mennen, 319
Wilson, Woodrow, 17
Wisconsin: archival development and legislation, organization for archival service, the archives function, records management and records disposition, care of local records, 296–302. *See also* 4, 19, 33, 105, 314, 325, 330, 332, 337, 338, 339, 346, 347, 376, *and Appendix B.*
Wisconsin Department of Administration, Records Management Supervisor, 296, 300–2. *See also Appendix B.*
Wisconsin State Historical Society, Division of Archives and Manuscripts, 22, 296–300, 302, 312, 320, 342. *See also Appendix B.*
Woods, Henry E., 15
Woodward, Dorothy H., 192
Works Progress Administration, 28, 176, 196, 212, 259. *See also* Historical Records Survey.
Workshops, S.A.A., 36
World War II, 34; records management in, 31, 32

Wright, Carroll D., 15
Wyllie, Robert C., 89
Wyoming: archival development and legislation, organization for archival service, the archives function, records management and records disposition, care of local records, 302–7. *See also* 4, 309, 310, 318, 322, 323, 325, 327, 341, 342, 346, 376, *and Appendix B.*
Wyoming State Archives and Historical Department, 302–7, 312, 337. *See also Appendix B.*